Christian Ethics

"In some of the clearest prose I have encountered, Cunningham speaks directly to undergraduates in their own language, artfully weaving in a myriad of allusions and illustrations from contemporary culture, unpretentiously explaining unfamiliar words and concepts, and astutely naming the assumptions that shape their lives and voicing the questions they raise. He deftly takes them by the hand and walks them, step by logical step, into and through the discipline of Christian ethics as an ethics of character rooted in Scripture, worship, and the Trinity. This is really a wonderful book—a long-needed gift to all who teach Christian ethics, whether in the classroom or in the congregation."

Therese Lysaught, Associate Professor, Department of Theology,
Marquette University, Milwaukee

"One of the best introductions to Christian ethics available. An essential tool for all students who want to explore the connections between Christian understanding of God, worship, community life, the reading of Scripture, and moral formation. The pace is lively, the text fluent and easy. David Cunningham opens up the rich resources of what Christian tradition says with respect to 'peaceableness,' justice, grace, love, courage, stewardship of the created order, giving and receiving, sacrifice and companionship, music as a Christian practice, and much more."

Esther D. Reed, Associate Professor of Theological Ethics,
University of Exeter, UK

"David Cunningham's enjoyable and highly readable textbook is an excellent introduction to contemporary Christian ethics and is ideally suited for those who have little prior knowledge of Christian belief. His use of literature, film, and music is notably refreshing, as is the imaginative way he draws on the virtues to illuminate practical judgements in different parts of everyday life.

This book will deservedly find its way onto the reading lists of many introductory courses on Christian ethics."

Robert Song, Senior Lecturer in Christian Ethics,
University of Durham, UK

What does it mean to study Christian ethics today? For many of us, the historical and cultural impact of Christianity has been so great that, in order to make sense of the world in which we live, we need to understand the beliefs and practices of this extraordinarily influential faith and the worldviews that accompany it.

David S. Cunningham has written an introduction to Christian ethics with a difference. His imaginative and lively approach is designed for today's students, who have a keen interest in theology and ethics, but who find traditional biblical and theological narratives daunting. He draws on film, literature, and music as well as the experience of everyday life to provide students with a vivid and accessible introduction to the field. Topics covered include the nature of human action, the narratives and discourse of ethics, and the development of a virtue ethics approach in its Christian context. He also tackles key contemporary issues in Christian ethics: the ethics of business and economics, politics, the environment, medicine, and sex. Vivid examples, questions for discussion, summary boxes, and lists of further reading all help the reader to a better understanding of the material.

Students and indeed anyone wishing to learn more about Christian ethics will find this engaging book the perfect introduction.

David S. Cunningham is Professor of Religion and Director of the CrossRoads Project at Hope College, Michigan. He has published widely on the subjects of systemic, doctrinal and philosophical theology, and Christian ethics.

Christian Ethics

The End of the Law

David S. Cunningham

For Rev. David Shaw —
With many thanks for your
good work in Green Mt. Falls,
my family's "second home" —
Grace & peace
David S. Cunningham

P.S. See pp. 365–367
for some "local color"!

Routledge
Taylor & Francis Group

LONDON AND NEW YORK

First published 2008
by Routledge
2 Park Square, Milton Park, Abingdon, Oxon OX14 4RN

Simultaneously published in the USA and Canada
by Routledge
270 Madison Ave, New York, NY 100016

Routledge is an imprint of the Taylor & Francis Group

Typeset in Sabon and Helvetica Neue by
The Running Head Limited, Cambridge
Printed and bound in Great Britain by
Antony Rowe Ltd, Chippenham, Wiltshire

British Library Cataloguing in Publication Data
A catalogue record for this book is available from the British Library

Library of Congress Cataloging in Publication Data

Cunningham, David S., 1961–
    Christian ethics: the end of the law / David S. Cunningham.
      p.   cm.
    Includes bibliographical references and index.
    1. Christian ethics. I. Title.
    BJ1251.C84 2008
    241—dc22

                                2007037780

ISBN10: 0–415–37599–1 (hbk)
ISBN10: 0–415–37600–9 (pbk)
ISBN10: 0–203–92975–6 (ebk)

ISBN13: 978–0–415–37599–3 (hbk)
ISBN13: 978–0–415–37600–6 (pbk)
ISBN13: 978–0–203–92975–9 (ebk)

To Margaret Adam

and to her family—Nathaniel, Josiah, and Philippa
(and AKMA, of course)

For Christ is the end of the law,
that everyone who has faith may be justified

Romans 10:4 (RSV)

Contents

Preface   ix

Introduction: the thin line   1

PART 1
Narrating the Christian life   **19**

1 Character and community, or: Why ethics probably isn't
   what you think   21

2 Identifying who(se) we are: what's God got to do with it?   42

3 Reading in communion: how stories structure our lives   59

   Interlude 1 The narratives of Christianity   76

4 From story to morality: proclaiming, inhabiting, and performing   85

5 A journey without maps: professing, praying, and repenting   103

PART 2
Practicing the Christian life   **125**

6 Forgiveness, reconciliation, and nonviolence:
   distinctive practices in a fallen world   127

7 An offering of souls and bodies: the life of virtue   145

8 Calling upon the triune God: the divine formation of
   Christian virtue   166

Interlude 2 "Those who sing well, pray twice": music as a Christian practice 185

9 Nourishing the body: sacrifice, companionship, and abundance 191

10 Sent forth into the world: taking character beyond the community 208

PART 3
Living the Christian life **227**

11 Monday: back at the office 229

12 Tuesday: at the voting booth 257

Interlude 3 Wednesday: back to church 286

13 Thursday: at the hospital 292

14 Friday: out on the town 320

15 Saturday: a walk in the woods 348

Sources cited and suggestions for further reading 375

Permissions 387

Index 389

reface

This book arises from two strongly held convictions, both of which have grown from nearly twenty years of teaching Christian theology and ethics in the classroom. The first of these convictions is that, somewhat to my surprise, students care deeply about these issues. Common wisdom suggests that most students take religion courses only when forced to do so, and that those who choose such courses voluntarily are few and far between. In fact, some cynics might imagine that most university students' interest in ethics would be stimulated only when someone was willing to confirm their own strongly held assumptions. In my experience, such stereotypes are only rarely borne out in actual practice.

Quite the contrary: throughout my experience—at colleges, universities, and seminaries, both Catholic and Protestant—I have met hundreds of students who are genuinely eager to learn about these subjects. They want to understand what Christians believe and why; they want to think about what kind of people Christians believe they are called to be and how they are called to act. This desire to understand and to learn about theology and ethics is quite widespread; it is not limited to those students who describe themselves as Christians or to those who participate heavily in worship and other church-related activities. Most students realize that the historical and cultural impact of Christianity has been so great that, if they hope to make sense of the world in which they live, they will need to understand the beliefs and practices of this extraordinarily influential faith and the worldviews that accompany it.

My efforts, as a teacher, to respond to these students' deep desire to learn has given rise to the second conviction that informs this book, which might be stated as follows: almost every textbook published on this topic *assumes far too much* about the background knowledge that students bring to this subject. Note well: I am not suggesting that the students are not smart enough to handle the available textbooks, or that they are incapable of stretching their minds to reach something that may, at first glance, appear to be beyond their grasp. The problem concerns not the reading level of the texts, or the implicit demands that these books make on their readers. The problem is, rather, the assumption that students (whether Christian or otherwise) have been well schooled in the traditional narratives and the everyday practices of Christianity, such that one can refer to (say) a particular biblical story or to some aspect of a worship service and assume that everyone will know its essential outlines. Even at many historically Christian institutions, only a small minority of students have grown up on the stories of the faith in ways that would make these narratives part of their basic mental furniture. Fewer still have been thoroughly "catechized" in the faith, such that they could articulate a detailed account of the basic beliefs of Christianity; and this remains the case, in my experience, even in those venues where most of the students would describe themselves as Christians. I have spent my entire career teaching at church-related colleges and universities and at theological seminaries; and, given that the students at *these* institutions find that their textbooks assume too much background knowledge about Christian belief, how much more will this be the case at more secular institutions.

A textbook is useless if it assumes that students bring much more background knowledge to the topic than is actually the case. Of course, an instructor can supplement any textbook with biblical, historical, and theological texts; but anyone who adopts this approach may well wonder whether the textbook is really fulfilling its purpose, which is to free up the professor's time and energy so that she or he can bring more detail, nuance, and specificity to the subject-matter. Moreover, given the limitations of class time, as well as the two-thousand-year history and theological complexity of the Christian faith, any textbook that demands a great deal of supplementation risks making a course in Christian ethics into a complete survey of Western civilization—in which theology and ethics must, of necessity, be consigned to the margins. Under such circumstances, many students may indeed learn something about Christian ethics, but only after they have digested the historical, philosophical, and literary exploits of the past two millennia.

Most of the textbooks in the field are written for a hypothetical student of fifty years ago: someone who was brought up in the Church, who had learned its narratives and its practices, and who would likely take for granted the reasonableness and the potential universality of the Christian worldview. Today, such students are rare—and they are rarely the most interesting students. The typical student today has no more than a passing familiarity with the Bible, does not attend church with any regularity, and is often deeply suspicious of the claims of Christianity and especially those of individual Christians. Discussions about Christian ethics, in particular, are seen by many students as a plot developed by the strong for the purpose of tyrannizing the weak. Moreover, many students find the typical discourses on Christian ethics to be rife with hypocrisy, particularly when the moralizing speakers are eventually found to be engaging in the very practices that they so bitterly denounce. This can lead students to develop a distorted picture of Christianity in general and Christian ethics in particular—a serious disservice both to the subject matter and to the student.

This book makes a genuine effort to take nothing for granted: to make as few assumptions as possible about the theological background that students will bring to the text. It recognizes that many readers will be non-Christians or nominal Christians, and that they will not stand for having fire and brimstone heaved in their general direction. This book does not dilute the ethical claims of Christianity, but neither does it assume that its readers have necessarily chosen to submit to them, nor that they will eventually do so. And although it makes regular reference to the biblical narratives and to the practices of the Church, it explains these in the text and provides additional detail in textboxes and interludes. It makes use of generalized descriptions of human experience in order to provide a way in to the conversation for those students who are relatively unfamiliar with the teachings of the Church. It does this even though, in my view, human experience in general cannot provide an interpretive key for understanding Christian ethics (and even though there may actually be no such thing as "human experience in general"). Nevertheless, experiential vignettes can be a heuristic tool for introducing the questions that I am attempting to explicate and address. This is especially the case in the "Questions for discussion" that end each chapter: they are designed not to make "experience" the arbiter of judgment, but to provoke thoughtful responses. Students need to be able to speak about these issues from their own experience, even if they also need to recognize that their own experience will not always be normative.

I am describing my assumptions in detail here primarily for the sake of those who *do* bring considerably more background knowledge in Christianity to their study of this book—including, of course, most instructors and scholars of Christianity. I humbly ask that such persons be patient with my "populist" explanations of highly complex theological concepts. I recognize (of course) that everything is more complicated than it is here presented to be; I am painting with broad strokes. I do not believe that I am diluting the discipline of Christian ethics, nor do I have any desire to do so. But I have seen too many students toss aside the texts that they are assigned because these books make too many assumptions about their own background knowledge, and because the instructor lacks sufficient time and space in the classroom (or a sufficiently homogeneous group of students) to provide that background. As an alternative, this is a book that students can take and read, with the expectation that they will be able to do so on their own. This means that classroom time can be spent working through more difficult texts and dissecting more complicated questions. This is how I plan to use it in my own classes, and I am hopeful that other instructors may find it useful for their purposes as well.

Books like this one are always multi-authored works, whatever names may appear on their covers. For what I have to say in this book, I am largely indebted to long and thoughtful conversations going back to my graduate school days—conversations among my teachers, my fellow graduate students, and the students in preceptorials and discussion sections upon whom I first began to try out my ideas. Those early teachers, colleagues, and students included A. K. M. Adam, Margaret Adam, Mike Cartwright, Bill Cavanaugh, Steve Fowl, Stanley Hauerwas, Greg Jones, Phil Kenneson, Nicholas Lash, Steve Long, Therese Lysaught, David Matzko McCarthy, Carole Stoneking, Ken Surin, Geoffrey Wainwright, Rowan Williams, and Jonathan Wilson.

In more recent years, I have benefitted greatly from the professional collaboration that occurs at the Society of Christian Ethics, the Society for the Study of Christian Ethics, and the Ekklesia Project—particularly at their respective annual meetings. Through these organizations, I have been able to maintain contact with my graduate school friends—as well as meeting (and learning much from) new colleagues such as Nick Adams, Scott Bader-Saye, Dan Bell, Nigel Biggar, Mike Budde, Rodney Clapp, David Clough, Amy Laura Hall, Kelly Johnson, Brent Laytham, Gil Meilaender, Neil Messer, Michael Northcott, Charlie Pinches, Ben Quash, Tim Sedgwick, Robert Song, David Stubbs, Paul Wadell, Bernd Wannentwetsch, Sam Wells, and Bill Werpehowski—among many others.

Anyone who saw fit to dissect this book and determine the ultimate provenance of each of its sentences and all of its ideas would be able to trace most of them back to one or more of these thoughtful scholars. For fifteen years, my students have been learning Christian ethics from these people, because—in the aforementioned absence of any suitable textbook—I have used the writings of these ethicists in order to give my students some idea of the nature and scope of the field. While these authors' writings are frequently mentioned in the further reading lists at the end of chapters, my decision to forgo all footnotes and other bibliographical citations in the text of each chapter has often prevented me from giving due credit in precisely those places where it is due. But given the emphasis that this book places on the notion of *community* in Christian ethics, it will not surprise most readers to learn that any idea that might be "credited" in this book would be credited to several of these thinkers simultaneously, rather than to any one of them in particular. I hope that, if this book accomplishes nothing else, it will make the insights of these thoughtful and creative scholars available to more students of Christian ethics.

My own students also deserve a word of thanks—particularly those enrolled in my Fall 2006 course at Western Theological Seminary, who read early drafts of chapters and offered helpful feedback. But the students in all my Christian ethics courses over the years have contributed to this book in more ways than they know. As I pieced together those courses, drawing on many works written by those listed in the preceding paragraphs, my students have had to labor alongside me as I tried to describe my vision of how all these various elements held together as a coherent whole. They have endured my efforts to teach my way toward a systematic account of Christian ethics, and they have often had to make bricks without straw. I know that my offer comes rather late, but to them I want to say: "Remember that textbook you asked for, back in class? Here it is." I am grateful for their patience.

Thanks are also due to Lesley Riddle, my editor at Routledge, who approached me some years ago with the notion that I might be able to write an ethics textbook that would be useful on both sides of the Atlantic. I am not sure where she came by that idea, and even less sure that I have succeeded; but in any case, I am grateful for her confidence, her support, and her seemingly infinite patience as the writing process went on (and on). She also sent the manuscript to three excellent anonymous readers; I am grateful for their feedback, which was very thorough and thoroughly helpful. Thanks also to Gemma Dunn, Lalle Purseglove, Sarah DeVos, Francesca Filippelli, and everyone at Routledge for making the publication process a smooth one, and to Carole Drummond for expert copy-editing. And thanks to my home institution, Hope College, for providing excellent support for my scholarship over the years.

My daughters Monica and Emily continue to be my most committed teachers; their own consistent manifestation of the fruits of the Spirit—particularly love, joy, kindness, and patience—reminds me that I remain a mere novice in the Christian moral life. They, along with my parents, Donald and Patsy Cunningham, are among my strongest pillars of support. Finally, in the early stages of writing, my friend Lisa Hackney provided all manner of encouragement—regularly reminding me that creating this book was mainly a matter of "writing down your ethics course." I have been blessed by the presence of such people in my life.

This book is dedicated to a person from whom I have learned a great deal about narrating, practicing, and living the Christian life: Margaret Adam.

Our paths first crossed because her husband, a New Testament scholar, was one of my closest friends in graduate school. I began to understand parenting by watching her interactions with her remarkable children—Nate, Si, and Pippa. Later, my own children also benefitted from Margaret's care, first as their godmother (a role she took more seriously than most) and then as a next-door neighbor. Ms. Adam (soon to be Dr. Adam) is also a first-rate Christian theologian; over the past two decades, she has helped me to think through complex issues, given helpful feedback on my writing, and provided much food for thought. The publication of this book marks our twentieth year of friendship—a friendship for which I am deeply grateful.

The Feast of St. Peter and St. Paul
Anno Domini 2007

*I*ntroduction

The thin line

There's a thin line
Between wrong and right, between black and white
It's been a long time
Since I could close my eyes and see the light
But there's some sunshine, baby,
Shinin' down on me, and it's all I need
To see the thin line
Between me and you, and you and me.
Yes, it's a mighty thin line.

The Dixie Chicks

The field of study that we call *ethics*—also sometimes called *morality*—is often concerned with judgments about doing good and doing evil, judgments about right and wrong action. For most people, this basic distinction—between right and wrong, or between good and evil—is classified among those definitive either/or conditions, in which there are only two options. Just as we would not describe a person as "slightly pregnant" or an event as "a little bit unique," we would hesitate to describe a morally inappropriate action as "somewhat evil" or a morally correct choice as "moderately right." If we assign any moral status at all to a particular human action or activity, it's typically either *right* or *wrong*; we're distinctly dissatisfied when told that something is "both right and wrong" or even that "it just depends on the situation." It makes no more sense to describe a moral action as "almost good" than it does to call someone "practically perfect" (except, of course, when referring to Mary Poppins).

The two-choice system

Our tendency to think of right and wrong as polar opposites is both caused by, and also contributes to, the most common modern approaches to thinking about ethics. Typically, such approaches pose questions that give us only two choices: to judge something as right or wrong, and often to put that judgment into action by doing something, or by refraining from doing it. (Of course, in some cases, refraining from doing something may result in the need to face the same choice again at some future time; but at that time as well, we will again be given exactly two choices.) This two-choice approach seems to have a fairly strong hold on our imaginations, regardless of whether the ethical question is posed in terms of a personal decision (Should I buy this item, knowing it was made in a sweatshop? Should I throw this candy wrapper out the car window? Should I have sex with this person I'm dating?) or judgments about larger questions of public policy (is it right for the state to execute criminals? to condone assisted suicide? to sanction same-sex marriage?). Although a thousand minor nuances could be offered in response to each of these questions—making the answer depend on certain specific conditions—the questions themselves are designed to elicit a yes-or-no response. Just as a teacher might object if a student answered "maybe" on a true-or-false test, we feel uneasy if the answer to every yes-or-no question about ethics is "it depends." And yet, most of the time—frustratingly enough—that is precisely the answer that we want to give.

In the first chapter of this book, I will raise some concerns about our tendency to discuss ethics strictly in terms of yes-or-no judgments and decisions; in fact, I will question the assumption that ethics is primarily about *decisions* at all (at least as we typically use that term). For the moment, however, we should note that our tendency to phrase ethical questions in this form was not simply invented out of thin air; many people *do*, in fact, face real decisions in which they must make a choice between two options. In some cases, the two options—about which one must render judgments and make choices—will be equally unattractive options. A person who is facing an end-of-life decision—trying to decide (for instance) whether to remove a loved one's life-support system or whether to assist a terminally ill relative to commit suicide—does not have the luxury of an abstract discussion in which the conclusion is some version of "it depends." Nor is there any way to take such an action "partly" or "a little bit." There are only two options: to do it, or not to do it. We sometimes describe such decisions as "black and white" decisions: the two choices are diametrically opposed to each other, such that a choice in favor of either option completely excludes the other from consideration. When considering the question of turning off someone's life support, we can admit all kinds of nuances and conditions to the discussion; but for the person who actually makes the decision—to do it or not to do it—there are no shades of gray.

The "either/or" structure that seems to be demanded by many of our decisions (and by the manner in which most ethical questions are posed) makes the whole enterprise of ethics seem like fairly dangerous territory. Add to this the definitive opposition between good and evil, and it's not surprising that most ethical debates become quite polarized. When people feel very strongly that one option is good and that the other is evil, they will naturally tend to emphasize the differences between the two spheres to an extreme degree. This tendency toward ethical polarization leads us to think of wrong and right as clearly labeled points on a moral map of the universe—and to think of them as located about a thousand light-years apart. Those who favor a particular ethical position will describe their own stance in ways that sound perfectly rational and obvious, while painting the opposing position in the most vilified terms imaginable. Consider, for example, those who hold a strong view about the morality of abortion during the first few months of pregnancy: one side labels itself "pro-life" and claims that anyone in the other camp is essentially countenancing murder; the other side labels itself "pro-choice" and describes its opponents as favoring the virtual enslavement of women. Each side gathers as a like-minded group whose participants have been carefully screened for appropriate partisan judgments and behaviors. Each side fires its heaviest artillery in the direction of the far-away camp, which it describes as located at the opposite (evil) end of the moral spectrum.

Questioning the dichotomy

But here's the rub: the two camps—whether they focus on abortion or on any other moral issue—are typically *not* located at opposite ends of the universe. The people who make their home in one of these two groups will regularly cross paths with people in the other group—in fact, they will do so thousands of times every day. They live in the same neighborhoods and the same apartment blocks as those who hold (what they consider to be) the wrong position. They go to school and go to work with people from the opposite camp. They talk with them and transact business with them and may even find them to be pleasant company. No matter how invested we are in a particular ethical position, we often find ourselves in contact, and even in fairly close relationships, with people who have a completely different view.

In fact, even among those who share the same ethical stance on a particular issue, uniformity is not always easy to achieve. Although a group of people may agree about one particular moral issue, they may disagree profoundly on another one; so even after we retreat back into our respective camps of like-minded people, we sometimes find ourselves setting up new mini-fortresses within that larger fortress. Moreover, a great many of us find that we do not feel comfortable in any particular camp—we don't like the way that the questions are being asked, and we find ourselves vacillating, first persuaded and then repelled by the arguments of one side of the debate. Still others among us may be mortified by the whole conversation; we just want to throw up our hands (or, sometimes, just to throw up) and to refuse to engage in *any* discussion of ethical questions. In the end, the field of ethics is not well served by the claim that all questions are constituted by two camps in polar opposition and separated by great moral distance; the metaphor simply breaks down. The difference between wrong and right, between black and white, is not a yawning gulf that stretches from one end of the moral universe to the other. The difference between wrong and right is, as the Dixie Chicks remind us, "a mighty thin line."

I appreciate this metaphor of "the thin line" because it helps us to realize that, when it comes to moral questions, the sides are not really very far apart. The faithful followers of each position live in the midst of one another and interact with one another; they often belong to some of the same communities and engage in some of the same pursuits as those whose moral positions they oppose. They also interact with people who would not identify with either side; in fact, those people—who find themselves unwilling or unable to choose a side—are often the majority. They, especially, appreciate *just how thin* the line is; in fact, most of the time, they find themselves standing directly on it, forced to give it the same kind of anxious attention that would be required if they were standing on a tightrope. It would be much less taxing to follow the tightrope to one of the two points where it's attached—to the safety of a solid platform, where we could relax into the knowledge that some things are known for certain. In fact, we're pretty sure that we can't stay up there forever; not only is it very hard work, but we also realize that we have other tightropes to walk. We need to move—but to which platform?

Part of the reason that we find ourselves walking an ethical tightrope is that a good case can often be made for planting our feet firmly on either side of most of these either/or decisions. While it's always possible to focus on a largely hypothetical issue about which nearly everyone will agree (often focusing on another culture or a different historical period), these are not the issues that engage us in the present moment. For most moral arguments which are likely to be of immediate concern to us, a good argument can often be made for either of the two opposing perspectives. And yet, precisely because there are exactly two opposing perspectives, we worry that the choice that we are facing must make *all* the difference: we only have two choices, and surely only one of them can be right. We fear that the smallest of miscalculations will lead us to choose the wrong side, and that we won't even be able to recognize the error of our ways until it's too late. Worse yet: as we continue to hesitate to choose one of the two available platforms on which to plant our feet, we may lose our balance and fall off the high wire altogether.

The challenges—and how to meet them

This "thin line" between wrong and right is what makes the field of ethics such a challenging subject for investigation—for at least three reasons. First, it makes it very difficult to discuss ethical issues in fruitful and productive ways. We only tend to talk about them when we're safely back in our camps of like-minded people—not while we're walking the thin line. The assumptions that seem obvious to one person seem ludicrous to another, and the action that seems so clearly right to one group seems morally bankrupt to their opponents. We have not yet hit upon the right vocabulary and the right set of conversational tools for working through our ethical disagreements in a civilized and productive way. We tend just to shout very loudly at each other from our opposite sides of the thin line. And since we're in such close proximity to each other, all that shouting tends to give us some pretty severe headaches.

Second, the *very existence* of two very vocal and (often) equally significant groups—each of which stakes its claim on different sides of the issue—makes it difficult for many people to feel perfectly comfortable with either one. Those people over on the opposite side often seem to be decent, thoughtful people; how could they possibly be so very misguided on this particular question? In fact, we might even get to know some of those other people and find ourselves attracted to their side. But if we were to join them, we'd be asked to vilify the very people with whom we've made common cause all these years, and *those* people seem to be decent and thoughtful as well. We may begin to suspect that, if right and wrong actions were as clear-cut and easily identifiable as some people seem to claim, we wouldn't have to spend so much time arguing about them in the first place.

A final challenge presented by any discussion of ethical issues is that the thin line that differentiates wrong from right is not always a straight and straightforward line. Here we need to set aside the tightrope metaphor and think instead of a road that winds through the countryside. We're fairly certain that the land on one side of the road is fertile and productive, while the land on the other side will yield nothing but weeds. But looking at the land on each side won't help us determine which is which; in fact, there appear to be quite a few people on both sides, actively plowing and planting, and many people in each group are ridiculing those on the other side. They are also trying to convince the rest of us, who find ourselves traveling along the narrow road that separates the two sides, that their choice is the right choice—that if we go along with them, we too will be rewarded.

Now, it so happens that we can turn around and look back down the road at a great distance, in the direction from which we've come. By doing so, we see a few signs of where the fertile land must be located: a patch of green here, a source of water there, a few buildings where grain is being stored. If the road were straight, these signs would be useful to us; they would let us know which side to choose. But in fact, the road isn't straight. Those who built the road had to work around obstacles and follow the contours of the hills and valleys that were encountered along the way, and it's not perfectly obvious to us, as we look back into our history, to which side we are being directed by the signs of our past.

The search for principles

Given all these complexities, it's hardly any wonder that many people have spent a good deal of time and energy trying to devise a method for evaluating human actions and decisions in order to render a judgment about whether they are wrong or right. (Nor is it any wonder that some people have given up on trying to do so, having found the whole process frustrating and unproductive.) Over the centuries, various cultures have developed principles that have governed human behavior; they have done so not just as a means of encouraging order and structure within a society, but (often) because they were convinced that certain behaviors were right and others were wrong. Needless to say, not all cultures have been identical in their choices; for example, some have considered human sacrifice to be a horrific crime, while others have believed it to be an essential act of devotion.

But even though civilizations have varied enormously as to *what* principles they hold, most have held to *some* set of principles; hence, we are often tempted to believe that our ethical disagreements might be resolved through the formulation of the right principles. If we could just agree on a set of principles for good behavior, we would dramatically reduce the degree of conflict over the moral worth of particular human actions. Many such notions have achieved a fair degree of support over time; two of them deserve mention here, though for the moment we will keep their treatment extremely brief. Although these approaches are not used in this book, students of Christian ethics (and of ethics generally) will find frequent references to them in the literature. Students seeking more detailed and nuanced accounts of these views will find them in books that make use of these perspectives in developing their ethical frameworks.

The first of these approaches focuses on *duty*, and is thus sometimes called deontological ethics, from the Greek word for duty. The German philosopher Immanuel Kant believed that we should act such that our choices could be formulated into a universal principle; so for example, we ought not to strike another person just because that person made us angry, because we would not agree with the principle that all people should be free to strike those who anger them. On the other hand, we might well argue that a particular murderer should be executed by the state because we believe that the state is duty-bound to execute all murderers. Kant believed that this approach could provide a framework for ethics without reliance on religious perspectives, or on any concept of God whatsoever.

The second approach is well articulated in the work of the English thinkers Jeremy Bentham and John Stuart Mill. They argued for a *utilitarian* approach to ethical decision-making, in which the basic rule was that we should seek the greatest good for the greatest number. More recently, a Christian ethicist named Joseph Fletcher offered a particular version of utilitarianism: one in which the principle of love should be our guiding light. What would love do, in any particular situation? By asking this question, he believed that he had formulated a decision rule that could guide us through most of our ethical conundrums.

While these perspectives continue to have their champions, they do not (in the humble opinion of the author of this book) truly provide what we seek in understanding what Christian ethics should be. Obviously, a detailed critique of either of these positions is well beyond the scope of this introduction; and in any case, I want to suggest that their faults are not just a result of the specific assumptions of each system. Rather, the inadequacies of these standard approaches to ethics result from the fact that, when it comes to ethical judgments, *rules* and *principles* are extremely difficult to formulate and to apply with any degree of specificity and consistency. Either the principle will be so abstract (as Kant's) that it will require detailed specification in order to be useful at all (and his position does not give us much guidance as to those specifications); or it will require such detailed foreknowledge about the outcomes of our actions (as does utilitarianism) that it will prove to be little more than a guessing game; or, finally, it will be so vague (as is Fletcher's principle of love) that it will allow anyone to make a moral argument for just about anything. (Plenty of slaveholders will explain, at length, just how good slavery is for their slaves—and how "loving" an act it is to enslave them.)

If not principles, what about rules?

Of course, these difficulties in formulating principles could be avoided if we were able to offer more concrete and specific rules about the rightness and wrongness of very specific actions. In order for such rules to be effective, they would need to be designed by a competent authority, and people would need to be inclined (or forced) to follow them. This has been a very common approach to ethics at various times in human history, including the present day. The word that we usually use to describe such approaches is "law." A *law* is "a rule of conduct or procedure established by custom, agreement, or authority." When a particular society customarily expects people to behave in a certain way, or agrees that they should, or submits to an authority that declares that they should, they are acting on the basis of law.

We often assume that the best way to handle our ethical disagreements is to create and enforce laws that define, in the very specific terms that laws typically employ, just which behaviors are right and which are wrong. Sometimes people will claim that "you can't legislate morality," but they usually mean only that one can't change people's minds about what is right and wrong simply by enacting a law. (And this is true enough; we could enact a law that authorized all people to throw their garbage in their neighbors' gardens, but this is unlikely to convince most of the recipients of the garbage to declare such actions to be morally justified.) Nevertheless, one can, in fact, legislate morality in the broader sense of enacting laws that take a particular position on moral issues. In fact, most of the laws that are enacted—whether by custom, agreement, or authority—do in fact have significant moral implications. Even something as bureaucratic as laws about taxation require moral judgments about, for example, the relative fairness of the distribution of the tax burden throughout society.

The kind of law that we are discussing here would be more specifically labeled, by many moral philosophers and ethicists, as "positive law." These same commentators would stress that *law* is a broader concept and that it can take many forms, including those that we might call natural law and moral law. We will return to these concepts later in this book. For the moment, we will concentrate on positive law, since it is the sort with which readers will be most familiar—precisely because such laws are written down and incorporated into the governing structures of institutions that seek to exercise authority.

We know of many examples throughout history in which law has functioned as the primary indicator of morality. The Code of Hammurabi, the Levitical laws of Judaism, and the laws enacted by the Roman Senate provide us with copious examples of how ethical behavior among human beings and

Navigating the Bible

If you have not previously spent much time with the Bible, the following information may be of use. The Bible is composed of a series of books of varying genres, including narrative, poetry, and epistles (letters, usually addressed to a group or community). The first and larger section of the Bible, commonly called (by Christians) the Old Testament, includes roughly the same texts that make up the Hebrew Bible, which is the sacred text of Judaism. This material consists of the *Torah* (Law), the *Nevi'im* (Prophets) and the *Ketuvim* (Writings). Collectively this material is sometimes called the Tanakh, an acronym created from the initial letters of each of the three sections.

The second, shorter part of the (Christian) Bible is called the New Testament. Its first four books are the four Gospels (a translation of the Greek word *euangelion*, meaning "good news"), which describe the life, death, and resurrection of Jesus Christ, believed by Christians to be the Son of God, the Messiah ("anointed one"). The four Gospels tell this story in four different ways; in fact, they tell four different, though related, stories. These are followed by one book of narrative material describing the early spread of Christianity (the Acts of the Apostles, usually just called "Acts"); a series of Epistles (letters written to various early Christian communities), most of which were authored by (or in the name of) Paul of Tarsus, an early convert to Christianity; and one book of dramatic and prophetic material, cast in the form of a vision, and entitled the Revelation to St. John the Divine (usually simply called "Revelation").

Most of the Old Testament was originally written in Hebrew, and most of the New Testament in Greek. The Hebrew Bible had been translated into Greek well before the birth of Jesus, and the entire Christian Bible was translated from Greek (and in the case of certain books, from the original Hebrew) into Latin in the late fourth century after Jesus' birth. The first English translation of the Bible was made in the Middle Ages; a definitive translation appeared in the early seventeenth century, known as the King James Version or Authorized Version. Since that time a large number of English translations have appeared. The current definitive translation, at least for academic purposes, is the New Revised Standard Version (NRSV); this is the version that will usually be quoted in this book unless otherwise specified.

The books of the Bible are subdivided into chapters, and these chapters are further subdivided into verses, which are typically one sentence each (more or less). Biblical texts are traditionally cited by book, chapter, and verse:

Genesis 3:21; John 4:11. The four Gospels have many texts that are parallel to, or even identical with, one another; sometimes two parallel texts are indicated by writing two parallel lines between them: Matt. 4:1 // Mark 1:12. Another form is simply to cite one of the four Gospels and then follow the citation with the abbreviation "par." which means "and its parallels in the other Gospels": Matt. 16:15 par.

among communities shaped, and was shaped by, the law. These laws declare what is right and what is wrong. They recognize that, even though people live on both sides of the thin line between wrong and right, they still live very close to one another; hence, laws are written in order to settle their disputes. As a result of the law, the ancient Hebrews, for example, knew for certain that murder was wrong (and knew what counted as murder); they also knew exactly what to do if one of their oxen fell into their neighbor's pit. (Yes, really: see Exodus 21:33–34.) Of course, it was always possible that a question of right and wrong would arise that was not specifically covered by the law, so a certain amount of judgment and interpretation was still necessary. But the codes of law in ancient civilizations could often be very detailed and complex, attempting to cover most of the cases that were likely to arise.

We continue to rely heavily on law in the present day. When people become convinced of the rightness of a certain activity that was hitherto prohibited by law, they work to have that law repealed. Conversely, they campaign in favor of legislation that would assess penalties for, and thereby deter, actions that they consider morally wrong. Those who find homosexuality to be a moral fault will seek to enact legal descriptions of marriage as exclusively heterosexual. Those who are concerned about the environmental effects of carbon dioxide will seek legal restrictions against those who contribute excessively to its production. In sum, the link between morality and law seems so obvious to us that it scarcely requires mention.

And yet, that link actually turns out to be rather weak—for a number of reasons. First, the law (at least, the positive law with which we are primarily concerned here) tends to be focused primarily on preventing bad behavior, rather than encouraging good behavior. We can't enact a law that will require all human beings to be people of good will. We can make it illegal to kill another person, but we can't make it illegal to harbor nasty thoughts against someone, nor can we forbid people from imagining that killing someone might be pleasurable. We can legislate the terms of marriage—who can marry, at what ages, and so on—but we cannot design a law to ensure what most of us would probably think of as one of the most important features of marriage: namely, that the two people love one another.

A second reason for the weak relationship between law and morality is that, ironically enough, the law can actually tend to encourage bad behavior. Because it tends to be written in an attempt to restrict the worst possible forms of behavior (and can do little to encourage good behavior), people often tend to push their own bad behavior right up to the very limits of the law—and occasionally beyond it. This is true not only of individuals, but of communities and institutions as well. For example, in the 1970s, the United States and the Soviet Union were engaged in a series of diplomatic overtures called the Strategic Arms Limitation Talks, in which they attempted to negotiate limits on the number of nuclear weapons that each side could build. But every time a limit was set—which would always be somewhere beyond the numbers of weapons that each side had at the time—each nation would immediately build weapons right up to the numerical limit. The law, which was intended as a restraint, actually became an incentive to work *against* that intention. This feature of the law is so commonplace that it is inscribed in one of the oldest stories we know. In the biblical account of creation, the man and the woman are given an abundant garden; everything they need is provided to them. They have only one rule to live by—and that is the rule that they immediately break (Gen. 3:6). The human spirit often seems to be somewhat allergic to whatever imposes any form of restraint on our actions. We tend to test limits and push up against them; and, not infrequently, we break out of them altogether.

A third and final weakness in the relationship between law and morality is that we can sometimes be led to believe that, simply because we have met all the conditions of the law, we are therefore good people. We follow the rules, but if the rules have left a loophole that allows us to avoid incurring any penalty, we happily take advantage of that loophole. We can even come to pride ourselves on our thoroughgoing adherence to the law, while engaging in behavior that most people would label morally dubious, or wicked, or just plain evil.

The end of the law

In the face of these inadequacies of the (positive) law as a basis for moral judgment, a wandering preacher and teacher in first-century Palestine began to speak about moral behavior in a different way. He believed that, rightly understood, the law—particularly the Jewish law, which was so much a part of the culture in which he lived—need not have all of the negative consequences that we have outlined here. Quite the contrary: the law could be understood in such a way that it did *not* encourage bad behavior; that it in fact could encourage good behavior; and that it did not automatically lead people to treat it as a minimum standard or to take advantage of its loopholes. He never argued that the law was a bad thing, but rather, that it could be abused in ways that led to negative consequences.

In order to address this abuse of the law, that wandering Palestinian Jew—Jesus of Nazareth—emphasized a theme that was not at all new to his culture, but may have too often been neglected. His theme was that ethical behavior depends, not just on whether or not one has obeyed the relevant laws, but on *the attitude and disposition* with which a person acts. So, for example, concerning the laws against murder and adultery (particularly in the form that they took as part of the Jewish law), he suggested that it was not enough to refrain from these acts if one retained the dispositions and attitudes that might lead to these acts (such as anger or lust). He argued that those who obey the law against murder are not necessarily behaving well; in fact, if they retain a disposition of anger against another person, this is itself tantamount to murder (Matt. 5:21–22; on adultery, see Matt. 5:27–28).

Needless to say, a person's attitudes and dispositions cannot be legislated by the government, nor can they even be determined (with any degree of certainty) by anyone other than the person who is thus disposed. (Even that person may be subject to considerable self-deception about her or his attitudes and dispositions.) Nevertheless, Jesus insisted that judgments about right and wrong action must necessarily pay attention to the attitudes and assumptions with which we undertake those actions. He repeatedly pointed out the problems inherent in relying only on the positive law for morality: it could easily be abused in such a way that it failed to encourage good behavior, encouraged bad behavior, or allowed people to mistake their observation of the letter of the law for truly good moral behavior. Even the divinely-given law, he suggested, could be (and sometimes had been) interpreted in ways that led to these morally troublesome consequences. Despite his concerns about these abuses of the law, however, Jesus emphasized that he did not seek to abolish it, replace it, or render it irrelevant. Rather, he sought to *fulfill* it (Matt. 5:17): that is, to bring its morally positive intentions to full fruition.

This element of Jesus' teaching was strongly emphasized by his most articulate and prolific early interpreter, Paul of Tarsus. Paul emphasized that the law, however good, could not by itself make for a good life: he himself had tried to be blameless under the law, and yet could not declare his life to be a good life. He knew that he had done all sorts of moral evil, even while adhering strictly to the law. He therefore argued that a truly good life could never rely solely on obedience to the law; it would require another source. This "other source" would need to be something in which we could put all our trust: not in the law, but instead, in a *person*. For Paul, that person was Jesus of Nazareth, whom he believed to be the Son of God, the promised Messiah—the one who had been anointed by God, singled out as a special divine messenger. (The ancient Greek word for anointed was *christos*, so the title *Christ* is used to indicate this special role.) Jesus' authority was based on his status as a spokesperson for God; in fact, Paul often implies (and the later Christian tradition would explicitly claim) that, in some sense, Jesus Christ *was* God.

Paul affirmed Jesus' own claim that he, Jesus, was the *fulfillment* of the law. Paul claimed that Jesus was able, in his person, to provide what the law had not provided, especially given the way that it had been abused by those seeking to maximize their own self-interest. According to Paul, the very nature of the law prevented it from becoming the source of a truly good life; the true source was Jesus Christ. And so Paul wrote that "Christ is the end of the law" (Rom. 10:4).

"End"—in what sense?

Unpacking Paul's description of Jesus Christ as "the end of the law" will require most of the rest of this book. For the present moment, however, we need to focus on one word in particular: the word "end." This word, which is a translation of the Greek word *telos*, has multiple layers of meaning. On the one hand, it means "end" in the sense of the last item in a sequence—as when the words "The End" appear after the last line of a story. So, on the one hand, Paul seems to be saying that, after Jesus Christ, there is no law—the law has come to an end. And in a sense, he does mean this; he understands the law as something that was necessary for a time, to provide guidance and discipline, but that has been replaced by a new standard of morality (Gal. 3:23–25). But this is not all—for the word "end" has another significant meaning as well: we use it to refer to the *goal* or *purpose* of something, as in the question "to what end?" or the phrase "the end justifies the means." So Paul also seems to be saying that, in his view, Christ is the *end* of the law in the sense that he is the goal or purpose of the law: the reason for the law's existence, the final standard to which the law points us. This accords with Jesus' own description of himself as having come not to abolish the law, but to fulfill it.

What might it mean to think of morality as something that is based, not on a principle or a rule, but on a *person*? At first glance, the idea seems to hold some promise; but it leads to some difficult questions as well. For one thing, what if the person upon whom we base our entire ethical framework turns out to be a crackpot or a charlatan? Can we ever be sure enough about a particular person's character that we would be willing to use that one life as the basis for our entire notion of the good? Many commentators believe that these matters pose significant challenges to the basic assumptions of Christian ethics.

And the questions don't stop there. Even if we were able to develop enough confidence in one person's life that we were willing to base our ethics on it, what would that mean? Would it mean following that person's ethical injunctions? (If so, wouldn't that just be another form of basing our ethics on principles or rules?) Or does it mean that we are behaving morally only when we behave as that person did? If so, how should we address the questions that did not confront him but which do confront us (because of differences in geography, in human culture, and especially in technology)? Should we try to use the scant historical evidence about his life to determine what his view would be on the ethical questions that confront us today, asking "What would Jesus do?" Or does that approach simply lead to speculation and self-deception, since we tend to shape our assumptions about what Jesus would do in ways that will justify whatever we were planning to do anyway?

These are all legitimate questions. In fact, they demonstrate just how complicated an idea it is to replace some of our typical assumptions about ethics or morality, as being based on law or rules or principles, with an approach based on a person. But that is precisely what Christianity has sought to do. Of course, alongside this approach, systems of ethics based on law, rules, or principles have continued to develop and to gain a certain amount of acceptance, even among Christians—so much so that an account of ethics based on a person is one that some people find difficult to think of as ethics at all. In the contemporary era, the word "ethics" usually leads us to think of rules, or principles, or laws, or some kind of definitive standard by which decisions can be made. Instead, we find—a person? A person who lived over two thousand years ago, and on the other side of the world? A very particular person, with certain attributes (male, Jewish, itinerant, unmarried) that make it very difficult to extrapolate his circumstances to those of people who are not like him in one or more of those ways? How can one person be the standard for morality?

Again, it will take us most of this book to wrestle with and understand even the *nature* of that question, let alone provide an acceptable answer to it. For now, it may be enough to recognize that we may have to redefine the terms of the discussion in order to make sense of this claim. We enter into the process of thinking about ethics with such strong predispositions about the meaning of the term that we may have to reorient ourselves rather radically in order to understand what *Christian* ethics might possibly be. Indeed, one recent commentator (a British theologian named John Milbank) has suggested that, given the kinds of things that we commonly associate with the word "morality," it might not be possible to imagine that morality could ever be *Christian* at all. The title of one of his essays asks the question "Can Morality Be Christian?"—and it begins as follows:

> Let me tell you the answer straightaway. It is no. Not "no" there cannot be a specifically Christian morality. But no, morality cannot be Christian . . . Christian morality is a thing so strange, that it must be declared immoral or amoral according to all other human norms and codes of morality.

At various points along the way, we will come to recognize the importance of this claim. This book will, in fact, speak of Christian morality and Christian ethics, but with a recognition that in doing so, we are significantly redefining the terms "morality" and "ethics" as they are used in our prevailing cultural context.

Attention to the practices

In order to understand what Christian ethics might be, we will have to enter into the realm of Christian action. If ethics is concerned, at least in part, with *how we act*, then we will need to understand *how Christians act*—particularly in those fields of action which are most identifiably Christian. We need to begin, not with the difficult decisions and their either/or structure, but with the actions that constitute everyday Christian life. One such field of action is that of worship; whatever else they may do, and however else we might seek to identify and understand specifically Christian action, we can at least point to Christians' long tradition of worship as one indicator of how they act. And by examining Christian worship, we will be attending to the Christian understanding of God, of the significance of Jesus Christ and his teachings, and of the role that God is understood to play in the formation of the Christian life.

Thus the first two parts of this book are organized according to the structure of Christian worship, sometimes known as the *liturgy*. (The word "liturgy," defined as "the prescribed set of forms for public Christian ceremonies," comes from the Greek word *leitourgia*, derived in turn from the words *laos*—"the people"—and *ergon*, "work"; the liturgy is the "work of the people," thus the public services of Christian worship.) The most commonly employed Christian liturgy has two principal parts; this is mirrored by the division of parts one and two of this book. In adopting this structure, I do not mean to suggest that Christian worship must always and only take this particular form; in fact, even in the most highly structured worship services, the various parts of the service may well appear in a radically different order from what I offer here. The argument of the book does not depend on this, or any other, particular form of Christian worship; it only seeks to emphasize the close connections between Christian worship and Christian ethics.

The first part of the worship service, the Liturgy of the Word, involves the gathering of the Christian community into one place, a proclamation of its identity (what they hold in common and makes them who they are), and the recitation and interpretation of the stories of the faith. In the second part, the Liturgy of the Eucharist, the focus shifts to one of the central practices of Christian worship: the gathering around a table for a symbolic meal. This part of the service includes acts of peacemaking and forgiveness, the offering of oneself, the active remembering of God's work in the world, and the sharing together in a meal of thanksgiving. By working our way through the Christian liturgy, we will come to understand the stories and actions that are most formative for Christians, and will thus have a better idea of the assumptions that operate within Christian ethics.

At the end of the liturgy, the worshipers are sent out into the world to continue the work of the people outside the confines of the Church. Thus the final third of the book examines what might happen outside those confines, moving through a typical "week" in which people must face a number of complex issues: participating in the economic and political order of their culture, facing decisions relating to the health and well-being of the physical body, and negotiating their relationships with other human beings and with the environment. As we move through this hypothetical week, we will consider how a person's *formation* in the Christian life, through the stories and the practices of the faith, helps to shape that person's everyday life in the world.

Me, you, and us

Throughout our investigation, one theme will emerge repeatedly: that of *community*. This may seem to be an unusual emphasis, given the world around us. We live in a culture of radical individualism, in which we often assume that we can make all our decisions for ourselves (and largely *by* ourselves), in isolation from the influences of others. Our relative wealth, our desire for autonomy, and our easy access to technology all help to make such isolation possible in ways that were not the case for many of our forebears.

In spite of the prevailing perception, however, this individualism is ultimately an illusion. Practically everything we do while isolated from one another is actually dependent on the activity of other people: they record the music we listen to, they cook and deliver the pizza that we order, they write the instant messages back to us. But because these others are often not physically present, we suffer under the illusion that we are relatively independent of them. And when other people are completely absent—when they abandon and forsake other human beings altogether—then those who are isolated suffer even more: they will often be severed from sources of health care, transportation, productive employment, and healthy food. All these resources require the participation and labor of others, and those who are isolated by political, economic, and social structures may find themselves without even the most basic needs for survival.

Certainly, the individualism and isolating structures of our culture can lead to the illusion that self-reliance is the greatest good; and this in turn can lead to the illusion that ethics, too, is largely concerned with the decisions that we make as individuals. But throughout the long history of moral reflection, one theme has arisen again and again: that our ethical assumptions and our decision-making processes are heavily dependent on the *communities* within which we are nurtured. Our assumptions are largely inherited from those by whom we are surrounded. Even if we rebel against our communities of origin, we still find ourselves shaped by their structures—just as a jet of water is shaped and oriented by the pipe through which it is being pumped. We are connected to one another in deep and abiding ways, as we are sometimes surprised to discover. (The 2004 film *Crash* provided a good illustration of this surprising connection, as a series of apparently independent characters in the storyline eventually reveal themselves as intimately interconnected.)

This, then, is one final bit of wisdom that I want to glean from the words of the Dixie Chicks with which I opened this introduction: that "the thin line" is not only a good description of the subtle, easy-to-miss distinction between wrong and right; it's also a good description of the subtle, almost invisible distinctions among human beings. Regardless of how thoroughly we want to think of ourselves as self-contained individuals, and regardless of how little we imagine ourselves shaped by the communities of which we are a part, we will eventually come to see that there is only a thin line "between me and you, and you and me."

Yes, it's a mighty thin line.

Questions for discussion

1. Does the "two-choice system" described here resonate with your experience? Have you ever been frustrated by the either/or mentality that is sometimes associated with certain moral issues? How have you responded to this?

2. Think of a moral issue on which you hold, or have held, a strong stance. Have you typically thought of those who hold the opposite position as "very

far away" in terms of their moral assumptions? Have you had direct contact with such persons and, if so, what resulted from that contact?

3. Do you think of ethics as primarily associated with principles and rules? What are some of the ethical principles that you have heard about or incorporated into your life? Do these principles seem to you to be strong and appropriate, or do you have doubts about their applicability?

4. Discuss your experience of law, particularly with respect to how it shapes moral behavior. Do you agree with the concerns raised about law in this introduction? If so, provide at least one example from your own experience that corroborates what is said here. If not, provide your own perspective on the role of law and offer an example that illustrates it.

5. How familiar are you with the traditional Christian worship service as it is outlined here? Have you been present at such a service and/or participated in one? If you have had some experience of Christian worship, describe the degree to which it conforms to the description in this chapter. How have your own experiences differed from what is described here?

Sources cited in this chapter and/or recommended for further reading

Note: complete citations of these and all other works listed at the end of each chapter may be found at the end of this book.

Crash, dir. Paul Haggis, 2004

The Dixie Chicks. "Thin Line." Sony, 2006

Joseph Fletcher, *Situation Ethics*

Stanley Hauerwas and Samuel Wells, "Why Christian Ethics Was Invented," chapter 3 of *The Blackwell Companion to Christian Ethics*

Immanuel Kant, *Critique of Practical Reason*; *Foundations of the Metaphysics of Morals*

Neil Messer, SCM *Studyguide to Christian Ethics*

John Milbank, "Can Morality Be Christian?" in *The Word Made Strange: Theology, Language, Culture* (the quotation is from p. 219)

John Stuart Mill, *Utilitarianism*

Paul Ramsey, *Basic Christian Ethics*

Bernd Wannenwetsch, "Ecclesiology and Ethics," in Meilaender and Werpehowski, eds., *The Oxford Handbook of Theological Ethics*

Part 1

Narrating the Christian life

1

Character and community

or: Why ethics probably isn't what you think

If you were to ask a random group of people to tell you what ethics is about, you would probably receive a fairly predictable range of answers. "It's about the differences between right and wrong." "It tells you how you're supposed to act." "Rules for good behavior." "How we should live." But if you press a little further and ask for an example of a topic that might be discussed in an ethics course, I'll wager that almost all the examples would be of the same type: they would be about difficult decisions concerning hard cases. Most people think of ethics as a discipline that is designed to help us wrestle with complicated dilemmas: whether to turn off the life-support system for someone in a persistent coma; how to balance a region's economic dependence on the logging industry against the potential environmental degradation; whether to send soldiers into combat.

Climbing into the lifeboat

One particular example of these difficult decisions concerning hard cases tends to appear quite frequently in conversations about the nature of ethics. The example runs something like this: "You're one of five people stranded at sea in a lifeboat. You have food and water for only four people. How do you decide what to do?" This example is so common that it has provided a name for this way of thinking about ethics: "lifeboat ethics." The more technical term is "quandary ethics": you're in a difficult situation, a quandary. You are faced with competing goods—that is, more than one morally positive element—which can't all exist simultaneously, or else there are insufficient resources to meet the needs that are present. Your mission, should you choose to accept it, is to prioritize these goods—or to divide the scarce resources among the competing needs.

How economics influences ethics

Right away, we can observe how thoroughly this way of thinking about ethics has been influenced by the way that we think about economics. Resources are scarce; people with particular needs are in competition with each other for a slice of the pie; and you, the student, are expected to jump into the situation that has been described and to render a decision without asking too many questions about the context or the circumstances. In its form, at least, this is very similar to the way that we make economic decisions. I have only a little money and even less time; other people are getting ahead of me by buying the right things at the right moment; and so I need to jump into the marketplace and make my strategic purchase. If you start asking me questions about the working conditions of the people who produced the goods, or about the environmental impact of the material from which they're made, or about the impact they may have on my health thirty years down the line—well, I just can't deal with all those questions right now. I don't have much time or much money, and I have to make this purchase, and it's a good bargain, and that's the end of the story.

Of course, the dilemmas that are described under the rubric of "lifeboat ethics"—whether they are about lifeboats or about turning off life-support systems or about sending soldiers into combat—are usually much weightier matters than our decisions about which new consumer toy we're going to buy. (Note, however, that in the previous example, the questions that we tend to put off when we're trying to decide whether to buy something often have wide-ranging ethical implications. We'll return to this point in a moment.) In any case, these decisions—whether about our purchases, or about matters with more immediate life-and-death consequences—are very similar in structure: they're about limited resources and competing goods. Nevertheless, those lifeboat-style questions tend to be much more frustrating to us than are most of our economic choices, because we don't have such straightforward ways of resolving them. We would like to be able to resolve those life-and-death quandaries in the same way that we make economic decisions: by minimizing the costs and maximizing the benefits. But when it comes to something like turning off someone's life-support system, or throwing someone out of the lifeboat, the costs and benefits are not always easy to identify with precision. (Just how much is a human life worth, anyway? Are some worth more than others? Does my life lose some or all of its worth when

I'm in a persistent coma? How do we know?) In fact, when you get right down to it, the costs and benefits of our *economic* decisions aren't always very easy to identify. (Exactly how much will my life be improved by this new MP3 player? Will the iPod really provide me with seven more units of social approval than the off-brand model? Will it lose its value entirely if I can't stop thinking about how much damage its production is doing to the planet? How can I know?) The trouble with defining ethics as being about "hard cases" is that, when you think about them long enough, they're *all* hard cases.

In order to imagine an alternative approach, we can retrieve an insight that goes quite far back into the history of ethics—at least as far as Thomas Aquinas in the thirteenth century. We might put it this way: we're tempted to imagine that all of our actions as human beings might be divided into two types—those actions with moral significance and those without. In truth, however, *all* human action is moral action. This is so because, first, as human beings, we are possessed of an intellect and a will, and we're not constrained to act merely from instinct; thus, even at the most physical, bodily level of satisfying our appetites, we actually have considerable choice in what we do. Second, we can't always predict the consequences of our action with precision; one thing leads to another, and who knows whether the half-eaten sandwich that someone accidently leaves alongside a mountain stream might fall into the water, breed bacteria, and eventually poison someone who lives many miles downstream. We might have a spirited argument over whether or not the sandwich-tosser is *responsible* for the poisoning (indeed, moral philosophers have done exactly that!); but it would be difficult to imagine that the initial action was not, in some sense, a *moral* action—particularly given the effects that it eventually brought about.

Decisions, decisions

Nor are we on safe ground when we define ethics as being primarily about decisions. The trouble is that, in most cases, they're not really *decisions* at all—or rather, they *are* decisions, but not in the way that we typically think about making a decision. In other words, they are not carefully considered, thoroughly examined judgments that take all relevant data into account. We don't actually stop to weigh all the potential costs and benefits every time we make a choice about, say, our purchase of consumer goods; if we did, life would grind to a halt. The difficulties are already obvious enough to us, even when we limit ourselves to considering the immediate costs and benefits; as I've already suggested, we often end up comparing apples and oranges, trying to weigh social approval against growing credit-card debt, or measuring potential entertainment value against time lost from work. As we begin to consider the wider environmental and human costs of any particular purchase, the boundaries of the conversation expand infinitely. They stretch back in time to consider the origins of the materials from which the item is made; they also reach forward in time, leading us to ask how it will affect us a decade or two later (and how we're ever going to dispose of it). The boundaries also stretch out to other people—not just down the street but on the other side of the world: Who made this object? Under what conditions? With what degree of sacrifice? Do I want to be involved in that? These questions, in turn, lead us back to recalculate the original cost–benefit analysis, about the depth of our desire for the item, its potential usefulness or benefit, and all the other ways we could spend our paltry disposable income. And all the time, while we're standing at the register attempting to evaluate this potentially endless list of concerns, we realize we're late for dinner—and the people standing in line behind us are starting to get a little annoyed.

If it's this difficult to weigh the costs and benefits of purchasing an article of clothing or a small electronic item, how much more complex will be the decision-making process when the question involves human beings whom we know, and/or involves human beings in direct and immediate ways—perhaps facing matters of life and death? Precisely because the weighing of costs and benefits is so difficult, we don't actually do it in most cases. We make decisions, but rarely do we base them on a careful calculus; in most cases, we don't have the time to do so, nor the information that we'd need (particularly since some of that information would require us to be able to predict the future with stunning accuracy). But most of all, when we're in the moment and facing the actual choice of alternative paths of action, we don't even have the *inclination* to go through a careful decision-making process. We are too constrained by circumstances, too limited in our knowledge and foreknowledge, and—particularly since it's likely to be a matter of great personal interest to us (we're among the people on the lifeboat, after all)—we are too emotionally involved to sit down and make a carefully nuanced, wholly rational, truly unconstrained decision about the right course of action. Such decisions are only possible if made in the abstract, far away from the realities of the moment. In fact, the only place that ethical decisions of this sort are likely to be made is when analyzing case studies in an ethics course.

All of this suggests that, in the end, ethics is *not* primarily about making difficult decisions when faced with hard cases—and this for at least three reasons. First, *all* the cases are hard cases; in fact, they are even harder than we imagined, because their ramifications expand through time and across space. Second, all action is moral action; we can't limit discussions of ethics to an isolated subset of all the things we do, because everything we do has potential moral consequences. And third, because—while we do in fact make decisions—our decision-making usually will not (and, in fact, very often *cannot*) be based on a careful process of cost–benefit analysis that can be taught and learned in a class.

Babel: why all action is moral action

In Genesis 11, we read a story in which all people speak a single language. They decide to build a great city, including a tower that would reach to the heavens, in order to "make a name" for themselves. God is not impressed by their pretensions to grandeur, and confounds the building project by multiplying their languages and dispersing them. "Therefore it was called Babel, because there the Lord confused the language of all the earth; and from there the Lord scattered them abroad over the face of all the earth" (Gen. 11:9).

This story has proven to be very fertile soil for reflections on the human condition. It has re-appeared in many genres of art and literature—from the paintings of the Dutch masters, to the work of postmodern philosophers of language, to the inimitable comedy of Douglas Adams' *The Hitchhiker's Guide to the Galaxy* (where the "Babelfish" serves as an intergalactic translating machine and plays a fundamental, if somewhat ironic, role in a "proof for the non-existence of God"!).

In 2006, the story re-appeared in the title of an Academy-Award-nominated film that helps to illustrate the claim that "all action is moral action"—*Babel*. In its complicated, non-linear plot, an interconnected series of events transpire in three far-flung locations: North Africa, Japan, and the US–Mexico border. At various points during the film, we become aware that various characters have made certain decisions and taken certain actions that would seem to have no obvious moral implications: a sightseeing trip to Morocco; a trip to a cousin's wedding; a hunter's gift of a rifle to his African guide. But eventually, these seemingly benign actions lead to death and near-death, to arrests and international tension, and to a whole series of physical, emotional, and psychological wounds.

Of course, as a genre, film is well known for tying together events that appear to have no obvious relationships; but in this case, the connections are not just coincidences. Rather, the film helps us understand the reasons why minor, casual decisions can have such significant moral consequences. Ours is not a world of perfect communication; we are divided, not only by our differing languages, but also by national borders, by differences in age and socio-economic class, and by a whole range of customs that seem perfectly natural to one group but are totally incomprehensible to others. We live, as one philosopher has put it, "after Babel": we are separated from one another by a whole host of political, economic, and linguistic structures. We are scattered abroad over the face of all the earth.

And this means that we often cannot predict the consequences of our actions. If we lived in a single closed system in which every part of the system was in tune with every other part (as in a well designed computer program or a perfectly functioning automobile engine), then we would know exactly what ramifications would ensue from an action taken in one part of the system. But our world does not experience the perfect communication and interlocking structures that mark a computer program or a car engine. It is filled with human actors who have a certain degree of freedom, and whose actions— undertaken, as they must be, in the absence of perfect communication with other human beings—will often lead to consequences that could never have been predicted. And thus, no human decision or action is entirely void of moral implications; we just don't always know what those implications will be.

Well then, what is it?

If this commonly assumed definition of ethics as difficult decision-making provides an inaccurate portrait of the enterprise, then exactly how *should* we define it? For a hint about the answer to that question, we need to go back to the ancient Greeks, and to the Greek word *ēthos*, from which our word "ethics" is derived. We also have the English word "ethos," which we use to describe the general atmosphere of a place or an institution; the ethos of a good college or university might be described with phrases such as "intellectually stimulating" or "encouraging and caring" or "a 'work hard, play hard' environment." That same word "ethos" can be applied to people as well as places; but rather than speaking about a person's "atmosphere," we speak about her or his "character." That word—"character"—is probably the best English translation of the Greek word *ēthos*. And *character* is the ultimate answer to the question we've been examining throughout this chapter: it's what ethics is all about. Ethics concerns the study, evaluation, and formation of *people of good character*.

At first glance, this may seem to be an odd claim. We usually prefer not to evaluate a person's moral standing until we've had a careful look at what they actually *do*. We might not care for that man who lives down the street, but we're not about to make a judgment about his *character* until he does something that gives us some evidence for doing so. Thus in our culture we have devised a method for gathering, sifting, and examining such evidence, and for making judgments about people based on that evidence. It is a relatively reliable method, but—as we will soon see—it also has some significant disadvantages.

The role of law

In making judgments about character, at least in our culture, we rely very heavily on *law*. (I raised this point in the introduction to this book, but now we need to examine it in more detail.) We live relatively private, isolated lives, and so we rarely know enough about the actions of "that man down the street" to make a judgment about his character. But if his name were suddenly to appear in the local newspaper as having been indicted on a charge of, say, domestic violence—well, *then* we'd feel we could safely make a judgment, because we would have learned something about his actions. (However, if we know very much about the law, we'd recognize that an indictment does not give us direct access to knowledge of exactly what the defendant has *done*; so even then, we would be wise to wait until we were more certain that he had actually done what he was said to have done.) And because we rarely have any direct access to that information, we're not very comfortable pronouncing on a person's character—at least not until after some kind of broadly recognized external authority (such as a court of law) has rendered some form of judgment, so that we might be reasonably certain about that person's actions.

But by that point, of course, *it's too late*. If we are studying ethics in order to think about how people should act and about how to judge human action—and yet, if no judgments can be rendered until those people have acted and have been examined by an external authority—then we can only profit from such an analysis after the fact. Only after the man has admitted his guilt (and/or has been sent to jail on a charge of domestic violence) do we feel fully comfortable declaring that his behavior was wrong. His victims have already suffered abuse (indeed, with respect to this particular form of wrongful behavior, statistics suggest that they probably suffered it for some time before it ever came to light). While those victims may be relieved by the actions of an external authority (which forcibly removes the threat from their presence), they would have been much better off had there been some way to rearrange things so that the abuse had never happened in the first place.

How do we prevent wrongdoing from taking place? Again, in our culture, our efforts at prevention also rely heavily on *law*. We have developed certain rules about what one can and cannot do, and although these rules are subject to a great deal of interpretation, most people understand them fairly well. For those who break the rules, certain penalties are imposed or certain privileges are denied. The man down the street has broken the rule that says that you can't do bodily injury to another person except in certain limited circumstances. You may be inside your own home and doing that injury to the members of your own family, but this does not count as one of those exceptional circumstances. The rule, which in this case takes the form of a law, also says that those who break it will be subject to criminal prosecution and punishment.

This is certainly an improvement on a system that simply waits until after the fact to render a judgment about one's actions. It provides a guideline for action ahead of time; and, while some elements of the law can be rather obscure, this one seems relatively clear. Most people know that they should not do bodily injury to the other members of their own family, and that they may face criminal penalties if they do so. Of course, this knowledge does not always deter a person from acting—and this for a variety of possible reasons. People sometimes imagine that they will never be caught, and so feel free to ignore the rules. Others would never break the rule under most circumstances; nevertheless, because they are in a crisis situation or are experiencing a moment of extreme emotion, the rule seems to evaporate and they act without thinking about the consequences. Still others are perfectly aware of the rules, but they develop a series of rationalizations as to why those rules don't really apply in their particular case.

These factors may seem like nothing more than attempts to excuse bad behavior; interestingly enough, however, they all have some basis in the law. The law itself does create exceptions and loopholes; moreover, this does not always happen at the time of their legislation, but sometimes occurs precisely because a person thinks that a law doesn't apply in his or her circumstances and breaks it as a way of challenging it. (A court may eventually rule in favor of the lawbreaker.) So when people disobey the law because they think it doesn't apply to them—for instance, because they believe that a certain situation or motive on their part puts them beyond its reach—they can sometimes cite reasonable legal precedents for doing so. And what about those who disobey because they think they won't be caught? Sadly, the statistics are apparently on their side. Of all the crimes that are committed, the number in which the crime is even *reported*—let alone in which the perpetrators are detected, arrested, successfully prosecuted, and appropriately punished—makes for a very small percentage indeed. And we have not even considered the degree to which certain persons are privileged (because of their age, sex, ethnicity, nationality, profession, or social class), making it extremely unlikely that they will ever come up against the force of law—even if they repeatedly violate it.

Another route to character

Thus far, we have discovered that ethics, if it is to be useful at all, cannot wait until a person has committed wrongdoing; nor can it rely solely on rules and laws to prevent wrongdoing. And in the end, we might well want to set our sights higher than just discouraging those acts of wrongdoing that are so extreme that we have enacted laws against them. In fact, in the best of all possible worlds, we would like ethics not just to discourage these and other forms of bad action, but *actively to encourage good action*. If ethics is about the formation of people of good character, then its goal ought to be to direct us toward the good.

This helps us understand why we need to make judgments about character long before the rules are broken (and even, in some cases, before we've decided or figured out what the rules *are*). We would like not just to punish bad actions, and not even just to *deter* bad actions, but to encourage good ones. In order to do so, we must focus our attention not only on the actions themselves but also on *the kinds of people who act in those ways*. We expect to find a certain continuity between how people act and the kinds of people they are—that is, their character. We can often predict how they will act, even in those crisis situations or experiences of intense emotion, by examining their *character*.

For a good illustration of how this works, think about the characters in a novel or a play. The good writer knows about this relationship between character and action, and writes accordingly. It's not that we, as readers, can predict everything that all the people in the novel are likely to do based on their character; but once the character acts, we should be able to recognize certain lines of continuity between that action and everything that has preceded it. In an early scene in Charles Dickens' *A Christmas Carol*, we are not terribly surprised that Ebenezer Scrooge turns away two men who have come to his office to ask him for a charitable donation to help those who find themselves in desperate poverty at Christmas time. After all, everything we have seen in him thus far has suggested that he is unkind, miserly, and focused almost entirely upon his own self-interest. Of course, Scrooge does not merely turn these gentlemen out (and impolitely, too); he adds a few words of his own philosophy about the poor, to the effect that they should be driven into workhouses and, if they cannot work, into prison. This may surprise us, because—at this early point in the story—we have not yet understood the depth of his cruelty (or any of the possible reasons for it). But this new event gives us a further indication of Scrooge's character; and the more of his actions we observe, the more accurately we will be able to describe just what kind of person this is. After this incident, for example, we are not all that surprised when Scrooge lambasts his clerk for requesting leave not to come to work on Christmas day.

So although we cannot be expected to predict every action on the basis of character, we can discern a close and reciprocal relationship between the two. We can usually understand how particular actions fit into our picture of a person's character as a whole; and these actions in turn contribute to a fuller understanding of that person's character. As readers, we *would* be surprised if, after what has transpired in the opening scene of *A Christmas Carol*, Scrooge suddenly reached in his pocket and gave a handful of change to a beggar on the street. At the very least, we would need to re-evaluate his character: perhaps he is simply confused about the notion of charity, or perhaps he prefers to help people in secret while maintaining a gruff exterior. But in fact, as the story goes, he maintains his miserly character throughout its opening day (and part way into the night), just as we expect him to. No significant change in his character will occur without some kind of outside intervention—and even then, it comes very slowly. Here, as elsewhere, we expect a certain degree of consistency between a person's character and his or her actions.

This is why ethics properly focuses its attention on character. If a person has a courageous character, she will be likely to do courageous things. Misers do miserly things and blowhards do boastful things. People typically act in the ways that they do, not because they pause to work out the ethical ramifications at every instant, or even because the rules tell them to, but because they are people of a certain character. Thus certain kinds of actions just seem natural to them: they take these actions for granted and often do them without much thought. Brave soldiers do not pause before a battle and work out whether or not to fight, and how hard; fighting bravely just seems to them to be the right thing to do. Generous people do not stop and develop a detailed cost–benefit analysis every time someone asks them for money. They just give, because they take it for granted; for them, that's just what one does when asked. Ethics is about character, and our character indicates what kinds of actions we will take for granted as the obvious course of action.

Of course, character is not always good character; one can have a kind of character in which *bad* actions are taken for granted as the natural thing to do. A well disciplined torturer, for example, does not pause before each session and go through a crisis of conscience about how horrible this action is going to be. The torturer has come to think of his work as the natural thing to do; if someone asks him whether it isn't rather obvious that he's doing a wicked thing, the suggestion will sound foreign to him. Part of his character is to regard individual human lives and human suffering as less significant than his obedience to those who have commanded him to do this deed, and to the larger cause to which he and his compatriots are committed. He has developed the character traits needed to be a "good"—that is, a bad—torturer (good at his job, though evil from a moral perspective). The question of how we come to distinguish good character from bad is a matter that will take up most of the rest of this book.

In the meantime, let us summarize: ethics is about *ēthos*—character—and character is what constitutes the moral framework within which we operate. Our character determines what kinds of things we will take for granted, what will seem natural to us, and the degree to which we even bother to stop and think about an action before we undertake it. Character is what leads us to pay very little attention to whatever rules and laws have been devised with the goal of shaping our behavior, and to get on with living our lives according to our character. Like the characters in a novel or a play, we mostly act as one might expect a person with our particular character traits to act.

Of course, unlike the characters in a novel or a play, we are not "written" by an author; we have a great deal of freedom to act as we might choose. We also have a great deal of control over the character of our own lives. (Actually, most novelists and playwrights will tell you that their characters, too, often seem to have that same kind of control over their own (fictional) lives—doing things that the author had never planned for them to do. This itself is a testimony to the continuities between character and action—thoughtfully explored in a number of films such as *Adaptation* (2002) and *Stranger than Fiction* (2006).) In any case, the development of our character results from a complicated blend of our own choices and external influences on us; we therefore need to spend some time investigating how this process works.

How is character formed?

The single most influential factor in the formation of character is *habit*. The things that we do over and over again, and eventually that we do almost without thinking about them at all, form the basic structures of our lives. These structures are seen and evaluated by others, who use these observations to form judgments about our character. If we arrive on time to work every day, we will develop a reputation for punctuality. And this won't be a mere façade; we will, in fact, be persons of punctuality. We didn't begin life with this character trait as an inborn disposition; we developed it over the course of our lives by doing the same thing over and over again (namely, being on time).

This very basic observation about the formation of character may sound a bit strange to us, primarily because it goes largely unnoticed. We rarely pause to examine our lives and to say to ourselves, "Ah, I see that I am coming up with a new excuse every time I have the chance to get some physical exercise; therefore I am developing habits of laziness and lethargy, which are endowing me with the character trait of *sloth*." If we were that firmly aware of the relationships among our actions, our habits, and our character, we would probably take a great deal more care about what we do. But in actual practice, almost all our habits, and therefore our character traits, are being formed while we're paying attention to something else. Certainly, we can make a diligent effort to adopt a new habit and to do certain things with regularity and with energy. But we are busy people, and our lives do not usually allow us to give full, individualized attention to the hundreds of things that we do every day that have become, for us, matters of habit.

Most of our habits fall into two categories: the stories that we tell repeatedly and the activities in which we regularly engage. (It may seem odd at first to think of storytelling as a habit, but I have a particular kind of story in mind; I hope this will become clear momentarily.) We need to spend some time examining each of these forms of habit; they will, in fact, provide the overarching structure for the first two-thirds of this book. Part 1 will examine the stories that form Christians most deeply, and Part 2 will focus on some of the activities in which they are habitually engaged.

Stories and narratives

We tell stories for a variety of reasons: to remember our past, to entertain ourselves in the present, and to give ourselves some direction for the future. We tell stories to our children from long before they are able to understand them; practically as soon as they can talk, they begin to tell stories to us and to one another; and soon they begin to devour them through reading. Human beings seem to be storytelling animals.

Many of the stories that we tell, particularly when we tell them regularly, become *more than just stories* to us; they become *the stories that we live by*. In this book, I will refer to such morally formative stories as "narratives." This is not a hard-and-fast distinction; in fact, we often find that human lives are shaped and formed in significant ways by narratives that most people might regard as "just a story." Nevertheless, I am introducing the term "narrative" here as a reminder that the stories that we tell have differing effects on us: some are told once and quickly forgotten; others are told repeatedly but with an ironic or skeptical tone that allows us to keep them at a distance. But many of the stories that we tell will come to have a morally formative influence on our lives—whether we realize it or not. These are the stories that I refer to in this book as narratives.

Some of our narratives might be drawn from the bedtime stories that we heard as children or the novels that we read as adults, but we are at least as likely to be morally formed by the historical events that we've heard recounted time and again, the tales told by and about our immediate families and friends, and the television shows that we watch religiously. Our narratives also include—and this point is crucial—the *implicit* stories that lie behind some of the most basic assumptions of our culture.

For example, many writers have pointed out that our economic system functions as a story about *scarcity*. We make our economic decisions on the assumption that there is not enough to go around, which is why we pay higher prices for goods in short supply. We save for retirement and guard our pension plans zealously because we just never know whether there will be anyone around to help us out when we're old. We are certainly willing to spend more than we earn—we carry enormous loads of personal debt—but even that action can be motivated by the idea of scarcity: we are afraid that we might, at some moment of our lives, have nothing to do. So we make purchases to insure that there is never a shortage of consumer goods and new adventures to fill up our lives.

Now, most of us did not grow up hearing stories that explicitly described a world of scarcity and explained to us, in vivid detail, that we must always be scrambling to get the goods before someone else gets them first. In fact, many of the stories that we tell to children, and that we enjoy as adults, paint pictures of abundance and generosity. (As one example among millions, think of Max in Maurice Sendak's *Where the Wild Things Are*. In spite of being sent to his room without his supper, he manages to sail across the ocean, to luxuriate in a lush jungle, and to engage in an exuberant "wild rumpus" with the creatures that he finds there.) Sadly, however, these stories become nothing more than a distant childhood memory (or possibly a form of escape) if we don't actually *live by them*; and in our culture, economic concerns tend to dominate our lives, so our narratives are more likely to be the stories of scarcity that we associate with economic structures. Such stories are implicit in the very way that our economy functions; it works through structures of supply and demand that make scarce goods seem more valuable and abundant goods seem relatively less appealing. Because our economic exchanges are dominated by this model of scarcity—because we are in the *habit* of living according to a narrative of scarcity—this actually becomes the narrative that governs our lives.

Of course, this is not *necessarily* the case. We can allow alternative narratives to become more salient in our lives: we can read *A Christmas Carol* and the novels of Barbara Kingsolver and the *Harry Potter* series and other tales of abundance and freely-given gifts. These stories compete with the stories of scarcity that are woven into our economic culture. Which set of stories will have a more morally formative influence on our lives? This will depend entirely upon which ones we habitually live by—whether we do so by making a definitive and explicit choice, or by simply allowing ourselves to be swept along with the crowd. In either case, the stories that we habitually live by will become the narratives that form us most deeply.

Certain stories—like that of scarcity—are more likely to become morally formative narratives simply because they are built into the structures of our daily lives and thus are widely told and retold. Often they are very difficult to avoid; even if we do not actively choose to tell and retell them, they circulate constantly through various forms of popular culture and are transmitted through the ever-present media. For many of us, our most deeply habituated narratives will include (in addition to those that are related to our economic system) those that concern the founding and the history of the nation-state; those that stress self-reliance and individual freedom; those that emphasize the possibility and even the likelihood that disputes are best settled through competition and, if necessary, violence; and those that place a high value on physical pleasure and on the prolongation of a pleasurable life at whatever cost. These stories are so regularly told and retold that they tend to drown out anything that might be posed by way of an alternative.

And yet, these dominant stories will not inevitably become the narratives that form us. We can, as I have suggested here, habituate ourselves in an alternative set of stories that form us in very different ways. As we will see throughout Part 1 of this book, Christians have often sought to undertake an alternative plan of moral formation in precisely this way. They have told and retold a set of stories that are meant to become their narratives—the stories that they live by—even though the moral implications of these narratives may differ radically from those that dominate their particular time and place.

Activities and practices

The second major form that habits take is that of *activities*. In addition to telling stories, we *do* things. Doing them over and over again allows them to take on the quality of a habit, such that we give little thought to the activity. Many of our habitual activities involve attending to the various physical demands of our bodies—moving them from place to place, interacting with our immediate environment, and tending to our needs for nourishment, protection, and rest.

From the point of view of morality, a subset of our activities is of particular interest to us: these are our *practices*. Practices are those habitual activities that have an internal goal that functions, in itself, as the end of the practice:

that is, its purpose, what we're trying to get out of it. In other words, practices are those activities in which we engage, not just in order to achieve some other result that is essentially unrelated to the activity, but as *an end in itself*. They are not just instrumental, comparable to a tool that we might use to achieve some other goal; the goal of a practice is simply to undertake the practice.

Practices also have standards of excellence (even if these are often under serious debate); one can make judgments about whether a practice has been done well or poorly. Sometimes the practice has built-in structures that render this judgment; the excellence of the player of a particular game, for example, may be determined by the ability to win the game. Other practices require judgment calls, which may often be disputed but which, again, are (at least in theory) based on standards internal to the practice. These judgments are sometimes aided by the fact that practices are extended through time, such that we can compare our own participation in a practice to that of people in other times and places.

Thus playing chess is typically a practice; we usually do it not for some larger goal, such as sharpening our mental skills (though that can certainly happen); we play chess in order to play chess. We might play it well or poorly, and there are standards (even if not entirely objective ones) against which we can measure the quality of our play. We might also wait at the train station every day to catch the 6:42 am train to work; but this isn't a practice, because the goal of this activity isn't just to develop the skill of waiting on trains. Waiting for the train isn't an end in itself; we wait for the train in order to catch the train—in order to get to work. The goal of the action of waiting on trains is *external* to the activity itself.

So we catch the train and arrive at work. Is our work a practice? That will depend on several factors. If we undertake it for the primary purpose of making money in order to buy things, then it's not a practice in the sense I'm describing here—its purpose is primarily to satisfy some other need or desire. But if we work because it gives us pleasure to use our gifts in the enterprise of completing the work that we have been given to do, and if there are standards of excellence that we can use to judge whether we do our work well or poorly, it may very well function as a practice.

Of course, we engage in a great many habitual activities that wouldn't fall into the category of practices as I've described them here. Nevertheless, those activities may sometimes develop into practices, since a habit that once had only external goals can sometimes come to generate internal goals as well. A person may have taken a particular job primarily for the money, but over time has come to love the work itself and to rejoice in a job well done. Other activities will rarely become practices, because they just don't have any goals that are internal to the activity itself. It's hard to imagine, for example, the habit of waiting to catch the 6:42 am train becoming a practice; what would be the good of that, in itself? One would have to imagine going to the station, waiting for the train, and then not bothering to take it because one had accomplished the goal of waiting.

At the same time, an activity that isn't a practice can still be formative of our character: by waiting for the train every day, we might well develop certain character traits, such as patience, fortitude, and hope. We might become more observant of and attentive to other human beings, or we might learn to use "empty" time more wisely. Nevertheless, these habits are unlikely to shape us as significantly, or to form our character as deeply, as would a practice that we undertook for the sake of its own internal goals. Waiting for the train *might* make me a little more patient; it might just as easily make me more resigned to the fate of being at the mercy of odd fluctuations in the train schedule. On the other hand, if I understand my work as my true calling in life, and if it takes some time before I can see the actual results of my labors, I'm likely to become a more patient person. The results of my labor are, in this case, internal to the practice of work; and that will always be worth waiting for, whereas the train won't ever be worth it (even though, on a very cold or very hot day, it may feel that way). In the final analysis, waiting on the train is merely a means to a very different end.

Again, practices are here defined quite widely: not just the things that we have *chosen* to do every day, but many of the things that we get drawn into without even noticing. Watching television is a practice because it has goals that are internal to the practice itself: we watch for the sheer pleasure of watching. (It has external goals as well—gathering information, staying in touch with popular culture, and so on—but these are not essential to the practice; one can watch without these external goals.) But watching television is not one of those practices that results from a definitive decision to engage in it ("From this day forward, I shall be a television watcher!"). Rather, we watch television just because it's there: it's a part of our culture. Even that small minority of people in the industrialized West who *don't* own a television cannot completely avoid the practice of watching it; we encounter TV screens in airports, bars, restaurants, and increasingly in other common spaces where, at one time, the more likely practice would have been to gather for conversation. Sometimes we end up engaging in certain practices—and living according to certain narratives—not so much because we have chosen to do so, but because *we haven't chosen not to.*

In other words, certain practices are such an essential part of our culture that the "default" option is to engage in them. When we described stories and narratives, we indicated that some stories are so commonly told and so deeply rooted in our particular time and place that they will automatically become our most morally formative narratives unless we deliberately choose some alternative approach. Matters are analogous here: some practices are so prevalent and assumed that one has to opt out—sometimes at considerable personal cost—in order not to be drawn into these particular practices. The practice of watching television is probably one such example; it has become deeply formative of our character, and this is true regardless of the content of its programming. Consider, for example, how it has altered the likelihood that we will engage in lengthy after-dinner conversation with one another—or that we will pursue any other highly relational activity—when the alternative of turning on the television has become a nearly automatic response.

Some of the most common practices in our culture are watching television; attending sporting events; working at our paid employment; raising children; maintaining a household (including cooking, cleaning, home repair, and the like); participating in voluntary associations such as clubs, team activities, and support groups; playing games; and attending entertainment events (films, theater, concerts, and so on). Obviously, we don't all engage in the same practices, and certainly not to the same degree; but to whatever extent we do engage in them, they form us as persons of a certain character. Precisely *what* qualities of character will result from a given practice is highly variable; one cannot always predict the results. Clearly, some people are strongly shaped by their habits of, for example, television viewing—they become people with short attention spans, prone to imagine simplistic solutions to complex problems and expecting most issues to be resolved, often on a fairly light note, and typically within a reasonably short period of time. Others can watch a great deal of television and never develop these character traits; however, the degree to which they can resist such formation of character may depend upon the other practices in which they are engaged. Thus, while we cannot necessarily predict exactly *what kind* of character formation will result from which practices, we can certainly acknowledge that engaging in a practice—particularly if we do so regularly over time—will form us as people of a particular character; and this will, in turn, strongly influence how we will act, both in everyday situations and in moments of dramatic consequence.

The power of the gathering community

So far, we have observed that (1) how we act is integrally related to our character, and that (2) our character is formed by the narratives that we live by and the practices in which we are regularly engaged. But to many people, this seems to get things exactly backwards. A typical response might be: "I'm not the person I am because I go to football games! I go to football games because I'm the kind of person who wants to!" Well, yes—in a way. But no one just wakes up one morning, having had no contact with the game whatsoever, and decides to become a lifelong devotee of football. One becomes an enthusiast through exposure to the game; one learns to like watching football by—well, by watching football. There's just no other way.

And this leads to the real surprise, for most of us—the surprise about stories and activities, about narratives and practices, about character development, and about ethics as a whole: namely, that our ethical judgments are formed *in the midst of our relationships with others.* I alluded to this at the end of the introduction, noting that the "thin line" between wrong and right is also a thin line "between me and you." In spite of the individualistic structure of our culture, in spite of our belief that we can make all our decisions on our own and that we can pull ourselves up by our bootstraps, and in spite of our culture's almost religious devotion to privacy and isolation—even in the midst of all these cultural forces, our ethical judgments are formed *in our encounters with other people.*

In spite of all our claims of independence, we remain incredibly social animals. We like to be with other people, and they have an enormous influence on us. Human beings *gather together* for various reasons and with a wide range of purposes. In fact, many of the practices that are most significant in our lives are much less attractive to us unless they are done in the company of others; this fact is reinforced by many of the narratives that shape us. A great many of our favorite practices—playing many kinds of games, experiencing live entertainment, participating in voluntary associations—are actually *impossible* without others. Consequently, we are drawn to gather together. It's just something that we do; and when we do it, we rub up against other people and take on certain aspects of their character—the good aspects and the bad.

Part of this has to do with group dynamics; we often gather with a common purpose in mind, and we enjoy acceptance within a group, so we tend to do what the group does. But any gathering of people also operates with its own set of narratives and practices, and these are the channels through which character formation takes place. When we gather, we are united by common goals, a common description of our activities, and a common story of the group's origin, its history, and the obstacles that it has faced and overcome. Moreover, when we gather, we typically engage in certain practices, and these reinforce certain habits; these in turn contribute to a person's overall character. Thus the kind of people we become is dependent, to a surprisingly large degree, on the character of those with whom we spend our time.

When I was young, my mother occasionally reminded me of that well-worn adage: "You'll be known by the company you keep." In other words: if you hope to have a reputation as a diligent, hard-working person, you'd better not spend all your time with lazy slugs. If you want to be an honest person and stay out of trouble, don't hang out with shoplifters and cut-throats. And of course, we begin "keeping company" with other people long before we make a *decision* about doing so: parents, extended families, and those whose company *they* keep will also be the company *we* keep—and to whom we may return throughout our lives, even if we imagine ourselves to have "broken free of all that" as we grow older.

But while the adage "you will be known by the company you keep" certainly points to an important truth, it may not go far enough. Specifically, it may create a loophole by relying too heavily on the notion of *perception*. It claims that you'll merely be *known* by the company you keep, that people will *perceive* you to be like those with whom you spend your time. That is to say: those who observe and judge you will map the character of your friends and fellow-travelers onto you, even though you might not have that character at all. This fact might lead us to discount the idea a little bit—it's not *our* fault if some people make the mistake of thinking that we are just like the people with whom we spend all our time.

But in fact, this adage is pointing to a deeper reality that isn't captured by a literal account of what it means to be "known" by someone (in the weak sense of "perceived"). We will understand its significance more fully if we think of the word "known" in the strongest possible terms: "known for the people we really are." To suggest that one's company leads only to a certain perception actually *underestimates* the significance of our voluntary associations and friendships. The reality is stronger: you won't just be *known* by the company you keep; you will gradually *become* the company you keep. Over time, the stories that those other people live by, and the practices in which they are engaged, will become *your* stories and *your* practices as well. And your character will be formed by those habits, just as surely as theirs have been.

So, to summarize again: ethics is about character, and character is formed through the habits of living according to particular narratives and engaging in particular practices. We are drawn into certain narratives and practices because of the communities of which we are a part, and these communities have the most significant impact on us when they (we) gather together with a common purpose. The communities to which we devote the most time, talent, and treasure will be the communities that will have the most significant influence on the formation of our habits and thereby on the formation of our character. By gathering regularly with a particular community, we learn to live by its stories and to engage in its practices, and thereby take on the character of the members of that community.

Questions for discussion

1. To what extent have you been influenced by the "lifeboat" or "quandary" approach to ethics? Is this how you understood the enterprise of ethics before you began the formal study of the field?

2. An underlying assumption of the first part of this chapter is that all decisions turn out to be significant decisions, and that all human actions are ultimately moral actions. Do you agree with this premise? Can you offer any examples of human actions and decisions that don't fit this assumption?

3. What are some of your own habits that you consider to be most morally formative? (Be sure to include at least one habit that you think may be forming you badly!)

4. What narratives and practices have the strongest hold on your moral imagination? Again, it's wise to include a few that you're not particularly proud of. (For example, I know that the standard story of economic advancement, in which one always seeks to move on to higher and higher paying employment, has a strong hold on me—even though I often tell myself that it's not *really* why I do my work.)

5. Consider your gatherings with other human beings. With what groups or communities do you gather most regularly, and to what purpose? What stories and practices are most central to the collective life of these groups? To what degree do you see yourself formed by these communities through their narratives and practices?

Sources cited in this chapter and/or recommended for further reading

Adaptation, dir. Spike Jonze, 2002

St. Thomas Aquinas, *Summa Theologiae* Ia–IIae.1.3

Babel, dir. Alejandro González Iñárritu, 2005

G. E. M. Anscombe, *Intention*

William T. Cavanaugh, *Torture and Eucharist: Politics, Theology and the Body of Christ*

Charles Dickens, *A Christmas Carol in Prose: Being a Ghost Story of Christmas*

Brad J. Kallenberg, "The Master Argument of MacIntyre's *After Virtue*," chapter 1 of Murphy, Nation, and Kallenberg, eds., *Virtues and Practices in the Christian Tradition*

Philip D. Kenneson, "Gathering: Worship, Imagination, and Formation," in Hauerwas and Wells, eds., *The Blackwell Companion to Christian Ethics*

Alasdair MacIntyre, *After Virtue: A Study in Moral Theory*, 2nd edition, chapter 14

Charles Pinches, *Theology and Action: After Theory in Christian Ethics*, chapter 4

Edmund Pincoffs, "Quandary Ethics," in Hauerwas and MacIntyre, eds., *Revisions: Changing Perspectives in Moral Philosophy*

Maurice Sendak, *Where the Wild Things Are*

George Steiner, *After Babel: Aspects of Language and Translation*

Stranger than Fiction, dir. Marc Forster, 2006

Samuel Wells, *Improvisation: The Drama of Christian Ethics*, chapters 2 and 3

2 Identifying who(se) we are
What's God got to do with it?

At the end of the last chapter, we observed that *communities* create the spaces within which character is formed. When people gather in community, they participate in common practices and rehearse the narratives that undergird their life together and propel it forward. This is true not just for communities that are designated as religious, but for all the various formations in which human beings gather together: families, extended families, schools, civic groups, clubs, interest groups, and crowds that gather to watch sporting events, to listen to concerts, or to take part in any kind of public spectacle. The stories that we tell and retell, the common practices in which we engage, and all the other ways that we adjust our lives in order to be together—all these events work together to form in us certain habits of mind and body that shape our character. This in turn makes certain kinds of decisions and judgments appear to be the natural or obvious ones; our communities lead us to take certain kinds of things for granted, thereby shaping our character.

Powerful communities

My account thus far may make it sound as though these communities wield an enormous amount of power over our lives—and in fact, they do. To use a visual metaphor, we might say something like this: the communities of which we are a part don't merely tell us where to look and what to look for; they actually shape the lenses through which we see the world, such that whatever is "out there" will be processed, by our optic nerves, according to the patterns that the community has come to expect. This explains why most communities, to whatever extent they recognize that they are forming people in particular habits, will typically assume or argue that these are the *right* habits for a person of good character. No community claims, other than in a tongue-in-cheek fashion or with a deep sense of irony, that its purpose is to perpetuate its members in bad habits. No group says, to its own members or to others, that it seeks to carry out a process of negative formation such that the end result will be a worse life rather than a better one. Every group believes that it is creating people of good character—assuming, of course, that it even acknowledges that it is having any moral effect on them whatsoever.

As this last comment suggests, many communities assume that any effect that they might have on their members will be morally neutral. This point of view would be commonly taken, for example, by those gathering for something like a sporting event or a fireworks display. The purpose of the gathering (so the argument goes) is just to relax and have fun; it's not meant to shape people in ethically significant ways. But the study of ethics reminds us that such gatherings always have *some* kind of morally formative effects— and this is even more fully the case when the group gathers repeatedly, re-enacting a common set of narratives and engaging in a common set of practices. And because most communities often don't take much note of their own narratives and practices, they can often be unaware of the degree to which these habits *form* people—even if they do so in ways that turn out, on further reflection, to be morally troublesome.

All this can be a bit disconcerting. It seems to grant the gathering community an inordinate degree of power over people's lives and, further, to insulate the community and its members from any kind of external critique. But even this way of putting the concern exposes a flaw in any such analysis: it makes it look as though we have a choice as to whether to allow the various gathering communities (of which we are part) to form us in morally significant ways. It's not actually a choice; if we spend enough time with a particular group of people, taking part in their common practices and living by the stories that they tell, we will become like them. This is not a prescriptive claim (for example, that we ought to do so, or that we ought not to); it is, rather, a *descriptive* one (that's just what happens, whether we want it to or not). We will be known by, *and we will become*, the company that we keep.

Evading the role of community

This analysis helps to explain why people in the modern age, particularly in democratic societies, have been so easily persuaded to adopt a model of ethics as applying only to those difficult decisions about hard cases. This approach allows us to imagine that we can set aside the sticky business of our moral formation within our gathering communities, suggesting instead that all people of good will can make right judgments about any particular ethical quandary. If we could just convince ourselves of this idea, then we could imagine that we become good people by making the right decisions in individual cases—and that we could do so regardless of the communities to which we belong or the habits that we develop as we gather in those communities.

Keeping our "ethical behavior" separate from our "community-formed habits" thus allows us to be modern, democratic people—choosing our communities on the basis of pleasure and interest, rather than thinking about how they might be forming or deforming our moral sensibilities. If I like auto racing, I ought to be able to go with my friends to see auto racing; I don't want someone telling me that doing so will shape my moral character such that I won't be able to make a good ethical decision when the time comes. In fact, I don't even want to hear the opposite argument, by do-gooders of one sort or another, that my appreciation of auto racing will somehow make me a better person. I want my moral qualities—as well as all those ethical decisions that I make—to be independent of my hobbies and my interests and the people with whom I spend my time. And if this represents a common thought-pattern among most of us, then it also explains the attraction of "lifeboat ethics" as a way of thinking about moral judgments—since that approach allows us to minimize the morally formative character of our gathering communities, concentrating instead on an abstract decision that is isolated from the actual events of our lives.

Moreover, as long as we understand ethics as focused on making hard choices about difficult situations, we will imagine that we can formulate universal rules and principles that can always be applied in those situations. These rules and principles, in order to remain truly universal, would have to be independent of the various communities of which we're a part and of the specific moral formation that we've received as members of those communities. One of the seductive features of this approach to ethics (as I suggested in the introduction) is that it gives us the impression that we're standing on firm, unshifting ground: solid, definitive rules and principles, universal and unchanging, and therefore not dependent on the people with whom we associate, the stories that we live by, or the practices in which we are engaged. While standing on such firm, unshifting ground, a person faced with an ethical decision could operate independently of all these particularities, needing only to apply the right rules in a given situation. As I have repeatedly observed, we don't actually make decisions this way; but we certainly do like the idea of having solid ground under our feet. To suggest that the gathering community sets the standards by which we render these judgments—well, that begins to make it sound as though we're just making it up as we go along.

But in fact, we're not. A great many of our narratives and practices are widely shared, and are deeply a part of a long-standing, continuous way of thinking and acting. Narratives tend to endure over the generations; practices have standards of excellence and are sustained across time. Many of these ways of thinking and acting are so deeply ingrained in us that, in most cases, we don't even have to think about what we're doing. That's part of what gives the *appearance* of firmness and solidity with respect to those moral principles: often, we just don't have any reason to question them. Hence, the idea that certain moral assumptions are shaped by the communities of which we are a part does not necessarily mean that everything is "up for grabs." We share enough assumptions with most other human beings that we can feel comfortable with the specific claims of the communities of which we are a part.

Admittedly, many people feel a great deal of anxiety if they sense that moral norms may lack a fixed and permanent quality. We will examine this anxiety in detail when we consider the notion of "moral relativism" in chapter 10. For the moment, our topic is somewhat narrower: we need to focus on the fact that, even though we draw much of our moral formation from our gathering communities, we need not imagine that such formation is arbitrary or that its specific assumptions are unwarranted. Part of what allows formative communities to endure over time is their ability to form people *of good character*—and to have that goodness recognized and appreciated even by those who are not part of the community itself.

Learning to play the game

An example may help. Think about a sport that you might want to be able to play, but with which you are largely unfamiliar. Think about fast-pitch softball, or cricket, or curling. (Depending on which part of the world you live in, one or more of these is likely to be largely unfamiliar to you.) Now, imagine that you'd like to play this game. Note well: not that you'd like to be able to *watch* the game and understand it, or that you'd like merely to *talk* with people about it, but that you'd like to *play* it. How would you go about achieving this goal?

One option would be to read the official rulebook of the game, from cover to cover. This might be a marginally successful (if incredibly boring) approach to the problem, but I doubt that many people would choose it voluntarily. Even if one had a taste for that kind of thing, the rules wouldn't tell you how to play the game well; in fact, most of the rules are limitations of one sort or another, telling you what you must do and what you cannot do while playing the game. (The rulebooks for a game or sport have some of the same dis-advantages, in this sense, that we discovered when examining the use of rules and law in discussions about ethics.)

Another option would be to pick up some books and magazines about the sport, and to read as much as one can about it. This might help a bit, but a great deal of the material is written for an audience that already understands the game quite well, and thus would address a great many issues that won't help a beginner learn to play. We might be better off focusing our reading on a "how-to" book of some description, a sort of instructional guide. But because these sports are physically-involved activities, a guidebook has lim-ited usefulness; at the very least, you will have to set the book down in order actually to pick up the ball, the broom, or the bat, and to try your hand at the activity. Moreover, each of these is a team sport, which means that you will need other people around to fulfill the various roles that are required for everything to happen as it should.

This is why most people learn about these games *by participating in them.* We usually do this passively at first—watching the game in order to develop a sense of what is supposed to happen, and (if we're lucky) having an experi-enced spectator or player close by, so that we can ask questions and start to understand some of the nuances of the game. We get together with friends to try out a few of the game's more elementary features—pitching (or bowl-ing) and batting (or sweeping). An experienced player, or eventually a coach, helps us improve our technique at certain aspects of the game—again, not by sending us to the rule-book or to *Sports Illustrated*, but usually by taking the game's equipment in hand and going through the motions: "not like this; like this." As we learn how to position our bodies and to train our minds in ways that allow us to play the game, certain questions arise that have not arisen before; and this takes us back into the theoretical side of things, in which we might read about (or more likely, ask someone about) how to handle a spe-cific situation or what strategies to employ under particular conditions. We won't all get the same advice, nor will we all go through the same training practices; and yet, we will all learn how to play the game. And most of the time, it won't even cross our minds to worry that everyone who tells us some-thing about the game might just be making it up as they go along.

When we're learning a new sport, we make use of knowledge, theory, and practice; these elements all inform one another, without any expectation that there will be one single, definitive training program to provide the perfect "solid foundation" for our participation. The same is true in life: when we're learning to act rightly, we don't just read the rulebook (even if we could get everyone to agree on one such book); we watch others, ask questions, take a turn trying it out, ask more questions, read the advice of some experts, ask someone to show us how, and then ask more questions. There just isn't any other way.

The key, in sports as in life, is to surround ourselves with the right people: to meet regularly with those who are good at the game, so that we can model our own practices on those that are known to work. And the only way to know who "the right people" are is to look at how they play the game. Those who play it well are those whom a person would seek out, in order to learn how to play. This process may sound circular, and perhaps it is; but it represents the give-and-take, trial-and-error, theory-and-practice approach that we almost always have to take when we allow ourselves to be formed in particular habits.

And so we return, as in chapter 1, to the gathering community: those who come together on a regular basis and, in the process, form one another in good habits for living well. Early in life, we don't have much choice about the communities within which we gather: our parents, extended family, schools, and neighborhoods provide obvious limitations (though with more and more electronic communication at our fingertips, our reach is wider all the time—even at a very young age). As we grow older, we make these choices for ourselves: where to go to university, which student groups to join, with whom to gather on the weekends, and how to interact with others in person and online. Eventually, most people join the workforce; the choices are then about jobs, socializing, and where to live. Or perhaps even these options are not open to us because of constraints imposed by our circumstances (immigration status, single parenthood, socio-economic class, racial stereotypes, inadequate health care). In any case, when we connect with a particular community, this does not result solely from an evaluation of the character of the people with whom we will be associating. We choose a profession because we feel called to it; we choose a club because its activities interest us, or a neighborhood because we like the house and the price is right; we join a support group—or a gang—because there seems to be no other choice. Whether we're conscious of it or not, the communities with which we affiliate ourselves will significantly affect our ethical framework in the long run, because they will put us in contact with the kinds of people that we will, over time, become.

Giving the community its due

If the foregoing analysis is even partially correct, this means that we probably should be paying more attention to the morally formative character of our communities than we tend to do. As I noted in the previous chapter, we typically gather on the basis of common interests or because we enjoy a particular activity—we don't usually undertake a moral evaluation of those with whom we're gathering (at least not explicitly). But if we realize that the company that we keep will have a strongly formative influence on us, it would behoove us to think about its character.

Identifying who we are

The first step in this process is to examine how a given community *identifies* itself. It might be helpful to think of this as a series of concentric circles, in which each successive identifier further narrows the field. So, for example, a group of eight women who gather every Thursday morning to play eighteen holes of golf might identify themselves as "people who like golf," then further as "people who like golf and who are able to spend Thursday mornings on the course," and then as "Thursday-morning golfers who play at a certain skill level, neither beginners nor professionals"; then further as "Thursday-morning amateur golfers who enjoy conversation about politics, health insurance plans, and dentistry." (They all happen to be dentists, so that's what they talk about—but they don't think of "being a dentist" as a rule for membership in the group.)

The interesting thing about the description that I've just offered is that, of course, very few groups of Thursday-morning golfers would ever provide an explanation of themselves that sounded anything like this. In fact, under most circumstances, they probably wouldn't describe themselves at all; they wouldn't be asked to do so by some curious passerby, nor even by the writer of an ethics textbook. Nevertheless, they *would* do things that indicate who they are. By their very actions—particularly when gathered as a group—they would signify their identity.

Some of the ways that they would do this are obvious: they would play golf, they would do it regularly on Thursday mornings, and they would talk about politics, health insurance, and dentistry. By engaging in these practices, they would be signifying their identity as people who do these kinds of things. Anyone who observed their behavior, even for a brief period of time (say, by walking along with them for three or four holes of golf) would be able to give a fairly detailed description of what held them together as a group—even if the observer had never previously met any of them.

How is the common identity of these eight golfers related to the rest of their lives, beyond those Thursday morning gatherings? At first glance, the relationship might seem rather tenuous; one might imagine that those Thursday mornings existed in isolation from the rest of their lives, and that the golf games weren't much affected by the rest of the week's activities. But in spite of the blocks of time that are laid out in a grid in our Day-Runners and Blackberrys, our weekly activities don't really exist in isolation from one another. Our lives tend to be fairly integrated, in spite of all the forces that work to break them down into small components. We anticipate future events and remember past events; we carry our joys and sorrows, our hopes and anxieties, from one activity to the next (even when the two events are largely unrelated). If one of our golfers spends the rest of the week worrying about her daughter's recent eating habits, that anxiety won't necessarily evaporate when she comes to play golf on Thursday morning. If another member of the group got into an argument with one of her fellow golfers during last Thursday's game, that may well gnaw at her all week long. Communities are morally formative, and they help us identify who we are; but these identities are not limited to those occasions when the community is present in an immediate way. By their very nature, our identities "stick" to us as we move into other communities of which we are a part.

Gathered communities have a great many other ways of helping us identify who we are. Some use a certain form of words every time they gather; for example, someone might read out a common statement of purpose, or the members may engage in some kind of well-practiced dialogue. If we hear someone say, "Hello, my name is John; I'm an alcoholic," and everyone in the room responds, "Hi, John," then we know that we are at a meeting of Alcoholics Anonymous: the dialogue itself is one possible description of the group's identity. We identify ourselves by how we dress (think of fans at a sporting event), by our physical posture (think of the crowd at a rock concert—or at a symphony), and by how we greet and treat one another.

Identifying *whose* we are

When we gather as a community, in addition to identifying *who* we are, we also identify *whose* we are. We make a statement about where we *really* belong—our "true homeland"—and to whom we owe our allegiance or fidelity. Compared with the process of identifying *who* we are, this process of identifying *whose* we are is typically more subtle, and the reason for this is obvious: even though we're gathering with a particular community, we all bring to the gathering other allegiances, other bonds of fidelity and care, that we don't necessarily hold in common. Two men enjoy each others' company at the Rotary Club, but their daughters play basketball at two different high schools—so when their teams meet, they won't be sitting on the same side of the arena. Two people care for each other deeply at their weekly support group meeting, but they have diametrically opposing political views and so, except at their meeting, they can't seem to have a conversation without getting into a fight.

In any given community, we usually find a fair bit of agreement and comfort around the question of "who we are," but we often find significant tension when the question shifts just slightly to *whose* we are. Let's return to our Thursday-morning golfers: three of the women are single, and they'd like to spend a little less of the morning golfing and a bit more time socializing with other groups in the clubhouse, with an eye to possible romantic involvements. But the other five women are married, and whether or not they have any interest in this activity (let's be kind enough not to ask them about that), most of them suspect that engaging in it publicly wouldn't be a very good idea. The various members of this group are of one mind in identifying *who* they are, but they have different assessments of *whose* they are: their allegiances and commitments outside the group are focused in different directions, and (at least in this case) they might want to give those commitments priority over accommodating the preferences of the group.

In fact, when we begin to think about all the varying allegiances that we bring to any communal activity, it's a wonder we can get together at all. In any given gathered community, the various members of the group would probably all have a different answer to the questions "To whom do we belong?" and "To whom do we owe our greatest allegiance?" And while most communities hope that the community itself will be fairly high on everyone's priority list, they also recognize that—again, in a modern democratic society in which free association is a given—most people will bring a variety of commitments to any gathering of which they are a part.

Consequently, most groups don't tend to put too many restrictions on their members, at least with respect to any commitments that don't seem essential to the group. The golfers don't require everyone in the group to be a dentist, or single, or married; the Rotarians don't require that everyone cheer for the same school team; the support group doesn't require conformity to a particular political platform. Admittedly, if such requirements existed, this might strengthen the cohesion of the community; but these same requirements would also limit its range. Many members would be placed in a situation where they had to negotiate among conflicting allegiances, and in some cases the community's priorities might not carry the day. We often try to avoid such circumstances by narrowing a group's focus of activity: we make it clear that "we're just here to cheer for the team" (or listen to the band, or support one another in our fight against an addiction); we may carry other commitments to and from our gatherings, but we don't let these interfere with everyone else's opportunity to engage in our common practices.

All this is well and good, and we have sufficiently narrowed the focus of most of our communities that we're able to avoid most of the potentially conflicting allegiances. But what happens when one particular allegiance claims to take over all the rest?

Enter God, stage right

In a course in Christian ethics that I recently taught, just as my class was taking up this chapter's topic, a banner headline appeared on the front page of the widely circulating daily newspaper *USA Today*. The headline read "View of God can predict values, politics." The article reported on a study by researchers at Baylor University, who had undertaken a careful examination of political and moral attitudes among a wide range of test subjects. The researchers also included questions that allowed the interviewees to talk about how they understood God.

The study's theological vocabulary was not very sophisticated; understandings of God were classified into the four broad categories of authoritarian, benevolent, critical, or distant. Most students of theology know that these four categories do not come close to exhausting the descriptive language about God; neither are they mutually exclusive. (Even as a matter of emphasis, it would be problematic to label God as, say, "more benevolent than authoritarian," or to use any other description that placed these categories in tension with one another.) Be that as it may, this broad formula allowed the researchers to demonstrate a high degree of continuity between a person's political and moral judgments, on the one hand, and, on the other, that same person's understanding of God.

A long, ongoing conversation

What is most surprising about this study, however, is that it could possibly qualify as *news*. Throughout most of the history of human thought, commentators have been nearly unanimous in their view that a human being's understanding of God, or of "the gods," will be one of the most profound and accurate indicators of the shape of that person's life. The ancient Greek poets and tragedians—Homer, Sophocles, Euripides—clearly believed this; they interwove their stories of heroes and villains with stories of the gods, whose actions and attitudes sometimes affected, and nearly always *reflected*, the actions and attitudes of the human characters. The later Greek philosophers had less use for the traditional pantheons of gods and goddesses, but they still used those figures in their stories and examples; they also wrote about a being, sometimes called "God," who created the world and who ultimately causes things to be and to act. Jewish tradition clearly states that human behavior, particularly within communities and tribes, is guided (and to some extent prescribed) by God's good judgment. Jesus of Nazareth taught his followers both to enter into a particular kind of relationship with God, and to adopt a certain way of life that was compatible with that relationship.

The early Christian communities took up this same claim, often putting the two features of the new faith side by side: because God has a certain character, so should they; and since God has done particular things for them, so they felt called to act in certain ways. Islam even made the word "obedience" the very name of its faith: living and acting rightly is, by definition, a willingness to be *obedient* to God's commands.

Only in the modern age do dissenting voices begin to arise. This is the era in which human beings first suggested that a detailed plan for a way of life could be constructed without reference to God. In the ancient world, the word "atheism" referred only to a belief in a *different* god or gods from those that held sway in the culture as a whole; no one imagined the possibility of complete disbelief in *any* god. Beginning in the seventeenth century, however, this assumption began to change; people began to imagine what various human enterprises would be like if God were not a part of the picture. In the case of ethics, some thinkers began to believe that moral judgments might be made dependent on human reason alone, without ethical conversations being complicated by various groups invoking their particular understandings of God.

A number of structures have helped to strengthen the credibility of this way of seeing things. Our political system encourages it; in a democratic society, the very basis for a common culture would begin to erode if each religious group's understanding of right action were based on a framework specific to its particular theology. Therefore, citizens are encouraged to keep their religious views private, whereas public debate is supposed to take place without reference to specific convictions about God (or even about the relationship between God and human beings). Even churches have contributed to this situation; just like the other groups that were mentioned in the previous section, churches in the contemporary setting rarely want to limit their numbers by imposing too many requirements about their members' allegiances.

But while this strategy may work as a means of keeping a golfing group together, it cannot work, in the long run, for any group that expects to have a more significantly formative influence on the moral assumptions of its members. This is because any assessment of moral character will require some notion of what counts for "good," and this in turn is always related to how a particular community understands God, or the gods (or whatever it treats like God or the gods). Faith—whether faith in God or in something else—has sometimes been defined as "ultimate concern"; in other words, when we speak of "what we believe" in the strongest sense of that word, we are designating whatever is most important to us, what concerns us in an ultimate way and therefore takes priority over everything else. That which we believe in most ultimately might best be described as *God*. In other words, a person's "god" is—by definition—whatever ranks highest in that person's list of allegiances. Even those who do not believe in God will have certain strong allegiances, and will therefore have certain things that function as "god" in their lives; and this in turn will always have a very significant impact in shaping their character and their judgments. This will be the case even if we set aside, either temporarily or permanently, all claims about belief in a being called "God."

Another factor that leads us to blur the distinction between belief in *God*, on the one hand, and belief in something else that is treated as God, on the other, is the attempt among some religious believers (including some Christians) to make God accessible, relevant, and timely. These efforts are understandable, particularly when many people have indicated that they are not interested in a God who is primarily characterized as distant or irrelevant. Paradoxically, however, when God is envisioned as more accessible and relevant, it becomes harder to tell the difference between God and anything else that we might hold in high esteem. If, for example, God is described with popular adjectives of praise ("cool," "awesome," "a great guy," and so forth), this may make God seem less distant; but if the same epithets that are used to describe God are also used to describe everything else—from that "cool" sociology professor, to the "great guy" who lives down the hall, to the "awesome" dessert last night at the cafeteria, then it becomes more difficult to understand what makes God different from anything else that we hold in high regard. God becomes just another one of the gods.

What are our "gods," in modern culture? To what do we give our highest allegiance? What do we believe in most firmly? I want to suggest that for many people—including many Christians—what functions as "god" in their life is not actually *God*, a supreme supernatural being. Instead, the candidates for the role of our gods include many things other than the being that they name "God" (regardless of whether or not they actually *believe* in that God). For example, many people put their trust in the nation-state and its government, or in money and the economic system, or in a set of creature comforts that make life tolerable. These are some of the answers that we use to answer the question "to whom or to what do we belong?"; these are some of our strongest allegiances; these are, in fact, our gods.

If we begin to think of our gods in this light, we will soon realize that all discussions of ethics must take into account the discipline of *theology*—the study of God (or the gods) and the things related to God. We often speak of theological ethics as though it were a particular subset of a larger field called ethics, alongside non-theological or secular or philosophical ethics. But to the extent that we all have certain allegiances that we prioritize over others, we all can be said to have gods; and to that extent, we all operate with *theologies*—implicitly, at least, if not explicitly. These theologies shape our character and our judgments; thus it is no exaggeration to claim that all forms of ethics are, at least implicitly, *theological* ethics, in which our judgments about God (or our gods) definitively shape our character, our habits, our judgments, and our actions.

The significance of God in ethics

This throws a slightly different light on the perennial question of whether one can be "good without God." This question has at least two meanings, and the resulting conversations are often somewhat confusing because the two meanings tend to slide into one another. One interpretation of the question is whether an ethical life is possible without a conception of God as traditionally defined in monotheistic faiths such as Judaism and Christianity. Clearly, the answer to this question is very likely to be "yes"; most people can cite examples of atheists or agnostics who have lived according to certain moral principles and whose lives are routinely recognized, even by religious believers, as "good." However, a second interpretation of the question "Can a person be good without God?" concerns whether it is possible to avoid theological questions altogether when exploring the field of ethics. Here, we would have to give a different answer: in order to speak of *good* behavior, we have to develop some notion of the good; and this requires us to be clear about who or what receives our highest priorities and our commitments of allegiance. A belief in "the good" turns out to work in ways that are similar to a belief in God. Thus when the field of ethics is explored by someone who does not explicitly believe in God, that person may choose to omit all reference to God; but to the extent that the concept of "the good" has a sovereign, god-like function in that person's discourse, theological questions will never be entirely excluded from the discussion.

Another way of examining this question is to consider the role of *worship*. This concept plays an important role, not only in those gathering communities that identify themselves as "religious" and that focus their allegiance on God, but also in many communities that *do not* identify themselves in such terms, but which expect members to offer their full allegiance to some other being or person or idea. If we can recognize the degree to which many communities operate with certain implicit practices of worship, we may be able to understand the degree to which they also operate with certain implicit understandings of God or the gods.

When human beings gather, for whatever purpose, they often share or develop a common sense of what is most worthy of love, respect, and honor. When people gather to watch their team play in a sporting event, they share a common focus on the team and they hope for its victory. When they gather for social action—say a group of students gathering to protest a new policy at their college or university—they share a common desire to see the policy overturned. Whenever we gather, we are encouraged and sometimes inspired to focus our love and devotion on a certain person, process, or outcome.

The question we must ask is this: when does this love and devotion, which plays some role in almost all human gatherings, become *worship*? We often associate the word "worship" with religious institutions such as synagogues, churches, or mosques, and we assume that the word only applies when the love and devotion in question is directed toward God. But it is certainly possible, and often happens, that people who gather in communities that do not understand themselves as "religious" can nevertheless find themselves offer the full measure of their love and devotion toward a particular object or person or idea. When attending a rock concert, one can enjoy the music and the spectacle; but one can also devote oneself to the superstars on the stage in ways that are not obviously different from worship. At a football game, we're focused on the team; we cheer them on and hope for a victory. But we may also raise up the team and the victory to such a degree that it eclipses all other concerns; and again, at this point, the line between appreciation and worship becomes very difficult to discern. (In fact, the level of devotion exhibited by some football fans toward their team far outstrips that which is exhibited by some Christians toward God!) In any gathering community, those who offer complete devotion to a particular being or idea might best be described as engaged in an expression of worship.

This last point is important because, although this book is focused on *Christian* ethics, we shouldn't imagine that its observations apply only within the specifically Christian context. The formation that occurs within the Christian community is different in *content*, but not necessarily in *structure* or *intensity*, from the formation that occurs in other kinds of gatherings. So although we will eventually turn to very specific discussions of the content of the Christian faith, other approaches to ethics must still grapple with the observations in these early chapters—about the nature of ethics as focused on character, and about the role of the gathered community in forming our character through narratives and practices.

This raises some questions as to whether there can be any such thing as ethics in a general sense, as opposed to ethics that are specific to particular gathering communities—whether they are religious communities in the traditional sense (Christian ethics, Jewish ethics), or communities that are identified with a particular profession or career (medical ethics, business ethics), or communities that identify something else as their highest good (creation ethics, humanist ethics). Because of the essential role of the gathering community in the definition, identification, and formation of character, "ethics" in the sense that we have been developing it here must always be associated with the particular allegiances that inhere in specific communities.

Hence, Christian ethics examines the understanding of good character as defined by those gathering communities that understand themselves to be Christian, and it has the strongest hold on those who identify their primary allegiances as aligned with the members of those communities. This does not mean that one needs to *be* a Christian in order to study Christian ethics; one need only recognize the importance of Christian communities for the identification of what counts as good character for the members of those communities. We will come to understand Christian ethics when we understand the formation of character that these communities seek to carry out; this will require us to have a close look at the stories that they live by and the practices in which they are engaged.

God in Christian ethics

Given the foregoing discussion, it will be fairly obvious that the Christian understanding of God will play a significant role in Christian ethics. We might say that Christian ethics differs from other forms of ethics, not in the sense that God has a role to play (this is in some sense true, as we have suggested, for all forms of ethics), but rather in the particularities of the *Christian* understanding of God and of God's relationship to the world. Christians identify both *who* they are and *whose* they are by aligning themselves with a very specific account of God.

In order to see how this takes place, we can consider the beginning of a typical Christian worship service. Often the very first words spoken will include some kind of reference to the God in whose name Christians gather. This may come in the form of a greeting, echoing the greetings offered in the New Testament epistles that were written to the early Christian communities: "Grace to you and peace from God our Father and the Lord Jesus Christ." Alternatively, it may be a call to engage in an act of worship: "Come, let us worship the Lord our God." Or, it may simply be a statement that what is to take place in this gathering is to be done in God's name: "In the name of the Father, and the Son, and the Holy Spirit, Amen." What do such statements mean?

A detailed analysis would require us to delve deeper into the field of Christian theology than is warranted at this point in our discussion. The first statement, for example, would necessitate an analysis of the person of Christ, who is considered fully human and fully divine; we will return to this point in chapter 8. The second statement would demand at least a basic articulation of one of the most complex Christian beliefs—the belief that God is Trinity, that is, simultaneously three and one. (We will have some cause to explore this notion in chapter 7, as well as several later chapters of the book.) For the present, it is enough for us to note that, by invoking the name of God at the beginning of the worship service and describing God as the ultimate reason for and focus of the gathering, Christians are doing the kind of thing that we have discussed in this chapter: identifying *who* they are and *whose* they are. Of course, these very abbreviated descriptions of God will not be very meaningful to anyone who has not already been drawn in, at least in a provisional way, to the narratives and practices that in Christians are habituated. Thus, in the following chapter, we will begin to analyze those habits by considering, first of all, how stories structure our lives.

Questions for discussion

1. Do all of our communal gatherings have a morally formative impact on us? Or are there some things that we do "just for the fun of it" without any moral implications? (It may help to construct the best argument you can for each side of this question.)

2. Do you find yourself worried or annoyed by the notion that moral formation is primarily a product of gathered communities? How might one differentiate this from a notion of moral relativism?

3. Think of a community (other than a church community) of which you are a part, and think about the ways that the community identifies *who* they are and *whose* they are. What might function as "God" or "the gods" within that community's structure?

4. Do you think it's universally the case that a person's moral and political outlook is always affected by that person's understanding of God? (In this question, the word "God" means whatever the people in question define as "god"—in other words, that to which they give their ultimate allegiance.) Is it possible to separate these two?

5. To what extent does the language of "worship" serve to describe the activity that goes on, at least among some of the members, within the gathering communities of which you have been a part? Who or what is the object of that worship?

6. Construct an argument on both sides of the following proposition: "All forms of ethics are theological ethics."

Sources cited in this chapter and/or recommended for further reading

Michael J. Buckley, SJ, *At the Origins of Modern Atheism*

Michael Budde, *The (Magic) Kingdom of God: Christianity and Global Culture Industries*

Cathy Lynn Grossman, "View of God can predict values, politics," *USA Today*

Philip D. Kenneson, "Gathering: Worship, Imagination, and Formation," in Hauerwas and Wells, eds., *The Blackwell Companion to Christian Ethics*

Philip D. Kenneson, *Life on the Vine: Cultivating the Fruit of the Spirit in Christian Community*

Nicholas Lash, *Believing Three Ways in One God: A Reading of the Apostles' Creed*

Alasdair MacIntyre, *After Virtue: A Study in Moral Theory*, 2nd edition

Iris Murdoch, *The Sovereignty of Good*

Paul Tillich, *Dynamics of Faith*

3 Reading in communion
How stories structure our lives

The previous chapter focused on the ways in which gathering communities define themselves, both in terms of their own identity (who they are) and with respect to their primary allegiances (whose they are). The chapter ended with a recognition that many communities specifically name their allegiances, and that, for Christians, this involves an invocation of God. However, we also recognized that the theological language that Christians use to describe God may not have much meaning for those who are unfamiliar with the faith's narratives and practices. Therefore, in this chapter, we will begin the process of making those narratives and practices more familiar. Our first goal will be to emphasize the important role that stories play in structuring our lives; we will then turn to the Christian stories in particular.

Telling stories

When communities gather, they tell stories. They tell stories about the members of the community, about the community as a whole, and about outsiders, strangers, and other communities. They usually tell some of these stories repeatedly—either in an identical form each time or, more commonly, with certain elements remaining open to alteration, expansion, or omission. Within these repeatedly-told, sometimes-altered stories, one can often discern the outline of a plot or at least the description of certain characters. These plots and characterizations may sometimes be reducible to a single sentence or moral; more often, though, they are complex and nuanced, like the plot or characters in a short story or a one-act play. If we listen carefully to these stories, we will learn a great deal about the character of the communities in which they are told, and about the people who constitute (and are themselves *constituted by*) these communities.

Family stories

Consider one of the most common examples of this phenomenon: the stories that are told within a family structure. From time to time, most extended families gather together—perhaps for a holiday meal, an annual reunion, or a funeral. The stories that they tell are likely to include, among other things, accounts of their travel to the gathering, news about any members not present, and autobiographical descriptions of what they've been doing since they've last seen each other. But once these new stories have been covered, most family conversations will turn to the shared history of the clan: something that happened to grandma when she was growing up, the hilarious moment three years ago when the dog upset three picnic tables, the vivid memories of a journey taken together. Many people will have heard these stories before, but they are not told simply in order to provide information. They actually serve to undergird the family structure: they point to the facts that it existed in the past and that it has been constituted by some of the same characters over time. This in turn implies that it will continue to exist in the future.

Many families will have a few stories that are told fairly often, though perhaps in differing forms, when the family gathers together. These might include stories that tell about how the family came to settle in its present geographical location, how a distant ancestor immigrated from Ireland to England two centuries ago, or how a great-grandfather moved his family from Ohio to Oklahoma in the 1920s. It might be a story of family unity at a critical moment, like that time after Aunt Edna's stroke that we all gathered around her bed and sang and cried and fully expected that she would die, but she recovered and lived a good life for many more years. In my own family, one of the oft-repeated stories tells of the days when a cousin of mine was courting his wife-to-be; both of them discovered, at a fairly early stage of their relationship, some of the more (shall we say) idiosyncratic characteristics of the other person's family—and decided to get married anyway.

These stories don't usually have a single form or format. They typically aren't written down for posterity; some of the details change on each telling. But the essential outline of the story remains fairly consistent, as do most of the characters that inhabit them. And because they are told repeatedly, they make a statement of sorts about the way the family is constituted. They describe the strength of resolve and the willingness to take risks that were exhibited by an ancestor who moved to a new land. They make reference to the family's compassion and its unity in caring for its own members, particularly those who are ill or otherwise incapacitated. They display a family's foibles and quirks, as well as its tolerance and its willing acceptance of those who don't necessarily conform to certain societal standards of behavior. And—at least in some cases—they characterize how the family treats outsiders and strangers, and the degree to which its members are willing to show hospitality to those who don't, or don't yet, belong to the family.

Community stories

The examples that I have offered concerning family stories also apply to the stories of other kinds of communities. While I will eventually suggest that practically all gathering communities rely on a certain set of stories for maintaining their identity, the process may be easiest to imagine if we think of a community that is small enough, and whose members live in close enough proximity to one another, that at least some of their members are able to gather fairly often. One of the best examples of this kind of community is the small town or village; here, because people live very close to one another and have come to rely on one another, they tend to gather fairly frequently. They also tend to tell stories. The role of storytelling in a small town or village is frequently celebrated in fiction writing; one example is the work of the American writer Garrison Keillor, whose stories about a fictional Minnesota town called Lake Wobegon are poignant reminders of the importance of storytelling in shaping and maintaining a community's identity. The African-American novelist Toni Morrison frequently emphasizes how various stories are handed down by means of an oral tradition through family structures. For many black communities in the US context, this served as a significant means of forging and maintaining identity, particularly in the face of sustained efforts by others to efface or distort that identity.

A single story does not, of course, constitute the character of an entire community. But when certain stories are told repeatedly, and when they become a staple of the gatherings of a particular community, they take on a greater significance. Stories that are told repeatedly are often particularly entertaining as well; but most communities have a huge repertoire of entertaining stories, so the only way to account for a story's *frequent* retelling is to recognize that its significance transcends its mere entertainment value. Particularly when a community repeatedly tells a story *about itself*, it is remembering and reasserting certain shared assumptions, beliefs, and practices that bind the community together.

At the same time, these stories *shape* the community and its members in certain ways. This may be more obvious in the case of relatively new members of the community; such persons need to learn these stories in order to understand the group and their own potential role within it. But stories are not just for newcomers; they are also for those who have lived in the community all their lives and know the stories by heart. By telling a story, we remind ourselves of certain qualities that we may already know we possess, but which we don't often actively bring to mind. We often allow certain features of our identity to recede into the background; we're busy doing other things, or it doesn't seem all that important to reiterate, or perhaps we're simply modest about it. But part of what helps a community to maintain a particular character over time is precisely the telling of the story that demonstrates and emphasizes it.

For example, the members of a small town may particularly pride themselves on their willingness to help one another out in moments of extreme need. They don't feel any desire to boast about this; they don't announce it on a plaque at the town hall or fashion it into a motto to attach to the welcome signs at the town limits. But these moments of extreme need don't come along every day, so they aren't always being reminded of this element of the town's character by simply doing it and watching it happen. However, they do tell stories about it: specific, concrete stories, about the time the pipes froze at Mark Johnson's house and how George down at the supply store brought his friends and a whole case of propane torches to thaw them out. How the neighboring town's school bus broke down three miles out of town, and how Evelyn Rockwell saw it and drove straight to Pat's beauty parlor, and how all seven women who were there at the time, even though none of them had kids or grandkids on that bus, got in their cars and drove out there and took all those kids to school. Everyone in town knows these stories; they've heard them hundreds of times. They don't end with a moral ("and this shows that we help each other out"); they don't have to, because everyone knows that already. Nevertheless, by telling the story repeatedly, the community reinforces its own understanding of its identity: this is the kind of people they are. The stories emphasize particular qualities that help to characterize, and to constitute, the community.

These stories, which help communities to identify who they are, don't have to be told in a traditional "storytelling" setting. In fact, under current cultural conditions, it may be fairly uncommon for people to gather around in a circle while someone "tells a story." More often, we learn the stories of a community in a much more diffused way, over a long period of time: we hear the pieces of stories in brief vignettes, pick up threads here and there, and catch snippets that we only later piece together. The stories that constitute a community and give it its identity are not often told in a continuous, straightforward way; but this fact does not prevent a particular narrative from emerging and becoming clear over time.

Broadening the picture

The significance of stories and storytelling is not limited to small, tightly-defined communities. It also helps us identify much more amorphous groups—for example, the citizens of a particular nation-state, or all people in a particular age group, or everyone who uses a particular category of consumer goods. While these are not regularly gathering communities in the sense that a family or a church congregation might be, the members of these groups do engage in certain practices and rituals that draw them together, in spite of the fact that they may be too large to gather as a unit or too diffuse to think of themselves as a community. Any group in which the members have a particular identity that is sustained through common practices probably also shares a common story or set of stories—even if they never gather as a single group.

A few examples may be in order here. Most nation-states have identity-forming stories of their own, even though all the citizens never gather in a single place at any one time. Young people often learn these stories from their parents and in schools; American children will tell the story of Paul Revere's ride or of George Washington's hard winter at Valley Forge as narratives that identify the ingenuity, determination, and perseverance that is thought to characterize Americans. Or, to take an example from another sphere of life, consider the community of people who regularly purchase a certain kind of consumer good. These people will rarely gather in any combination whatsoever, and would not usually tell a certain story to constitute their identity. Nevertheless, these stories are often implicit both in product advertisements and in the accounts that people offer as to why they purchase a particular product. For example, when tobacco products were more widely advertised, the images that marketers employed often told an implicit story in which the smokers of a particular brand were successful in their work, their friendships, and/or their romantic and sexual relationships. The implicit narratives of these visual advertisements had a formative effect on the consumers, who then came to see their own lives through these same categories. This example is also a reminder that the kinds of moral formation that stories can bring about are not always salutary ones; we can be formed in bad habits by stories, just as we can be formed in good habits.

Storytelling and moral formation

As the previous paragraph was already beginning to suggest, stories play a highly significant role in the process of moral formation within a community. This is why stories are such an important (and contested) aspect of child-rearing: the stories that we tell our children will shape their moral and imaginative universe. Needless to say, there is no one-to-one correspondence at work here; one cannot easily predict the precise outlines of moral formation that are taking place as stories are being told, and parents do not need to screen every story in order to excise whatever they may regard as moral turpitude. But the themes, plots, and characters of the stories that we tell will certainly come to have an effect on the overall structure of our moral lives.

The various ways that this occurs are well illustrated in Richard Adams' novel *Watership Down*, in which the primary characters are rabbits. The book focuses on a group of rabbits who leave the apparent safety and comfort of their home warren and strike out across the countryside to begin a new community. They are a motley crew: misfits, weaklings, rabbits who hold something against the leadership of the warren. Many of them didn't know one another before they gathered in preparation for leaving. The ragtag quality of their group doesn't seem to bode well for their success. But they do succeed, primarily because they find ways of developing and strengthening the identity of their new community. One of the most important ways that they do this is by telling stories.

The stories that these rabbits tell are often about their hero, El-ahrairah, whose name means "the prince with a thousand enemies." The heroism of El-ahrairah stems from his ability to use cunning, trickery, and speed to outwit the many predators that rabbits always face. The stories are tried-and-true; the rabbits don't tell them in order to learn some new fact. Indeed, they tell them precisely because they know them so well. These are their narratives: the stories they live by, that give them their identity, that tell them who they are.

Within the structure of Adams' novel, the formal "storytelling" moments occur at rather critical junctures: times when the rabbits need to remember who they are and whose they are, which in turn provides some guidance for the ongoing structure of their life together and for the overall shape of their moral lives. Through their stories, they learn how to live as a community: they gain confidence to take on hazardous tasks, they are comforted in times of hardship and loss, and they are reminded that being a rabbit means not giving up—even though it seems that the whole world is against you (since, it fact, it pretty much is). One of the stories, in particular, tells them that El-ahrairah once offered his own life to release his people from captivity; and so it is through stories, as well, that they are reminded of one of their most important beliefs: namely, that a gift has made them safe, and has thereby set them free.

In addition to helping them build up a common moral life, the rabbits' storytelling also provides them with a means for comparing themselves with other communities that tell different stories—or that tell no stories at all. One warren that they encounter is located near a farmhouse, where human beings regularly scatter tasty food nearby. It seems, at first, like a dream come true: abundant provisions, well protected shelter, and nothing to worry about. But something is wrong: the rabbits in this warren have stopped telling the traditional stories of their trickster prince and his thousand enemies. In fact, these rabbits appear to *have* no enemies; the people from the farmhouse drive their usual predators away. And these rabbits have stopped doing the usual digging, running, playing, and foraging that mark all rabbits' lives. They've grown fat and lazy, and have taken to odd practices like carrying and storing food, creating representational art, and reciting abstract poetry about the inevitability of death. Strangest of all, they never answer any question beginning with the word "where."

Early one morning, while exploring the area around the new warren, one of the traveling band of rabbits gets caught in the wire of a deadly snare. When his companions run to get help from their hosts, the resident rabbits turn away silently. And thus we discover that, every now and then, the people at the farmhouse set snares in the grass and kill one or two rabbits for their meat and fur. The snares are not set so frequently or in great enough quantity as to drive the rabbits away; but from time to time, a member of the warren is killed and taken from their midst. This is the price that these rabbits must pay for their otherwise carefree existence. It is a morally painful price, which is why they don't talk about it, and why they don't allow people to ask questions about "where" a particular rabbit might be found. It also explains why they don't tell stories about their hero El-ahrairah; with his acts of heroism, and particularly with his willingness to give good gifts to make all his rabbits safe, his stories highlight the comparatively shameful legacy of a community that is willing to sacrifice its own members in order never to have to exert themselves too much.

Upon discovering harrowing truth, our group of intrepid rabbit-adventurers strike out on their own again (picking up one refugee from the troubled warren—one of several ways that they demonstrate their ability to incorporate new members into their community). After many further adventures, they eventually establish a new home for themselves on a high down where they can dig a beautiful warren, stay dry, and keep a good lookout for predators. They are able to establish a successful new community because they continue to affirm their identity through their stories and practices.

To summarize: storytelling is a critically important aspect of a community's process of moral formation. Our narratives—the stories that we live by—help us understand both our identity and our allegiances. By telling and retelling these stories, a community testifies to its own endurance through time; it thereby helps its members understand their place within its structure, and it helps outsiders and newcomers to find their way into its common life. Thus, if we want to understand the most strongly held moral assumptions of a particular community, we would be well advised to begin by paying attention to the stories that it lives by.

The ambiguity of stories

Of course, stories are ambiguous. This is especially true with reference to their moral implications; audience members may all understand and agree upon the basic structure of the plot and the nature of the characters, and yet carry away radically different interpretations of the story's moral meaning. If a group of people listen to the story of *Romeo and Juliet* (or of *West Side Story*), some of them might suspect that the message is ultimately "don't fight with rival gangs," but others might imagine that the play demonstrates how important it is to protect one's turf and one's compatriots. Still others might imagine its primary moral imperative to be "don't be blinded by love; it may lead you astray," while others would see it as a celebration of love and a glorification of those who will pursue at any cost, even unto death. And while *Romeo and Juliet* is a complex, multi-layered story in which multiple interpretations are clearly possible, even the shortest and most straightforward stories can lead to interpretive disputes.

This is especially true when it comes to texts that a community holds in high regard. The multiple and even conflicting interpretations of *Romeo and Juliet* have kept scholars and graduate students busy for centuries, and will no doubt continue to do so into the indefinite future; however, very few communities think of it as one of the stories that its members live by. This is not to say that it doesn't have some significant symbolic weight in our culture; its themes of young love, feuding families, and strife between parents and children are clearly germane to our lives. But very few people have structured their lives according to the text of *Romeo and Juliet*; therefore, they can live with a certain amount of ambiguity about its interpretation.

Some stories, however, play a much more formative role for certain communities. In my home state of Kansas, for example, the history of the state's admission to the United States has this kind of foundational quality. In the 1850s, the US Congress had sought to keep the peace within an increasingly divided nation by admitting states that allowed slavery at the same frequency as those that had outlawed it. But some people believed that the better course would be to adopt a policy of popular sovereignty, in which territories that were about to be admitted as states were allowed to vote and thereby to choose their state's position on this highly contested issue.

Kansas was one of the first states to be admitted under this approach, and the efforts by both pro-slavery and anti-slavery forces to achieve victory at the ballot box led to arguments, border skirmishes, and something resembling a small-scale war. Newspapers across the nation reported what was taking place in "Bleeding Kansas." Eventually the Kansas state capital building would come to be decorated by a larger-than-life mural by John Steuart Curry that depicts the era; in the center stands the anti-slavery campaigner John Brown—sporting a tremendously long beard and looking for all the world like everyone's image of a fiery Hebrew prophet—holding a Bible in one hand and a rifle in the other.

This story is taken, by most Kansans of my acquaintance, to underscore certain characteristics among the state's citizens: independence of mind, integrity of convictions, and the right to defend oneself—with firearms if necessary. By telling this story repeatedly, passing it down among schoolchildren, and memorializing it in the artwork decorating official buildings, the state and its citizens emphasize some of their strongest convictions and identify themselves as a people who came into being through the apocalyptic strife of a ferocious gun battle.

Needless to say, one could offer an alternative interpretation of this story. It might be that "Bleeding Kansas" could remind us of how much damage can be done when people defend their moral convictions with deadly weapons. One could focus on the number of people who died, the number of families who lost loved ones, the number of children orphaned. One might see it as a strong argument in favor of strict gun control and of insuring, through whatever means necessary, that armed citizens would never make the state bleed again. And yet, this is not the interpretation that the story, and its various representations in art and literature, typically evokes.

If stories are this ambiguous, how do they come to have morally formative power? How did the citizens of Kansas decide that they would read the story of Bleeding Kansas as, for example, an argument in favor of an armed citizenry instead of an argument against it? Why does the Curry mural portray John Brown as a heroic (if slightly eccentric) figure? What leads people to adopt one particular set of interpretations, rather than a very different but equally plausible set?

Ultimately these interpretive choices are made by the communities themselves. The community reads the story with a certain interpretive "spin"; the story is told and retold in ways that emphasize certain features over others. In the case of Bleeding Kansas, the emphasis is typically placed on the importance of holding firm to one's convictions and to defending oneself against encroachment by others, rather than on the lives that were lost and the strife that was perpetuated. These beliefs become the lens through which the story is told. Consequently, while a story *appears* to support a particular set of ideals and practices simply by being the story that it is, it actually accomplishes this feat only because it has been *interpreted* in a particular way. (This is, in fact, one reason why stories are such successful instruments of moral formation: the listeners imagine that it's "just a story," but all the while, they are being shaped to draw certain kinds of moral conclusions from it.) Thus the story itself is not the only morally formative force in the equation; a particular *reading* of the story also contributes to the formation of character and the shaping of the moral life of the community.

One might imagine that the role of interpretation would become less significant when the stories themselves are considered especially important, as is the case in many religious communities. Here, many of the most important stories have been enshrined as sacred texts. Surely these stories, we might imagine, influence people *directly*, rather than being mediated by varying interpretations. But in fact, the opposite is true: the more significant the story, the more investment people have in identifying its "proper" interpretation. The decision that the interpreter makes—to emphasize certain parts of a story and to marginalize others, to tell stories in a particular order and with a certain emphasis, to choose to tell certain stories in certain circumstances and contexts—all these factors become much more critical when the story is one that the community holds in particularly high regard.

This point is further accented by the fact that most communities have a very large stock of stories, and that some degree of selection is always necessary. Interpretations are strongly influenced by the very decision to tell certain stories, or certain parts of a story, rather than others. This is as true for the stories of Christianity as it is for those of Bleeding Kansas, or of a particular town's or family's stories. We will therefore need to return, in the upcoming interlude and the chapter that follows it, to the interpretation of the Christian narratives; this will set the stage for understanding the role that these narratives play in the shaping of Christian character, and therefore their role in Christian ethics. Before turning to that task, however, we need to undertake a brief investigation of the role of narratives for the Christian faith.

The narratives of Christianity

What are the stories that Christians tell? Clearly, the range of possible stories is enormous. In addition to the entire Bible, which contains hundreds of stories, the Christian faith has been around for some two thousand years—and the written records of the faith are vast. If we include not only the officially sanctioned stories of saints and martyrs, of bishops and priests and pastors, but also the stories of ordinary Christians who have acted in particularly noteworthy ways, the number of potential stories approaches the infinite. How could anyone possibly choose?

Canonical scripture

The centerpoint of the Christian faith is the person of Jesus Christ, who is understood to be unique—not simply because of his teachings and his actions, but because he is believed by Christians to be God incarnate: both human and divine. Because of his centrality to the faith, stories about his words and his actions are of paramount importance. Of course, because he was a historical person, stories about him will always be in some dispute. Within the first century after Jesus walked the earth, a great many stories were circulating about him in the ancient world, but four particular accounts—the Gospels—emerged as definitive. The process by which these four, and not any of the others, came into prominence is a long and complicated one, and has recently been the subject of much conversation and argument, not only among scholars but in the popular media as well. For the moment, however, we are concerned less about the interior workings of the process and more about the result: that certain stories eventually emerged as authoritative for the community's life. These stories are its *canon*. The word "canon" was the Greek word for a measuring rod or ruler, and it applies outside the religious context as well: we also speak of the canon of texts of recognized importance within a particular field or discipline. The narratives that come to be seen as essential and authoritative for a particular community are its *canonical* texts.

(At this point, readers may wish to consult some of the other resources in this book, depending on their level of familiarity with the Bible and its contents. For those who have very little acquaintance, a review of the textbox entitled "Navigating the Bible" (in the introduction) may be helpful at this point. Those seeking more information as to why certain texts appear in the Bible will be interested in this chapter's textbox on "The canon battle." Those seeking a brief summary of the *content* of Christian scripture will find some help in the Interlude that follows this chapter.)

The canon of texts that emerged as important for the earliest Christian communities included, in addition to the four gospels, two other significant sets of texts. The first of these were the Jewish scriptures. Since Jesus and his earliest followers were Jews, and since certain texts had already emerged as the canon of their faith community, these texts continued to function as scripture in the newly forming groups of Jesus' followers. These texts, eventually canonized

The canon battle

The canon of Christian scripture has been relatively fixed since very early on in Christian history. Occasionally, proposals arise—both explicitly and implicitly—to alter the canon in some significant way: removing a text that is thought by some to be no longer relevant or detrimental to the shape of the faith, or adding an ancient text that was recently discovered or was, for whatever reason, excluded from the canon in the early days of the faith.

Such proposals raise the question of how the canon was formed, which is a matter of considerable dispute among Christians. One view holds the process to be God's work alone—with texts dictated to human scribes and thereby selected by God. A second view gives credit to the human authors alone, seeing them as no different than other historians and writers of their era, and understanding canonization as a process of persuasion and power-plays among competing groups. But these are both minority opinions; most Christian theologians would argue that both God and human beings play a role in the process, using language of divine inspiration to describe both the writing of the texts and their selection for the canon. The canonization process involved paying attention to which texts were being used in worship and in teaching in the various Christian communities; but this usage, too, was understood as guided, in some sense, by a divine hand. All the same, different views persist as to whether the community ultimately determines its canon of scripture (the common view among more Catholic elements of Christianity) or whether the canon of scripture, as divinely ordered, constitutes the community (as the more Protestant elements of Christianity would tend to insist).

Fortunately, we do not need to settle this dispute in order to move forward with the argument of this book. Most Christians continue to make use of the same canon of scripture that has been in place for centuries, and widely accepted changes are extremely unlikely to occur. Christianity's sacred texts have had such a profound impact on the shape of the faith, that changes in the canon would require an extraordinary degree of deliberation, agreement, and willingness to persevere in maintaining the newly revised version as definitive. The obstacles for such change are overwhelming, which helps to explain why no significant changes in the canon have occurred since very early on in Christian history.

for Christians as the Old Testament, were often given a new interpretation; they were understood as pointing forward, often toward the life of Jesus. The texts were interpreted *Christologically*—that is, Jesus was understood to be the interpretive key for understanding the text. He was also understood to be the long-awaited *Messiah* to whom some of these texts referred.

The other set of texts that emerged as canonical were written during the formation of the earliest Christian communities. These include an account of the formation of these communities by Jesus' followers (the Acts of the Apostles), as well as a collection of letters attributed to various disciples and to Paul the Apostle. These texts helped to set out the meaning and significance of Jesus' life, death, and resurrection; they also provided considerable guidance as to how the emerging Christian communities might build up their common life, particularly with respect to worship, ethics, and mutual care.

Christians are in fairly wide agreement about the specific texts that constitute its canon of scripture, though some slight differences exist among the major branches of the faith (Roman Catholic, Eastern Orthodox, and Protestant). Moreover, since most contemporary Christians read their canonical texts in translation, not everyone reads "the same" biblical texts. But even if everyone agreed on exactly the same texts and read them in their original languages, the *interpretation* of these texts would still remain an open question. For this reason, the stories found in the Christian scriptures, while remaining formative for Christian identity, will always have more the character of an ongoing conversation rather than a definitive pronouncement. To tell the stories of the faith, as with the stories of any community, is to open up a conversation about the community's identity. Through the selection, interpretation, and performance of particular texts by Christian communities, their members give shape to the community and establish its character.

Reading the Bible in public

A community's narratives have the greatest power when they are told within the context of a gathering of that community. When Christians gather for worship, they tell the stories of their faith; these stories are read aloud, recast into prayers, and sometimes performed in dramatic readings or fully staged scenes. In the early centuries of Christianity, of course, these live readings of the text were the only ones available to most people. By the sixteenth century, the invention of moveable type and printed books—as well as a somewhat greater literacy rate—began to make the stories available to people well beyond their bodily performance at gatherings of the community. Nevertheless, Christians continued to read their stories aloud—and they still do so today. This practice strikes some observers as old-fashioned or simply eccentric, particularly in the modern West, where literacy is widespread and most people could simply read the stories on their own. But if we recognize the important role of these stories in the moral formation of the community, we should not be surprised that they continue to be read aloud. This is done in order to familiarize the community with a particular set of texts—to make them part of the mental furniture of its members. As in the case of a family or a small town, the stories that are told repeatedly and aloud are usually those that most clearly represent, and thereby reinforce, the specific character traits of that community. These stories create a framework within which the community's other experiences find their meaning and significance.

The morally formative quality of the stories of the faith is recognized in the Christian and Jewish scriptures themselves, in a story in which God instructs the Israelites to make the words of scripture a part of their identity:

> Keep these words that I am commanding you today in your heart. Recite them to your children and talk about them when you are at home and when you are away, when you lie down and when you rise. Bind them as a sign on your hand, fix them as an emblem on your forehead, and write them on the doorposts of your house and on your gates (Deut. 6:6–9).

The stories of the faith should be so familiar, so well-worn, that they provide the structure for the world that the faithful inhabit. They should be kept ever before the eyes of the believers: on their lips and their tongue, on their doorposts and gates, even worn upon their bodies. They should be the stories that they know best, that they can most easily retell, and that give shape to all the other stories of their lives.

Competing stories

In those cases in which people gather to rehearse their central narratives as part of their *daily routine*, this will probably be sufficient in itself to give these stories a real prominence in the life of the community. But when, as for many Christians, people gather for this purpose only once a week at most (and often much less frequently than that), these stories are unlikely to become the structural principles of one's life. After all, churches are not the only communities that tell stories; human beings are typically engaged in a number of communities simultaneously, and all these groups have their stories to tell. Whether they undertake this work explicitly or implicitly, the stories with which we have the most, and the most regular, contact will be the ones that most significantly influence the shape of our moral lives. And for most people—including most Christians—the stories with which they have the most contact will not be the stories of Christianity.

Consider this rather straightforward example. Throughout the stories that are told, both in Christianity and in Judaism, one of the most regular features is the idea that God is the one to whom our love and worship is properly due. The first commandment in the law, echoed by Jesus, is that one should love God with all of one's heart, soul, strength, and mind. Parables and vignettes tell of the foolishness of those who place their trust and offer their worship to that which is not God. The theological term for this—treating something as God when it isn't God—is "idolatry." (An *idol* is something that is accorded the treatment that is properly due to God, even though it isn't God. Therefore, whether someone is willing to describe something as an *idol* depends on what they describe as *God*.) The biblical narratives are replete with exhortations against various acts of idolatry; again and again, people are counseled to reserve their worship and praise for God alone, and not to give it over to anything that falls short of the reality of God. In spite of all the divisions and varying interpretations of scriptural texts throughout the Jewish and Christian faiths, this is one element of the story that seems to be fairly constant and broadly agreed upon. Most Christians will hear at least one story that implies this idea during every single worship service that they attend. They hear the story told aloud, in the midst of the community, and they often hear it commented upon and commended to their use.

But most of them hear it only once in the week at the very most. And throughout the rest of the week, they are bombarded with a very different set of stories, most of which not only fail to reinforce the message of this story; they actively contradict it. The alternative stories constantly raise other aspects of life as those in which we should put our trust and our hope, and to which we should pledge our love and loyalty. We tell stories about people who achieve the good life by trusting and loving money and everything that it will buy. We tell stories in which the nation-state, and that for which it stands, makes our lives worth living and offers us peace, prosperity, and security. The stories that are told throughout the week provide all sorts of candidates for what people should trust and love with the greatest fervor: the family, the school, the political party, the market, the job, the bank account. How, in the face of these competing stories, can the stories that describe God as the one and only being who deserves humanity's faith, hope, and love—how can such stories ever hope to find a foothold?

The only solution, of course, is to make sure that the members of a community encounter their stories more than once a week. Thus many Christians try to extend the influence of their narratives by reading them to their children at bedtime or reading them throughout the week as private devotions. They form Bible study groups and discussion groups. But in spite of all these efforts, most Christians (like members of other communities) usually realize that other stories—many of which serve as the narratives of other communities—will also have a considerable presence and power in their lives. One can attempt to organize boycotts and protests in order to keep these alternative stories out of hearing range, but these strategies often backfire; the organizers often seem strangely fearful that their own stories will have no persuasive power unless competing stories are held at bay. And given the technological access that we have to so many forms of media, we are quickly reaching the point at which each community's narratives are available to everyone; all that is needed is enough time and energy to learn them. Thus, no matter how thoroughly a community may try to insulate itself from stories that at least some of its members may consider deformative of moral character, these stories will eventually be heard.

We will return to this point in chapter 10, where we will confront the question of what happens when Christians encounter people whose primary allegiances are formed in other communities and whose lives are shaped by a different set of narratives and practices. This will in turn prepare us for the last third of the book, where we will examine the shape of the Christian life within various other spheres of action, including economics, politics, health care, sex, and sexuality, and the natural environment. Part of our concern in those chapters will be to explore how Christians go about making their own stories their primary point of reference in addressing these spheres of activity, even in the midst of others whose moral formation may differ considerably from their own.

At this point, however, we have said enough about stories, their role in moral formation, and their particular significance in the Christian community. We now need to return to a point made in the previous section, concerning the ambiguity of stories. How does one move from the morally ambiguous character of the story to a more concrete moral claim? This will be the focus of the following chapter; first, however, a brief interlude will introduce the most significant narratives of the Christian tradition.

Questions for discussion

1. Think of one community (other than a church community) of which you are a member, and consider the story or stories that are told repeatedly when that community gathers. Think of both implicit and explicit examples.

2. What are the "larger" stories that dominate the culture in which you live? Think about the political system, the economic system, the educational system, and the news media in your cultural setting.

3. Speaking personally, which stories have had the greatest impact on you? Which have been most important in giving you your identity, and in forming your moral landscape? Be sure to include examples both of the *specific* stories that are told in gathering communities, and the (often more implicit) stories of the larger culture of which you are a part.

4. Provide at least one example, either from a church community or some other gathered community of which you are a part, where there is dispute about the interpretation of a particular narrative that is significant in the community's life. How does this dispute get aired? If it has been resolved to any degree, how did resolution come about?

5. Within the context of Christianity, what difference might it make to interpret stories Christologically? Consider one example, such as the story of the creation of the world, the flood, the promise to Abraham, the binding of Isaac, or the crossing of the Red Sea. Pick one of these and offer a description of a Christological and a non-Christological interpretation of the significance of the story for the moral formation of Christians.

Sources cited in this chapter and/or recommended for further reading

Richard Adams, *Watership Down*

David S. Cunningham, *Friday, Saturday, Sunday: Literary Meditations on Suffering, Death, and New Life*, chapter 7

Stephen E. Fowl and L. Gregory Jones, *Reading in Communion: Scripture and Ethics in Christian Life*

Stanley Hauerwas, "The Story-Formed Community," in *A Community of Character: Toward a Constructive Christian Social Ethic*

Stanley Hauerwas and L. Gregory Jones, eds., *Why Narrative? Readings in Narrative Theology*

Garrison Keillor, *Lake Wobegon Days*; *Leaving Home*; *We Are Still Married*

Toni Morrison, *Beloved*; *Song of Solomon*

Brian Wicker, *The Story-Shaped World*

*I*nterlude 1

The narratives of Christianity

At this point, the author of a textbook encounters a dilemma. Given that readers will vary enormously as to their acquaintance with the biblical narratives, how much of that information should appear here? The sheer size and complexity of the Bible makes it impractical for students simply to be sent away to read it, as they might be asked to read a novel or a history text as part of a course assignment. Nevertheless, without a working familiarity with the narratives of the faith, the study of Christian ethics is simply not possible.

The compromise reached here is to list a small selection of biblical texts with which students need to be familiar in order to proceed. These are texts that have had a particularly significant influence on the Christian faith and, in particular, on its account of the moral life. Those students with little or no acquaintance with this material are strongly urged to pick up a Bible and *read the texts listed here*, rather than simply relying on the summaries offered. Others may wish to use the summaries as a way to determine which of the texts they need to read or reread.

In any case, this list is *not* an attempt to name the only relevant biblical texts, nor merely to prioritize the really important ones. The entire Bible has served, and continues to serve, as a source of ethical reflection for Christians, and no subset of texts can provide a substitute for the whole. Nevertheless, given the limitations of time (and of the reader's energy), some such list is essential; readers need to have some knowledge of at least some of the Bible in order to make sense of what follows.

The Old Testament

As noted in the previous chapter, the Old Testament includes the books of the Hebrew Bible, the canonical texts of Judaism. These were the scriptures of Jesus and his first followers, and as such they provide the essential background against which his life, death, and resurrection can be understood. Christianity adopted these texts as part of its own canon of scripture in order to acknowledge its roots in Judaism and to maintain continuity with that tradition. Although Christians and Jews interpret many of these texts differently, these shared scriptures are an important part of the mutual heritage that ties these two faiths inextricably together.

Genesis 1–22

God creates the world and everything that is in it, declaring this created order to be good. Human beings are created in the image of God and blessed with reason and will. But rather than placing their trust in the God who created them, they trust that which is not God and do things which, though they seem to be to their advantage, turn out to be to their great disadvantage. They use their freedom and their will, not to put their trust in God, but to turn away from God. Nevertheless, God always finds ways to set them on a new course, to give them a second (and third and fourth) chance, and to help them learn to use their freedom more wisely.

Eventually, God calls Abraham and Sarah to be the parents of a special tribe of people who will have a special relationship with God and who will serve as a means through which all people can eventually be called back into a right relationship with God. This tribe will extend through many generations and its numbers will multiply. Abraham believes God's promise, and this marks the beginning of the restoration of the relationship between human beings and God. Even when his faith is severely tested, Abraham seeks to do whatever God asks of him.

Exodus 1–20

God's chosen tribe, the Israelites, have been taken captive in Egypt, and have been enslaved. God decides to set them free, and chooses as an emissary an unlikely Israelite named Moses, who has lived as an Egyptian for his entire life. God sends a series of plagues on the Egyptians in order to convince them to let the Israelites go free. The culminating plague is one in which the first-born of every household dies; the Israelites are "passed over" by this plague, and they mark the event with a ritual meal and by telling the story of their victory over their captors (the origins of the Passover). They depart *from* Egypt, narrowly escaping the pursuing Egyptians; they then wander in the wilderness for generations, receive a set of laws and commandments from God, and eventually arrive at the land that God has promised them.

2 Samuel 7–12

The Israelites were ruled first by a series of judges, then by a series of kings. One of the greatest kings of Israel was David, who was a military leader, a poet, a musician, and a devoted believer in God. But he was also a human being with human failings. This section of 2 Samuel is one of many stories that display both the greatness and the weakness of the Israelite kings. David wants to have a sexual relationship with the wife of one of his generals, so he sends the general into a disastrous combat situation in order that he will be killed. The plan succeeds, and David imagines that he has gotten what he wants; but through the use of a story, the prophet Nathan helps David to see the evil in what he has done.

Psalms and Proverbs (selections)

These books provide examples of Hebrew poetry. Because we read them in translation, they often don't seem very poetic to us, but the psalms in particular are finely-wrought poems that were often set to music. They are written in the form of prayers to God, and they express a variety of emotions and attitudes: joy, anger, grief, lament, injury, gratitude, and thanksgiving. The psalms play an important role in both Jewish and Christian worship, even today; they provide believers with an opportunity to express the various emotions and experiences of the community in addressing God. The book of Proverbs seems at first glance simply to provide a great deal of commonplace advice. On closer inspection, however, many of its sections provide some information about God and about God's relationship to the world.

Isaiah 40–44, 52–53

This is a good example of prophetic literature, and it is often read and understood on multiple levels. It was probably written around the time that the Israelites were conquered by the Babylonians and sent into exile. The prophet's words express God's desire to bring comfort to the people and, eventually, to bring them out of their exile to their homeland. Some readers and listeners might have understood these words as referring to specific historical events in the near future; for example, the "servant of the Lord" might be taken as an oblique reference to Cyrus of Persia, who conquered Babylon and allowed the Israelites to return home. Or it might refer to the promise of a Messiah, a specially anointed messenger of God, who would eventually restore the people of Israel to their former glory and their former intimate relationship with God. Finally, many Christians interpreted these prophecies as referring to Jesus as having taken on the role of the Messiah and having suffered on behalf of others.

This last point is important for understanding how Christians made use of the Jewish Bible. Since Jesus himself was a Jew, and since many of the earliest Christians were as well, they earnestly desired to give a special place to the Jewish scriptures. These were eventually canonized as the Christian *Old Testament*, but the texts were often interpreted in ways that differed significantly from how the same texts were understood by those Jews who did *not* become Christians. The various interpretations of Isaiah provide a case in point; Christians often interpreted these and other Old Testament texts Christologically, that is, as referring implicitly or explicitly to Jesus as the Christ, the Messiah.

Amos

Many of the shorter prophetic books, sometimes called the Minor Prophets, focus on particular issues or actions. Often they include some form of critique about current religious practices, and some kind of higher goal toward which the community should be striving. The book of Amos is well known for raising significant concerns about social and economic justice for the less fortunate. Its author speaks scathingly of the luxuries enjoyed by the wealthy in contrast to the sufferings of the poor. A number of social reformers, including Martin Luther King, Jr., often pointed to Amos and to other prophetic books as a critique of some contemporary practices and a directive toward a more just society.

The New Testament

The New Testament begins with four Gospels—accounts of the good news of the life, ministry, death, and resurrection of Jesus of Nazareth. Of the four accounts, Mark is the shortest, and is thought by many scholars to have been written earlier than the others. Three of the four Gospels—Mark, Matthew, and Luke—are often referred to as the *synoptic* Gospels. This is because they all follow the same basic timeline and can be set side-by-side with one other in an approximate parallel structure. Most of what is in Mark also appears in Matthew and Luke, but these two Gospels have about half again as much additional material compared to Mark, and much of this additional material is common to both Matthew and Luke. This has led some scholars to speculate that Matthew and Luke used two sources to write their Gospels, one of which was Mark, and the other was a collection of narrative material that is now lost.

The Gospel of Mark

Of the four Gospels, Mark is the easiest to read at a single sitting, and it provides a good outline of the story of Jesus; having a good grasp of this story is absolutely central for a good understanding of Christianity and of Christian ethics. The gospel divides neatly into two halves. The first half describes the ministry of Jesus, from his baptism by John, through a series of teachings, healings, and other miraculous signs, to the point at which he reveals his special divine status to his disciples. The second half focuses on his suffering and death; this part of the story is sometimes called the *Passion narrative* (drawing on an older meaning of the English word "passion," which in turn comes from the Greek word that means "to suffer"). The Passion narrative includes Jesus' predictions of his own suffering and death; his last meal with his disciples; his arrest, trial, execution, and burial; and his followers' discovery that the tomb where he was laid to rest was now empty.

Matthew 26–28 or Luke 22–24

Because the Passion story is such a central part of the *good news* of Jesus, students should read at least one other synoptic account in addition to that of Mark. Moreover, most scholars believe that Mark originally ended at verse 8 of the last chapter, and that the rest of the Gospel was added later; this means that Mark probably did not originally contain any direct account of Jesus' resurrection, nor of his appearance to his disciples in the days that followed that event. Because these post-resurrection appearances have had such a significant impact on the shape of the Christian faith, students should read one or both of these sections in order to get some sense of these narratives.

Matthew 5–7

This passage is particularly important for the purposes of the study of Christian ethics. It is a long, interrelated series of teachings that are described as having been delivered by Jesus while standing on a high place above the crowds. It is therefore often called the Sermon on the Mount. In these chapters, Jesus speaks in broad terms about human behavior, often emphasizing the inward disposition of human beings when they act. In this section of the text, Jesus returns time and again to several themes that are particularly important for Christian ethics. First, he shows how the law often fails to provide a sufficient indicator of good human behavior, since it is relatively easy for people to fulfill the letter of the law while operating against its spirit and purpose. Second, he describes God's approval of certain kinds of character traits and actions, some of which (such as meekness, sorrow, and being persecuted) might not often be considered in a positive light. And third, he cautions against certain kinds of behavior that might typically be thought to be good and appropriate: praying in public, making plans for the future, and judging others. These three chapters of text contain the sources of some of Christianity's most distinctive ethical claims.

Luke 10 and 15

These two chapters contain some of the most well-known and best-loved stories from which Christians have drawn inspiration for their ethics. As we have noted throughout this book, stories help to orient communities toward the character traits and behaviors that they consider most important and praiseworthy. The material in these two chapters of Luke provides an excellent example of this phenomenon, as well as providing us with clues as to the most important Christian character traits and behaviors. Four important stories can be identified:

1. A story about the sending out of the apostles, from which Christianity draws its missionary impulse.
2. The story of the Good Samaritan, in which an injured man is ignored by the religious leaders of the day but is shown extraordinary kindness by a foreigner whom most of Jesus' listeners would have considered to be a person of dubious character.
3. The story of Jesus' visit to the home of Mary and Martha, in which attention to and acceptance of his teachings is described as being at least as important as the accomplishment of one's work.
4. Three stories in which things that were formerly lost—a sheep, a coin, and a son—are found, often after great exertion; the last of these stories is the lengthiest and best known, often referred to as the story of the Prodigal Son.

All three stories illustrate the emphasis that Christianity places on repentance, that is, allowing oneself to be turned away from bad behavior and toward good behavior: "there will be more joy in heaven over one sinner who repents than over ninety-nine righteous persons who need no repentance" (Luke 15:7).

John 1 and John 13–17

The Gospel of John differs significantly from the three synoptic gospels. Its author seems less concerned about placing events in a particular order (except for the Passion narrative, which is somewhat similar to that of Matthew and Luke). Rather, John concentrates on Jesus' signs and his teachings, and the author also inserts more theological commentary than do the other Gospel writers. The first chapter, for example, begins with an extended description of Jesus as the Word of God; after describing the relationship between God and God's Word, the author tells us that this Word "became flesh and dwelt among us" (1:14) in the person of Jesus. In chapters 13 through 17, often referred to as the Farewell Discourse, Jesus speaks at length to his disciples in anticipation of his own death. He warns them that he will be leaving them, and counsels them to continue to follow his teachings even in his absence. He also tells them that God will send them the Holy Spirit as a counselor, advocate, and comforter. Finally, he describes his own role in detail, making clear his own relationship to God and to his disciples. The discourse ends with a prayer (often called the "high priestly prayer"), in which Jesus prays for himself, for his disciples, and for those in the future who will believe in him through the disciples' preaching.

Acts 1–9

The Acts of the Apostles is a collection of stories about the work that Jesus' disciples carried out after his death and resurrection. Many of these stories are about a particularly zealous persecutor of the early Christians, Saul of Tarsus, who was converted and became one of its most ardent advocates of the new faith, becoming known by his Roman name, Paul. These stories describe the dedication, energy, and zeal of these early witnesses to the life, death, and resurrection of Jesus, and thereby help to explain the rapid spread of Christianity into many different parts of the Roman Empire. While the entire book is of great profit, the first nine chapters are important in their description of the divine inspiration of these witnesses through the descent of the Holy Spirit at the festival of Pentecost, the work of the Spirit in their lives and the lives of others, the specific form of the message they preached, and the conversion of Saul.

The Epistle to the Romans

Most of the rest of the New Testament is in the form of *epistles*, that is, letters written to a community of believers according to a particular form that was common in the ancient world. The longest and, in later Christian history, probably the most important of these was Paul's letter to the Romans. Reading this letter from beginning to end can be a challenge for modern readers, because Paul makes a number of assumptions that are different from ours, and he uses a number of terms that may be unfamiliar or might be used in a different sense today from their original sense. Nevertheless, students are strongly encouraged to read this letter in its entirety, given its influence and its integration of theology and ethics. If possible, it should be read with the help of a study Bible, paying close attention to the footnotes for an explanation of Paul's assumptions and terminology.

The first half of the letter provides Paul's summary of the good news brought by the life, death, and resurrection of Jesus: namely, that human beings—who, because of their sinful nature, are estranged from God—are, through Jesus, brought back into right relationship with God. In this account, Paul emphasizes the universality of sin, the insufficiency of the law as a vehicle for getting beyond our sinful state, and the significance of *grace*—God's gift of mercy to human beings. Although Paul's account of sin leads some readers to feel put off or excessively chastised, his account of God's grace leads him to end this first half of the letter with what might be described as the most gloriously positive and hopeful sentence in the Bible: "For I am convinced that neither death, nor life, nor angels, nor rulers, nor things present, nor things to come, nor powers, nor height, nor depth, nor anything else in all creation, will be able to separate us from the love of God in Christ Jesus our Lord" (Rom. 8:39).

The second half of the letter includes a long, important, and often misunderstood section on the role of the people of Israel in God's plan of salvation (Rom. 9–11). The ultimate conclusion of this section is that the salvation of the entire human race is possible only because it was first offered to the Jews and that, in the end, all the people of Israel will be saved. The remainder of the letter includes a good summary of Paul's ethical teachings, which arise directly from his account of God's plan of salvation. Most commentators have pointed to a very high level of compatibility between Paul's account in these chapters and the ethical teachings of Jesus, as they are laid out in, for example, the Sermon on the Mount, and as they are exemplified in the stories that he tells.

Students should also become acquainted with at least one other Pauline epistle, such as 1 Corinthians, Galatians, or Philippians—as well as one by another author, such as 1 John.

The Revelation to St. John

The last book in the New Testament is also one of the most controversial. It offers an apocalyptic vision of the final consummation of history—the end of the world. As was typical for this genre of ancient literature, it relies heavily on vivid and colorful descriptions, dramatic narratives of action and battle, and the secret meanings of signs, symbols, and numbers. Many readers assume that its primary purpose is to describe how the world will end; but literature of this type often had a purpose other than predicting the future. Its real significance lay in its subtle ethical implications: i.e., that those who behaved in certain ways would be rewarded, while others would be punished. We can make some guesses about exactly what kinds of behavior the author had in mind, given the details offered in the seven letters to various Christian communities in chapters 2 and 3; however, we don't really have enough information about these communities and their contexts to know precisely what kinds of moral judgments were being made. In its original day, the book was probably understood by Christians as a call to hold firm to their faith and practices, even in the midst of severe persecution by the Roman Empire.

4 From story to morality

Proclaiming, inhabiting, and performing

At this point in our journey, we find ourselves awash in stories: childhood stories, family stories, small-town stories, and stories that describe a community's origins. We have also recognized that certain *implicit* stories are deeply woven into the structure of our lives; these narratives may shape us in ways of which we are not even aware. At the end of chapter 3, and in the interlude that follows it, we have begun to focus our attention on those stories that are particular to the Christian tradition, especially the biblical stories; but we still face a very long list of options. Even the small set of biblical narratives that we have just reviewed cover a very wide swath—in fact, they stretch from the creation of the world to its final consummation (and it's difficult to get much broader than that). How can all these diverse stories possibly lead us toward an account of the shape of the Christian life? Isn't this likely to turn into a very large muddle?

This might well be the case if we were simply to read the stories and go no further. But in fact, in the Christian tradition, the stories themselves are not, so to speak, the end of the story. The whole enterprise of Christian ethics depends upon a deep and expansive knowledge of these stories, but it also depends upon a series of additional steps, through which these stories become more deeply rooted in the lives of Christians. Our goal in this chapter will be to explore the process whereby a community moves from story to morality.

Stories and their interpretive discontents

Two of the claims of the previous chapter bear repeating at this point. First: the stories that we live by—our narratives—form us deeply. They do so in subtle ways, such that we are not always aware of their importance in our lives. They become part of our mental and spiritual landscape—part of the air that we breathe—such that we have to exert a certain amount of effort even to recognize the strength of their effect on us. Their effects may even pull us in different directions simultaneously; since we all belong to multiple communities, we find ourselves listening to widely varying stories and trying to follow multiple scripts. These conflicting plot-lines of our lives can sometimes create deep tensions within us. Often we don't even realize that these tensions are present; much less do we fully understand their causes and their nuances.

A second point: these stories are ambiguous. They are capable of multiple interpretations, and the same story may be heard in very different ways by two people, even if they are members of the same community. All language bears certain marks of ambiguity, but stories are a special case. In and of themselves, they are nothing more than a simple recounting of a series of events, whether fictional or otherwise. Nevertheless, because they help us to create an imaginative internal landscape that provides the backdrop for our moral reasoning, we often draw from them certain implications for how we should act and who we should be. At the same time, we all hear these stories with different sets of ears—having had differing experiences from one another, and having been influenced in our interpretations by other stories and other communities. As a result, the same story can easily give rise to several different sets of moral assumptions.

Two stories, four interpretations

Consider an example of this ambiguity. In the early centuries of Christian history, certain forms of thought—now grouped under the general label of *gnosticism*—were very popular. Our word "gnostic" (pronounced "nostic": the "g" is silent) comes from the Greek word *gnosis*, which means "knowledge." (Many English-speakers will be familiar with the word "agnosticism"; the "a" at the beginning of a Greek word is a negative, so the roots are "no" and "knowledge": a denial that one can *know* something—for example, whether God exists.) Gnostic thought urged human beings to strive toward an understanding of the deep interior knowledge that they already possess. The gnostics told various stories of how we came to possess this secret knowledge, as well as why it is so difficult for us to remain focused on it.

One of these stories provides the first half of our example. It tells of a pantheon of lower-order gods and goddesses, all of whom have within themselves a true spark of divinity, a gift from the one true God who is above them all. These demigods are spiritual beings, free from the constraints of physical bodies. But at some point, one of these demigods made the mistake of creating *matter*, and this introduced chaos into an otherwise rosy scene. After a series of further errors on the part of one or more demigods, the material world (as we know it) was created. This world is considered to be a very unpleasant place: prone to change and decay, misleading in its tendency to confuse appearance with reality, and weighing down the true spiritual nature of all being. All in all, the creation of the material order was seen as a great mistake—both by the gods and by those who dwelt within the created order.

This is a very different story than the one told by Judaism and Christianity. As we have observed, the story of creation—as it is told in the book of Genesis—describes the created order as good. God declares it to be good and offers it to human beings as a glorious gift. This creation narrative endows the material world with a purpose and a degree of majesty that is a far cry from the accidents, mistakes, and sheer incompetence that mark the creation of the material world in the gnostic stories. The gulf between this version of the creation story and the gnostic one could hardly be any wider: we are given two very different stories, and the communities that sought to live according to these stories developed very different accounts of the ethical life.

But this is not all. Each of these stories gave rise to two very different ethical perspectives; that is to say, two stories led to four interpretations. Even more interesting than the contrast between the two *stories* is the contrast between the two *very different ethical perspectives* that developed from each of the two stories—*even among those who were in agreement* about which of these stories they wanted to live by. In other words, even when a group of people had come to an agreement about the story that they were taking on as the narrative of their lives, they still found themselves in disagreement about the moral implications of that story. Thus four different sets of ethical assumptions arose from these two different stories.

Those who had made the gnostic story their own agreed that the material order was disordered and corrupt; nevertheless, various groups diverged as to its ethical implications. At one end of the spectrum (call it Gnostic 1) was a willingness to indulge the human body in all its desires; the justification for this view was that, since the material order is corrupt anyway, it doesn't really matter what we do with it. The other perspective (Gnostic 2) was exactly the opposite: it argued for mortifying the flesh and subduing the desires of the body, because these were thought to get in the way of adequate attention to the soul as the only thing that was good about humanity.

Similarly, the account of creation in the book of Genesis has led to its own kind of ethical divide. One perspective (call this one Christian 1) believes that, since God gave this good creation to human beings, they ought to be free to make use of it. One passage in particular—"fill the earth and subdue it; and have dominion over . . . every living thing" (Gen. 1:28) was some-times taken as enjoining human beings to take charge of the earth for their own purposes. Various forms of environmental degradation thus came to be seen as the necessary result of the proper exercise of human free will in mas-tery over the creation. An alternative reading (call this one Christian 2) is that, since the created order is given and entrusted to human beings, they should be good stewards of its bounty, as a way of offering back to God the gift that they have been given. Here the master image is of the first human being naming the animals (Gen. 2:19–20); human beings have dominion over creation, but the goal is one of care and tending, rather than domination and exploitation. We will return to the substance of this disagreement when we examine the implications of Christian ethics for the environment in chapter 15; meanwhile, it will suffice to observe just how diametrically opposed these two perspectives are to one another.

In each case—gnostic and Christian—the ethical implications of a partic-ular story are believed, by their adherents, to have arisen straightforwardly from the stories themselves; and yet, in each case, two very different ethical claims are made. And because these stories and their interpretations became such an essential part of the moral universe for their respective communi-ties that have told these stories, it can be very difficult for those who advo-cate one or the other interpretation to see the logic of those who view things differently, despite being a member of the same community. What happens in these situations? Do communities necessarily divide when they differ on the interpretation of a particular story? How can the meaning and significance of a story be re-envisioned or revised? How do we know when we've hit upon the "right" interpretation—or does such an animal even exist?

Interpretation and the evaluation of practices

Part of the problem we face is that, although *interpretation* of our stories sounds like a worthy goal, it's not actually our final goal. Searching for a descriptive phrase that describes the *meaning* or the *significance* of a story might be useful when we are attempting to summarize its relevance, but eventually, we want to understand how it structures our moral universe—and therefore how it leads us to evaluate certain kinds of actions and activi-ties. We might be able to deduce the meaning of a particular story and state it in abstract terms; but if we don't actually *do* whatever that description demands, then we aren't really living according to the story.

The ancient Greek writer Aesop wrote a number of short fables that have endured, over the years, as children's literature. They offer moral instruction by telling the tale of, for example, a hungry fox who enters a vineyard and tries several times to steal a bunch of high-hanging grapes. His efforts fail, so he trots off, muttering to himself about how bad the grapes probably are, and how he never really wanted them anyway. At the end of the story, we are given a moral: "Fools can easily despise what they cannot get." The moral is almost unnecessary, because the story is written primarily for the purpose of providing the moral message; most readers—even very young children—will often deduce the moral without much assistance. This pattern holds for many story collections that are intended for children—from Beatrix Potter to the *Uncle Remus* tales of the American South. By their brevity, their definitive descriptions of character, and their simple plot structure, they leave little room for ambiguity with regard to their moral message.

But of course, the simpler and more straightforward the tale, the less likely it is to become one of those "stories that we live by." Once the single, straightforward moral message is obtained and internalized, the story can be forgotten; it becomes a mere nostalgic memory, rather than a story that is retold time and again throughout one's life. Compared to the single phrase of the moral, the story is lengthy and provides a great deal of unnecessary detail; if its purpose is simply to lead us to a single, straightforward moral injunction, why should we bother to remember the story? We can just memorize the moral; in fact, in the case of Aesop's Fables, that's often exactly what we've done. (Many people would recognize some of Aesop's morals, such as "Don't count your chickens before they are hatched" or "Prepare today for the wants of tomorrow," but would not necessarily be able to tell the story from which they arise.) In contrast, the "stories that we live by" are those that are worth remembering in their entirety *precisely because* they are not so straightforward; they therefore lend themselves to diverse interpretations and seem to have different nuances every time we tell them. This makes them much more useful for framing a moral universe—even while their ambiguity makes them frustrating to those who would like to have more definitive answers to life's persistent questions.

During the modern era of biblical criticism, one group of scholars proposed that certain genres of biblical literature ought to be read in the manner of Aesop's Fables. The temptation is understandable; many biblical stories are relatively brief and have stock characters whose moral outlooks are fairly obvious. Very few of these stories have an explicitly-stated moral, but we could easily write one for each of them. This is particularly true of the *parables*, a special genre of story that the Gospels describe Jesus as telling. His story of the two men who built their houses on different foundations—one on solid ground and one on sand, with predictable results—has a fairly obvious moral, along the lines of "plan wisely to protect against future disaster." Almost all of Jesus' parables could conceivably be read this way. For example, the parable of the Good Samaritan tells of a man who was beaten and robbed; two religious leaders pass by him and do not offer to help, but an outsider, a Samaritan, not only tends to the man's wounds but pays for his future care. One might well argue that the moral of this story is "One should stop to help those in need." Other parables might have morals such as "Those who forgive are more likely to be forgiven" and "Only a fool begrudges a good gift." Through an extension of this method, it is possible to boil the entire Bible down to a series of hints for better living. (In fact, some editors of the Bible make this move explicitly: they insert, in an edition's first few pages, a list of quick references that lead the reader to certain passages based on their needs and moods: "If you are experiencing grief, turn to Psalm 23"—and so on.)

But other biblical scholars have argued for a position that is diametrically opposed to this one. They suggested that the parables (and most other genres of biblical narrative as well) don't really work this way. First, most of them *don't* actually have a moral attached, so assigning one always requires a bit of speculation on our part. Two listeners might take away significantly differing moral injunctions from the same parable. (Is the parable of the Good Samaritan primarily about the importance of generosity, or is it about the hypocrisy of religious leaders who refuse to help? Or is it perhaps about our difficulty in imagining that a social outcast—the Samaritans were a marginalized and much-hated group—could be the hero of the story?) In addition, the community that values these stories has taken care to preserve (and frequently to reread) the stories themselves, rather than simply a summary of their moral significance. As the community tells and listens to these stories over time, its members hear them differently, depending on the context in which the stories are told. In fact, one might well argue that the *reason* that the biblical narratives have endured over time is precisely because they seem fresh to us in every new context.

Of course, we have not yet noted the most important argument against the attempt to draw out the moral from the stories that a community lives by. If the stories are ultimately reducible to a series of morals or moral principles, then we are right back where we started, in chapter 1: facing a series of moral rules and wondering how we might use them to wrestle with the specific dilemmas that we face. The desire to extract a moral from the story is very similar to the desire to develop a system of lifeboat ethics, in which the solutions to our moral quandaries are discovered by applying the right rules to the situations we face. But it was precisely the inadequacies of this approach that helped us recognize the significance of our habituated narratives and practices in the first place. Admittedly, if the question is a straightforward one that can be resolved by accepting a commonplace judgment about human nature ("Fools easily despise what they cannot get"), then a story with a simple moral will do quite nicely; in fact, this helps us to understand why Aesop's Fables and similar stories have endured through time, in spite of their somewhat platitudinous morals. If, on the other hand, the issue is more complicated—such as the question that led Jesus to tell the parable of the Good Samaritan in the first place ("Who is my neighbor?"), then a simple moral platitude may not be immediately available. Thus any effort to evade the ambiguity of the stories of Christianity will always take us back along a path that leads to the same set of obstacles: simplistic principles that often don't seem to apply to the case that we're facing; rules that appear to contradict one another or require us to predict the future; and, most significantly, the fact that we nearly always make our most morally significant decisions out of habit and based on our character, rather than by consulting the rules.

How shall we then proceed?: three strategies

If these narratives—the stories that Christians live by—do not carry their moral significance on their backs in the manner of Aesop's Fables, and if we're not really interested in extracting a single moral principle from them anyway, how exactly do we wrestle with their ambiguity? How do we go about drawing out their moral significance, particularly when different people have, over historical time and across geographical space, believed them to have such widely varying moral implications? Three theological strategies can provide some help in answering this question, each one with its advantages and disadvantages. All three, however, provide some hints for a way forward.

Emphasizing the contemporary context

One strategy for approaching the stories that we live by is to set them alongside the other stories that circulate widely in our culture. This allows us to make straightforward comparisons and to draw out the implications of the stories *in the present context*. A community's most important narratives will look different in differing cultural contexts, so it becomes important to examine them alongside the stories that dominate those contexts, in order to understand some of their moral features.

A great many examples could be offered, but most of them will be deferred until later in the book. In Part 3, we will return to this approach as we consider the kinds of character traits that might best help Christians face the moral questions that arise most frequently in the present cultural context. Meanwhile, two examples will suffice to provide a sense of how this approach helps the Christian community to make the transition from story to morality.

One set of examples concerns our contemporary assumptions about economics. As I have already noted, our economic lives are governed by a model of *scarcity*: there are only so many goods to go around, and the price that we pay for them depends on their supply and our demand. Things become more valuable when they're more difficult to obtain, and whatever is plentiful is practically free. Scarcity tends to create anxiety; we worry that we will not have enough, and sometimes we actually *don't* have enough; so we tend to hold on rather tightly to whatever we *do* have. We worry about spending too much, giving away too much, or finding ourselves in an emergency situation and being unable to attend to it. This is one of our culture's most significant narratives, the economic story that we live by: there is not enough to go around, so accumulation is the key to a good life.

A few biblical narratives tell this story, but they are relatively rare. Instead, most of the characters in the biblical stories who attempt to store up goods and treasure routinely run into difficulties, whereas those who have accumulated little suddenly find themselves overwhelmed with abundance. When the Israelites are wandering in the wilderness, they are given manna to eat every day; when they try to store it up, they find that their efforts are wasted, because the stored manna becomes rotten (Exod. 16:14–20). Jesus is in a boat with his disciples who have caught nothing and are anxious about their circumstances; he tells them to put down their nets again, and they fill the boats so full that they nearly sink (Luke 5:4–6). Jesus also tells a parable about a father whose son has squandered all his resources; but when the wayward son returns home, his father greets him with a feast of abundance (Luke 15:11–24).

Needless to say, these stories are still ambiguous; they do not provide us with a single moral principle that will guide all our economic choices. However, when placed alongside the dominant stories of our culture, they help us to identify some of the background assumptions with which each story operates (scarcity vs. abundance; individualism vs. mutual care in community; providing for oneself vs. dependence on God). If we were to read these stories within a context of certain other forms of economic organization—for example, socialism instead of capitalism—the shape of the narrative would seem very different to us; its background assumptions would stand out in different ways. However, in no case would our context (as readers of the story) be precisely the same as that of its authors and/or its original audience. This is why it is so important to set the narratives of a community alongside the dominant cultural narratives: doing so will help us understand, *in our particular circumstances*, what aspects of the community's stories give the community its identity, and therefore have the most significant moral implications.

A second example comes from the realm of politics, and concerns the stories that we tell about the "natural" world—that is, the world as it exists before human beings impose political order on it. The dominant story is the one passed along to us by Thomas Hobbes, who, in his *Leviathan*, describes life in the state of nature as "nasty, brutish, and short." His view was that, without governments to control people, we would all simply kill each other. He referred to this "natural" condition of humanity as "the war of all against all." The natural world is bad, and governments come along to make it better.

The biblical narratives, by contrast, tell just the opposite story: the natural world is not a bad place; in fact, it is created by God and declared, by God's own voice of authority, to be *good*. The natural state of things—the state in which God creates them and the state to which, through God's ongoing work, they will someday return—is one of peace and harmony. Far from *improving* this condition, human intervention tends to have just the opposite effect: it creates dissension and conflict where there was none. Specifically, the creation story in Genesis suggests that the actions and reactions of human beings eventually lead, not only to their own expulsion from paradise, but also to an overall worsening of the relationships among various elements of the created order.

The contrast between these two stories—that of the book of Genesis and that offered by Thomas Hobbes—not only demonstrates how differently the biblical authors and modern political commentators understand the world; it also helps us to understand how significant a role these narratives play in forming our fundamental assumptions. For many people (including most Christians), the story of creation is either "just a story"—a legend that explained the origins of the world to a pre-scientific age, but today has only sentimental value—or else it is a literal documentary history of how the world began, useful primarily in fighting against contemporary theories about the age of the earth and the process of evolution. Similarly, Hobbes' description of the state of nature in his *Leviathan* is, for most people, little more than one of those "great texts of Western civilization" that we're supposed to know about in order to prove that we are well-educated people. But when we set these two stories alongside each other, their moral implications for our current circumstances are highlighted. This is not to say that we can easily extract from them some kind of prescription about what we should do; that, again, would be to reduce these rich, nuanced stories to a mere set of principles. But the contrast between the two stories helps us to envision just what moral difference it might make for people to make the biblical story of creation one of those "stories that they live by," rather than constructing a life that assumes the necessity of Hobbes' "war of all against all." (We will return to the contrast between Hobbes and the book of Genesis when we examine the question of nation-states and governments in chapter 12.)

In their communal gatherings for worship, Christians have traditionally made use of one particular moment to offer an analysis of the relationship between the biblical stories and the contemporary context. This occurs in the *sermon* or *homily*, which seeks to read and think through the biblical texts in light of contemporary circumstances. This often involves the offering of additional stories—not only the stories that are canonical for the faith, but others that are told for the purpose either of aligning them with, or contrasting them to, the biblical narratives. This requires the preacher to have not only a thorough grasp of the biblical stories (and of a moral framework that is formed by those stories), but also a thorough grasp of the contemporary circumstances in which we live. Only with a detailed understanding of the stories that our world tends to live by can we also understand the moral significance of the stories that Christians seek to live by in the biblical texts. One twentieth-century theologian and preacher, Karl Barth, repeatedly suggested that a sermon needs to be delivered with the Bible in one hand and the newspaper in the other.

But as useful as it may be to point to the *sermon* as the place where this comparison of stories takes place, it would be wrong to *limit* this work to that one moment in the worship service, or to imagine that it can only be undertaken by those who are prepared and willing to ascend the pulpit. All members of the community have to be about this business all the time. They have to know their own stories, and to know the prevailing stories of the world in which they live; unfortunately, both of these tasks are ever more difficult to accomplish in our increasingly busy lives.

The task of attending to the world's stories is not made any easier by the constant blurring of the lines between news and entertainment; much of what is offered in the way of "news" (particularly in local newspapers and on local television stations, but increasingly in the national media as well) is designed primarily to appease a widespread taste for gossip, sensuality, and the macabre—or to offer information that will be perceived by their audiences (i.e., consumers) as useful and practical.

Of course, the current state of the news media reminds us of another of the narratives that is deeply embedded in our culture, to the effect that the stories that are most important to us are those that affect *us*: our health, our pocketbooks, our government's actions (but only when they actually bear on us; what the government does to other people is *their* business). We will better understand the specific nature of the Christian story if we set it alongside stories such as these—precisely because of the contrast that will come to the fore. Because so many of the Christian stories point away from self-interest and toward the interests of other people, they contrast fairly clearly with a mode of storytelling that always accents the extraordinary relevance of oneself.

In comparison to an approach that derives a single moral from each story, the Bible-and-newspaper approach has a number of obvious advantages. It puts the Christian story into the contemporary context, thereby highlighting the differing assumptions with which it operates. It provides for a certain degree of temporal and geographic flexibility, recognizing that the stories—while enduring through the ages—will take on a particular coloring in light of the context in which they are read and exemplified. And it sets aside the necessarily abstract quality of "the moral of the story" and provides a concrete instance that helps us to imagine what it might mean to live according to a particular narrative.

But neither is this approach a cure-all to the question that occupies us in this chapter. Setting two stories side by side is certainly concrete, but it often doesn't bring the issues home to us directly. To use one of the previous examples, we can say that we *understand* the difference between the Christian account of creation (in which God creates the world as good, whereas discord and wickedness arise through the actions of human beings), and the Hobbesian account (in which the world is "naturally" corrupt and human beings must fix it). But how, exactly, should this affect how individual human actors should act? We can't just pretend that the world is still in the perfect state that God made it, so how will the contrast between these two stories affect our behavior? One solution that we often adopt is to hold these stories at a certain distance from the actual living of our lives; it's much easier to examine and evaluate them from afar. In doing so, we hope to avoid having to make moral judgments about what it might mean to live according to one story rather than the other. But this alternative has problems of its own (as we will see in the next section of this chapter); meanwhile, we are left with the problem of negotiating among the conflicting stories that our various communities hold up as significant for the shape of the moral life.

Another flaw in this approach is that it can encourage us to relativize the biblical texts in ways that make them infinitely malleable in every situation. In one cultural context, a story tends to point us toward one set of actions, while in another context, it seems to point us toward precisely the opposite action. One nineteenth-century biblical scholar worried that this approach would make Scripture into "a wax nose" which could then be twisted in whatever way a person wants to twist it. These worries are probably a bit overdrawn, for reasons mentioned in previous chapters: over time, the community of readers tends to be self-correcting with regard to interpretations of its own texts. But the concern needs to be acknowledged because historians can certainly cite numerous occasions when the contemporary context came to have the upper hand over the biblical texts (see the textbox for some frequently cited examples). Those who employ the Bible-and-newspaper approach need to invest a fair amount of vigilance in assuring that an altogether appropriate level of attention to the contemporary context does not slide over into a willingness to reshape the biblical stories such that they conform to every nuance of that context, leaving only one voice in the conversation.

Performing the scriptures

A second strategy gives due attention to the contemporary context, but uses a different set of metaphors to explain how it affects the interpretation of the biblical text. The metaphors come from the world of the arts—particularly theater and music. The key term is that of *performance*: interpreting the biblical texts in light of the contemporary context has certain resemblances to performing a classic work of drama (like a Shakespeare play) or performing a well known piece of music (like a Beethoven symphony). The texts—the script of a play or a musical score—are well known, and generally agreed upon (as are the texts of the biblical stories themselves); but their performance (the interpretation) must often take account of a different set of circumstances than those that accompanied their original creation. New musical instruments, new interpretive styles, a different cultural setting, and the shifting structures of language—all contribute to the fact that a performance of a work a century ago, or even a few decades ago, will have different nuances from performances of the same dramatic script or musical score today.

In the Christian context, we can again see why the *sermon* is a particularly apt moment for this to occur. Preachers do not only set the biblical narratives alongside the dominant stories of the world in which we live; they also give us some sense of what it would mean to *inhabit* the world of the story, to *embody* it, and to make it one's own. Consider again the parable of the Good Samaritan, which we have discussed above. There is much to be gained by setting this story alongside contemporary accounts of people who are offering and refusing to offer help to those in need, as well as accounts of needs that are going unmet. (People often fail to see that there is, in fact, the equivalent of a wounded person in the ditch by the side of the roads along which they themselves travel every day.) Listeners may come away from this comparison with a new appreciation for the ways that the parable mirrors certain aspects of our contemporary situation. But the preacher's job is not merely to inform; it is to exhort the audience, to move people to action. Part of what it means to proclaim the biblical stories is to help people understand what it might mean to live them and to perform them in the world in which they live. And this may require going beyond merely setting two stories alongside each other; it may require guidance and suggestions about how to "perform the scriptures" in the present-day context.

At this point, we are reminded again of why the sermon cannot be the *only* place in which the narratives of Chrsitianity are interpreted. Consider an analogy from the theater: an important moment in a play's rehearsal process occurs when the director offers to the actor an account of what attitudes and assumptions a particular character should have. In this moment, the actor receives not only certain kinds of *information* about the emotions and psychological depths that should be portrayed, but also some *guidance* as to *how* that portrayal should occur. Nevertheless, as every actor knows, there is no painless, trouble-free path from the receipt of that information and guidance to the actual performance of it on the stage. The actor has to work hard—to try out particular phrasings and uses of the voice, to rehearse scenes both alone and with other actors, and, in short, to develop *habits* which allow the character's inner psychological states to come through in performance. Just as the actor cannot simply *receive* the director's insights but must repeatedly *enact* the character's role, so the Christian believer cannot simply receive the preacher's insights but must determine how to embody them such that they become habitual and formative for the shape of one's moral life.

How might we evaluate this second strategy for drawing out the moral implications of a particular story? The analogy of performance maintains the concrete emphasis of the first strategy, while reducing its tendency to keep us at a distance from the texts. It's one thing simply to *examine* an ancient text (or script or musical score) in light of current circumstances; it's quite another to be asked to *perform* it. The notion that human beings are called upon to perform their narratives brings a whole new level of existential involvement into the picture. Christians are asked to embody these stories, to enter the story's world, and to let the story enter their own world, such that their lives become more and more closely conformed to the moral landscape that is given shape by a particular set of stories.

The disadvantage of this approach, as some commentators have noted, is that most narratives—whether those of a family, a community, or of the Bible—do not come to us in the shape of a script or a musical score. There are no specific lines to be learned or rhythms to work out, in any straightforward way; and although we may be able to draw very useful analogies to these elements of the artistic performance of texts, the performance of the Scriptures will always be a bit more complicated. And since the performance of a play

The shifting contexts of biblical interpretation

The interpretation of biblical texts has varied greatly over time and in differing cultural contexts. In slaveholding cultures, for example, many people cited evidence that slavery existed when the Bible was written and that its authors seem to accept the practice. Paul even returns a runaway slave to his owner (see his letter to Philemon). But in those contexts where slavery is opposed or when people are fighting for its abolition, they appeal to other biblical passages, such as Galatians 3:28 which declares that "there is no longer slave or free . . . for all of you are one in Christ Jesus." Which one is the *biblical* perspective?

Clearly, one's context affects how one reads the Bible. It can be difficult to determine, particularly in the moment, to what degree one is reading one's own self-interest into a particular interpretation. For those who live in countries in which slavery has been abolished, it is easy enough to look back and see that slaveholders argued as they did because it supported their economic way of life. But it may not be so easy to see how we, in our own current circumstances, also argue for (or just assume) certain interpretations of the biblical stories because they provide warrants for the way that we live today. A few generations from now, will people look back at us with a knowing smile, amused at our naively self-justifying interpretations, in the same way that we today look back at the views of slaveholders?

We are also particularly good at criticizing the biblical interpretations of defeated political powers—from the too-willing support given by Roman Catholics and most Protestant denominations to the government of Nazi Germany, to the long-term support of the Dutch Reformed Church for the system of apartheid in South Africa. Why, we wonder, could these people not see that their interpretations of the Bible were so thoroughly tinged with racism? The answer is related to the general argument of this book—namely, that morally formative communities have a great deal of sway over their members, and that even the existence of a canonical set of scriptures cannot prevent such communities from interpreting the texts according to their own self-interests, if they choose to do so.

What, then, can be done to avoid morally defective interpretations that will be scorned by future generations? Three factors can play a role here. First, time: an interpretation needs to withstand the test of time. If a certain biblical narrative looks roughly the same to us today as it did to readers of a century ago, in spite of so many changes in culture, then we can feel more confidence about it than about an interpretation that seems to change with every shift in the wind. Second, breadth: Is the interpretation persuasive to the community as a whole, or do certain members have to be excluded in order for a particular account of the biblical text to have staying power? When entire categories of people are marginalized by a particular interpretation, history will often eventually show that the "excluders" were primarily operating out of their own self-interest. Third, coherence with Christ. Since the biblical narratives are diverse and sometimes even appear internally contradictory, most theologians argue that a particular criterion should serve as the determining factor in the interpretive process. Some would put heavier emphasis on the role of the institutional church, while others would give more weight to the individual Christian conscience; but most would see the person of Jesus Christ, as God incarnate, to be the best criterion for biblical interpretation.

Of course, none of these factors is absolutely definitive; one of the empirical realities of any moral community is that it can always make arguments for its own positions. This has led some commentators to argue very strongly for some form of "ethical humility" in the process of biblical interpretation: a realization that communities are flawed in various ways and that they may make assumptions that, in the light of some new context, will come to be seen as morally wrong. This doesn't mean that no new interpretations are possible; it only encourages interpreters to admit that their own perspectives, no matter how firmly held, may eventually be understood as errors.

or a symphony is already a very complicated affair—requiring deep familiarity with the texts, the gift of creative insight, and years of technical training—the performance of the scriptures may strike us as a useful analogy but not a particularly practical approach for human beings who are trying to inhabit a particular moral framework.

Improvising on the text

A more recent strategy builds on the notion of "performing the Scripture," but seeks to modify the notion in recognition of the differences between the biblical text and the script of a play. The Bible is not a script, but is rather a diverse collection of material that Christians are asked—in some rather mysterious way—to inhabit, enact, and embody in their lives. We therefore need other metaphors, in addition to that of performance, in order to understand precisely how the process by which Christians seek to undertake this process of inhabiting and embodying the narratives. The language of *improvisation* may be helpful here—building on the analogy of musical or dramatic improvisation. But for this approach to be useful to us, we need to understand what improvisation means for those who are involved in it; otherwise, we are very likely to misunderstand both its approach and its goal.

Those who have had little experience with this particular art form may be tempted to imagine that it consists primarily in "making it up as you go along." This is partly due to the fact that good improvisation gives the illusion of being wholly spontaneous and instantly creative; in reality, however, a good improviser must work very hard ahead of time to develop the fundamental building blocks for good improvisation. This requires a substantial collection of tools and materials from which the final product can be built, and it requires good habits of thought and action that allow a person to use these tools well—and to do so without much apparent exertion of effort and complicated planning for each individual case. Finally, when more than one person is involved in the process of improvisation, it requires that each person pay close attention to the actions of everyone else. The improviser needs to be deeply familiar with the skills, assumptions, and probable actions of others in the group, and to be prepared to respond to the ways that those other artists, actors, or musicians are likely to behave.

The application of this way of thinking to the business of ethical reflection provides some useful food for thought. The members of a particular community of moral discourse certainly need to know their stories well—just as a jazz musician must know chords and rhythms and structures of music. Similarly, the members of a community need to be well acquainted with one another—just as the members of an improvisational comedy troupe must know the other members of the group and be prepared for at least some of the directions in which the improvisation is likely to develop. And finally, improvisers need to develop certain habits, so that the process of improvising on their stories—something that will take on different contours in each given situation—will be something that they do almost automatically, naturally, and without needing to stop and consult a handbook in order to offer an analysis.

All of these strategies, but especially this last one, underscore the importance of *habit* for a person's formation in the moral life. Anyone who hopes to be a good improviser must *get in the habit* of reacting in a certain way to a certain kind of situation, and must *get in the habit* of anticipating the moves that fellow improvisers are about to make. Developing these habits requires practice: one must do the same kinds of things, over and over again, in order to develop the mental agility, emotional preparation, and physical reflexes that will be required, regardless of the specific content of a given improvisation. Thus, in the next chapter, we will begin to move toward an examination of those habits that take the form of *practices*—in an effort to consider how Christians might habituate themselves to offer good performances of, and improvisations on, the narratives that they seek to live by.

Conclusion

Regardless of which of these three approaches (or some other approach that we might develop) seems to be most appealing, all ethical reflection has to grapple with the movement from story to moral claim. This necessity arises, not just from the ambiguity of stories, but from the ever-changing fields of thought and action in which we live. Even if we believe that our ethics must have continuity over time, we are faced with the reality that our language, our circumstances, and our knowledge will continue to change; and so paradoxically, against this background, our assumptions must change even in order to maintain continuity. As John Henry Newman, a nineteenth-century teacher and preacher at Oxford, once famously remarked: "In a higher world it is otherwise; but here below to live is to change, and to be perfect is to have changed often." So must it also be in the field of Christian ethics: the narratives of the faith must be brought afresh into every new context, where we will discover that they may well point us toward a different conclusion than that to which they pointed a generation ago. To some readers, this idea might seem very worrying (we will address the potential concerns that it raises in chapter 10); but I suspect that to many others, the recognition of this need for "changing often" may well offer some hope of redemption to the whole enterprise of Christian ethics.

Questions for discussion

1. Give two or three examples of stories that have been important in your own moral formation. In each case, imagine how someone with a different set of experiences from your own might take that same story to imply a very different moral framework than the one that you derived from it. Is it difficult to imagine a radically different interpretation of the story than your own?

2. Have you typically thought of the parables of Jesus as stories with a moral? What sorts of experiences of these parables have most profoundly shaped your assumptions about them? Pick one of the parables (other than those mentioned in this chapter) and offer examples of two significantly different moral claims that might be made on the basis of the parable.

3. Pick a biblical story that you find particularly interesting, and consider the degree to which the dominant stories of your culture seem to stand in solidarity with, or in contrast to, the biblical story. What kinds of insights might arise from setting the two stories "side by side," as that process is described in this chapter?

4. Pick two biblical stories—one each from the Old and New Testaments—and describe how the metaphors of performance and improvisation might help us make sense of the moral implications of these stories. What would it mean to "perform the Scriptures" in the case of the stories that you have chosen? What would it mean to "improvise" on the story? Both of these questions—but particularly the latter one—may require you to imagine some concrete situations in which a person might "perform" or "improvise on" the text(s) you have chosen.

5. What other models or analogies, other than those described in this chapter, can you imagine for undertaking the process of moving from the biblical stories to moral claims? Pick several biblical stories to test the viability of your approach. What do you see as its advantages and disadvantages?

Sources cited in this chapter and/or recommended for further reading

A. K. M. Adam, "Twisting to Destruction: A Memorandum on the Ethics of Interpretation," in *Faithful Interpretation*

St. Augustine of Hippo, *De Doctrina Christiana*

Scott Bader-Saye, "Listening: Authority and Obedience," in Hauerwas and Wells, eds., *The Blackwell Companion to Christian Ethics*

Jeremy Begbie, *Theology, Music, and Time*

William T. Cavanaugh, "Politics: Beyond Secular Parodies," in Milbank, Pickstock, and Ward, eds., *Radical Orthodoxy: A New Theology*

Thomas Hobbes, *Leviathan*

Nicholas Lash, "Performing the Scriptures," in *Theology on the Way to Emmaus*

John Henry Newman, *An Essay on the Development of Christian Doctrine*

Francesca Murphy, *God is Not a Story: Realism Revisited*

Charles Pinches, "Proclaiming: Naming and Describing," in Hauerwas and Wells, eds., *The Blackwell Companion to Christian Ethics*

William C. Spohn, "Scripture," in Meilaender and Werpehowski, eds., *The Oxford Handbook of Theological Ethics*

Kevin Vanhoozer, *The Drama of Doctrine: A Canonical-Linguistic Approach to Christian Theology*

Samuel Wells, *Improvisation: The Drama of Christian Ethics*

A journey without maps
Professing, praying, and repenting

Thus far, our investigations into the role of narrative in shaping the moral life have focused on what we might call the "macro" level: broad, general claims about the relationship between particular communities and the stories that give shape to their moral assumptions. We have considered how the telling and retelling of stories, and the proclamation and performance of those stories, form the background against which we evaluate right and wrong behavior and good and bad character. Now we need to consider how this operates at the "micro" level: how specific human actors come to make their way in the world, on the basis of the narratives that they live by and that their communities take for granted. At various points in this chapter, I will employ a geographical metaphor to describe this process: it is something like trying to make one's way across a landscape without recourse to a map. Our first step in that process will be to try to figure out where we are.

"You are here": finding our place in the moral universe

So far I have emphasized the importance of the gathering community in setting the basic moral assumptions by which we operate. But even if we recognize that we are formed, at least to some degree, by the narratives of our various communities, we still have to live as *agents* in the world—making decisions and taking action. We may often do this in a rather passive way, going along with the crowd and asking few questions; but we will also regularly reach those moments in life where the narratives of our community have not trained us as to what we should take for granted. Even if our assumptions and actions are decisively shaped by the stories of those communities of which we are members, we are still free beings and our actions are not wholly determined by those stories. We each find ourselves in a particular location within the larger moral universe. How do we discover where we are, and how do we decide what direction we should move in the ongoing journey of our lives?

Freedom, determinism, and a possible alternative

The typical answers to this question grow out of two opposing tendencies. On the one hand, human beings are endowed with free will; this means that they can choose their own paths in life, independently of their formation in particular narratives. We may be shaped by the stories of our lives, but we can always break away from them; we leave our families of origin and enter into new communities, leaving old stories behind and taking up new ones. And even in these new environments, we like to see ourselves as relatively free to take or leave whatever we may encounter.

The alternative account is one of "determinism": our backgrounds and previous experiences so thoroughly shape us that we really have very little control over what we do. According to this view, we are practically preprogrammed to behave in certain ways, based on the stories of which we are a part. Regardless of whether this programming is understood to be guided by the providential hand of God, or is simply considered to be an arbitrary result of a series of random experiences, the implications are the same: we are not, in the end, the masters of our own destinies. Our choices are, essentially, made for us—determined by the shape of our lives thus far.

Neither one of these perspectives can hold up under close scrutiny; in each case, we can think of plenty of counter-examples that disprove the rule. Moreover, both perspectives create real problems for any analysis of morality: the first position makes it very difficult to make any judgments about the rightness or wrongness of a certain act, since the human being is considered to be free of any moral community that might render a judgment on those acts. In the second case, judgments about right and wrong can certainly be made, but they seem largely irrelevant, since decisions are not really made by the people who act; they don't really have any choice in the matter, so it seems odd to describe what they do as "making moral judgments."

A helpful alternative to these two perspectives is found in the concept of *finite freedom*. While God may have infinite freedom to choose among all possible alternatives, human beings do not. We are not in the circumstances described in the first approach above, where all possible options are open to us. For one thing, our fleshly, bodily existence prevents us from doing quite a few of the things we might choose to do (flying through the air unassisted, for example, or being in two places at the same time). Beyond this, however, our experiences of the world so shape our perspective that, without even being aware of it, we never actually even consider more than a small proportion of the choices that are actually open to us. So, for example, I could (I suppose) learn Italian, move to Naples, and live out my life as a fisherman; however, the idea had never occurred to me before I wrote this sentence, and it will probably never occur to me again. And there are an infinite number of such sentences that we could write, describing an option that is technically available to us but which we would never bother even to consider. This is because our experiences and our communities of discourse actually shape and constrain our view of the world, such that we never achieve, nor would we really be interested in achieving, this kind of infinite freedom—the "God's-eye view" that we sometimes imagine ourselves to have.

But while our freedom is *finite*, we are still, nonetheless free: our actions are not wholly predetermined by our circumstances and our stories. We do make real judgments and we sometimes act in ways that might not be expected on the basis of our own moral formation thus far. Thus we are *neither* wholly determined by the stories that we live by, *nor* totally free of them.

Given this reality, however, we still need to ask ourselves: how do I, as a particular human being, fit into (a particular interpretation of) the stories of my community? To what extent am I shaped by their assumptions, and in what ways do I seek to strike out in a new direction, taking advantage of my (admittedly finite) freedom? More generally, how should people position themselves with respect to the web of stories into which their own lives are constantly being woven? Should they give each story or each set of stories its proper due within its own sphere of influence, "rendering to Caesar the things that are Caesar's, and to God the things that are God's"? Should they allow and encourage one community to transform other communities, thinking of that one community as sent forth in order "to make disciples of all nations," attempting to persuade others to live by the same stories that they have made their own? Or should they counsel a strategy of withdrawal from all other communities—reminding themselves that they "do not belong to the world" and that they have been chosen "out of the world"—advocating a form of insulation from its influences in order to maintain their true allegiances? Each of these approaches has certainly had its advocates over the history of Christianity, and each can be justified by citing the biblical texts (I've quoted from Mark 12:17, Matthew 28:19, and John 15:19, respectively; many other passages could be cited as well). Given the biblical and historical warrants for these claims, each of them probably has something important to offer. But none of these strategies—neither living in two realms simultaneously, nor converting others, nor withdrawing from their influence—none of these approaches adequately explains how we might come to understand the place of our lives and our particular stories within the larger contexts that we inhabit.

Why, in the end, are all of these approaches ultimately unsatisfying? Answering this question will require us to examine a very influential book in the history of Christian ethics.

Christ and culture

In 1951, an important Christian theologian and ethicist named H. Richard Niebuhr published a book called *Christ and Culture*. Niebuhr's goal was to face the same question that we are seeking to address here: how might people understand and find their own place within the complex relationships among the many narratives that are told, enacted, and performed by the various communities of which they are a part? How have they done so in the past and how might they best do so in the future? In particular, Niebuhr was interested in how people negotiate the relationship between the specific claims of the Christian faith and the more general claims of the wider culture (thus the title of his book). Although he did not focus on the ways that these perspectives are carried in *narrative* form (as we have done in this book), he was wrestling with a similar set of issues.

Niebuhr postulated five categories or types of response to the problem of Christ and culture. They might be best understood by placing them along a spectrum. At one extreme was "Christ against culture"—a withdrawal from the world in which Christians insulated themselves from the temptations of the broader culture. At the other end was "Christ of culture," in which Christian and cultural assumptions merged together to form a single perspective. Moving inward from these extremes, he spoke of "Christ and culture in paradox" and "Christ above culture"; in both of these cases, Christianity and culture retain their own separate spheres of influence, but the former version argues for a somewhat distanced relationship to the world, whereas the latter allows considerably more cultural involvement in spite of the separation. At the center of the spectrum is a position called "Christ transforming culture." This was Niebuhr's own preferred perspective, as evidenced by the fact that the section with which he ends all the previous chapters—in which he details the disadvantages of each position—is conveniently missing from this final chapter.

As an attempt to wrestle with questions about Christianity's relationship with the world, Niebuhr's book set the agenda for decades to come. By positing "Christ" and "culture" as two potentially separate realms and then "mixing" them (at various strengths and dilutions) to provide the varying gradations along a spectrum, Niebuhr offered a fairly simple tool for untangling a very complex problem. His typology allowed him to pigeonhole various theologians, and various manifestations of Christianity throughout history, according to their type: Thomas Aquinas and Anglicanism are of the "Christ above culture" type; Lutheranism holds to the position of "paradox"; monasticism and some strands of the Anabaptist tradition advocated "Christ against culture"; and so on. The invention of such a straightforward device—enabling readers to classify much of Christian history and to sort out their own perspectives in the process—was a theological coup of epic proportions. Not surprisingly, the book has been in print continuously since its publication. To this day, whenever the questions that I am addressing in this chapter are raised, someone is likely to remark, "Ah, the *Christ and Culture* problem!" or "Oh, you mean the question that Niebuhr examined in his typology." In fact, the book has such a strong hold on the collective mindset of those who study this issue that it can be difficult for many people to imagine thinking through the question in any other form.

Nevertheless, as influential as Niebuhr's book was (and continues to be), it tends to mislead people about the questions that we are pondering here. It does this by postulating two relatively distinct realms—labeled "Christ" and "culture"—and then examining the degree to which they can be mixed together and the ways in which the two realms might interact. Only in the modern age, however, does this way of seeing things even become *possible*; for only in modernity do people begin to imagine a "separate" realm of religious life that could be set apart, at least theoretically, from everything else that happens. One must first postulate a notion of "culture" that does not include Christ, in order to investigate whether, and to what degree, Christ can be mixed back into culture. This creates a problem, on three different levels.

First, it is empirically false. Even in the modern era (with all its secularizing assumptions), the basic structures of Christianity are very deeply woven into Western culture. We find its presence in our laws, our musical and artistic endeavors, and even in our weekly and yearly calendars. While it is certainly true that there are large swaths of our culture that bear no imprint of the Christian tradition, it is likewise true that we cannot move through the course of a typical day in any part of the Western world without experiencing significant elements of Christian symbolism, narrative, and practice along the way (even though we may sometimes be totally unaware of it). Similarly, one cannot experience Christianity in a culturally neutral form. Every instantiation of the faith, in a particular place and time, will take on elements of its context: its language, its art and music, its political and economic assumptions. It is therefore misleading to begin by postulating a realm of "culture" that is separate from a realm of "Christ"—and *only then* to think about whether, and to what degree, they can interact. In point of fact, they are already deeply woven into each other.

Second, the book's neat division of "Christ" and "culture" participates in one of the most widespread and most troublesome philosophical techniques of the modern age. This is its tendency to structure reality as a series of dichotomies: two opposing forces or powers, which are understood to be mutually exclusive, and which can be reconciled only at great cost. This dualism is certainly not unique to modernity; it was a signal feature of the Greek philosophical perspective and it has seeped into various forms of Christianity, both in its earliest forms and throughout its history. But this kind of dualistic thinking has been particularly popular in the modern age; René Descartes famously constructed a dualistic description of mind and body, while Immanuel Kant carefully distinguished between the external world of phenomena and the interior realm of the mind.

The trouble with such dichotomies, as I observed in the introduction to this book, is that they polarize us—implying that the "others" (against whom we define ourselves) are located far, far away, rather than just on the other side of the "thin line." They also lead us to define ourselves as "what we oppose" or "what we are not" rather than as "what we are." Moreover, these dichotomies tend to stifle our imaginative faculties; by assuming that everything must fall on one side or the other of a particular line, we discourage ourselves and others from postulating the possibility of a third (or fourth, or seventeenth) way that breaks away from the assumptions inherent in postulating only two poles or two options. Such dichotomous thinking about theology and religion, in particular, has frequently hampered intelligent thought about the subject. (Indeed, some commentators have wondered whether these dualistic structures might have become so popular in the modern age *precisely because* they encouraged the marginalization or elimination of certain questions about religious faith.) In any case, a great deal of recent philosophical inquiry has raised serious questions about the viability of these supposedly dichotomous distinctions, suggesting that they only appear to be so difficult to reconcile because of the fact that they were wrongly (or at least misleadingly) constructed as mutually exclusive realms in the first place.

Finally, the "Christ and culture" paradigm is theologically problematic—on at least two levels. With respect to the dualistic structures outlined in the previous paragraph, Christian theology has often sought to question such dichotomies: the Christian God is *both* transcendent (beyond all our categories) and immanent (immediately present to us); the person of Christ is *both* human and divine; human beings are *both* sinful and saved. In fact, some writers have suggested that the Christian claim that God is triune—one being who is also three—is itself an attempt to confound the dualistic assumptions of the thought-world into which Christianity was born and which it still encounters from time to time. Oppositional dichotomies of all sorts are brought under scrutiny by more imaginative and thoughtful investigations into the nature of God, of human beings, and of the entire universe.

A second theological objection to the "Christ and culture" paradigm concerns the Christian doctrine of creation. Christian theology postulates that the entire world is created, redeemed, and sustained by the triune God. This means that, at least according to Christian belief, the surrounding "culture"—no matter how it is defined—is already imbued with Christ at the very deepest levels: created by God, it bears the marks of its maker and reflects the glory of God, regardless of what kind of relationship one might postulate between Christ and culture. If Christians truly have the courage of their convictions when it comes to an examination of culture, they can never treat it independently of the God in whom, according to the Bible's quotation of a Greek philosopher, "we live, and move, and have our being" (Acts 17:28).

Given these significant criticisms of the "Christ and culture" approach, we need to find other ways of understanding the question that we are wrestling with in this chapter. If we are to find our way among the many stories that human beings live by—whether they be explicitly Christian, implicitly Christian, or something else entirely—we need to find a new way of asking the questions.

We have already begun that process in the previous chapters of this book—by focusing on specific stories and practices rather than on large-scale claims about whether a particular idea or activity belongs to "Christ" or to "culture." By recognizing that we are influenced by a wide range of narratives that are interpreted in a variety of ways, we are already developing a more nuanced account of how character is formed—and of how this affects judgment, action, and the overall shape of the moral life. Our challenge now is to think about how human beings might situate themselves—as members of a community but also as particular, finitely free beings—among the various stories and practices that are woven together in their lives. In order to do so, we will return to the geographical metaphor with which I began this chapter: the idea of the moral life as a "journey without maps."

Finding our way

Let us begin by examining one of the more popular ways of thinking about this journey (even though I will eventually want to raise some objections to it). We can refer to it as the "fork in the road" perspective: in this account, the moral life is compared to a path that one follows through the woods. At various points along the way, the path divides; we have to make a decision about which direction we will choose. There may be some signs along the way—indicators as to which path will lead where—but these signs will prove, over time, to be less than one hundred percent reliable. Each time the path divides, therefore, we must make decisions on the basis of imperfect information, and we need to be willing to retrace our steps whenever our choice of a particular path leads to a less-than-desirable destination.

Many readers of this book will recognize immediately how closely this "fork in the road" analogy corresponds to our earlier discussion of the "lifeboat"—that is, the ethical strategy that we described as quandary ethics. The analogy describes a solitary traveler who simply follows one single path most of the time, but who is occasionally presented with a difficult choice and who must make a fateful decision. The goal of ethics is thought to be that of providing rules and strategies for deciding, so that one will more frequently choose the path that leads to a better journey and an appropriate destination.

But our progress through life isn't like that—not at all. We are not alone; there is no path; our lives are not defined by a series of forks in the road; and, to whatever extent we do actually choose a particular direction, we probably will not be able to determine whether it is the right one until it is far too late to retrace our steps. The moral life does have certain features that make it like a journey, but it is not simply a series of forks in the road. We will therefore need to alter the analogy in significant ways. I would suggest that our lives are more like a movement across a vast landscape, in which there are hundreds of crisscrossing paths worn into the ground, but no real indications about which is the main road. There are many maps available to help us find our way; unfortunately, however, they are all very different from one another. One of them seems reliable for a while, then we suddenly encounter something that isn't on the map, and we find ourselves shuffling through a stack of alternatives to try to find something a little more reliable. As we wander through this space, we meet other people—traveling with them for a season, negotiating about which direction to travel, and eventually parting company with them. We do make choices, just as the "path in the woods" analogy suggests; but we make these choices, not just occasionally, but *constantly*; not alone, but in the company of others; and not in order to find the "correct" or "best" path (since we would rarely be able to recognize it as such, even when we're on it), but simply as a means of continuing to move across the landscapes of our lives.

This analogy makes ethics look much more complicated than do those accounts that simply offer us rules for negotiating difficult cases. It means, of course, that the process of finding our way will require, not a collection of tools for making good judgments at each fork in the road, but rather, a certain disposition and character that will enable us to chart a course, in the company of others, that makes for a good life. What can we do in order to prepare ourselves for this rather daunting undertaking? What are the key components of the traveler's character? What practices will form us into the kinds of people who can undertake such a journey?

Looking to the liturgy

Throughout this book, I have suggested that the most basic practices of Christian worship—as they have been practiced through much of the history of the faith—can give us a clue to understanding how we might proceed. In Part 1, we have made our way through the Liturgy of the Word: the community gathers; its members identify who they are (and whose they are); the community retells the narratives that provide the context for its understanding of the moral life; and it proclaims and enacts these stories in ways that are relevant in the contemporary setting. The process thus far might be imagined as something like a funnel: at the top, at the broadest point, a large group gathers. It then identifies itself in particular ways that narrow its focus and concentrate its energies. A yet sharper focus develops as particular stories are told and their yet-more-particular significance for the present moment is proclaimed and performed. Finally, we come to the concern of the present chapter: how the individual members of the gathered community might take these identities, narratives, and performances into their own lives in highly specific ways. We have reached the narrowest point of the funnel, where the energy of the flow is most concentrated and the focus is at its most specific.

At this point in the traditional Christian worship service, three events typically occur; all three help the participants to take the identities, stories, and proclamations into their own lives and to find ways of embodying these elements of the community in their specific circumstances. These three events are the profession of faith, the prayers of the people, and the confession of sin. These practices might be thought of as an effort on the part of Christian worshipers to face the fact that their lives are not, in fact, defined by a clear-cut trail through the woods in which they are only asked to make an occasional choice between two diverging paths. It is, instead, a journey across an uncharted landscape, in which they constantly make judgments concerning the hundreds of possible directions that are available. In the face of such circumstances, their only option is to put their feet down, at this time and in this place: to accept that life has taken them to this particular point, to state clearly where they think they are, and to ask for strength in taking the next step. This is the goal of the profession–prayer–confession sequence in the liturgy, and it may provide us with some insight as to how particular human beings might appropriate a community's moral insights and make them their own.

The profession of faith

The first of these three elements is the profession of faith; this typically occurs as a communal recitation of a *creed*, a statement of belief. The word "creed" comes from the Latin word *credo*, which is often the first word in a creed; translated, it means "I believe." Creeds are frequently misunderstood; they often seem, not only to outsiders but also to many Christians, to be something like a checklist of beliefs that one has to affirm in order to be considered a Christian (or at least, a Christian who believes in the right things!). This leads some people (and some entire Christian denominations) to object to creeds in general, or to amend the traditional creeds of the Church— either permanently and officially, or by individuals on an ad hoc basis (perhaps remaining silent during certain parts of their recitation, or altering a few words in accordance with one's understanding of a particular doctrine or belief).

It may well be the case that the precise language of the creeds may need to change, very slightly, from time to time—particularly since most creeds are recited in translation and since the nuances of each vernacular language are always changing. But the tendency to think of the creed as a checklist of beliefs—a checklist comprising some beliefs with which we can agree, and some to which we must object—is, I think, a misunderstanding of the nature and purpose of a creed. This requires a word of explanation.

The Christian faith certainly includes, and in some cases even requires, certain specific beliefs; but the creed is not primarily intended as a means of announcing that "we believe that x is the case, and also that y is the case," and so on. It is not worded in the form "we believe *that . . .*" but rather, "we believe *in . . .*" Note that the object of that preposition—that which the community believes *in*—is not merely a statement of fact or a logical proposition, but a *person*: namely, God. (To describe God as a "person" is not the same as calling God a human being; the word "person" is used here in a specific philosophical sense, meaning a self-conscious or rational being—someone with personal qualities such as character and intellect, and usually known by one or more proper names.) Christians who say "we believe in God" are not so much like the astronomers who announce to the newspapers that "we believe that Pluto is (or is not) a planet"; this is merely a claim about facts (or perhaps an argument over the definition of terms). Rather, those who say "we believe in God" are more like the parents who say to their children, "we believe in you"; this is an expression of their trust and a declaration that they intend to direct their lives in certain ways. The statements in the creeds are not simply claiming that "I (or we) have decided, upon rational reflection and examination of the evidence, that the following facts are true"; but rather, "this is what (or whom) we trust; this is the proper object of our faith and hope; this is the end toward which we orient our lives in significant ways." This is the sense of "we believe" that is encapsulated in the creeds as professions of the Christian faith.

Given this definition, a profession of faith can be understood as an important step toward preparing human beings to "find their way" across an uncharted landscape. In order to undertake such a journey, we have to know where we're headed and where we're willing to put our trust and our hope. By making the statement that "we believe in God," Christians are announcing a basic orientation of their lives toward God—a thoroughgoing reliance upon, trust of, and hope in God. They are also saying, conversely, that they do not believe in (that is, they do not put their ultimate trust in) all of the other things that might be candidates for such belief. In previous chapters, we have explored some of the possible candidates for these alternative "gods": political and economic structures, technologies that might capture our attention, or individual human beings who seek to win the allegiance of others through charisma or proffered rewards. All of these things exist, of course; those who "don't believe in them" are not attempting to deny their existence, but rather to say that they do not place their entire confidence and trust in them. The phrase "we believe in God" means that those who speak

The Apostles' Creed

One of the most ancient and enduring professions of the Christian faith is a short statement known as the Apostles' Creed. Its name springs from a legend that it was composed by Jesus' twelve apostles, with each one contributing a phrase. This is unlikely to have occurred, but the point of the attribution was to suggest that the particular beliefs that it names are foundational to the faith, and that they date very far back in its history. Along with the (somewhat longer and more elaborate) Nicene Creed, it is one of the two most commonly used professions of faith in Christian worship and practice.

The creed begins with the phrase "I believe in God, the Father almighty, creator of heaven and earth." In this single phrase, it encapsulates the essential

Christian beliefs in one God, and in an understanding of the created order that places it in complete dependence upon God. This is followed by a relatively lengthy section about the significance of Jesus Christ: his relationship to God; his birth, death, and resurrection; his descent to the dead and ascension into heaven; and the future expectation of his return. These details are important, not so much as a list of facts about Jesus' life (in the style of a biography), but rather, because of what they say about Christ's person (both divine and human) and about Christ's work (i.e., that his suffering and death were vindicated by God through his resurrection and the events that followed it).

The final section of the creed includes a series of very brief statements that came to be elaborated further in other creeds and confessions. These express Christian beliefs in the Holy Spirit; in the Church as the community of believers; in the forgiveness of sins (more on this in chapter 6); and in the resurrection of the body and eternal life. These last two elements are frequently misunderstood; they are sometimes taken to suggest that Christians are most concerned about what happens to them after they die, rather than the shape of their lives on earth. But in some ways, these beliefs should actually make the significance of one's earthly life of *greater* importance—not only because one's future fate is judged on that basis, but also because that future life apparently retains at least some of the bodily, material elements of the present life (hence the phrase "resurrection of the body," rather than merely the "immortality of the soul" or "ongoing spiritual existence"). This phrase—along with the idea that God actually took on human flesh and dwelt on earth in the person of Jesus—underscores the fact that Christianity is not only about spiritual realities but is deeply concerned with the material, fleshly reality of human existence.

Occasionally, some writers try to set the Bible and the creeds against one another, suggesting either that the Bible is too diffuse to provide a detailed account of Christian belief, or that the creeds are an unnecessary and misleading philosophical elaboration of biblical faith. Most Christian theologians, however, would argue for the importance of both the Bible and the creeds for a thorough understanding of Christianity, and would see them as very closely aligned with one another. The creeds are an attempt to summarize, in a clear and concise way, the much more extended biblical accounts of the central tenets of Christian belief; and, conversely, the Bible provides narrative accounts and detailed elaborations of the concepts about which the creeds can offer only the barest outline. As theologian Nicholas Lash puts the matter: "What the scriptures say at length, the creeds say briefly."

these words are claiming (or, at least, they are seeking to convince themselves!) that they do not *believe* in any of these other possible candidates for
their trust and devotion—at least not in any absolute sense. They thereby
announce that their orientation, as they undertake their journey, will be
directed toward and guided by God, rather than being directed toward and
guided by any of the many possible alternative gods that will be offered for
their consideration.

Of course, what this will mean in the concrete instance will need to be
fleshed out in detail, and that cannot be done in a few pages. Many, many
authors (and I am one of them) have written expositions of the Christian
creeds, describing what it might mean to orient one's life by, for example, a
belief in the Holy Spirit or in the resurrection of the body. In later chapters, I
will take up a few of these beliefs as particularly salient for Christian ethics.
My point in the present context, however, is not so much to work out the
specific implications of these claims, but rather to emphasize that the act of
pausing to profess one's faith—to state clearly what one most firmly believes
in—is part of what gives a person direction and forward movement in the
ongoing journey of life.

Prayer

Perhaps the most important, and the most frequently misunderstood, way in
which Christians learn how to "find their way" through life is that of *prayer*.
Christians pray: for themselves, for their loved ones, and for the Christian
community. They also pray for the world: for peace, for justice, and for an
end to suffering. This practice strikes many people as irrelevant at best; they
see it as a waste of precious time that could have been used "to do something that would really help." At the opposite end of the spectrum, some
people—including many Christians who regularly engage in the practice of
prayer—think of it as a means of "fixing" the world's problems; if we pray
hard enough for, say, an end to the HIV/AIDS epidemic in Africa, then that
is the result we will achieve. Neither of these accounts of prayer is adequate,
and neither explains the role that it plays in Christian ethics.

The reason that these accounts are inadequate is that prayer is *not* simply
an instrument for carrying out the work of solving the world's problems. It is
not a means to an end, whether that end is understood as something that God
causes to happen or something that human beings cause to happen. In other
words, prayer is not primarily focused on bringing about results; it is not a
form of divinely assisted wish-fulfillment. Whether or not something happens in the world is not the result of whether enough people spent enough
time praying for it. Certainly, many Christians have themselves contributed

to widespread misunderstanding on this point, through ill-conceived claims about "the power of prayer" or loud thanksgivings about how some good thing happened "because so many people were praying for it." Even by Christianity's own theological account of itself, divine favor is not bestowed on the basis of human works of any sort—whether words, deeds, or prayers. (I will return to the importance of this particular claim in chapter 8 and again in chapter 13.)

Why is this instrumental view of prayer so widespread? First, as I have noted at several points, our lives are dominated by models of economic exchange. We tend to think that in order to get something, we have to give something; this model drifts over from the economic sphere into all regions of our lives, including the relational and interpersonal spheres. Because prayer often occurs in the form of a request for something to transpire, we tend to map our understanding of other things that we ask for (a pay raise, a word of affirmation, or a candy bar) onto the activity of prayer. God is then imagined to be a tremendously powerful being with favors to be dispensed; human beings are the disempowered bargainers, either offering up good words and good works for a reward, or admitting their own powerlessness and simply begging for what they want and need.

Another factor influencing our misperceptions about prayer is our heavy orientation toward results and outcomes. Partly because of our economic and political systems, and partly because of our pragmatic efforts to get ahead (in whatever realm of life), we tend to evaluate actions on the basis of what they accomplish. Therefore, we assume that prayers, which seem to be requests for things to happen, will be more or less valuable depending on whether their outcomes are achieved. It doesn't occur to us, in most cases, to imagine that the purpose of prayer might be something other than maximizing the fulfillment of human needs through God's intervention. But in fact, this is not the purpose of prayer at all. What *is* that purpose?

First of all, prayer is a way for human beings to orient themselves toward God. In this sense it is very much like the profession of faith that we discussed in the previous section: prayer is a way for believers to state that they desire to focus their attention and their energies on God, and—at least for these few moments—on God alone. Human beings carry a great many burdens in their lives, and most people are well aware that there is no magic cure for them all. But for those who believe that God is ultimately in charge of the universe— that God is aware of all the burdens of humanity as well as its joys—turning to God in prayer provides a way of orienting their lives toward the divine.

Therefore prayer is also a means of acknowledging God's sovereignty. By praying, people admit that they are not in complete control of their lives, or of the lives of others; they accept the fact that they did not create the world, nor are they empowered to redeem it or to sustain it. The implicit message of every prayer is something like this: "we human beings are not capable of finding the perfect solution to this or that particular problem; we accept that God's provision for the world is something that transcends our power and our understanding."

In addition, prayer is a means of focusing one's attention on the fallen state of the world and on one's own failures to live in right relationship with other human beings. By praying for peace, people acknowledge that they have allowed conflict to spread; by praying for the hungry, they admit that they have not found ways to distribute the world's food such that everyone can be well nourished. The purpose of these admissions is not to make the petitioners feel guilty, so that they will get up and solve these problems themselves; rather, it is to offer an adequate description of the world and of the human role within it.

Finally, corporate prayer unites people in solidarity with one another. Those who pray together have to admit that their prayers are not simply a wish-list; for in that case, they would be unable to pray together, as a body, for anything. Every set of prayers would be different, because each individual would ask for whatever was most urgently important to that person. By collecting their lives into one set of prayers and directing these petitions toward God, they announce their connectedness to one another and their solidarity in faith and hope.

Confession of sin

The third element of preparation that Christians use in "finding their way"—that is, for locating their particular place within the Christian story—is also a prayer, but of a very particular sort. Here, Christians pray to God for the forgiveness of their sins; thus the various elements described in the previous section also apply here as well. However, understanding the confession of sin will require us to make sense of one of the most misunderstood of all theological terms: namely, that little word "sin."

Even those who consult an unabridged dictionary for a careful definition of the word will be seriously misled: there, the focus is on the violation of a rule or command. Whether in the dictionary or in everyday speech, sin is typically understood to be a form of rule-breaking, perhaps with particularly strong moral implications. And although sin has often been associated with some kind of transgression of a particular code of conduct, such as a violation of a divine command or a rule promulgated by the Church, its roots are really much deeper and its theological significance more profound.

Scholars of the Hebrew Bible remind us that the word "sin" might best be translated as "missing the mark." The analogy is to any kind of game or sport in which we aim at a particular target, seeking to hit the bull's-eye. When we fail to do so, we have missed the mark. Of course, if a person breaks a law or violates a particular code of conduct, one also "misses the mark"; but as anyone who has ever aimed at a target knows well, there are very many ways to miss without ever breaking a rule. One can fail to hit the target because of one's own inadequacies in strength or discipline or foresight; one can miss because of adverse conditions; one can even miss and have absolutely no idea why or how.

If we transfer this analogy of missing the mark to our relational lives, we might say that sin is best described as something like "falling away from right relationship with God and with others." We miss the mark in a moral sense when we are not in right relationship with others: when we offend them, or hurt them, or betray them. We might or might not break some rule or law when we do so; this "falling from right relationship" may or may not be our own fault; we might or might not understand what led up to this situation. None of these variables has any impact on the basic issue, which is that the relationship has somehow been compromised. This is the theological concept of *sin*.

This explains why the biblical narrative can speak about sin in circumstances where there is no law or rule that is being violated. The first occurrence of the word in the Bible is in the book of Genesis, where God uses it as a warning to Cain who is jealous of the divine favor having been bestowed on his brother. There is no law, at this point in the story, against anger or even against murder; but there is, apparently, a relationship that has been, at the very least, seriously threatened. God says to Cain: "Why are you angry, and why has your countenance fallen? If you do well, will you not be accepted? And if you do not do well, sin is lurking at the door; its desire is for you, but you must master it" (Gen. 4:6–7).

Note how sin is personified in this passage, described as "lurking at the door"—quite ready to catch us unawares. The point seems to be that our relationships are fragile things, and that it is fairly easy for us to fall out of right relationship, just as it's easy for the archer to miss the bull's-eye. Even without Cain's motivations of jealousy and anger, we often find ourselves "overtaken" by these relational failures, unaware even of what brought them about.

This is why theologians apply the language of sin not just to human beings, who are moral agents, but also to impersonal structures and systems. Structures, too, can lead us to miss the mark with respect to human relationships: political and economic systems, for example, can shape our assumptions about race and gender in ways that lead to distortions of our relationships. Whether or not a person has violated a certain rule or even knowingly fallen out of right relationship with others, that person can be involved in "structural sin" through systems that reinforce racism, sexism, or nationalism.

Given this very broad definition of sin, it should come as no surprise that Christian theology makes the claim that all human beings participate in it to one degree or another. Paul is very adamant about this in his letter to the Romans: "All have sinned and fall short of the glory of God" (Rom. 3:23); John makes the same point in different language: "If we say that we have no sin, we deceive ourselves, and the truth is not in us" (1 John 1:8). Thus the confession of sin in the Christian worship service is not primarily an exercise in enumerating the specific rules that a person or group of people have broken, or the mistakes they have made. It is, first and foremost, an acknowledgment of the pervasive character of sin: that it affects all human beings in one form or another, and that even with the best of intentions and the most brilliant execution of our plans, we are still caught up in sin. We continue to miss the mark and to fall out of a right relationship with God and with one another.

Obviously, the specific ways in which individual human beings will miss the mark are going to vary greatly from one person to another, and in that sense, this is one of the most *differentiating* aspects of Christian practice. Christians are not just asked to affirm some abstract claim about the general human tendency to be caught up in sin and to be in need of forgiveness and reconciliation of our relationships. Rather, they are asked to consider and examine the *specific* ways in which each person, as a moral agent and a member of various communities, has been caught up in sin and fallen out of right relationship. Human beings all have their own particular failures in this regard; the point of this moment in the worship service is to try to recollect and discern those failures. It is also important that this be done within the context of the community; confessing one's sins *privately to God* simply opens the door to an ever-greater degree of self-deception. Making oneself accountable to at least one other member of the community makes it less likely that people will fool themselves into imagining that an unresolved matter has been resolved.

The purpose of this process is not to wallow in one's sins or to engage in self-flagellation, as if to publicly demean oneself for having sinned; this would make little sense, given the universally sinful state of human beings. The point, as we will see in the following chapter, is for Christians to discern their own particular relational failures so that they can recognize them for what they are and, perhaps, begin to move beyond them and to restore those relationships to their rightful state. The only hope of moving into that more positive realm is to acknowledge the various ways in which one has not yet arrived there. We might draw an analogy to taking a trip to the doctor's office and asking to be healed, but refusing to say anything about the symptoms that we are experiencing. In order for healing to begin, we have to know where our wounds are to be found.

Of course, for many Christians, this process of confessing one's sins has taken a very particular form, in which one essentially enumerates the rules that one has broken. How does this idea square with the discussion of sin that has been offered here? Well, breaking a rule is certainly one way of missing the mark, and rule-breaking may in fact be the easiest form of sin to identify and describe. When children are first taught about the notion of confessing one's sins, they are often directed toward particular rules that they may have broken as easily identifiable (and not too terribly dangerous-sounding) ways that they have fallen out of right relationship with others. A child might find herself at odds with her parents because she keeps forgetting to obey a particular household rule—perhaps something about table manners or household chores. The problem here is less about the rule than it is about the *relationship*; the ultimate goal is for parents and children to have good relationships with one another. But children (and a good many adults) can't really be thinking through all the details of what makes for a right relationship at all times and in all places, so it's easier to focus on rules that have been broken or obeyed. This is a good way to begin the discussion, but unfortunately, it sometimes has the effect of leading children (and, again, a good many adults) to imagine that restoring good relationships is simply a matter of obeying all the rules. As we noted in the introduction to this book, rules and laws don't work this way; in fact, they can sometimes have precisely the opposite effect. Even when they are rigorously obeyed, they can strain relationships and give rise to bad behavior.

At some point, then, it becomes important to recognize that although rule-breaking might be one particular form that "missing the mark" can take, it is not the only one, nor is it the one about which we ought to be most concerned. Rather, our focus should be on the relationships that are damaged (whether by breaking a rule or by obeying one), and the interior dispositions of the people who are involved in these relationships, as well as the larger structures that push and pull us into and out of right relationship with one another.

Summing up and moving forward

In this chapter, we are drawing to a close our discussion of "narrating the Christian faith," which has been the focus of Part 1 of this book. We have examined how the narratives of the Christian faith are taken up into the actions and activities that Christians undertake, particularly in their worship services, so that they might begin to live into the moral framework that these stories construct for them. As we have noted, narratives are multifaceted and are quite ambiguous with respect to their moral implications; this means that they are in need of interpretation. But as we observed in the previous chapter, that process of interpretation is not merely a matter of stating the meaning of the story, as if reciting the moral to an instructive fable; rather, it involves living into the story's world, which might take the form of proclaiming it, or performing it, or perhaps improvising on its themes.

We are now beginning to get an initial taste of what some of these "performances" might look like. Although the forms that we have discussed thus far are limited to the highly stylized and particular structures of the traditional Christian worship service, they have a role in that worship service for a reason: they are designed to help Christians develop *habits* that will inform the practices in which they will engage when they are not in a formal worship setting. Professing one's faith, praying, and confessing sin are all efforts to develop habits that will inform Christian action in rather less formal, less stylized conditions.

In Part 2 of this book, we will delve into the practices of the Christian faith in much greater detail. Again focusing on the worship service, we will consider how the Liturgy of the Eucharist is designed to develop in Christians such habitual practices as forgiveness, peacemaking, giving, thanksgiving, and companionship. These are the practices that Christians seek to cultivate in their worship so that, when they leave the worship service, they take these practices with them into the rest of their lives. This movement out of the Sunday worship service and into the rest of the week's activities will prepare us to investigate, in Part 3, the essential role of Christian stories and practices in living the Christian life.

Questions for discussion

1. Where do you see yourself on the "free will and determinism" question? Do you think that you are largely programmed by the stories in which you were formed, or do you freely break away from them? Is the notion of finite freedom a helpful concept?

2. Before reading this chapter, had you come across the "Christ and culture" approach to the question of how we place ourselves and find our way within the various stories that structure our lives? If so, had the problems of that approach (as described in this chapter, or by others) been a part of your discussion?

3. What geographical analogies seem most appropriate to you as a description of the moral life? Is our journey along a path (with forks in the road), across an open landscape, or via some other option? (Feel free to alter the analogy in any way you choose; for example, if you conceived of the journey as taking place on water, would it be a canal or an ocean? Could you see the land? Would you be in a boat, with or without others—or would you be floating along alone? And so on.)

4. Discuss your experience of a creed, whether a particular Christian creed or some other statement of faith. (It needn't arise within a religious institution; many other kinds of associations and societies have creeds or statements of belief.) Do you think of it as a checklist of beliefs? How does your experience of creeds relate to the perspective offered in this chapter?

5. How do you understand prayer? To what extent has the language of "wish fulfillment" been part of your view? Can you think of other purposes of prayer, besides those described in this chapter?

6. How have you typically understood the word "sin"? Was this chapter's discussion of the theological significance of the term new to you? In what other ways, besides those discussed in this chapter, might this understanding of sin affect the broader cultural assumptions about rules, rule-breaking, and relationships?

Sources cited in this chapter and/or recommended for further reading

Books marked with an asterisk provide readings of the Christian creeds.

Nicholas Adams, "Confessing the Faith: Reasoning in Tradition," in Hauerwas and Wells, eds., *The Blackwell Companion to Christian Ethics*

*Hans Urs von Balthasar, *Credo: Meditations on the Apostles' Creed*

Hans Urs von Balthasar, "Infinite and Finite Freedom," in *Theo-Drama: Theological Dramatic Theory*, vol. II

John Berkman, "Being Reconciled: Penitence, Punishment, and Worship," in Hauerwas and Wells, eds., *The Blackwell Companion to Christian Ethics*

Craig A. Carter, *Rethinking Christ and Culture: A Post-Christendom Perspective*

*David S. Cunningham, *Reading is Believing: The Christian Faith through Literature and Film*

René Descartes, *Meditations on First Philosophy*

*David Ford, *Theology: A Very Short Introduction*

Hans-Georg Gadamer, *The Relevance of the Beautiful and Other Essays*

Kelly S. Johnson, "Praying: Poverty," in Hauerwas and Wells, eds., *The Blackwell Companion to Christian Ethics*

Immanuel Kant, *Critique of Practical Reason*

Philip D. Kenneson, *Beyond Sectarianism: Re-imagining Church and World*; *Life on the Vine: Cultivating the Fruit of the Spirit in Christian Community*, introduction and chapter 1

*Nicholas Lash, *Believing Three Ways in One God: A Reading of the Apostles' Creed*

H. Richard Niebuhr, *Christ and Culture*

Glenn H. Stassen, D. M. Yeager, and John Howard Yoder, eds., *Authentic Transformation: A New Vision of Christ and Culture*

*Rowan Williams, *Tokens of Trust: An Introduction to Christian Belief*

D. M. Yeager, "H. Richard Niebuhr's *Christ and Culture*," in Meilaender and Werpehowski, eds., *The Oxford Handbook of Theological Ethics*

Part 2

Practicing the Christian life

Forgiveness, reconciliation, and nonviolence
Distinctive practices in a fallen world

In the previous chapter, I suggested that the shape of the first part of the traditional Christian worship service, the Liturgy of the Word, might be compared to a funnel: it moves us from a broad embrace of the entire community into a more intense concentration on the particularities of specific human lives. The second half of the worship service, the Liturgy of the Eucharist, is like a funnel in reverse: moving us outward from the specificity of our lives toward a recognition of our essential connectedness to one another, to the entire universe, and to God. The two funnels are connected at their narrowest points to form a kind of hourglass shape: open and broad at both ends, but narrowing down to the specific and the particular in the middle.

In our journey through the liturgy, we have reached that narrowest point in the hourglass. In the last chapter, we examined the ways in which Christians take the narratives of the faith into their own lives, giving them concrete specificity in their own life journeys across an uncharted territory. In this chapter, we will examine three additional practices, in which believers turn outward toward others in anticipation of the movement of the worship service toward the rest of the community and the world. This part of the service encourages participants to consider the gifts that they have been given and to offer their own gifts in return—a mutual act of abundant giving that overflows the worship service and spills over into the entire world.

However, before we turn to the specific practices that constitute this outward movement, we need to reach back into our discussion in Part 1 and spend some time unpacking an important story within the Christian narrative. That story provides essential background for the practices that will become the focus of this chapter.

A fallen world

According to the Christian story, God created the world and saw that it was good. As we noted in previous chapters, this account of the natural order of things stands in striking contrast to the description offered by the political philosopher Thomas Hobbes. As mentioned earlier, he famously described the "state of nature" as the "war of all against all," in which a typical human life is expected to be "nasty, brutish, and short." According to the biblical narrative, however, the state of nature is best exemplified by the beautiful garden and peaceable community that is described in the first two chapters of Genesis. The Bible also suggests that this is the state to which everything will eventually return: the garden, and indeed a new city that will surround it, will be beautiful and peaceable at the end of time (Rev. 21–22). This, according to the Christian narrative, more accurately describes the true nature of the world in which we live.

If things seem otherwise to us—if we are more likely to be convinced by Hobbes' account than by that of the Bible—this may result from the fact that we ourselves do not live at the beginning or at the end, but in the middle: in a *fallen* world. According to the Christian faith, the less-than-perfect circumstances in which we now live are the result, not of God's miscalculations, but of deliberate human action. The Bible is hardly unique in its attention to the fact that human beings sometimes make unwise choices. But as I noted in the previous chapter, the biblical account recognizes that these choices are not always directly related to our intentions; sometimes we simply "miss the mark." Moreover, the Bible also offers us a more nuanced understanding of this phenomenon—one that can help us better understand our most fundamental predilections and tendencies. The most troubling aspect of our character (so the biblical narrative suggests) is that we sometimes give our ultimate allegiance—an allegiance that we should reserve only for God—to that which is not God. This notion is inscribed in a very specific narrative, in the third chapter of the book of Genesis. This narrative is known as "the Fall."

As the story goes, a man and a woman are enjoying a life of leisure in the beautiful garden. They do not need to work; their needs are all provided; they experience no shame or pain. At this point, a crafty trickster enters the scene and encourages them to disobey God by eating the fruit of a particular tree. Their allegiances are torn between God (who has given them every good gift and has told them not to eat of the tree) and the serpent (who has given them nothing at all, but has provided some persuasive arguments as to why they should). Faced with this situation, they do what human beings often do: they turn away from a trustworthy relationship (with God) and focus instead on the apparent advantages of an alternative course of action. They are led away from God by the trickery of others, by the allure of their senses, and by their excessive confidence in their own knowledge and judgment. They "fall" from a right relationship with God into a state in which they are granted the independence and autonomy that they sought—which, perhaps unsurprisingly to the readers of this narrative, turns out to be not such a good bargain after all. In their fallen state, they are oppressed by their own desires, at odds with one another, and subject to pain and death (Gen. 3:14–19).

A fallen world (so the story tells us) will be a world beset by conflict and strife; this is corroborated not only by God's description of their future life, but also by the next episode in the narrative: one of Adam and Eve's sons, Cain, turns away from his relationships both with God and with his family, and kills his brother Abel. This is followed by more and more violence—so much so that God actually regrets having created human beings and decides to blot them out from the earth, with only one family finding favor in God's sight (Gen. 6:5–8).

The fallen world is awash with wickedness, torn by conflict and strife, and given over to the worship of idols. What could it possibly mean to live a good life in the midst of such chaos? Given the prevalence of broken relationships and inappropriate allegiances among human beings in every corner of the world, how can one person—or even a thoughtful and devoted community—expect to avoid coming under the influence of these malign structures? How does the Christian faith propose to guide human beings into lives that do not capitulate to the typical practices of a fallen world?

One answer, which we have explored over the course of the first part of this book, is that individuals and communities might seek to embody and to enact a different set of narratives, rather than simply settling into their fallen state. In the case of the Christian perspective, that will mean attending to a set of narratives which, although they recognize the reality of the Fall, refuse to endow it with any ultimate significance. The world is fallen, yes; but transcending that reality are the facts that, first, it has been created by God as good; and second, that (as we will consider further in chapter 8) it is being redeemed and sustained by God as well. These elements of the story constitute its broader, more all-encompassing plotline; the Fall, while certainly part of the story, does not dominate its overall structure. In embodying and enacting the broad contours of the story, Christians affirm that God can ultimately bring about some form of healing from the negative effects of the Fall.

This story has considerable power to provide a moral structure for the shape of human living. Nevertheless, it is not sufficient by itself. After all, the man and the woman who inhabited the Garden of Eden were intimately acquainted with God's care for them, through their own creation and God's preservation of the garden; but this fact did not prevent them from turning away from God, or from disobeying God's one (and apparently, at least at this point, only) rule for their lives. According to the biblical text (Gen. 3:6), they were drawn away from God by the persuasive power of someone other than God—and by their bodily appetites (they see that the fruit of the forbidden tree is good for food and a delight to the eye). Thus their familiarity with the story of their own creation and preservation is not sufficient to insulate them against the persuasive appeal of a clever stranger and the delectable beauty of a tasty snack. If human beings hope to avoid the same fate at myriad points throughout their lives, they will need to do more than be willing to pay attention to a particular narrative. They will also need to engage regularly in certain practices, developing habits such that their lives are not dominated by their fallen state. Human beings live good lives when they allow themselves to be habituated in good practices.

But this is to get ahead of ourselves: the role of habit in the formation of practices will be the focus of the following chapter. Meanwhile, we need some examples of the kinds of practices in which Christians are regularly engaged.

Three distinctive practices

The three practices that will occupy us for the remainder of this chapter are forgiveness, reconciliation, and nonviolence. These three practices are among the most difficult for Christians to cultivate in our present cultural circumstances; and precisely for this reason, they deserve focused attention in this chapter. For each practice, I will begin by describing how it arises from the biblical narratives and how it is manifested within the Christian worship service. Then, after a brief discussion of the obstacles that make these practices so difficult today, I will say a few words about their implications for Christian ethics. We will return to these implications as we take up some particular ethical questions in Part 3 of this book.

Forgiveness

When we speak of living in a fallen world, we are pointing to the fact that human beings are prone to fall out of right relationship with others, to focus their allegiances in inappropriate directions, and even to commit thoroughly evil deeds against one another. According to the biblical narrative, human beings are good; but part of that goodness is their (finite) freedom. This freedom includes the freedom to do things that may not be particularly good for them or for others. Presumably, God could have made human beings in such a way that they would always act for the good, both for themselves and for the general harmony of the universe; however, such beings would not then be, in any meaningful sense of the word "free." However resolutely people might seek to embody the story of their own fundamental goodness in their lives, they will never fully achieve that goal; they will always fall short, will always find themselves distracted by one temptation or another, misled by someone who does not have their own best interests at heart. How should others react to those who act in these ways? How, according to Christians, does God react to them?

The story that is told, over and over again, both in the Bible and in the Church through its history and its worship, is quite consistent. While wrongdoing is indeed judged and even punished, the guilty party is also shown mercy and forgiveness. The pattern begins in the book of Genesis, in the stories that I described earlier in this chapter: the inhabitants of the Garden of Eden are exiled for their error, but they are not left without resources; God provides them with clothing, with a means for sustenance, and with children (Gen. 3). When Cain kills Abel, he is punished by being made a wanderer, but he is marked for protection (Gen. 4). When God floods the entire earth, one righteous family is spared, as is each species of creature (Gen. 6).

In the traditions that arise from the Bible, mercy and forgiveness are hallmarks of God's dealings with human beings; and for this reason, a similar pattern is expected of human beings with respect to one another. Many of the Jewish laws that are codified in the book of Leviticus focus on restraints against overly harsh punishments; as commentators have often noted, the phrase "an eye for an eye and a tooth for a tooth" (drawn from Exod. 21:24, Lev. 24:20, and Deut. 19:21) was not traditionally understood as countenancing revenge. Instead, it was a *limitation* on the severity of punishment: no *more* than an eye for an eye, no *more* than a tooth for a tooth. Other laws provide for mercy to those who act rashly or with insufficient information. God shows mercy as well—though not always in ways which are fully comprehensible to human beings. "I will be gracious to whom I will be gracious, and will show mercy on whom I will show mercy," says the Lord (Exod. 33:19). All the same, God's mercy is a sufficiently predictable character trait to make it a regular feature of the biblical narrative; it is, for example, consistently invoked as descriptive of God's character throughout the Psalms (see Psalms 23, 25, 40, 51, 69, 103, 119, and 123). The prophets proclaim God's mercy and are occasionally surprised by it—or even a bit put off by it, as when they are particularly eager for God to strike down the wicked with force (for example in Jonah 3:10–4:3).

God's forgiveness of others, as well as God's call for human beings to forgive one another, is further intensified in the ministry of Jesus. Here even the relative restraint of the Levitical law is abandoned in favor of total forgiveness, even to the point of allowing the offender to add more insults, more dispossession, and more demands:

> You have heard that it was said, "An eye for an eye and a tooth for a tooth." But I say to you, do not resist an evildoer. But if anyone strikes you on the right cheek, turn the other also; and if anyone wants to sue you and take your coat, give your cloak as well; and if anyone forces you to go one mile, go also the second mile (Matt. 5:38–41).

Forgiveness is at the heart of many of Jesus' parables (for example, the lost son, Luke 15:11–32); it is central to his model of prayer for the disciples (Matt. 6:12 par.); and, in several instances, it is directly commanded (Matt. 18:21 par.; Luke 17:3–4). The ultimate example is offered by Jesus himself, who asks (and proclaims) divine forgiveness even for those who have tortured and killed him (Luke 23:34). Forgiveness is an essential part of the Christian story; it is woven in at a deep level, and even makes an appearance as one of the few *practices* (as distinguished from beliefs) to be included in the Apostles' and Nicene Creeds.

Forgiveness plays an important role in Christian worship. The confession of sin, which we discussed in detail in the previous chapter, is always followed by an absolution—an announcement of God's forgiveness. This procedure strikes some observers as odd; how can anyone declare that the sins of all people present are forgiven, when the person making such an announcement doesn't even know what those sins are? But this is to mistake the theological concept of *sin* for the legal concept of rule-breaking or wrongdoing. As we noted in the previous chapter's discussion of confession, sin is not the same as "breaking the rules," or even simply "choosing wrongly." (Confusion on this point is quite understandable, since many Christians would themselves define sin in precisely this way.) As we observed, a more adequate definition of sin has more to do with being out of right relationship with God and with other people. On this account, the absolution of sin—asking God to forgive it, or announcing that it has been forgiven—is best understood as a proclamation that God recognizes our heartfelt desire for the restoration of our relationships with God and with one another—and that God does in fact restore them.

Absolution, then, is the reciprocal "other half" of the confession that we described in the previous chapter. In the confession, believers acknowledge their own failure to maintain right relationships; in the absolution, they are reminded that God can and does restore those relationships. This is simply the actualization, within the worship service, of the narratives that pervade the Christian story—enacting the claim that, in spite of humanity's repeated tendency to make wrong choices and to drift away from God, God is always about the business of finding the stray sheep and healing the wounded victim. The human propensity to choose wrongly, pervasive though it may be, cannot ultimately overcome God's desire for right relationships with human beings.

But regardless of how deeply entrenched this notion of forgiveness may be in the biblical narratives and in the practices of Christian worship, most people—including most Christians—find it very difficult to carry out. When we are wronged by another person, we want some kind of compensation; forgiveness can often seem to us to imply a failure to take the offense seriously, a failure to acknowledge one's own hurt and hardship. Our culture provides a great many countervailing stories that advise against mercy and forgiveness. In fact, some scholars have suggested that a refusal to forgive is written into one of the most fundamental stories of our culture: a story of "mimetic violence." (The Greek word *mimesis* means "imitation"—not in the pejorative sense of "fakery" but in the sense of acceptance and approval: imitation as form of flattery, or, in this instance, a way to "even the score.") In a system of mimetic violence, one group or tribe responds to any violent act carried out against one of its members by imitating it: they carry out a similar act—an act that is at least as, and often more, damaging and violent than the original act—against the offending group or tribe. Regardless of how foundational this story is for our culture, we can certainly provide hundreds of examples in which our legal system, our political structures, our schools, and even our churches often seek to carry out punishments without showing much mercy or forgiveness to the perpetrator.

So while we can certainly say that a *Christian* response to injury and evil would be one of forgiveness (rather than some form of reprisal or revenge), the cultural prevalence of an alternative set of narratives and practices can make this very, very difficult to do. When we read or hear the stories of people who have been able to extend forgiveness to those who have done great harm to them or to members of their families, we are often overwhelmed by such godlike displays of mercy, and sometimes—like Jonah—even a bit angry with them for so easily letting the offenders off the hook. In any case, we rarely imagine it as something that we could bring ourselves to do in similar circumstances; it seems to be the vocation of a saint, not of an ordinary person.

One of the most poignant stories of such superhuman forgiveness is told in Sr. Helen Prejean's book *Dead Man Walking*. One of the death-row inmates that she was counseling had killed a teenage couple; the young woman's parents could not imagine forgiving the perpetrator, but the young man's father spoke freely of the forgiveness that he was willing, because of his Christian convictions, to offer—even from the moment that he knelt beside his son's body in the field. Not that such forgiveness is easy to embrace; as Prejean says at the very end of her book, "each day it must be fought for, and struggled for, and won."

This is why the Christian faith has emphasized forgiveness not just in its stories, but in its *practices*. Forgiveness of any sort, let alone of such magnitude and depth, is not something that most people will just suddenly and miraculously find the strength to do, any more than they could win the French Open without ever having played tennis. Forgiveness, like any practice, takes *practice*. Christians are therefore encouraged to *get in the habit of* forgiving one another—asking for forgiveness for their own faults, offering forgiveness to those who have offended them, and praying both for forgiveness and for the ability and willingness to forgive. The importance of such practices is nicely illustrated in the example from *Dead Man Walking* to which I just referred: the young man's father had knelt beside his son's body and recited the Lord's Prayer, and, according to Prejean, "when he came to the phrase 'forgive those who trespass against us,' he did not hesitate, but said, 'whoever did this, I forgive them.'"

The goal of the habitual practice of forgiveness, and of praying for forgiveness, is to make it begin to seem like the *natural* thing to do. By being in the habit of forgiving one another, and of recognizing their own need for forgiveness, Christians are meant to become more likely to ask for and to offer forgiveness when an offense has occurred. The goal is to make forgiveness *habitual* so that it will become something that Christians simply take for granted, rather than something that they have to consider and convince themselves of in every instance in which it might be required.

Forgiveness is therefore something of a presupposition for the entire structure of Christian ethics. Ethics is about the formation of people of good character, and one can always hope that people of good character will live good lives by developing good habits, thereby taking for granted that a particular course of action is the right one. However, given the fallen state of the world, the propensity of human beings to fall out of right relationship with others, and the (often rather less-than-good) habits that our culture may encourage us to develop, human beings will sometimes act wrongly. They will find themselves in circumstances in which they end up hurting others, whether inadvertently or intentionally. They will look back on something that they have done and regret their actions. They will also find themselves injured by others. All of these difficulties are not merely *likely* to occur; the limited but (finitely) free nature of human beings makes such difficulties an absolute certainty. No set of rules or principles will prevent all conflict and injury among human beings; consequently, forgiveness will often be a necessary aspect of any process of human interaction. By practicing forgiveness in those circumstances in which it seems relatively easy to do so, people prepare themselves to forgive in those extraordinarily difficult cases—in which they or their loved ones have been directly harmed by another person. (I will return to this point below, when we discuss the Christian practice of nonviolence.)

We might also observe that a strong commitment to the practice of forgiveness helps to take off some of the pressure that people often feel when facing questions of ethics and morality. As I noted in the introduction, we can develop a fair bit of anxiety around the dichotomy of "good versus evil"; we worry that we may end up on the wrong side of the thin line between wrong and right. Ethical systems that rely heavily on rules, principles, and law are designed to ease that anxiety by assuring us that, if we just follow the rules, we'll always be on the right side. But in Christian ethics, as I have been describing it here, we have no unambiguous, universal principles or rules upon which to rely. It is more a matter of performance and improvisation, in which particular narratives and practices form Christians to be people of good character, so that they can negotiate each new circumstance that they face. In doing so, they are bound to make mistakes; they must therefore accept the fact that they will eventually look back on at least some of their actions and decisions with a significant degree of regret. Even people of very good character will sometimes fail; this is why they need to rely on, and practice, forgiveness.

With these considerations in mind, some people may find themselves a little less anxious about the highly ambiguous and improvisational character of the Christian life as it is being described in this book. Not everything depends on whether they make the right decisions, so they need not be paralyzed into inaction. In fact, the Christian practice of forgiveness ought to have a freeing effect: one can venture out into a variety of relationships with others, seeking to embody the narratives of the faith as fully as possible and to be well trained in its practices, while remaining aware that the occasional failure is almost guaranteed to occur. The practice of forgiveness is a reminder that such failures are part of our fallen human condition—and that they need not permanently estrange human beings from one another or from God.

Reconciliation

Closely related to the practice of forgiveness is that of reconciliation. Forgiveness is the first step, but the ultimate goal is not merely a willingness to show mercy on those who have injured us. The goal, rather, is that those who are estranged from one another because of an injury or failure do not remain in that state of estrangement, but are brought back into right relationship with one another. The human community is understood as a single fabric which, when torn apart, cannot merely be taped or stapled back together; the individual threads must be rewoven, so that the fabric becomes whole again.

The biblical narratives are filled with stories of estrangement that are overcome by gracious acts of reconciliation. In the latter chapters of the book of Genesis (42–45), the story is told of Joseph, one of the twelve sons of Jacob (eventually the symbolic heads of the twelve tribes of Israel). Joseph had been sold by his brothers into slavery in Egypt, but through a series of not-so-unfortunate events, he has become a high-ranking advisor to the Pharaoh. When a famine strikes and Joseph's brothers come to Egypt to beg for grain, they find themselves negotiating with the very brother that they had sold into slavery (although they do not recognize him). While some might well expect Joseph to use this opportunity to take revenge on his brothers, he does the opposite: he forgives them and re-establishes his fraternal relationship with them. (Though he does first play a few tricks on them—he is human, after all.)

Forgiveness and hope

Forgiveness is very closely related to *hope*—a word that will arise again at several points in this book, and which we will discuss extensively in the final chapter. The practice of forgiveness can give us hope for the future; it can also provide, in a strange way, a kind of hope for the *past*. It does this by releasing us from a permanent state of regret about how we might have behaved otherwise. Forgiveness gives us hope that our past, with its many mistaken judgments and wrongful actions, will not define our lives forever.

This connection between forgiveness and "hope for the past" is nicely encapsulated in a poem by David Ray entitled "Thanks, Robert Frost." Some readers will already be familiar with the celebrated American poet Robert Frost (1874–1963); at least two of his best known poems are relevant background for reading Ray's poem. "The Road Not Taken" begins with the line "Two roads diverged in a yellow wood," and concludes with the poet's rather regretful-sounding admission that "I took the one less traveled by, / And that has made all the difference." Another Frost poem, "Stopping by Woods on a Snowy Evening," describes a traveler who stops to gaze at the "lovely, dark and deep" woods as they "fill up with snow," but who must move on: "But I have promises to keep, / And miles to go before I sleep," he writes. David Ray's poem takes up these moments of judgment, decision, and potential regret in

Frost's poetry, and points us to the importance of "hope for the past"—and therefore to the practice of forgiveness. It reads as follows:

> Do you have hope for the future?
> someone asked Robert Frost, toward the end.
> Yes, and even for the past, he replied,
> that it will turn out to have been all right
> for what it was, something we can accept,
> mistakes made by the selves we had to be,
> not able to be, perhaps, what we wished,
> or what looking back half the time it seems
> we could so easily have been, or ought . . .
> The future, yes, and even for the past,
> that it will become something we can bear.
> And I too, and my children, so I hope,
> will recall as not too heavy the tug
> of those albatrosses I sadly placed
> upon their tender necks. Hope for the past,
> yes, old Frost, your words provide that courage,
> and it brings strange peace that itself passes
> into past, easier to bear because
> you said it, rather casually, as snow
> went on falling in Vermont years ago.

Another example is the story of Jonah, which was alluded to in the previous section. Jonah is sent to preach against the city of Nineveh for its neglect of God's commandments. The hearts of the people are drawn to Jonah's preaching, and they repent; they pledge to return to a right relationship with God. But Jonah finds himself disappointed by this sudden reconciliation between God and the people of Nineveh. He is looking for action on God's part—preferably including some fairly significant scenes of mimetic violence! Only after God directly demonstrates to Jonah the importance of right relationships can we imagine that he might eventually come to understand the importance of reconciliation over revenge (Jonah 4:6–11).

Of course, complete reconciliation is not always possible. The book of 2 Samuel tells the story of King David's enthusiastic sexual desire for Bathsheba, the wife of one of his generals, Uriah. In order to cover up his affair, he sends Uriah into battle in a way that virtually assures that he will be killed. When the prophet Nathan leads David to see the error of his ways, the king is stricken with remorse; but of course, a full and complete reconciliation is now impossible, because the person he most offended is dead. David suffers the further hardship of seeing the child of this liaison die (2 Sam. 11:1–12:23). (Some commentators have wondered whether this part of the story, as well as a number of other biblical scenes, doesn't align God fairly closely with a certain kind of mimetic violence. I will return to this question in the following section.) In any case, the story is a reminder that when an injury cannot be reconciled, this often results in further harm.

As was the case for the importance of forgiveness, the significance of reconciliation is also radicalized by the message of Jesus. When speaking of a breakdown in the relationship between two people, Jesus makes it clear that acts of worship and other duties to God do not release a person from restoring the relationship:

> When you are offering your gift at the altar, if you remember that your brother or sister has something against you, leave your gift there before the altar and go; first be reconciled to your brother or sister, and then come and offer your gift (Matt. 5:21–24).

Jesus quite clearly argues that reconciliation is a more important practice than are the various rules and requirements relating to ritual and worship. One of the most basic acts of Jewish temple worship—bringing one's gift to the altar—is here set aside as irrelevant if it is done as a way of evading the reconciliation of an estranged relationship.

Through biblical texts such as these, we can get some inkling of the importance of reconciliation as part of the overall Christian story. This gives us a better sense of why it is such an important element in the structure of Christian worship—and why the practices of confessing sin, receiving absolution, and being reconciled to one another are written into the worship service at the most basic level. Of course, reconciliation is obviously a practice that has to be carried out over a period of time, and for which the proof is in the pudding. It is easy enough for two people to declare, perhaps within the formal structures of a worship service, that their former estrangement has ended; but it is usually much harder to live out that reconciliation in practice. The only true reconciliation is that which can be sustained over time. Nevertheless, because Christian worship provides the paradigm and model for many Christian practices, it is important that reconciliation has a prominent place in the service.

The prayer of absolution, which follows the confession of sin, can often provide some emphasis as to the importance of reconciliation: one version includes a prayer that God might grant to those who confess their sins "time for amendment of life"; another asks God to strengthen the believer in goodness. Such prayers are followed by another practice through which reconciliation can sometimes be initiated or reinforced: the "passing of the peace." In the most common form of this practice, the worship leader offers some form of invitation ("Let us offer one another a sign of peace," or a similar phrase); the members of the gathered community then turn to one another and offer a customary form of greeting—which may range from a stiff handshake to an emotional hug and kiss. While this is not a moment in which severely estranged persons are likely to be reconciled to one another (they aren't likely to be sitting closely enough to each other for that!), it does have the symbolic significance of encouraging the worshipers actively to reach out in peace to those around them. Perhaps the willingness to address and greet one's neighbors—even those with whom one has very little contact, or with whom one has a particularly troubled relationship—can help to habituate a person in the dispositions and actions needed to bring about reconciliation in cases of more severe estrangement. This points us to the third and final Christian practice that we will consider in this chapter.

Nonviolence

Within the context of the worship service, at least, Christians practice nonviolence. But since nonviolence is a practice defined by the *absence* of something, it can be difficult to understand the role it plays as part of a community's identity. For this reason, some writers have spoken instead of Christian practices of "peacemaking," which is certainly a more active term and designates a positive practice. Several of the practices that we discussed in the previous section, under the heading of "reconciliation," could appropriately be named practices of "peacemaking."

Nevertheless, I here retain the language of *nonviolence*, in spite of the difficulties that we will have in identifying practices that contribute to it. This is because the Christian attitude toward the use of violent force is a highly contested issue, and it needs to be named and examined with some care. The language of "peacemaking" is too vague in our contemporary setting; we have been taught to think of peace as something that has to be defended and enforced, usually (ironically enough) through at least the threat of, and often the actual use of, violence. One can be a "peacemaker" while still counseling the use of, and even actively using, violent force. (In the 1980s, the United States military developed a new form of nuclear weapon called the MX Missile, for which at least one government entity proposed the name "Peacemaker"!) What is different about the commitment to peace and peacemaking in Christian narratives and practices is its commitment to forswear the use of violence in bringing about that peace.

Records are sketchy, but most historians of Christianity agree that in its earliest days, the adherents of this new religion were absolutely committed to practices of nonviolence. This was partly due to the new faith's identification of itself in contrast to its surrounding context—a context that depended heavily on strategies of violent force. In the world within which Christianity was born and nurtured, local religious leaders and minor political officials often attained and maintained their positions by appeasing the Roman imperial government, and that government had no qualms about carrying out its conquest and subjugation of foreign lands by force. Rome had found Judea to be a particularly troublesome province to govern, with its inhospitable climate and a people who were fanatically devoted to their decidedly non-Roman religious practices. The Romans adopted something of a shock-and-awe approach to colonial governance, carrying out a great many public executions by nailing criminals up on crosses—a method that was not only drawn-out and cruel, but religiously offensive to the Jews ("Anyone hung on a tree is under God's curse," Deut. 21:23).

Some militant revolutionary groups fought against Roman rule through various forms of subversion, including violent ones. But there seems to be no evidence that Jesus and his followers were engaged in anything of the sort. On the contrary, Jesus' teachings seem to be quite straightforward in their counsel of nonviolence: "If anyone strikes you on the right cheek, turn the other also" (Matt. 5:39); "Love your enemies and pray for those who persecute you" (Matt. 5:44). When Jesus is arrested and his disciples try to defend him with violence, he stops them: "Put your sword back into its place; for all who take the sword will perish by the sword" (Matt. 26:55; cf. John 18:11). About the closest Jesus ever comes to an act of violence is his dramatic act of driving out merchants and moneychangers from the temple, having made "a whip of cords" (John 2:15). Throughout Jesus' ministry and in the early days of the Christian community, the chief weapons that were employed were words of persuasion; no one seemed to imagine that anyone should take up arms in defense of the faith. In fact, precisely because Christianity, like Judaism, was heavily persecuted by the Roman government (often with lethal force), those who employed violence thereby identified themselves as allied with forces *opposed to* the Christian faith.

All of this changed rather dramatically when Christianity rose to become the official religion of the Roman Empire, which occurred under the emperor Constantine in the early fourth century. Having allied itself with power-structures that depended on sanctioned violence for their very existence, Christianity gradually started developing justifications for the use of force in certain circumstances. Although these justifications often sought to limit and constrain the use of violent force, such limits did not always have much impact in practice. Eventually, the Church was willing to adopt violence as a method of protecting its own interests; in fact, for a certain period of its history, it did so with at least as much enthusiasm as did governments and empires.

Even after the demise of the Christian empires of the Middle Ages and the Christian states of the post-Reformation era, Christians often continued to operate with the mindset that violent force was an acceptable way of addressing problems—though they also tended to believe (or at least to claim) that it should be a last resort. Oddly, though, this conviction did not square very well with the narratives of the faith, and particularly those of the New Testament, where the only references to violence are of something that others, i.e., non-Christians, would engage in; the only interaction that Christians seem to have with violence is to suffer it. This dissonance between the stories and the evolving acceptance of violence in Christianity has been noticed by more than one theologian, and much ink has been spilt trying to explain it. This process has sufficiently muddied the waters on this question that a few words of explanation are in order at this point.

Through much of the last two centuries, the standard ethical response concerning the use of violence was simply to announce that Jesus' teachings, particularly those related to nonviolence, could not possibly function as a basis for social ethics. One of the strongest and most influential voices in this regard was that of Reinhold Niebuhr, the brother of H. Richard Niebuhr (whose influential book *Christ and Culture* we examined in the previous chapter). Reinhold Niebuhr argued quite adamantly that the various immoral and amoral forces at work in the world had to be met in the strongest terms possible, including by Christians; and for him, that meant that the use of violence was sometimes necessary. Given the time-period in which he wrote (his career spanned both World Wars), his voice was often gratefully received.

But it was, of course, a voice that could make little sense of the teachings of Jesus and the stories that Christians had told, throughout the centuries, about the absence of any appropriate role for violence in Christian practice. And this point was made with force by another of the most influential books in Christian ethics to have been written in the twentieth century: John Howard Yoder's *The Politics of Jesus*. Yoder worked through each of the arguments that had been made, whether by Reinhold Niebuhr or by other theologians of his convictions, to the effect that Jesus' teachings could not possibly form the basis of a workable system of ethics. Yoder dismantled each of these arguments, one by one. Yoder also sought to analyze and explain those parts of the biblical narrative in which God seemed to be engaging in acts of violence (as with the death of the son of David and Bathsheba that we encountered earlier in this chapter). Yoder argued that the primary purpose of these passages was to emphasize God's sovereignty and God's willingness to protect the people, which in turn helped to bolster the claim that they should not be exercising violence on their own behalf—not even for their own protection, which was ultimately the sovereign work of God. Over the last several decades, John Howard Yoder's work has led a number of Christian ethicists to reconsider their assumptions about the use of violence, and whether Christians could ever countenance it.

I tell this long and convoluted story because I believe that the practice of nonviolence is a very important Christian practice, very much aligned with the practices of forgiveness and reconciliation that we have described in this chapter. Many Christians have written passionately about the importance of this practice, and have argued against the use of violence for any purpose. By their account, Christians should not serve in the military; they should not own weapons (such as handguns and assault rifles) that have no other purpose than inflicting violence on other human beings; and they should not engage in violence against others, even for the purpose of defending themselves or others against attack. If all this sounds rather radical, it simply goes to show how very far modern forms of Christianity have drifted from the faith's original insights about violence. Its own stories—from the teachings of Jesus to the lives of the saints—point precisely in the direction of the steadfast practice of nonviolence.

From narratives to practices

In this chapter, we have sought to complete the transition from *narrating* the Christian life to *practicing* the Christian life. We have attempted to understand how the Christian narrative of the Fall leads directly into the practices of forgiveness, reconciliation, and nonviolence that are central to the Christian life and that are emphasized at this halfway point in the traditional structure of the worship service. Now that we have some sense of the relationship between narratives and practices, we are ready to develop a vocabulary for describing the kinds of character traits in which we can expect Christians to be formed, on the basis of these narratives and practices. This will be our focus in the following chapter.

Questions for discussion

1. Do you find the Christian account of the Fall resonates with your own experience of human nature? Do you see human beings as essentially good but *fallen*? Or would you provide a different account of what it means to be human?

2. Consider several recent news stories in which an offer of forgiveness either was made or could have been made. What arguments would you advance in favor of, or against, such an offer? Do you think that a Christian perspective should necessarily opt in favor of forgiveness? Why or why not?

3. Think of a time in your own life when you fell out of right relationship with someone who was close to you. What would have been necessary for that relationship to have been restored? Was it eventually reconciled, and if so, how?

4. Discuss your own assumptions about the use of violence. Do you think it is ever justified, and if so, under what circumstances? Does the account of Christianity's opposition to violence that is offered in this chapter square with your own previous understanding of the Christian perspective on this question? What might account for the tensions among Christians on this question?

5. Choose an ethical issue or question about which you are personally undecided. How do you think a Christian who was deeply schooled in the three practices described in this chapter would approach that question? What elements of the practices of forgiveness, reconciliation, and/or nonviolence might most shape a person's response to the issue that you have raised?

Sources cited in this chapter and/or recommended for further reading

Erich Auerbach, *Mimesis: The Representation of Reality in Western Literature*

Scott Bader-Saye, *Following Jesus in a Culture of Fear.*

Steven Bouma-Prediger, *For the Beauty of the Earth: A Christian Vision for Creation Care*

Robert Frost, "The Road Not Taken," from *Mountain Interval*; "Stopping By Woods on a Snowy Evening," from *New Hampshire: A Poem With Notes and Grace Notes*

René Girard, *Violence and the Sacred*; *Things Hidden Since the Foundation of the World*

L. Gregory Jones, *Embodying Forgiveness: A Theological Analysis*

Thomas Hobbes, *Leviathan*

Reinhold Niebuhr, *Moral Man and Immoral Society*; *The Nature and Destiny of Man*

Sr. Helen Prejean, *Dead Man Walking: An Eyewitness Account of the Death Penalty in the United States*

David Ray, "Thanks, Robert Frost," from *Music of Time: Selected and New Poems*

Timothy Sedgwick, *The Christian Moral Life: Practices of Piety*

John Howard Yoder, *The Politics of Jesus: Vicit Agnus Noster; What Would You Do? A Serious Answer to a Standard Question*

7

An offering of souls
and bodies
The life of virtue

I grew up attending church fairly regularly, and I still have a number of very strong memories of those days: sights, sounds, and smells that all signified "church." Whether I am remembering the Sunday School rooms, where I faithfully glued pieces of dry pasta onto posterboard to depict a biblical story, or envisioning the movements of the various worship leaders as seen from my family's habitual seats in the balcony, or imagining myself listening to the organist hold forth at the console—the memories are all still quite strong.

One part of the service was called the offertory. I remember just where it occurred, about halfway through the service. As far as I can remember, the word "offering" or "offertory" had only one clear association for me at the time: it was *money*. The offertory was the time when we took up the offering, which meant passing around a set of large plates into which we would place our money. Even as a child, I had my own set of offering envelopes and I contributed to the offering every week. Of course, it was really my parents' money, funneled to me in the form of an allowance or a last-minute loan when I realized, during the church service, that I'd forgotten to bring anything. But I was doing my part—putting my money in the offering—because that's what an offering seemed to be: money.

It didn't ever strike me, through all those years, that what we called "the offering" was—well, an *offering*. It was presented, by those of us sitting in the pews, to the people who were standing at the front of the church to receive it—and they in turn presented it to God. I suppose that, over time, I began to develop some inkling that, in depositing my weekly pledge into the plate, I was offering something to God. But the word that we used to describe this part of the service—the offertory—never seemed to me to be as closely related to the action (to offer) as it did to the object that I was putting into the plate (money).

In the traditional liturgy of the Church, the collection of money as part of the offertory is actually rather incidental to the primary focus of the event. In Roman Catholic theology, what was "offered" at the offertory was understood to be in preparation for a sacrifice. Building on ancient Jewish rituals of the sacrifice of the firstfruits of the harvest, the Christian liturgy called for an offering of bread and wine that would be sacrificed by the priest, on behalf of the whole congregation; it would be taken up by God and transformed into a form of nourishment for the people. (There will be more on this in chapter 9.) Even in those churches that did not have a strongly sacrificial understanding of this rite, however, the idea that the people "offered" to God the produce of the land—bread from grain and wine from grapes—has continued to play a fairly strong role. This is sometimes accented by the procession of these elements forward, out of the congregation and up to the altar; the people symbolically offer up the gifts that they have made from what the earth has produced. A traditional liturgical prayer, sometimes spoken at this point in the service, emphasizes that these elements are being offered to God as gifts: "Blessed are you, Lord God of all creation; through your goodness we have this bread to offer, which earth has given and human hands have made." It is an offering by human beings to God; yet at the same time, they acknowledge that they only have this gift to offer because God had already given it to them—in the form of grain that has sprung forth from the earth.

Protestant theology was not enthusiastic about the traditional Roman Catholic language of "sacrifice" with regard to this part of the worship service. Protestants preferred to emphasize the sacrifice of Christ as something that had happened once and for all; it did not need to be (and in fact could not be) repeated or even re-enacted. But they did sometimes retain the word "sacrifice" in a more specific sense, referring to the worship service itself as a "sacrifice of thanksgiving and praise," or speaking of the worshipers as a "living sacrifice" whose gift to God is their presence and their praise. Such descriptions helped to emphasize that human beings give something up to God—that they give something *away* to God—in the worship service. Whether that gift is understood as the produce of the land, the money that they offer, or the act of worship itself, the essential claim remains fairly constant: human beings present *something of themselves* to God.

In the *Book of Common Prayer* (one of the first efforts to translate the traditional liturgy of the Church into English), this idea is made explicit. In a long prayer that accompanies the offering of the bread and wine to God, the following sentence occurs: "And here we offer and present unto thee, O Lord, our selves, our souls and bodies, to be a reasonable, holy, and living sacrifice unto thee." In this phrase, the element of sacrifice is combined with that of self-giving; the offering that human beings make to God is one in which they offer *their very selves*.

I have described the liturgical concept of offering in some detail here, because it bears on the discipline of Christian ethics in a very significant way. In order to be a person of good character—from a Christian perspective, at least—one must be willing to offer something of one's self to God. This reminds us, once again, that ethics cannot be limited to mere obedience to a set of rules; nor does it consist primarily in the application of abstract principles to concrete circumstances. Neither of these actions is likely to take the form of an *offering*. But human beings are capable of allowing their lives to be shaped in certain ways, in order to become people of a certain character. In doing so, they allow their "selves," their "souls and bodies," to be made into a "reasonable, holy, and living sacrifice" to God.

Our work in this chapter will be to focus on the specific elements of character that Christians are seeking to offer to God—and to build up a vocabulary that can describe these character traits in detail. To do so, we will turn to a rather unlikely theme from an unlikely source: the theme of *happiness*, as exposited by a thinker who lived several centuries before the birth of Jesus of Nazareth.

The significance of Aristotle for ethics

The ancient Greek philosopher Aristotle spent a great deal of time observing the world around him and trying to describe the nature of things. As a result of his careful attention to his surroundings, he developed a number of important insights about the world in which he lived and about human behavior within that world. While some of his observations are highly specific to his own historical context, many commentators have applied his insights much more broadly. His work is, in fact, partly responsible for many of the claims about character, stories, and practices that we have discussed throughout this book—claims that came to inform much of the history of ethics in general and Christian ethics in particular.

Habits and happiness

Aristotle argued that a considerable portion of human action was not so much the result of carefully calculated decisions at a given moment, but the natural outworking of *habits* that are ingrained in us over a long period of time. This is not to say that we have no control over the shape of our lives;

in fact, we can choose to develop certain habits (and we can also get rid of them—though this sometimes takes an extraordinary amount of effort). But when the time comes for action, the habits that we have developed will limit the range of (what we are likely to consider) our possible responses. This is the case, not because we are *unable* to perform any action outside our usual habits, but because other options simply don't appear on our internal radar screens.

Sometimes we develop habits rather randomly or accidentally; at other times, we allow our friends and acquaintances to lead us toward or away from certain habits. Most of the time, however, habits develop because we tend to do certain things over and over again in pursuit of a goal. Those who love a particular meal will develop the habits of purchasing the ingredients and cooking them in a certain way, because they know that such actions will result in the fulfillment of the goal. When they reach the step in the recipe when they are supposed to whip three eggs, they don't pause to consider whether they should use two eggs, or four, or whether they should forgo whipping them altogether. In a technical sense, they are still making *decisions* about each of these things, since they could theoretically do something else; they could, for example, choose to change the proportions as a kind of experiment that might improve the dish. Most of the time, however, such notions will not even occur to them, because they are in the *habit* of doing things a certain way.

Aristotle believed that, while individual human actions have individual goals, all human action also has, in a larger sense, a single goal—a goal that all human beings pursue relentlessly and that shapes their habitual actions. This goal is *happiness*: according to Aristotle, all people seek happiness. This is what ultimately drives their actions, leading them to develop certain practices through repetition and to ingrain these practices into their lives as habits. We develop habits of cooking in a certain way because we are pleased by the taste and presentation of the outcome. We develop habits like watching television (or not watching it) because doing these things makes us happy. And yes, we even give money away to others because, ultimately, we are happier people when we do so.

At first glance, Aristotle's focus on happiness strikes some people as very odd. They imagine all kinds of habitual activities that do not make anyone happy: people continue to do a particular job even though they hate it; they give their time and money to a good cause, but do so begrudgingly and complain about it; they mow the lawn, peel potatoes, and lay the table, annoyed the entire time. In response to these apparent counter-examples, Aristotle would say: in each case, there is some larger goal that, in the mind of the person doing the (apparently unpleasant) task, brings a kind of happiness that outweighs the annoyances of the moment. People stick with a job they hate because they seek the happiness that is brought by the money they earn; they do chores around the house because they enjoy the eventual result, or because they find happiness in the approval of others, or perhaps simply to decrease the probability that domestic tranquility will be interrupted by anger and frustration. Even the child who complains loudly about doing her homework may choose to do it anyway—even if only because she finds happiness in the lack of complaints from her parents and teachers once she has finished it.

The truth of Aristotle's claim that all people seek happiness may become more obvious still, if we pause to look closely at how he defined the term. His understanding of happiness differs, in significant ways, from the most common uses of the word today. For us, happiness is primarily a *feeling*—when we pursue happiness, we typically mean that we want to experience pleasure, to feel good. We think that the man who complains loudly as he mows the lawn must not be doing it for the sake of happiness, since he clearly isn't feeling happy at the moment. Indeed, if this notion of "feeling good in the moment" were the only definition of happiness, Aristotle's claim would make all human beings sound frivolous—as though they never had anything better to do than to try to have a good time. But Aristotle's word for happiness—the Greek word *eudaimonia*—suggests something deeper, broader, and more enduring than the temporary high that we often mean when we speak of being happy. We might retranslate the word as something like "the good life"; Aristotle's claim would then be that all human beings seek the good life. But again, in our culture, this phrase tends to carry a connotation of wealth, fame, and leisure—and such an outcome is, likewise, not quite what we have in mind. Another possible translation might be "wellness," denoting an overall positive disposition of body and spirit; unfortunately, this word too has become captured in our culture, most recently (in the United States, at least) by insurance schemes and employee health programs developed by employers who are seeking to reduce their medical care costs. Rather, the kind of wellness that I'm pointing to here might be best indicated by a nineteenth-century hymn, the refrain of which is: "It is well with my soul."

Other languages may help us. French has the word *content(e)*, which usually translates as the English word "happy"; but in French, the meaning is less about a momentary burst of pleasure, leaning more toward a steady state in which matters are "well with one's soul." (This is suggested by the word's English cognate; when someone says "I'm content," this implies a deeper and more sustained experience than does the phrase "I'm happy.") The German word *Glück* is probably closer to the ordinary English use of happiness as a positive, pleasurable feeling—with the additional complication that *Glück* is also the German word for luck or fortune. This point may help us as well;

"It Is well with my soul"

I have suggested that the word "well," as it appears in this well known and much-beloved Christian hymn, might help us to translate Aristotle's notion of *eudaimonia*, which is frequently rendered as "happiness." In the text of the hymn, "wellness" is not confused with a feeling of temporary elation, momentary pleasure, or merely physical well-being; it is, again, a much more sustained and profound notion, including ideas of being content and fulfilled in a deep and abiding way. The chorus of the hymn simply repeats the phrase "It is well with my soul" several times. The original three verses of the hymn are as follows:

> When peace like a river, attendeth my way,
> When sorrows like sea billows roll,
> Whatever my lot, Thou hast taught me to say,
> It is well, it is well, with my soul.

> Though Satan should buffet, though trials should come,
> Let this blest assurance control,
> That Christ has regarded my helpless estate,
> And hath shed his own blood for my soul.

> And Lord, haste the day when my faith shall be sight
> The clouds be rolled back as a scroll,
> The trump shall resound, and the Lord shall descend,
> Even so, it is well with my soul.

This hymn's portrayal of "wellness of soul" is quite different from our contemporary conception of "happiness" as a passing feeling of pleasure. Just how different is amply demonstrated by the story of how this hymn came to be written.

Its author, Horatio Spafford, experienced one trauma after another: his only son died very young and, shortly afterwards, he came to nearly complete financial ruin during the Great Chicago Fire of 1871. Two years later, he planned a trip to Europe with his wife and four daughters; he sent his family ahead while he concluded some business. The ship on which they were traveling collided with another ship and sank within a few minutes; his wife was rescued but all four of his daughters died. Some time later, when Spafford was crossing the Atlantic and was told that they were passing the spot where the tragedy occurred, he penned the words to this hymn.

A happy life? Certainly not according to the common usage of that word in our current context! Nevertheless, Spafford's own habituation in the stories and practices of the Christian faith had taught him that human happiness, in the more profound sense described here, did not depend upon whether one's lot in life were marked primarily by "sorrows like sea billows" or by "peace like a river." Rather, because of God's work in Christ, our lives are marked primarily by the "blest assurance" that allows a person to say, "It is well, it is well with my soul."

perhaps happiness is not so much something that one pursues, but rather is something that "just happens" to a person. (Aristotle would certainly recognize this aspect of its meaning, since the idea of luck or fortune was a standard element in Greek tragedy and philosophy.) A related German word is the verb *erfreuen*; to express happiness, one might say *ich bin darüber erfreut*, which would typically be translated "I'm happy about that," but is etymologically closer to the (now archaic-sounding) English phrase "I rejoice over that." This again comes closer to Aristotle's meaning, because it implies a sustained response of the whole person, rather than a narrowly focused emotional reaction of pleasure. All in all, it can be very difficult to find an English word that precisely captures the meaning of Aristotle's concept of *eudaimonia*. Perhaps we can evoke this sustained, integrated idea by translating Aristotle's concept of the life of *eudaimonia* as "a fulfilled and fulfilling life."

However we choose to translate Aristotle's word, the concept is that of a state that designates something deep within our being, that can be sustained even in the most difficult moments of our lives, and that endures over time. Those who lead a truly happy life, in this sense, are happy at a more profound level—which is not to say that they never cry or are never in a temporary funk. These are emotional reactions to circumstances; they are the negative equivalent of the rather more fleeting idea of happiness-as-a-feeling that is so commonly sought in our culture. The more enduring idea of happiness as "fulfillment" is not diminished by emotional moments of sadness. This helps explain why Aristotle thought that it probably wasn't possible to know whether a person had truly experienced a good or "happy" life until that life could be viewed as a whole: only a survey of one's entire life at the time of one's death would really provide a true picture.

Of course, most people make a great many mistakes as they attempt to determine what would make for a happy (or good or fulfilled and fulfilling) life. Their attention is captured by objects that they expect would give them a temporary feeling of pleasure, or that they think might make them happy in the long run (often because other people tell them that it would), and they pursue those goods accordingly. We have many examples of this process in our culture: advertising aims to convince us that a certain product or service will make us feel good. The product may often do so, at least for the moment; it may even provide more sustained happiness over a certain period of time. But eventually its power over us wears off, and our gaze is captured by a yet newer product, also promising to make us feel good (if we are only willing to buy it). But the deep, broad, lifelong happiness that Aristotle calls the goal of all human beings is nothing that can be purchased; it doesn't come in a box. This kind of happiness can only be experienced over time, through the development of certain character traits that contribute to a good life.

As I have observed at various points throughout this book, good character traits are developed through the cultivation of good habits; our explorations in previous chapters have provided some examples of the habits (in the form of narratives and practices) that Christians seek to cultivate. For example, they tell stories about Jesus as a healer of disputes, and they engage in practices of reconciliation, because they seek to become the kind of people who think of practices like forgiveness and nonviolence as the natural thing to do and who take these kinds of activities for granted as the appropriate course of life. They also believe that the life that a human being lives is not an end unto itself, but that it is properly directed toward a higher end (God); moreover, it is not strictly limited by the birth and death of the physical body, but involves resurrection and eternal life. According to the Christian perspective, these beliefs and practices (and the habits that they develop in us) will lead to a good, fulfilled, and fulfilling life: a *happy* life, in the most profound sense of the term.

A life of virtue

Aristotle's next step is to consider the specific character traits that will lead to this kind of life. He calls these traits the "excellences" of character, or *virtues*. A virtue, for Aristotle, is a specific account of a particular character trait that can contribute to a happy life: a life of *eudaimonia*, a fulfilled and fulfilling life. For example, Aristotle tells us that one of the excellences of character is *generosity*. A good life, a fulfilled and fulfilling life, will be a life of generosity—a willingness to give to others. How do we know this? Aristotle's answer is: from empirical observation. We look around and see people whose lives we would describe as good and happy (fulfilled and fulfilling), and we observe that such people are, among other things, *generous*. In contrast, those who hoard up everything that they have for themselves, even though they may find pleasure in the short run, will eventually feel empty and unfulfilled; and, at the end of their lives, few people will judge them to have lived a good life. The happy (or fulfilled or good) person is the generous person. Thus generosity is a *virtue*.

Aristotle offers a long list of such virtues. Unlike Plato before him and unlike many thinkers who were to follow him, Aristotle does not provide a carefully constructed, orderly account of the virtues, nor does he place them in a hierarchical relationship to each other. He simply lists them—moving from one to another in ways that strike most readers as somewhat random. His lists include not only Plato's four cardinal virtues (justice, courage, temperance, and practical wisdom), but also truthfulness, gentleness, magnanimity, wittiness, and a number of others (some of which do not have readily available names, even in Aristotle's Greek, and others which do not translate particularly well into English).

At this point, we are interested less in Aristotle's particular list of virtues, or even his specific definitions of those that he does list. (Some of his virtues and much of their content are quite specific to his historical context, and they do not always translate into ours. We will return to the question of the *content* of the virtues in the next section.) For the moment, we are more interested in Aristotle's *concept* of a virtue: its status as *an excellence of character* that we can name and describe. The virtues provide us with a vocabulary for identifying the habits that we believe people should develop if they are to become people of good character. Instead of simply designating someone as a "good" person, we can say that she is a generous, or courageous, or truthful, or witty person—perhaps all of these. Or we might describe a person of our acquaintance as having cultivated the virtues of temperance and courage, but as having had less success in developing the virtues of kindness and gentleness. The language of the virtues gives us a more precise set of tools for describing and analyzing what makes for a truly *good* human life.

In this respect, the virtues offer a useful contrast to another term that gets bandied about a good deal in conversations about ethics: the term "values." This is not a term that has appeared much in the book (nor will it); in fact, in my own courses in Christian ethics, I counsel my students to avoid it altogether, for three reasons. First, the word promotes a kind of self-insulating individualism in ethics. Throughout this book, we have emphasized the importance of the *community* as the touchstone of ethical deliberation, but the word "values" is individualistic to the core. We speak about a person's values, and how they differ from another person's values, as though these were determined in the privacy of one's room: "I think I will make the desire for vengeance one of my values." If a person does set a high regard on the idea of seeking revenge, it will not be because that person decided to do so alone; one's surroundings and one's formation in a particular moral tradition will be what leads a person to approve of, and to develop, a particular character trait. And yet those communal elements of moral formation are easily shunted aside when we describe this process as adopting a particular set of "values," perhaps comparing it to another possible set. We are able to insulate ourselves from the community's reflection and discernment by distinguishing "my" values from the values of others.

A second reason: the word "value" finds its ultimate frame of reference in the marketplace: an item that has *value* is one on which we can put a price. That item can then be exchanged for a certain amount of money; in fact, in our economic system, the way we determine something's value is precisely by naming an amount of money for which the item can be exchanged. I do not mean to suggest that those who speak of "moral values" are necessarily suggesting that they can or would put a price on their ethical perspective. Rather, I am suggesting that this language encourages people to think of ethical claims in much the same way that they think of other commodities—weighing competing goods against one another, calculating probabilities and risks, and making choices based on an essentially economic calculus. This is why some ethical debates are cast in terms of a cost–benefit ratio; this is an attempt to weigh outcomes and principles against one another, to determine whether the value that we place on a human life, and particularly a life of a certain quality, is great enough to justify the amount of time and money that must be spent to maintain it. These ethical debates are rarely cast in such stark language; nevertheless, by thinking of our moral assumptions as *values*, we encourage this kind of exchange-mentality.

Finally, as a result of Enlightenment-era attempts to make discussions of ethics more "scientific," the word "value" has been given a lower standing in the realm of moral discourse—in other words, the word "value" has been (let us say, without *too* much irony) *devalued*. In particular, certain writers tend to distinguish between "facts" and "values"—the former being empirical truths that can be known for certain, and the latter being subjective states that are determined by individuals. In addition to contributing to the two problems that I have already described—the individualism and the commodification of *values* language—this development has had the further effect of locating all moral discourse in a place that was considered subordinate to the "hard science" of fact. This in turn has helped to escalate the process whereby morality was largely assigned to the emotions, such that a person's interpretation of his or her own experience and feelings becomes the trump card in making a moral argument.

In contrast to the problematic nature of the language of *values*, the language of *virtue* has a long and venerable history. As we have seen, it stretches back to Aristotle; and as we will see in the chapter that follows, it has undergone considerable refinement and nuancing over the course of Christian history. It also avoids most of the problems that we have identified with the language of *values*. For example, it cannot be used to isolate or insulate a particular moral actor, since the virtues can only be defined by a morally formative community through its narratives and practices. It does not lend itself to commodification, because, unlike a value, a *virtue* does not play a role in our usual conversations about economic exchange, and is not reducible to a particular cost. Finally, because the language of virtue arises from empirical observation, it cannot be so easily divorced from hard fact and assigned a lower order of significance. It therefore provides a much more reliable vocabulary for our investigation of the specific character traits that we believe should be cultivated in order to live a good, fulfilled, and fulfilling life.

The language of virtue also gives rise to its opposite—the language of *vice*—which provides additional helpful vocabulary as we attempt to map out the territory of Christian ethics. It allows us to specify the kinds of character traits that should *not* be cultivated—that one should, in fact, attempt to work *against* in order to live a life that is rightly ordered toward the good and is therefore likely to produce true happiness. Aristotle saw the vices as describing those traits of human character in which we find ourselves to have too much or too little of a certain virtue. Thus, if generosity is a virtue, it can give rise to two related vices: miserliness, when we give too little, and profligacy, when we give too much. At first, this may seem odd; can we really give too much? Aristotle has in mind those persons who give so wildly and extravagantly that they neglect their other responsibilities. He also suggests that the spendthrift is often more interested in making a good impression than in being truly generous to others. Thus, for Aristotle, the question is not only the amount that is given; it is also relevant how one gives, with what degree of fanfare, and so on.

Aristotle thought of a virtue as a "mean" between two extremes. The extremes, in which one had too much or too little of a certain quality, were the associated vices. The mean is the point where (as Goldilocks might appreciate) everything is "just right"; this is because it lies in the middle, between the vices at each extreme. Aristotle's point here is not so much that we should have "moderation in everything," but simply the idea that excellence is always a delicate balance. If there were only one virtue, one might well seek to take it to the positive extreme; but Aristotle senses that by doing so, we would probably be ignoring other excellences of character that we might be cultivating. Because there are many virtues, and because a life that is oriented toward the good must pay some attention to them all, we have to reckon with the possibility that we might end up cultivating too much of a certain quality, just as we might cultivate too little of it.

This in turn reminds us of a final feature of Aristotle's account of the virtues. If there are many virtues, we might well imagine that they could come into conflict with each other—not just in terms of the time that we spend cultivating them, but in their actual execution. For example, one might imagine that *courage* and *kindness* might be in some tension with each other: an act of bravery might well seem unkind to a neutral observer, and similarly, an act of kindness might be seen as cowardly. But Aristotle says that, if we find ourselves making these sorts of claims, we have not adequately defined the virtues. If they are all excellences of character, and if a good and happy life is one in which they are all cultivated to the proper mean, then they cannot be in essential conflict with one another. This notion is referred to as "the unity of the virtues."

The unity of the virtues reminds us that, if we were to imagine that a true act of kindness was also an act of cowardice, this would only demonstrate that we simply don't understand the virtues of courage and kindness very well. Conversely, if we identify something as courageous and yet also believe it to be an unkind act, something is wrong with our definition of either courage or kindness (or both). As we try to give specific substance to the language of the virtues, we will need to keep this detail in mind. Otherwise, we will construct an impossible moral program, in which people are expected to compartmentalize their excellences of character in order to prevent them from coming into conflict with one another. Moreover, we might imagine that the virtues are something like the various offerings at a food court, in which we can pick and choose among our favorites and leave the others behind. But because the virtues are interconnected, they are all necessary. As the great Roman orator Cicero put the matter, "If you admit to not having one particular virtue, it must needs be that you will have none at all."

Which virtues? Why?

Having praised the language of *virtue* as a means of establishing a good vocabulary for evaluating morality, I must now insert an important caveat—one to which I alluded briefly at the beginning of the previous section. This concerns the *content* of the virtues: that is, the specific behaviors that we associate with various excellences of character. These behaviors vary considerably, depending upon the social and historical context in which the language of the virtues is employed. By themselves, the words that we use to identify the virtues—words like generosity, courage, kindness, or wit—are hollow and empty. Although these words may have fairly clear dictionary definitions, they do not really achieve any concrete specificity until we know what kinds of acts qualify as generous, or courageous or kind acts. Different cultures and different communities all tend to define the virtues differently; so, for example, while Aristotle might assume that courage would require someone to kill in certain circumstances, a Christian description of courage might claim that a true act of courage would always require a willingness to refrain from killing.

Thus, although our first step will be to identify certain virtues as significant for Christian ethics, we will have to go further: we will have to flesh out the concrete content of these virtues by considering how they are informed by Christian narratives and practices and are thereby given specificity. In fact, for Christians, one of the most important features in describing a particular virtue will be to consider whether, and to what degree, it marks the character of God; for this will often determine whether it should mark the character of human beings (though a particular character trait will often look rather different when applied to God than when applied to human beings). A more detailed examination of the *content* of the virtues will have to wait until later chapters; for now, suffice it to say that in naming the virtues, we are only taking the first step toward developing an account of their usefulness in ethics.

All the same, our first step will indeed be to name the virtues—and, more specifically, to construct a "table of the virtues." This isn't a literal chart with rows and columns, but rather something more like a list: a description of those excellences of character that Christians might want to hold up as worthy of offering up to God. Some of these character traits will have the same names as certain virtues that were held in high regard in the ancient world, in the work of Plato and Aristotle; however, in their specifically Christian use, they may take on slightly different definitions, or at least different resonances and connotations. Other virtues may not have appeared among the ancient Greek philosophers at all; rather, they developed as important understandings of the character of God in Judaism and Christianity, and emerged over time as morally significant notions.

How does one develop a table of the virtues? Clearly, the primary sources for these "excellences of character" are the narratives and practices that give a particular community its identity. By being deeply embedded in those narratives and practices, one can begin to discern certain traits that arise repeatedly and positively, both with respect to God and with respect to human beings whose moral behavior is being praised. Fortunately, in the Christian tradition, we do not have to create a new list of virtues from whole cloth; in fact, Christian thinkers have been enumerating lists of the virtues from the very earliest days of the Christian community. Some of them appear in the Bible itself; however, they are not labeled with the term "virtues." Nevertheless, they have the same function: they name the character traits that Christians believe they are called to cultivate. Other lists are appropriated from the ancient Greek or Roman philosophers and given a particularly Christian interpretation. Still others are developed by theologians over time, as they attempt to find contemporary language in which to express the essential elements of the Christian faith.

In this chapter, I have chosen to offer a sampling from several different Christian traditions concerning the virtues. One list offers a Christian interpretation of ancient Greek wisdom on the four cardinal virtues; another list of nine virtues comes from a passage describing the "fruits of the Spirit" in the book of Galatians; a third list represents a theological shaping of three character traits named in 1 Corinthians; and a fourth list offers three trinitarian virtues, developed in our contemporary context. The four lists together name eighteen such "excellences of character"; two of these are duplicates (occurring in two different lists), so our resulting table will have sixteen Christian virtues for our consideration.

The virtues that are listed here are clearly not the only possible options for Christians. One might draw on other sources that have sought, over time, to name those characteristics that best describe the shape of the Christian moral life. However, most of the traits named here have been particularly influential, and many of them would appear in any effort to compile a reasonably thorough list of Christian virtues. So it will certainly serve for our purposes in this book.

However, this chapter will make no attempt to spell out the specific features of each virtue in detail. Before we are able to take that step, we will need to think about God's role in the cultivation of the virtues, which is our topic for the following chapter. Even then, we will need to defer any thoroughgoing description of the virtues until after we have completed our exploration of Christian practices and entered into a discussion of the implications of these practices for the overall shape of moral life. Therefore, in chapter 10, I will map out how we will explore each virtue in turn; then, over the course of the chapters in Part 3, I will take up each one in relation to a particular set of ethical issues. In the present chapter, I will offer only the briefest thumbnail definition of each virtue.

The cardinal virtues

Plato lists four cardinal virtues; these have made their way into Christian tradition through writers such as St. Augustine and St. Thomas Aquinas, who endow them with a more specifically Christian focus. The cardinal virtues are justice, courage, temperance, and practical wisdom. *Justice* involves the proper ordering and distribution of rewards. The word "courage" means roughly the same for Plato as it does for us, though Christian writers tend to take it out of the largely military and conflictual context that it carried in ancient Greek culture. Sometimes also called "fortitude," *courage* requires the strength of will to face situations that might endanger a person's life, health, or soul. *Temperance* is something like "self-control"; it is not limited, as in its occasional modern usage, to the denial of certain pleasures to the body (the campaign against the public sale of alcohol, for example, was known as the "temperance movement"). For Plato, it means something more like the wise arrangement and ordering of all one's desires.

Finally, *practical wisdom* is a kind of master virtue that binds all of these elements together; it is the character trait that helps us to make the right choices under the right circumstances at the right times. Sometimes called "prudence," it is nevertheless very different than the idea (sometimes conveyed by that word in the modern context) of a cautious calculation of advantages and disadvantages. Practical wisdom is more akin to the kind of character trait that the improvisational artist requires: something like an "instinct" for doing the right things at the right time.

Together, these four cardinal virtues have had a tremendous effect on the history of ethics, and have been taken up into Christian ethics in particular (though with certain modifications). Again, we will explore these in detail in Part 3.

The fruits of the Spirit

We often speak of "cultivating" the virtues; this is just one example of the agricultural metaphors that often come into play on this topic. In Paul's letter to the Galatians, for example, he employs the metaphor of *fruit*. Such language is useful to him because the virtues, like apples, tomatoes, or walnuts, are the eventual product of a long process of cultivation—a process in which both human beings and God have a role to play. When we plant a fruit tree, we do what we can to encourage it to bear good fruit; but some of its productivity will be out of our immediate control: it will depend upon the bees that pollinate the flowers, the rain that falls (or doesn't), and the birds that don't (or do) eat all the buds. If good fruit is eventually produced, it will not be simply because we are such skilled gardeners; it will be because all the various elements necessary to the production of good fruit happened to come into confluence at the right time.

The virtues are similar: they require us to engage in a process of cultivation, but they also require the right growing conditions. From a Christian perspective, this means that they need a certain degree of divine assistance—the work of the Holy Spirit, who dwells in human lives and brings forth what is best in them. (This point will receive more detailed attention in the following chapter.) Paul offers a list of the kind of good fruit that the Holy Spirit can produce in human beings: "the fruit of the Spirit is love, joy, peace, patience, kindness, generosity, faithfulness, gentleness, and self-control" (Gal. 5:22–23).

As many commentators have noted, this is, in fact, a list of virtues. These are excellences of character that Paul is holding up as worthy of emulation; moreover, they are also characteristics that find their true standard in the character of God. Paul was a passionate practicing Jew, and he knew his scriptures well; most of the terms that he uses here are Greek translations of Hebrew words that are quite frequently applied to God in the Hebrew Bible. Both in the narrative accounts of God's actions, and in the poetic and prophetic descriptions of God in the Psalms and in the books of the prophets, these characteristics appear over and over again to describe the nature of God. No surprise, then, that Paul believes that, when human beings allow God (the Holy Spirit) to work in them, these same kinds of character traits will be produced.

Clearly, these "fruits of the Spirit" overlap with other lists of the virtues. In the following section, for example, we will see that one of the fruits, *love*, is also described as one of three "theological virtues" by Thomas Aquinas. Similarly, the fruit of the Spirit that Paul calls "self-control" is very closely related to Plato's cardinal virtue of *temperance*. These overlaps should not surprise us, since these various lists of virtues are not at all meant to be complete unto themselves or exclusive of other possible lists. In fact, the appearance of a particular virtue in more than one place in the Greek, Jewish, and/ or Christian traditions is a reminder of its significance.

I will not enumerate each of the nine "fruits of the Spirit" here; rather I will employ them in the various chapters of Part 3 to illuminate one or another set of ethical issues that we will discuss in that section. At that point, I will say more about the biblical origins of each word and its meaning as applied to God and to human beings. For the moment, it will be sufficient simply to note the presence of this list in the biblical text as a reminder that, despite our focus on the Aristotelean origins of the language of the virtues, it is hardly foreign to the biblical narrative. On the contrary, it provides a very useful way for the biblical writers to describe the character of the Christian life.

The theological virtues

Christian writers found it notable that the biblical narratives seemed to consider certain character traits to be virtues, even though these traits receive little or no mention in the classical writers. Chief among these are a triad of virtues named by St. Paul in his first letter to the Corinthians: "And now faith, hope, and love abide, these three; and the greatest of these is love" (1 Cor. 13:13). These came to be understood as character traits that were particularly descriptive of God's character, and therefore to be among the most worthy virtues to which Christians could hope to aspire. This is why they came to be known as the "theological virtues." Again, only a few brief words of explanation can be offered here.

Faith is often misunderstood to be a kind of inferior form of knowledge, as in the phrase "a leap of faith." But, as we noted in chapter 5, in our examination of the role of "confessing the faith" in the words of a creed, it might better be defined as *trust* or as a definitive orientation of one's life toward a certain object or goal. (This is why God can be described as exhibiting this virtue: it does not represent a lack of knowledge, but a loyal orientation toward the other. The same Greek word is also translated "faithfulness"; more on this in Part 3.) A famous passage in the letter to the Hebrews defines faith as "the assurance of things hoped for, the conviction of things not seen" (Heb. 11:1); here again, what appears to be a lack of definitive knowledge is actually focused on the idea of trust and confidence.

Hope is defined as a positive expectation that one's desires might be fulfilled—with the caveat that, in the case of human beings, we tend to desire things that might not be for the best. Again, the naming of hope as a *theological* virtue is a way of pointing to God as the referent of all true desires; to cultivate the theological virtue of hope is to seek to align one's own desires with God's desires. Again, the virtue of hope might seem not to apply to God; but since human beings are endowed with free will, we can still speak of God's hope that their judgments and actions will be aligned with God's desire, which is always for their good. It is therefore closely related to the third theological virtue, to which we now turn.

Love is understood as "desire for another"—and, more precisely, for the *good* of another. As we will note in a later chapter, it is a particularly complex character trait, since one English word is used to translate four different Greek words. The word that Paul uses in 1 Corinthians, *agapē*, came into Latin as *caritas* and thus into an older English idiom as "charity"; this word has the advantage of distinguishing it from other Greek and Latin words for love, but the disadvantage of aligning it with our more common use of the word "charity" to mean generosity or philanthropy (usually in a monetary form). We will return to these distinctions in chapter 14; meanwhile, suffice it to say that Christians believed God to offer the ultimate manifestation of the virtue of love, particularly in God's self-offering to the world in dwelling among human beings. This divine love became the standard through which human love would, according to Christians, be rightly understood.

Trinitarian virtues

One of the more distinctive claims of the Christian faith is its understanding of God as *trinitarian*—that is, as characterized simultaneously by unity and by plurality. This belief grew out of the earliest Christians' experience of God as simultaneously *transcendent* (i.e., beyond all human categories), *incarnate* (i.e., having taken flesh in the person of Jesus), and as an *ongoing presence* (i.e., the work of the Holy Spirit in the community). And yet, in spite of these three apparently different experiences of God, Christians continued to claim that there was only one God. These simultaneous claims of unity and three-ness in God have given rise to some additional descriptions of God's character which have developed in the theological literature over time and have been outlined in more detail in the contemporary period. My own account of these "trinitarian virtues" offers three such terms: "polyphony," "participation," and "particularity."

Polyphony draws on a musical analogy, denoting the possibility that several different notes, or even different series of notes, can be sounded simultaneously to positive effect. We sometimes imagine that human beings should only do one thing at a time, and that mixing together a variety of differing ideas (or thoughts or concepts) will only result in chaos and confusion. But polyphonic music suggests otherwise: it is, in fact, possible to mix together multiple strands in ways that not only allow each line of music to be heard as part of the whole, but may in fact enhance the overall effect precisely because of the ways that the various strands combine and interact. In the context of the moral life, this virtue may help us imagine the possibility that two or more apparently contradictory narratives or practices might jointly contribute to the pursuit of a fulfilled and fulfilling life.

Participation designates the ability of one person (or idea or structure) to become a part of another person (or idea or structure), without thereby losing its own identity. Like the virtue of polyphony, it encourages us to find ways of breaking down harsh oppositional categories, in which we are forced to choose between sharply contrasted alternatives. For example, our culture can sometimes imagine marriage and other long-term committed relationships as the dissolving of each person's identity so that the (former) individuals "vanish" and a new reality is created. But it is also possible to understand marriage and similar unions as a form of mutual participation, in which each person retains her or his identity while still inhabiting the life of the other. This virtue has particularly significant implications for questions related to medical and sexual ethics, as we will note in Part 3 of this book.

Finally, *particularity* is a virtue that helps us understand the differences among human beings without resorting to the extreme individualism that so pervades our culture. By empirical observation, we know that we are separate from one another: physically, emotionally, and psychologically. And yet we are often uncomfortable with the claim that we can or should exist in complete isolation from one another; we recognize that we are connected to one another as members of the human community, and of many smaller communities within that larger reality. The term "particularity" seeks to give full weight both to our independent existence and to our interdependence on one another. We are all strongly influenced by the communities of which we are a part; and yet we are unlike any other person, because each of us is influenced by a different combination of communities, and to a different degree by each. Hence we are rightly understood, not as individuals, but as *particular* human beings.

Conclusion

This chapter has sought to introduce the idea of the virtues, and to offer a preliminary description of one possible table of the virtues that has grown out of the Christian tradition. These virtues describe the habits that, according to Christians, should be cultivated in order to pursue a happy life, a fulfilled and fulfilling life. And yet, we began this chapter by focusing on the idea of offering; we suggested that an essential part of a person's formation in Christian ethics has to do with one's willingness to offer one's self, one's soul and body, to God. How are these concepts—virtue and offering—related to one another?

Christianity has always struggled with the question of whether the human capacity for the good is primarily the work of human beings or of God. On the one hand, Christians believe that God is ultimately in charge, and that all that is good must ultimately find its source in God rather than in the creatures of God. Thus Christian theology has argued very strongly against the notion that human beings are capable of achieving the good all by themselves; they are dependent on God for their good lives. On the other hand, this would seem to absolve human beings of all responsibility; if their goodness (or lack thereof) is simply a result of God's work in them, they would seem to have very little role to play. Why should one even *try* to embrace the good, if it's all God's doing anyway?

This apparent paradox makes the notion of *offering* particularly useful. Like the elements of bread and wine that are offered in Christian worship, a good human life really does involve human work. It doesn't just happen; human beings have to cultivate certain habits just as surely as they have to knead the dough and bake the bread. On the other hand, no human being can make bread out of nothing: we are dependent upon the natural world, with its processes of growth and renewal, for the grain and water from which the bread can be made. From a Christian perspective (and from the perspective of many religious traditions), this means, ultimately, that what we have to offer *to* God actually comes *from* God. Thus both human beings and God have a role to play; it is not an equal partnership, but human beings do contribute something—if only in allowing God's good work to bear fruit in their own offerings and in the good character traits that mark their lives.

Questions for discussion

1. What experiences do you have, outside of any specifically religious context, of the idea of "offering" something to another? To what extent do you think of this as a transaction, and to what extent an act of self-sacrifice? Think about a variety of examples—giving a birthday gift, falling in love, doing work for an employer or a teacher, and/or volunteering one's services to an organization.

2. Do you agree with Aristotle's claim that, ultimately, "all people seek happiness"? What examples can you give of this phenomenon? Can you think of examples that seem to deny this proposition?

3. Make a list of three or four people that you consider particularly *good* people. They may be personal acquaintances, people who are in the current headlines, historical figures, or even fictional characters. What words would you use to name their specific excellences of character? Try not to limit yourself to the character traits that are described in this chapter—allow your thoughts to range widely. In some cases, you may not be able to come up with a specific word that names the trait you have in mind; in that case, offer a sentence or two of description, or perhaps tell a story about the person that illustrates your point.

4. Do you find Aristotle's concept of "the unity of the virtues" to be a useful idea? Do you think that most people operate under this assumption, or do they tend to evaluate certain traits positively even though they understand these traits to be in essential contradiction with one another?

5. Drawing on your own knowledge of Christianity, what other virtues (in addition to those named here) would you describe as functioning as "excellences of character" for Christians? Are there some character traits that, even

though they are held up as positive among Christians, you would not consider to be positive traits at all? If so, how do you account for this difference?

Sources cited in this chapter and/or recommended for further reading

Aristotle, *Nicomachean Ethics*; *Politics*; *Rhetoric*

Cicero, *Tusculan Questions*

David S. Cunningham, *These Three Are One: The Practice of Trinitarian Theology*

Stanley Hauerwas, *Character and the Christian Life: A Study in Theological Ethics*

Stanley Hauerwas and Charles Pinches, *Christians among the Virtues: Theological Conversations with Ancient and Modern Ethics*

Philip D. Kenneson, *Life on the Vine: Cultivating the Fruit of the Spirit in Christian Community*

D. Stephen Long and Tripp York, "Remembering: Offering Our Gifts," in Hauerwas and Wells, eds., *The Blackwell Companion to Christian Ethics*

Martha C. Nussbaum, *The Fragility of Goodness: Luck and Ethics in Greek Tragedy and Philosophy*

Jean Porter, "Virtue," chapter 12 of Meilaender and Werpehowski, eds., *The Oxford Handbook of Theological Ethics*

Ben Quash, "Offering: Treasuring the Creation," in Hauerwas and Wells, eds., *The Blackwell Companion to Christian Ethics*

St. Thomas Aquinas, *Treatise on the Virtues* (*Summa Theologiae* Ia–IIae.49–67)

Jonathan R. Wilson, *Gospel Virtues: Practicing Faith, Hope & Love in Uncertain Times*

Calling upon the triune God
The divine formation of Christian virtue

We have reached the central chapter of this book—both numerically and thematically. In our explorations thus far, we have developed an account of the nature of ethics in general and of Christian ethics in particular; we have traced the contours of the Christian narrative; and we have examined how that narrative is enacted and embodied by Christians in the activities of proclamation and profession, confession and absolution, prayer and nonviolence. Finally, we have examined the case for using the language of the virtues as our central vocabulary for ethical reflection.

We have also noted, however, that any list of virtues is, by itself, a morally hollow notion; the words themselves can be made to justify almost any sort of behavior or circumstance, as when state security forces in Chile describe the forced "disappearance" of government opponents as an act of *justice*, or when someone with a severe eating disorder describes it to others as merely an act of *self-control*. The virtues only come to have meaning in the context of a particular set of narratives and a particular context of discourse within which those virtues can be defined and exemplified. While the last chapter gave us an opportunity to name and describe several virtues within the Christian tradition, the current chapter will broaden that discussion by examining the relationship between Christianity's virtues and its description of the character of God.

Specifying the content of Christian virtue

As we have already observed, the stories of the Bible and of the history of the Christian faith provide a backdrop against which one can recognize certain actions and dispositions as properly virtuous. In addition, the virtues will only come to acquire substantive content when they are embodied in the life of a gathered community—particularly as it is expressed in that community's habitual practices. Throughout this book, we have been gathering up these elements of the Christian life, and our accounts of Christian narratives and practices will certainly help us to provide more specific accounts of the content of the virtues.

Excellence of character and the character of God

In the case of Christianity, however, we need to address an additional facet of this question. Christians believe that their narratives, their beliefs, and many of their practices find their ultimate source, not just in their own best efforts to discern the good and to calculate the best way to achieve it, but in God's *revelation* of these elements of their faith. This claim was implicit in the last chapter, in that we turned to the Bible and to the theological claims of the Church in order to develop a Christian account of the virtues. We did not simply offer a rational assessment of potential outcomes, nor did we cite social-scientific research into what behaviors or dispositions would be the most "healthy" according to modern psychology. Instead, we observed that Christians shape their account of the virtues by *calling upon God*: their understanding of what makes for excellence in human character depends quite heavily on their understanding of *God's* character.

In fact, since virtues are defined as "excellences of character," a specifically Christian account of the virtues might understand them as, first and foremost, descriptions of the character of God. Christians come to know the shape of a particular virtue because they understand it to be descriptive of God's character first. We might put it this way: Christians understand the virtues to be those dispositions that *God has by nature*, and in which human beings *can participate by grace*. (The word "grace" here should be understood, not in terms of its common meaning of "style" or "elegance," but with attention to its Latin root *gratia*, which means "gift." Human beings can participate in God's excellences of character, not through their own efforts, but because God offers them the opportunity to do so as a gift.) In other words, God gives people the opportunity to participate in the virtues by cultivating in human beings the same character traits that God possesses by definition. Because this is a *gift*, it is not forced upon human beings; nevertheless, people can allow the virtues to be cultivated in their lives and, thereby, to form their moral outlook. In doing so, they allow God to bring their own lives into alignment with the divine character.

These claims raise two interrelated questions. First, how does one come to know, with any degree of reliability, the *character* of God? And second, does this create an impossible standard? Can human beings really be expected to emulate the character of *God*?

Discerning God's character

For Christians, knowledge about God's character traits comes not through some supposedly neutral analysis of human religiosity, but from God's revelation of these traits through the witness of the Bible (as its canonical scripture) and through the Church (as its living tradition). By paying close attention to the descriptions of God in the Bible, the liturgy, and other long-standing Christian narratives and practices, we can begin to get a sense of how Christians understand the shape of God's character, and can thereby begin to give more specific content to the virtues.

Because of the significant stake it places in God's character as a guide to human character, Christian ethics sometimes makes larger claims for itself than might be the case in other ethical paradigms. For example, Christians will sometimes speak of ethics as having "objective moral norms." Unfortunately, this claim is sometimes misunderstood as aligning Christian ethics with the Enlightenment project of conceiving a purely rational basis for morality—one that does not rely on God's action in revealing God's own character to human beings. But most Christian assertions about objective moral norms are different from generalized philosophical claims about this same topic. For Christians, moral norms are "objective," not because they are independent of God, but precisely the opposite: because they conform to the one true "object" of morality (in the sense of its *goal* or *focus*): namely, God. While Christians recognize that such objective (that is, God-focused) moral norms will not be immediately obvious to all people, they do nevertheless believe that they are the *right* ones: that these norms are actually appropriate for all, even when they are not recognized as such. Their "objectivity"—if that is the right word to use—is not a result of their rationality or their self-evidence, but of their conformity to the nature of God, as that nature comes to be known through God's revelation to humanity.

Needless to say, this claim needs to be treated with special care. Whenever we hear an appeal to God as the ultimate source and guarantor of someone's beliefs, we are rightly wary. Such claims are not verifiable in the way that, for example, a newspaper reporter might check the facts that she has been given by a source simply by making a phone call or two. Moreover, it is very tempting for those who are setting forth arguments (of whatever kind) to turn to God to back up those arguments; history is replete with examples of people who did exactly this, and did so strictly for the purpose of wielding more power or making more money. At their best, Christians have been rather hesitant to pronounce a particular claim to have the status of divine revelation; the Bible came to canonical status over a very long period of time, and church teachings are typically handed down only after councils and synods have deliberated long and hard about them. In addition, most Christian denominations are wary of claims to "private revelation"—that is, when an individual claims that God has chosen to unveil a divine secret to that person alone. More often, such claims turn out to be efforts to lend credence and authority to some individual's grasp for wealth, fame, or power.

But beyond the rather daunting difficulties of sorting out true revelatory claims from sham and artifice, we face an additional problem. When it comes to the moral life, matters are always more complicated than merely appropriating certain bits of information and making decisions about them. Thus, even if we somehow managed to agree upon a complete set of terms and definitions that described the character of God, we would still have to take another step. Mental acts alone will not form people in a particular set of virtues; that will require habits that are developed and practiced over time. This is not to deny the work of the intellect in discerning God's character traits (whether that understanding is gained through revelation or otherwise), nor to deny the work of the human will in seeking to embody those same traits to whatever degree possible. These elements are necessary, but not sufficient; the human intellect is easily distracted and the human will is rarely unwavering. People need help in concentrating their minds on the importance of particular character traits, and in directing their wills to make those traits their own.

One of the chief sources of this help, as we noted in the previous chapter during our discussion of Aristotle, is our cultivation of habits. Aristotle insists that we become people of virtue by cultivating good habits: so, for example, we become courageous by acting courageously—and not just in crisis situations, but every day. We do not become generous simply by waking up one morning, declaring ourselves so, and making one large, publicly observable act of generosity (such as a large monetary donation). Rather, we have to develop habits of generosity, giving regularly over time, such that doing so becomes an almost instinctive action: we see a need, and we give. The intellect and the will are involved in this process, but a casual observer would never notice that fact. It would not *appear* as though the person had mulled it over, thought twice, come to a difficult decision, and then finally decided to give. That might be an act of generosity, but not the action of a generous person. The generous person has so trained the mind and the will (through long habituation in acts of generosity) that, just as soon as the need is seen, the desire to give is felt—and, when possible, the action follows accordingly.

This much is true for human beings in general: since we often act from habit, embodying the virtues requires the cultivation of good habits. But this presents something of a problem for Christians, because they define the virtues according to the character of God. This would seem to suggest that they have to get in the habit of being very much like God—and that would seem to be a rather tall order. Therefore, we must now consider our second question about the Christian account of virtue: how can Christians hope to emulate the character of God?

God's role in cultivating the virtues

At the very end of the previous chapter, we considered the paradoxical nature of Christian virtue: its cultivation is not merely a human action, and yet human beings must participate in this work in order for it to occur. We reiterated this observation at the beginning of the current chapter, describing the virtues as those dispositions that *God has by nature*, and in which human beings *are invited by God to participate*. This aspect of Christian ethics can be particularly difficult to understand; we are accustomed to thinking about ethics as focusing primarily on what *human beings* do, rather than what God does. But Christian ethics offers a radically different claim: that the good habits of human beings are cultivated—in an ultimate sense, at least—not by those human beings themselves, but by God.

In fact, Thomas Aquinas goes so far as to describe the virtues as "good habits that God cultivates in us, without us." He wants to emphasize that the virtues that Christians cultivate are not their own good works which they are able to develop in themselves through some flamboyant act of moral bodybuilding. The virtues are, rather, *God's* work *in* human beings: a divine initiative that nudges them toward the cultivation of good habits. But lest God be seen as the great puppet-master who controls our every movement without any involvement on our parts, we should also note that Thomas goes on to say that the cultivation of virtue "is caused in us by God without our action, but not without our consent." In other words, although Christians believe that God is the supreme cultivator of the virtues in human lives, they also recognize that they are capable (nevertheless) of resisting God's work. (This might be described as an instance of the "finite freedom" that we discussed in chapter 5.)

So, for example, Christians believe that God desires human beings to cultivate the virtue of generosity—and that God nudges them toward habits of generosity in various ways. Of course, people can place obstacles in the way of that process: as free beings, they do not need to yield to the hint, the nudge, or the urge to be generous. They can steadfastly refuse to allow such a habit to be developed in their lives. However, according to Christian belief, this does not deter God's efforts; the divinely directed work of cultivating generosity is always ready and available, always waiting to be allowed in to a person's life. In some sense, then, Christians might admit that, with respect to God's power to cultivate the virtues in their lives, it may often seem as though "resistance is futile"—since God will typically have a greater degree of resolve, perseverance, and patience than will those who resist the divine initiative.

But in theory, at least, anyone can refuse to "give consent" to God's desire to cultivate the virtues in one's heart. Thus the Christian account of the cultivation of virtues does not make God the *only* agent involved: human beings have a role to play as well. As Thomas Aquinas puts it, a virtue bears fruit only when we are active as well: "As to those things which are done by us, God causes them in us, yet not without action on our part, since God works in every will and in every nature." Thus a Christian account of the virtues emphasizes both God's activity and that of human beings. In order to attend to both these elements, we might define the virtues (from a Christian point of view) as "the presence of God's gifts in the development of good habits."

In the remainder of this chapter, we will attempt to understand how this takes place, and in the process we will begin to get some sense of how Christians might define the character of God. We will undertake this work, first, by examining how God's presence, agency, and character is understood within the context of the liturgy, and particularly in that section of the worship service that we have been examining in Part 2: the Liturgy of the Eucharist. Second, we will broaden the scope of our inquiry, looking at a series of more general theological descriptions that have developed over time to describe God's work in the world: the divine activities of creation, redemption, and sanctification.

God's work in the liturgy

"It is right to give God thanks and praise." At the outset of the Liturgy of the Eucharist, the congregation speaks these words at the beginning of the eucharistic prayer. Because of its structure, this prayer includes a lengthy description of God's character: it declares why God is to be praised, what God has done for human beings, and how God is present in the eucharistic feast. There are many forms of this prayer, which takes on different emphases in different Christian denominations. But its elements follow a standard pattern: a declaration of God's holiness, a remembrance of God's actions, and a request for God's presence.

At the outset of the prayer, the congregation often says or sings a declaration of God's holiness. (The traditional form of this declaration is the *Sanctus*, which is the Latin word for holy; for more on this part of the liturgy, see Interlude 2 which follows this chapter.) In declaring something holy, one acknowledges its special status: it is set apart, recognized as differing from everything else, and therefore worthy of special treatment. By designating God alone as holy, Christians emphasize God's status as the only object truly worthy of worship and praise; this suggests in turn that God is the one true standard of goodness and truth. Whatever acts of goodness we may find in the world (that is, among human beings), they cannot be compared with the one true instance of the Good, namely God.

A eucharistic prayer

What follows is a shortened and slightly amended version of one particular eucharistic prayer; it originates in the Book of Common Prayer and is in relatively common use today. The first six phrases are typically spoken in call-and-response style, with the worship leader stating a phrase and the people responding with the following phrase. The rest of the prayer is usually spoken or sung by the worship leader, with a few sections spoken or sung by the congregation.

The Lord be with you. (Response: *And also with you.*)
Lift up your hearts. (*We lift them to the Lord.*)
Let us give thanks to the Lord our God. (*It is right to give God thanks and praise.*)
It is truly right to glorify you, Father, and to give you thanks; for you alone are God, living and true, dwelling in light inaccessible from before time and for ever.

Fountain of life and source of all goodness, you made all things and fill them with your blessing; you created them to rejoice in the splendor of your radiance. Countless throngs of angels stand before you to serve you night and day; and, beholding the glory of your presence, they offer you unceasing praise. Joining with them, and giving voice to every creature under heaven, we acclaim you, and glorify your Name, as we sing,

Holy, holy, holy Lord, God of power and might,
heaven and earth are full of your glory.
Hosanna in the highest.
Blessed is the one who comes in the name of the Lord.
Hosanna in the highest.

We acclaim you, holy Lord, glorious in power. Your mighty works reveal your wisdom and love. You formed us in your own image, giving the whole world in to our care, so that, in obedience to you, we might rule and serve all your creatures. When our disobedience took us far from you, you did not abandon us to the power of death. In your mercy you came to our help, so that in seeking you we might find you. Again and again you called us into covenant with you, and through the prophets you taught us to hope for salvation.

Father, you loved the world so much that in the fullness of time you sent your only Son to be our Savior. Incarnate by the Holy Spirit, born of the Virgin Mary, he lived as one of us, yet without sin. To the poor he proclaimed the good news of salvation; to prisoners, freedom; to the sorrowful, joy. To fulfill your purpose he gave himself up to death; and, rising from the grave, destroyed death, and made the whole creation new.

And, that we might live no longer for ourselves, but for him who died and rose for us, he sent the Holy Spirit, his own first gift for those who believe, to complete his work in the world, and to bring to fulfillment the sanctification of all.

When the hour had come for him to be glorified by you, his heavenly Father, having loved his own who were in the world, he loved them to the end; at supper with them he took bread, and when he had given thanks to you, he broke it, and gave it to his disciples, and said, "Take, eat: This is my Body, which is given for you. Do this for the remembrance of me."

After supper he took the cup of wine; and when he had given thanks, he gave it to them, and said: "Drink this, all of you: This is my Blood of the new Covenant, which is shed for you and for many for the forgiveness of sins. Whenever you drink it, do this in remembrance of me."

Father, we now celebrate this memorial of our redemption. Recalling Christ's death and his descent among the dead, proclaiming his resurrection and ascension to your right hand, awaiting his coming in glory; and offering to you, from the gifts you have given us, this bread and this cup, we praise you and we bless you . . .

Lord, we pray that in your goodness and mercy your Holy Spirit may descend upon us, and upon these gifts, sanctifying them and showing them to be holy gifts for your holy people, the bread of life and the cup of salvation, the Body and Blood of your Son Jesus Christ. Grant that all who share this bread and cup may become one body and one spirit, a living sacrifice in Christ, to the praise of your Name. . . .

Through Christ, and with Christ, and in Christ, all honor and glory are yours, Almighty God and Father, in the unity of the Holy Spirit, for ever and ever. AMEN.

The next section of the prayer is the *anamnesis*, which is the Greek word for memory or remembrance. This section "remembers" the most significant actions of God through history, with a particular emphasis on what God has done for human beings. In some sense, this part of the prayer serves as a recapitulation of the Christian narrative; it might be understood as a condensed version of some of the stories that we examined in Interlude 1. Typically, the prayer describes God's creation of the world, the election of the Israelites as the chosen people of God, the liberation of the people from their slavery, the establishment of the monarchy, and the prophetic voices that pointed toward the one who was to come: the anointed one, the Messiah. The prayer then describes the sending of God's beloved child, Jesus of Nazareth, who taught and preached a new concept of morality and community. At some point, it also describes, usually in some detail, his last supper with his disciples; this provides important background for the sharing of bread and wine in the eucharist (more on this in the following chapter). This section of the prayer also describes Jesus' arrest, execution, and resurrection. Finally, it describes the gift of the Holy Spirit, God's "own first gift for those who believe," who brings God's presence into the newly formed community of Jesus' followers and guides them into the future.

By collecting up and reiterating these basic narrative claims, the *anamnesis* reminds the gathering community of the essential character of God. God is the One who creates the world and cares for its people; God calls them back when they wander away; God becomes present on the earth, first in the person of Jesus and then in the person of the Spirit, in order to reconcile the relationship between human beings and God. By listening carefully to this narrative, we can begin to name some of God's more obvious character traits: compassion, faithfulness, persistence, strength of will, and love for humanity.

Finally, the last section of the eucharistic prayer is the *epiclesis*—the Greek word that means "to lean upon" or "to call upon." In this part of the prayer, the focus shifts away from a reiteration of God's past actions and toward a request for God's action in the present and the future. It asks God to bless and to transform the congregation's offerings of bread and wine, and of prayer and thanksgiving—turning them into a form of spiritual nourishment for those who have offered them. This last section of the eucharistic prayer invites God into the lives of human beings, asking that the divine power of transformation be brought to work in human lives. It is therefore a liturgical enactment of the divine work that we have been discussing in this chapter: human beings asking that God's character be brought to bear on human life and activity. The congregation gives its assent to this prayer with a final "Amen."

God's work in the world

As I have suggested, the liturgy provides us with a very useful microcosm to understand the Christian account of God's character and of God's work in human lives. In addition, however, these matters have been accented throughout the development of the Christian theological tradition, through its accounts of the entire scale of God's interactions with human beings. Thus, for Christians, God's character and God's agency can also be understood by considering the various elements of God's work in the world.

I want to examine three such elements here. Each of these aspects of God's work is traditionally associated with one of the three persons of the Trinity. (Theologians would be quick to emphasize, however, that none of these three divine activities is the exclusive work of any one "person" of the Trinity. Rather, all of God's work in the world is undivided. There are important reasons for this, to which we will return at the end of this chapter; for the moment, however, I must simply ask my readers to trust me on this point.) Each of these three descriptions has a number of advantages, but all are important; in fact, difficulties tend to arise when Christians rely too heavily on any one of these elements to give them a complete picture of the moral life. The three forms of divine cultivation of the virtues are associated with God's work of creation, redemption, and sanctification.

Creation

The first description focuses on the Christian doctrine of creation: because human beings are made by God and, in fact, made in the image of God (Gen. 1:26–27), they bear a certain resemblance—however distant—to their creator. Thus, even though they have fallen away from that original image, they continue to find it attractive and find themselves drawn back to it. Simply by being the creator and the archetype of human beings, God has formed them in certain patterns of thought and action that they can never fully abandon, or can do so only through the greatest effort and at the greatest expense. St. Augustine may have put it most clearly when, addressing God, he said: "You have made us for yourself, and our hearts are restless until they rest in you."

This understanding of creation is the ultimate Christian warrant for something called "natural law"—a collection of moral claims that all human beings know and intuitively recognize. St. Paul hints at this notion in the beginning of his letter to the Romans, when he speaks of those non-Jews who, though they "do not possess the law," nevertheless "do instinctively what the law requires" (Rom. 2:14). Thomas Aquinas describes the "natural law" as the way in which human beings participate in God's "eternal law." His reasoning is similar to Aristotle's, in that he makes a claim that he believes applies universally to all people: "good is to be sought and pursued, and evil is to be avoided." He notes that this is true for created things generally, for animals in particular, and for human beings in a supreme sense. But Thomas differs from Aristotle in the warrant that he offers to support his claim: while Aristotle based his view that "all human beings seek happiness" on empirical observation, Thomas bases his claim on the doctrine of creation: because God made all things, they behave "naturally," that is, in accordance with their status as creatures of the creator God.

Unfortunately, Thomas' teaching about the natural law eventually became uncoupled from his teaching about the doctrine of creation, and even uncoupled from God altogether. As the story is usually told, the role of the villain is played by a seventeenth-century Dutch political theorist named Hugo Grotius, who argued that we would still be compelled to obey the natural law, *even if there were no God.* In addition to undermining Thomas' claim that the natural law was based on the theological premise of God's creating work, this position fueled the Enlightenment notion that one could speak of morality in ways that completely skirted the question of God. Grotius was himself a Christian believer, and no doubt intended his claim to have the effect of demanding adherence to the natural law from all persons, regardless of their religious belief. In the end, it had the opposite effect: it made God irrelevant to the natural law, thereby undermining its theological basis. This in turn meant that the concept of natural law was easily ignored—not only by those at whom Grotius was aiming (i.e., those outside his definition of Christianity), but also by Christians themselves, for whom God was no longer the perceived authority who justified the natural law.

Because of this complicated history, I find the more general category of *creation* to be superior to that of *natural law* as a point of focus for this element of God's work in the world. Because the idea of creation naturally points us back to a *creator*, the idea cannot become separated from God in the same way that the natural law can. In addition, our focus on Christian ethics as encapsulated by Paul's claim that "Christ is the end of the law" would lose its sharpness if we were to re-introduce a different concept of law at this point—however nuanced a description we might give of it. As Paul states plainly and as we have re-emphasized from the outset, the law cannot, by itself, provide the kind of transformation of character that Christian ethics seeks to bring about. Moreover, and as the history of the term "natural law" clearly shows, any introduction of the concept of *law* to Christian ethics tends to obscure the fact that it is ultimately based on a *person*: Jesus Christ. To that person we now turn.

Redemption

A second way in which Christianity has traditionally described God's cultivation of the virtues in human beings is through its doctrine of redemption, which is primarily associated with Jesus Christ. It is usually considered under two headings: the *person of Christ* and the *work of Christ*. The first term refers to the notion that Jesus Christ, as God incarnate, provides one of the most straightforward and reliable indicators of God's character. Since this is God in human form, we can learn a great deal about the virtues simply by looking at Jesus. He provides us with a relatively clear picture of the life of virtue—a life characterized by those dispositions which (as we observed earlier in this chapter) "God has by nature, and in which human beings can participate by grace."

A strong focus on the person of Christ in ethics is often associated with the long-standing tradition of *imitatio Christi*—the imitation of Christ. If we want to cultivate the virtues, we need to do what Jesus did; and we need to do so repeatedly and habitually, so that his actions and his reactions in the circumstances that he faced are embodied in our actions and reactions as well. This approach has much to commend it, because the trinitarian logic of Christ as *God incarnate* means that God's character traits are certainly to be found in the person of Jesus. One difficulty with this approach, however, is similar to the one we faced when we examined quandary ethics in the first chapter of this book. The circumstances that Jesus faced do not always arise—at least not in exactly the same form—in our lives. Jesus lived as a practicing Jew in first-century Palestine under the imperial power of Rome; his world held views about politics and economics, about race, class, and gender, and about socio-cultural status that are very different from our views of these matters. We know what Jesus said about paying taxes to Caesar, but what would he say about paying taxes to the US government? Or to the Chinese government? We know that Jesus blessed the children, but does that really help us set public policy with respect to the foster-care system? Ironically, it is precisely that aspect of Jesus' life that makes the *imitatio Christi* tradition so appealing—its concrete specificity—that also makes it so difficult to use in making broad ethical generalizations. It particularly limits its applicability. The WWJD question—"what would Jesus do?"—can certainly be a fruitful starting point for Christian ethical reflection, but it can only carry us so far.

Having said that, it should also be acknowledged that Christian ethics has often failed to give adequate attention to the person of Christ in its description of the moral life. It has used the obvious differences in time, place, and circumstance between Jesus' era and our own to discount his life and actions as morally significant data for thinking about how one might live. We noted a clear instance of this in chapter 6, when we turned to the discussion of nonviolence as a Christian practice. Because of their involvement in world events, Christians tended to become enamored of accounts, like that of Reinhold Niebuhr, that discounted the character and practices of Jesus in favor of a doctrine of "Christian realism." Against this perspective, the work of a writer like John Howard Yoder attempted to give the life and actions of Jesus a more central role in the work of Christian ethics.

The work that Yoder and others have done to rehabilitate this element of Christian ethics is very important because, as Aristotle notes, role-models provide one of the most important ways that we learn how to be good people: we become magnanimous by watching and imitating a magnanimous person. In order to offer a Christian account of justice, we would need to make reference to how Jesus described the appropriate administration of justice—and to the ways that he administered it himself. Jesus' counsel to "Love your enemies; do good to those who hate you" (Luke 6:27), his parable of the father's warm welcome for his wayward son (Luke 15:20), and his response to the woman who was caught in the act of adultery ("Neither do I condemn you," John 8:11)—all provide a fairly clear indicator that justice is not to be allied with retribution or revenge, but rather with mercy and love. The facts that Christians throughout the ages have so often failed to show mercy, demanded retribution, and carried out acts of revenge, are evidence of just how easily Jesus' own words and deeds can sometimes be ignored in the understanding of the Christian life.

The other element of the doctrine of redemption concerns the *work of Christ*—the salvation of the world through his death and resurrection. Here, the claim is that in Christ, God reconciled the God–world relationship that had been damaged by the Fall. In dying, Christ sets people free from the sin that so often had become an obstacle to the cultivation of virtue. Human nature might be likened to a large reservoir of fresh water that is held back by a dam: the water is clean and pure, just as it was created, but it is unable to nourish the dried-out valley below, because the dam is holding it back. God's work in Christ bursts open the floodgates, so that the true reality of human nature—in all its God-created purity—can be the good gift to the world that it was meant to be.

Again, a too-exclusive emphasis on this aspect of God's work can lead to some misperceptions. One might argue that, since God has already reconciled the world through the death and resurrection of Christ, the cultivation of the virtues is not strictly necessary, and may even be misleading. How can human beings, through their habituated actions (even if they are ultimately cultivated in us by God) ever accomplish anything more than was accomplished by God in the death and resurrection of Christ? In fact, doesn't God's act of justification already cancel sin, such that it doesn't really matter what we do from that point onward? Or—to take the point to an even more radical conclusion—don't people actually re-emphasize God's saving work every time they act badly, by showing that God is able to redeem even *this* behavior?

Paul actually faced this question quite early on. In preaching the message of salvation through the grace of God (i.e., as God's freely given gift to humanity), Paul recognized that he might well be tempting some people to relax into a rather complacent state with regard to the shape of their moral lives. In order to pre-empt this line of thinking, Paul argues that the change brought about in Christ's death actually brings about a change in human beings as well: not just a legal transaction (i.e., whatever your sins have been or may be in the future, they are canceled), but rather, a metaphysical one (i.e., you have been transformed from your sinful state into a state that, by God's grace, has the potential to reflect—however dimly—God's own goodness; and this changes the way that you can and should live). Paul writes:

> What then are we to say? Should we continue in sin in order that grace may abound? By no means! How can we who died to sin go on living in it? Do you not know that all of us who have been baptized into Christ Jesus were baptized into his death? Therefore we have been buried with him by baptism into death, so that, just as Christ was raised from the dead by the glory of the Father, so we too might walk in newness of life. For if we have been united with him in a death like his, we will certainly be united with him in a resurrection like his (Rom. 6:1–5).

Thus, while Paul strongly affirms the once-for-all nature of God's act of redemption through the death and resurrection of Christ, he does not allow the centrality of this claim to eclipse the real transformation of life that it brings about in its wake. Human beings are redeemed, not just as a pretense (in which God knows that we're sinful but pretends that we're not), but as part of a genuine change. Redemption is therefore not merely a remission of sins but an entrance into a new form of life. Part and parcel of that new life is the cultivation, by God, of the virtues in the redeemed lives of human beings.

Sanctification

A third and final means by which God cultivates these virtues is through the work of the Holy Spirit. According to Christian doctrine, the Holy Spirit is fully God, a co-equal member of the Trinity. The Spirit is present in the work of creation and redemption as well, but Christians tend to focus their attention on the role of the Spirit in the work of *sanctification*: leading human beings ever more fully into the calling to which they are called. This suggests that, in the language that we have been using here, the Spirit leads Christians into a life of *virtue*.

Through God's work of sanctification, people are drawn in more closely to the divine orbit, moving ever nearer to the image of God in which they were originally created. The work of the Spirit and the language of sanctification is often seen as the most appropriate place to think about the cultivation of the virtues, since it has an ongoing, lifelong scope. According to the Gospel of John, the Holy Spirit continues the work of Christ after his death and his departure from earth (John 14:16–20). This makes the Spirit an especially helpful point of focus for present-day Christians, who live in the "time between the times"—that is, between Christ's first advent on earth and Christ's return at the final consummation of history. And since the Church, the body of Christ, is the vehicle for the Spirit's earthly activities, it comes to be understood as one of the places where the Spirit's activity is most discernibly carried out.

The Spirit's work of sanctification offers an important contribution to the ethical perspective that is being elaborated in this book. If Christian ethics can indeed be built on Paul's claim that "Christ is the end of the law," then we rightly focus our attention on the teachings of Jesus—particularly his insistence that the moral evaluation of an action depends not simply on its conformity to a rule, but also to the disposition and character with which that action is performed. But because the teachings of Jesus were offered in a particular historical, geographical, and cultural context, extending them through time and space can be a difficult task. The Spirit's work is to guide Christians in this task, helping them to make Christ present in other historical and cultural contexts. Consequently, the claim that "Christ is the end of the law" can also be extended into these new contexts, adapting the insights of Jesus to every new historical and geographical circumstance.

Here too, however, we must be cautious about the danger of overemphasis. By appropriating to the Holy Spirit a too-exclusive role in the cultivation of the virtues, the conversation can lapse into one in which "anything goes." "The Spirit blows where it wills" (John 3:8), and this has sometimes been taken to mean that practically anything can be justified on the basis of the testimony of the Holy Spirit. Those who have taken this view have understood the phrase "Christ is the end of the law" to mean that the law has simply vanished (a perspective sometimes referred to as *antinomianism*, from the Greek word *nomos*, law), having been replaced by the Spirit's guidance. Some very freewheeling forms of Christianity have developed during the course of its history on precisely this basis. As appealing as this may be at first glance, it always requires one or more human beings to announce just what it is that the Spirit is saying; thus certain charismatic individuals are easily tempted to use such claims to their own advantage. Or, in the absence of such interpreters of the Spirit's guidance, people can begin to feel so thoroughly adrift that they end up demanding a ruler who will put things in order (with an iron fist, if necessary). In either case, this helps us understand why, as the Anglican moral theologian Oliver O'Donovan has noted, most accounts of Christian ethics that have overly stressed the role of the Holy Spirit have eventually lapsed into the tyrannical rule of the few over the many.

At its best, however, an adequate account of the sanctifying work of the Holy Spirit can help us understand how divine guidance can be given to human beings in ways that bring the ethical influence of Christ into every new context, so that Christians need not rely only on a narrow set of rules or laws in order to develop a deep ethical perspective. The Spirit thus plays a particularly important role in the virtue of *practical wisdom*, which we described (at the end of chapter 7) as the master virtue that enables us to make good judgments and to act rightly in each concrete circumstance.

Keeping everything in motion

Too heavy an emphasis on any one of these elements—creation, redemption, or sanctification—can lead to an ethical framework which, while filled with insight, is ultimately out of balance in one way or another. In our explanation of these themes, I have mentioned four accounts of Christian ethics that lack this balance:

1. a focus on natural law, which is rightly based on God's work in creation but is too easily separated from its true source in God;
2. an overly simplistic account of the imitation of Christ, which rightly focuses on Jesus as God incarnate, but pays inadequate attention to his historical context;
3. the claim that God's work of redemption in Christ is the only thing that matters, thereby rendering our human judgments and behavior irrelevant; and
4. the antinomianism that can develop from an excessive reliance on the Spirit, encouraging self-interested "interpreters" of the Spirit's guidance to use this as a means of exerting power and control.

All four of these perspectives have played a role in the history of Christian ethics. Ultimately, however, each of them relies too heavily on an exclusive focus on one particular part of God's work in the world—creation, redemption (whether focused on the person or the work of Christ), or sanctification—without attending to the other elements as well.

But as I noted at the outset of this discussion (in a cryptic comment in which I asked my readers to trust me), Christian doctrine claims that "the works of God are undivided." That is, God's work in the world—including the work of creation, redemption, and sanctification—cannot be assigned separately to individual persons of the Trinity as if they were the exclusive domain of one or another. This is because, in spite of the "threeness" that is emphasized by the Christian belief in the Trinity, God is also *one*; God is not a three-person committee whose work can be divided as a kind of time-saving "division of labor," and whose members might ultimately push us in different directions. We would be wise to bear this doctrinal claim in mind with thinking about the works of God with respect to the overall ethical framework of Christianity. Too exclusive a focus on creation, redemption, or sanctification will tend to lead us to neglect the others; as a result, we will obtain a distorted picture of Christian ethics, in which one or more element of God's work will not be allowed to play its role. It is far better to keep all these aspects in play simultaneously.

Thus: God is the creator of the universe, so human beings do bear the mark of their maker and are drawn back to God in ways that feel almost instinctive or "natural." However, human beings are fallen creatures, unable to maintain the focus of intellect and will that would be necessary to conform their own lives to the character of God. They therefore need God's work of redemption—both the salvation of the world in the work of Christ, and the ultimate exemplar of good character that is provided by the person of Christ—in order that they might learn to set aside the obstacles that they have placed in the way of God's grace. But although God's work in the world is especially visible in one human (and divine) being at one particular moment of human history, that work continues across time and space: thus the importance of sanctification. This work includes the ongoing guidance of the Holy Spirit in the cultivation of the virtues, and particularly the virtue of practical wisdom, in the lives of human beings.

This trinitarian account of Christian ethics is reflected in the liturgy, particularly when the entire history of salvation is recapitulated in the form of the eucharistic prayer. Here, the entirety of God's relationship to the world is recounted: creation, fall, liberation from bondage, and the call of the prophets; the life, death, and resurrection of Jesus; the sending of the Spirit and the birth of the Church; and, looking forward to the future, the return of Christ and the consummation of the age. Without this holistic picture, something will be distorted; all these components of the God–world relationship need to be drawn together in a single narrative, in order to avoid lapsing into an oversimplified picture of that relationship—and with it, a distorted picture of the Christian faith and its ethical imperatives.

In this chapter, we have emphasized the role that God plays in the Christian understanding of the cultivation of the virtues. By focusing on both the human and the divine roles in this process, we are aiming at an account that supports the Christian claim that the virtues involve "the presence of God's gifts in the cultivation of good habits." In the next chapter, we will consider how those gifts take material form in the central Christian practice of the eucharist.

Questions for discussion

1. How do you understand "the character of God"? Based on your own background in Christianity (if any), as well as what you have learned about the faith from this textbook, try writing a short character sketch of God that might be used if, for example, God were appearing as a character in a play.

2. Using a Bible, and working in groups if possible, try to identify several passages in which God seems to offer some hints that might help us describe the divine character. Do these texts confirm, refute, or alter the character sketch that you developed in question 1?

3. Using a Christian prayer book or other worship resource, find an example of a eucharistic prayer (or similar liturgical text) other than the one included in this chapter. Try to identify the main sections of the prayer that are referred to in this chapter (declaration of God's holiness, remembrance of God's acts, calling upon God's presence). What further clues with respect to discerning the character of God are offered by the prayer that you examined?

4. How do you understand the concept of "natural law"? Do you think that there are laws that are more or less obvious to all people? Or does any understanding of law depend upon the authority of a particular lawgiver—whether that be God, the government, or an individual?

5. Describe your own understanding of the idea of "redemption." Is this a concept with which you were familiar before you read this section of the text? What had you heard about it, and how did this relate to what you read here?

6. How have you understood the role of the Holy Spirit in Christianity, or of an idea of "the Spirit" in some other expression of faith? Have you encountered examples of a too-exclusive focus on the Spirit that resonate with the description in this chapter? What do you see as the positive and negative features of an emphasis on the "spiritual" aspects of faith?

Sources cited in this chapter and/or recommended for further reading

Augustine, *Confessions*

William T. Cavanaugh, "Human Habit and Divine Action in Aquinas' Account of the Virtues"

David S. Cunningham, introduction to Part 2 in *These Three Are One: The Practice of Trinitarian Theology*

Richard Hays, *The Moral Vision of the New Testament*

L. Gregory Jones, *Transformed Judgment: Toward a Trinitarian Account of the Moral Life*

Nicholas Lash, *Believing Three Ways in One God: A Reading of the Apostles' Creed*

Bruce D. Marshall, *Trinity and Truth*

Oliver O'Donovan, *Resurrection and Moral Order: An Outline for Evangelical Ethics*

Oliver O'Donovan and June Lockwood O'Donovan, eds., *From Irenaeus to Grotius: A Sourcebook in Christian Political Thought*

Stephen Pope, "Reason and Natural Law," in Meilaender and Werpehowski, eds., *The Oxford Handbook of Theological Ethics*

St. Thomas Aquinas, *Summa Theologiae*, Ia–IIae.55.4

Paul Wadell, *Friendship and the Moral Life*; *The Primacy of Love: An Introduction to the Ethics of Thomas Aquinas*

*I*nterlude 2

"Those who sing well, pray twice"

Music as a Christian practice

One very important aspect of Christian worship has thus far made only a very limited appearance in this book: that of *music*. The notion that God might be praised with musical instruments and with song is of very ancient origin, with roots deep in the Jewish worship traditions from which Christianity took its bearings. Because of the deep and broad influence of Christianity in Europe through the Middle Ages and well into the modern era, a great deal of European music was composed for specifically Christian purposes: hymn tunes, together with a variety of arrangements and harmonizations of these tunes; settings of the mass or of particular worship services (such as the funeral requiem or the Passion); motets and anthems on a particular biblical or prayer-book text, for performance by a choir; and a wide range of incidental music for all kinds of religious occasions. This vast musical inheritance has both shaped, and been shaped by, the claims of Christian theology and ethics.

In this brief interlude, we have time and space for only the most cursory treatment of this phenomenon. But because music has been so influential in the Christian tradition, it seems very important to mention the most important ways that music contributes to the ethical formation of Christians.

The first of these is through hymnody and religious songs. When the narratives of the faith are set to music, they become easier to memorize and they therefore take a firmer hold on a person's psyche. Learning a spoken text by heart can take considerable time and many repetitions; but if the text follows a clearly defined meter (with a regular pattern of accented syllables across each line), the process can become much easier. (Many actors will testify that lines written in verse—or, like much of Shakespeare, in metrical prose—are much easier to memorize than are lines written in imitation of ordinary modern speech patterns.) If, in addition to being written with attention to poetic meter, the language is also set to music—well, this provides just one more element to aid the memory. Most people find that they can easily memorize all the words to a song or hymn just by listening to it a few times. Christianity has a long history of using songs and hymns, not only in worship services but as part of daily life. Many such hymns have endured over generations or even centuries; they have been carried along to new countries and new continents, and translated into multiple languages. Many people associate particular hymns with significant moments in their lives or with certain people who have meant a great deal to them. This is why, even though musical styles change over time and new church music is always being written, many people still find themselves drawn to hymns that have endured for many years. These hymns have helped to shape the moral and imaginative worlds of generations of Christians, and singing them today helps contemporary believers to participate in that same process of formation.

A second significant area is the setting of various verbal elements of the worship service to music. In its most basic form, this involves providing music for the six parts of the mass that are sung in response to the priest or other worship leader. We have made passing references to most of these six parts as we have moved through the liturgy, but it may be useful to point to them here, since their musical settings have had such a tremendous influence in western culture. They take their names from the initial Greek or Latin words in each part:

1. the *Kyrie eleison* ("Lord have mercy"), beginning the service with an invocation for God to be present and to be merciful on the worshipers;
2. the *Gloria* ("Glory"), a song of worship and praise;
3. the *Credo* ("I believe"), a recitation of the Nicene Creed (as discussed in chapter 6);
4. the *Sanctus* ("Holy"), together with
5. the *Benedictus* ("Blessed"), which begins the eucharistic prayer (as discussed in chapter 8); and finally
6. the *Agnus Dei* ("Lamb of God"), which accompanies the breaking of the bread and the distribution of the eucharistic elements to the congregation.

In traditional forms of the mass, these were the primary "responses" to the priest, who spoke (or sang) most of the remainder of the liturgy in a single voice. The musical setting of these responses made them memorable and beautiful, giving them a significance beyond their practical role. As is the case with hymns, setting the parts of the mass to music serves as an aid in their memorization and internalization; these texts, and the music that accompanies them, can thereby become part of the moral universe of many Christians, which in turn helps to shape their assumptions. When these texts are frequently on the minds and on the lips of believers, they begin to play a structuring role in their entire lives—uniting the narratives of the Christian faith with the practices of singing, worshiping, and rejoicing.

Some of these mass settings became sufficiently complex and multi-voiced that they were primarily sung by trained choirs; while this reduced the degree to which the music became a memory device for the congregational singer, it nevertheless tended to increase the sheer beauty of the music, so it became memorable and formative simply because of the aesthetic response that it evoked in the listener. Lyrics set to music often have this effect, particularly if we regard them as beautiful and hear them repeatedly. Many of the pop songs that we know so well contain lyrics that would not be memorable, and perhaps not even particularly meaningful, if we had not heard them repeatedly in the context of music. Thus, musical settings of these parts of the liturgy—whether designed to be sung by the congregation or by a choir—have had the effect of cementing these texts into the minds of those who hear and/or sing them regularly.

Music written for the worship service need not be in the form of a setting of the mass. As mentioned above, composers have also written anthems and motets, which set a particular text (often a text from the Bible or a prayer book) to music. Indeed, this practice expanded to the creation of an entire series of anthems that were held together by a common theme. Such pieces, often called *cantatas* or *oratorios*, were sometimes much too lengthy to be incorporated into a church service. (In fact, some of them were not composed for church services at all, but were designed to provide an upright religious purpose in response to public demand for vocal music. One of the most famous oratorios in English, Handel's *Messiah*, was written because the government had not allowed opera to be performed during Lent.)

In all these cases, however, what the composer seeks is a matching of musical rhythm, tone, and texture to the words that are sung, so that the music accents or reinforces the language. Two particularly well known and clear examples of this phenomenon may be mentioned here. In Johann Sebastian Bach's most famous setting of the mass (*The Mass in B Minor*), the section of the creed that narrates Jesus' crucifixion and death is slow, somber, and quiet. Then, at the words *et resurrexit* ("and rose again"), the music is loud, clear, and triumphant; a listener would certainly not need to understand the Latin words in order to know that a shift had taken place from death to life. Similarly, Franz Joseph Haydn's oratorio *The Creation* begins with a very slow section, marked *Largo*, in a frequently modulating C minor; the resulting musical texture matches the text, which describes the earth as "a formless void" in which "darkness covered the face of the deep" (Gen. 1:2). Then, at the words *Es werde Licht!* ("Let there be light"), the music shifts from C minor to the brightest C major *fortissimo* imaginable. Listening to the music, one can almost see the light bursting forth.

A third category is theologically inspired instrumental music. This is, I think, the most difficult for a non-specialist in music (like me) to understand; without the help of words, one must rely on one's knowledge of musical forms, their history, and the theory that undergirds them in order to take significant meaning from the music. On the other hand, most of us have "felt" something in certain forms of music that, while we may not be able to put it into words, still indicates that the music has conveyed something to us.

Here I will mention three composers whose music is often placed in this category, either because they declared that they wrote with specifically theological intentions in mind, or because their music has traditionally been interpreted through theological categories. The first of these is Johann Sebastian Bach, who also contributed a very large number of works in the two categories mentioned above (hymns and service music). He also wrote a series of *Three-Part Inventions*, in which three different tunes are placed in counterpoint with one another. Commentators have often remarked that these pieces provide interesting analogies to the Christian doctrine of the Trinity, in which each member has its own proper tune but in which all the aspects are held together in a coherent whole.

A second example is the twentieth-century French organist and composer Olivier Messiaen, whose works very often draw upon his own Roman Catholic faith in various ways. Messiaen was a deeply thoughtful composer with a great respect for the mystical traditions of Christianity; he also wrote at considerable length about the theological underpinnings of his own work, which often provide listeners—even non-specialists—considerable insight into their meaning. His *Quartet for the End of Time* was written in a Nazi prisoner-of-war camp where Messiaen was himself a prisoner. It is inspired by the Book of Revelation, and in particular the idea that "time shall be no more" (Rev. 10:6, KJV). Through its structures of rhythm and stillness, the piece explores the theological claim that time, like every other aspect of the world, is the creation of God; it came to be, and it will one day cease to be.

A final example is the composer and pianist Dave Brubeck, whose work brings together the classical musical forms and the rhythms, textures, and improvising style of American jazz. He has written cantatas and oratorios, and has also developed orchestral and improvisatory sections of these pieces into standalone jazz offerings. One such piece, "New Wine," comes from an orchestral section of an oratorio entitled *The Voice of the Holy Spirit*; it begins with a fast, sharply accented series of cadences that, for me at least, provide a detailed musical "picture" of the scene in Acts 2 when the Holy Spirit descends on the apostles, causing them to preach the gospel in many languages. (According to Acts 2:13, some onlookers sneer at them, remarking that "they are filled with new wine.") Another piece, "Lullaby," is an improvisatory section from Brubeck's Christmas cantata entitled *La Fiesta de la Posada*, and evokes (again, for me as a listener) a story that is told of a sixteenth-century Spanish monk known as St. John of the Cross. He was praying in the side chapel of a church which housed a life-size crèche scene (a set of sculptures depicting the infant Jesus lying in a manger just after his birth, surrounded by Mary, Joseph, and animals). Looking around and thinking that he was alone in the church, the monk gingerly lifted the statue of the infant Jesus into his arms and cradled it there, rocking it like a baby, singing a soft lullaby.

How much of my interpretation is due to the music itself, and how much results from my knowledge of other information such as the titles of the pieces, the biographies of the authors, and so on? This question is, of course, very difficult to answer. No one has yet provided a definitive account of precisely how music "works" to evoke in us memories, connections, and emotions. Perhaps this will always remain something of a mystery, but the fact remains that people find themselves deeply moved by music, and they often understand a strong connection between music and faith.

Sources cited in this interlude and/or recommended for further reading

Nicholas Adams, "Messiaen, Meaning, and the Transmission of Tradition"

St. Augustine of Hippo, *De Musica*

Johann Sebastian Bach, *Messe in h-moll (Mass in B Minor)*; *Three-Part Inventions*

Jeremy Begbie, *Theology, Music, and Time*

David S. Cunningham, "Polyphony," chapter 4 of *These Three Are One: The Practice of Trinitarian Theology*

The Dave Brubeck Orchestra, "New Wine" from *The Voice of the Holy Spirit*; "Lullaby" from *La Fiesta de la Posada* (both re-orchestrated and included in the album *New Wine*)

Franz Joseph Haydn, *Die Schöpfung*

Olivier Messiaen, *Quatuor pour la fin du temps*

Don Saliers and Emily Saliers, *A Song to Sing, a Life to Live: Reflections on Music as Spiritual Practice*

Brian Wren, *What Language Shall I Borrow?*

Nourishing
the body
Sacrifice, companionship,
and abundance

As philosophers and sages have noted throughout recorded history, human beings are interesting creatures. Creative, resourceful, and driven, they are capable of great accomplishments. They travel across such inhospitable spaces as deserts, seas, and the air; they exert mastery over species that are larger, and stronger, and swifter than themselves; they build towers that seem to scrape the sky. And yet, at the same time, human beings are biological organisms that are just as constrained by physical limitations as are animals, plants, and even rocks. We can't be in two places at one time; we cannot survive extremely adverse environmental conditions; and we depend upon a constant supply of food, water, and shelter in order to live.

Many religious faiths expend a great deal of energy trying to understand the special position of human beings, particularly with respect to their status or location as somewhere between the gods and the other animals. We share many of the intellectual and creative powers of God or the gods, but we lack the complete knowledge and power of such beings; we are smarter and more adaptable than other animals, but we seem to be just as dependent on our physical bodies as they are. The narratives that describe the origins of human beings—such as those found in the book of Genesis, shared by Christians and Jews—are examples of the effort to find a fitting place for humankind, in a special relationship to God but nevertheless to be found among the creatures, alongside animals, plants, and rocks.

In fact, this "both/and" character of human existence—resembling, in some ways, both God and the non-human animals—is part of what allows the discipline of *ethics* to arise in the first place. If we were truly gods, we would always know what to do; or, rather, our very actions would themselves define what would count as *good*. If we were identical to the other animals, we would act primarily from instinct; we would rarely face difficult decisions and we would not be in need of moral formation. Our free will and our intellect make us enough like God that we care about our decisions; but our physical limitations and our bodily appetites make us enough like the other animals to be aware that we are not completely the masters of our own destinies. Consequently, we are often on the lookout for ways of negotiating this peculiarly human state, in which we are (as a number of philosophers have emphasized) "neither beast nor God"—or perhaps, in another sense, we are equal measures of both.

The Christian faith has sought to negotiate the unique circumstances in which human beings find themselves by developing accounts of the ways in which humanity's connectedness to God intersects with its connectedness to the material realities of the creation. These "points of contact" may help us to understand the "both/and" quality of human beings: drawn to God at the level of the spirit and the intellect, but also drawn to the material world because of our physical bodies and our sensory desires. Because the discipline of ethics is concerned particularly with our location in this in-between space, the contours of Christian ethics are shaped in part by its understanding of that space—and in particular, by its understanding of the ways that the divine realm intersects with the material order.

For Christians, the most important form of this intersection is the *incarnation*—the claim that God took on flesh and dwelt in the material world, experiencing all of its glories and its sorrows. This degree of divine *involvement* in the material world makes Christianity a quite different kind of faith—different even from Judaism and Islam, two faiths to which it is very closely related. The Christian belief in the incarnation has two highly significant effects. First, it means that God and the created order are closer together than we might have imagined; thus the in-between space in which human beings dwell is perhaps not an isolated and lonely spot, but an exalted place in which communion with both God and the created order is possible. Second, the incarnation brings God's holiness into the created order, emphasizing its essential goodness and implicitly opposing any claim that the material world is fundamentally corrupt or corrupting. It is a reassertion of the claim, repeated on each day of the creation account in Genesis, that the created order is essentially *good*.

In addition to its claims about the incarnation, Christianity has a number of other ways of emphasizing the special status of human beings as related both to God and to creation. Among the most important of these are the rites and rituals that are known as *sacraments*. By examining these important practices and observing how they highlight the ways that God's action intersects with the created, material order, we will better understand the place of humanity in the midst of this intersection—and the role of ethics as a means of negotiating our way through that space.

Sacraments: visible words

The sacraments are visible signs of God's love and care; they are understood as indicators of just how dependent human beings are on God, and of God's willingness to enter into relationship with these peculiar creatures. The sacraments make use of physical, material realities—realities of which most human beings have at least some experience—to point toward the depth of God's care for the created order in general and for human beings in particular. They are often defined as "outward and visible signs of inward and spiritual grace"—grace being here understood in the sense of God's gifts of love and care to human beings. Because they point to physical material realities, the sacraments emphasize that the Christian faith is among the most *materialist* of all religious faiths. (Here, I use the word "materialist," not according to its common usage as "obsessed with the acquisition of goods," but rather as a way of affirming the importance and the essential goodness of the material order.) In spite of many claims to the contrary, Christianity does not concern the spirit alone, as though this could even be separated out from the bodily reality of human existence. Rather, Christianity is a faith that takes seriously the created material order as a gift from God that is declared to be good and to which human beings are inextricably bound. This positive account of the material order, and of its relationship both to God and to human beings, is underscored by the sacraments—since they stand at the intersection of the outward, visible, material world and the grace that God gives to human beings. According to the early Christian writer St. Augustine of Hippo, this point of intersection is given such clear and meaningful expression in the sacraments that they might well be called "visible words."

Of baths and meals

The sacraments make use of everyday, physical human activities—taking a bath, sharing a meal, falling in love—and invest these activities with a value and a significance that far outstrips their apparently mundane, ordinary status. We bathe in order to wash away the dirt from our bodies, to make ourselves clean, and to prepare ourselves properly for those who may enter into our physical presence. Christianity makes use of the familiarity of bathing in order to give extraordinary significance to the rite of baptism, by which new members are initiated into the faith. New Christians are symbolically washed in water as a means signifying God's desire to wash away the stain of sin, to symbolize the burial of their old life and their rising up into a new life with Christ, and to prepare them for reception among the members of the new community which they are joining. Of course, the actual rite of baptism is not a wordless affair; it includes many references to scripture, explanations of the ritual, and words spoken about, to, and by (or on behalf of) those being baptized. Consequently, the "signifying" nature of the rite is augmented by these verbal elements. But the spoken words alone would not be nearly as effective in pointing to the realities of forgiveness, incorporation, and death and resurrection if it were not for the everyday experience of *bathing*—which is referenced not just in words but by the actions associated with baptism. These actions, with their obvious associations to the taking of baths, are what give baptism its connection to daily life.

Nevertheless, because each Christian only experiences baptism once, it differs significantly from the ordinary experience of bathing, which is repeated throughout life. The situation is different with respect to the most regularly practiced Christian sacrament, which is known by many names: the eucharist, the Lord's Supper, communion, the mass, or the sacrament of the table. Just as baptism draws on the ordinary experience of bathing, so the eucharist draws on the ordinary experience of eating—together with everything that accompanies it: preparation, fellowship, and even the ritual of cleaning up the dishes afterwards.

The eucharistic rite is also closely connected to Jesus' last meal with his disciples—a matter that we will take up in more detail later in this chapter. Its origins in this "first eucharist" are made clear by the scriptural story that is usually told before, during, and after the event of eating. (For an example, see the eucharistic prayer reproduced in the previous chapter.) But even without this story to provide its context, the sacrament would function as a signifying event—a form of visible words—precisely because of its connection to the ordinary, universal, and frequently repeated experience of eating a meal together.

We will better understand the significance of the eucharist for Christianity, and for Christian ethics in particular, if we take a moment to consider the constituent parts of any meal that we share with others. The preparation process starts long before the meal takes place—not only with respect to the food itself (buying the ingredients, preparing them, cooking them, and so forth) but also with respect to the gathering for the meal: we plan ahead, we clear our calendars for the event, we dress for the occasion, and we arrive when expected. Often, we bring something along to the meal—a gift for the host, perhaps, or a contribution to the food; but even when this is not present, we offer ourselves. (Many a host, when asked by guests whether they can bring anything, will respond that "your presence is a gift in itself"—and this need not be a mere convention, for often the host is genuinely most grateful for the commitment of time and attention that is required simply to gather for a meal.)

The meal itself is an opportunity, not just to nourish ourselves physically, but to experience the very particular forms of fellowship and communion that accompany a meal eaten in common with other human beings. The very fact of physical appetite, common to all human beings, acts as a kind of "social leveler" at mealtime; and even though some people who gather may not be familiar with all the social customs and assumptions that surround eating in a particular culture, it is nevertheless the case that we all must eat; therefore, when we gather over a meal, we are reminded of just how very much we are like the person next to us, who must also eat. No surprise, then, that when universities or businesses or other organizations want to bring a group of diverse people together in order to make common cause and to agree upon a program for future action, they often plan that gathering around a meal.

The tradition of table-fellowship

In practically all human cultures and across the entire span of recorded history, the concept of "table-fellowship" has played a significant role in the formation and perpetuation of communities and cultures. Meals become an opportunity to celebrate our common humanity and to share the realization that, regardless of our social standing, professional class, income level, and so on, we all share the need to eat. As the community gathers around a common table, people who did not formerly know one another end up speaking with one another and perhaps becoming friends. Stories are told and ideas are exchanged. Sometimes this is done more formally, as when a single member of the group narrates a series of events for the benefit of all; at other times, a variety of smaller conversations break out around the table. In either case, the meal becomes an opportunity for the community to develop a clearer sense of its own identity as well as its diversity.

These elements of table-fellowship were particularly strong in the ancient near East—the culture into which Jesus was born. The Jewish people had developed a number of detailed rituals around mealtimes. In fact, one of their most significant and widely celebrated annual rituals was a meal: the Passover, which marked the Israelites' exodus out of their slavery in Egypt. The celebration of this feast is always accompanied by a narrative account of that great event, which gives deeper meaning and significance to the meal; however, many of its most basic symbolic elements lie close to the surface and connect it, in obvious ways, to all our experiences of eating. The

Passover feast was (and is) eaten in a hurry, for example, because the Israelites were told to leave Egypt with all deliberate speed. Anyone who has had to "squeeze in a meal" before some important event will immediately recognize the experience; and while the (perhaps more typical) experiences of conversation and leisure may be dramatically altered, a different set of realities emerge to build up the community: namely, the need for each participant to take part in the preparation, the eating, and the clean-up—so that everyone can get on to the event that lies ahead.

A meal is frequently the site of various kinds of expectations regarding behavior and disposition—all those elements that we frequently group together under the general heading of "manners." We often associate table manners with the extraordinarily stylized and refined functions of high society, in which everyone must learn which fork to use for which course, what to do with the table linens, and so forth. But table manners are not limited to these "refined" contexts; every culture and every setting carries with it certain expectations about how to behave at the table. This may involve eating with the hands (and, in some cultures, with the *correct* hand!), chewing loudly and energetically, or other behaviors that might seem completely *un*mannerly to those schooled in a different culture. In this broader sense, the word "manners" describes the communally-normed set of behaviors that are appropriate in a given setting, and common meals are one of the places where such behaviors are most frequently enacted, taught, and emulated.

Once the meal is finished, the process of cleaning up can also become a space for conversation, fellowship, and the cultivation of habits. Often a meal involves common serving dishes and utensils that have been used by everyone, so the process of clearing and cleaning often involves taking responsibility for items that were common to all or items that were primarily used by others. Some food may be stored away for later use, and dishes are cleaned and stored to be ready for the next meal. All these activities remind us that the meal is not just in the eating, but in the entire process—from preparation to putting away. This in turn helps us to understand that eating is not just as a means to a physiological end (that is, we need food to live, so we must eat), but as an end in itself: part of what it means to be a human being is to break bread together, to join with others in a time of companionship. In fact, although we rarely note this connection, our word "companion" is literally "one with whom we share bread" (from the Latin roots *com*, with, + *panis*, bread).

It must be observed, however, that ever fewer of our meals actually take the shape that I have described here. We purchase more food ready-made or at least ready-to-cook, or we pay for its preparation by others in a restaurant. We eat on the run, in our cars and on the train, without the presence of others with whom we are in relationship. We use disposable dishware and we throw away tremendous amounts of food, thereby eliminating the need to engage in any detailed rituals of clean-up. We have moved in this direction because of its convenience and our (perceived) shortage of time; but although we often feel some vague sense of disappointment about the demise of the home-cooked meal, we are rarely able to put our finger on precisely what has been lost in the process. If my description here is accurate, what has been lost includes communion and companionship, as well as opportunities to cultivate certain emotional and physical habits that were traditionally formed in us around the dinner table. While some of those lost opportunities can certainly be made up elsewhere in our lives, it is very difficult to replace the degree of focus, the regular rhythms, and the sheer amount of time that has, through most of human history, been involved in the preparation, partaking, and putting away of everything involved in sharing a meal together.

The eucharist as ultimate meal

In order to understand the relationship between eating a meal and partaking in the eucharist, we need to remind ourselves that, regardless of our experiences today, the culture in which the Christian faith had its origins was accustomed to meals that involved a tremendous expenditure of energy, a regular rhythm, and a significant time commitment. In such a cultural context, it should be no surprise that a ritual that closely resembled a communal meal became one of the most oft-repeated and time-consuming activities of the gathered community. In making this common meal a regularly practiced, repetitively structured, and fairly lengthy procedure, Christians were quite consciously imitating the significant role that the common meal played in the daily lives of most human beings. The frequency and regularity with which they participated in the eucharist reflected the regular rhythms of mealtimes; the presence of a group of people around a common table (and common serving utensils) called to mind the similar structure of a common meal. Like the Passover, this was a memorial meal, symbolizing and (in some sense) re-enacting Jesus' last supper with his disciples; thus the narrative of his life and death, and particularly of his institution of this particular sacrament, typically plays a prominent role in the rite. As I have already observed, however, the whole procedure would not have the deep symbolic significance that it has for us if it were not for the fact that we know something about sharing a meal together, and about everything that such an event entails.

One of the few aspects of the Christian eucharist that is not much like even the traditional version of the home-cooked common meal is the nature of the food on offer. Bread and wine hardly constitute a "meal" for most people in the West today, though these elements would have suggested something closer to a complete meal to the people of the ancient near East. On the other hand, they are quite basic elements; bread is one of the most common foodstuffs (and may be the only available food for people in much of the world); and wine is, for many cultures without ready access to clean water, the most basic drink. We still speak of bread as "the staff of life" and as a minimal description of what a human being needs in order to live. A minimal prisoner's diet consists of "bread and water," but only because we now think of drinkable water as readily available; in another age and culture, bread and wine would have been exactly what a prisoner would be allowed. Nor do these substances constitute a mere minimum, as though reflecting some kind of deprivation. However basic these foods might be, they can become—particularly when enjoyed in the presence of a dear companion—the most desirable and delectable forms of sustenance. There is a reason for that old clichéd adage in which the lover desires nothing more than "a loaf of bread, a jug of wine, and thou."

Those readers who have experienced a Christian eucharist will know that, in most cases, only a tiny quantity of bread and wine are on offer. This, too, is certainly different from a typical meal in contemporary Western culture—at least for most of us—and it certainly is not designed to evoke the same level of physical satisfaction (or, more likely in our context, that slightly overstuffed feeling) that we experience at the end of a well-prepared meal. The alteration of this one element is significant, because it points quite firmly to the fact that the eucharist is not merely "just another meal"; it certainly incorporates many of the elements of an ordinary meal, but it also has a significance that transcends those everyday events. By providing only a tiny portion of the essential mealtime elements of bread and wine, the eucharist focuses the believer's attention on the significance of the meal as a remembrance of Jesus' death, a community-strengthening act of fellowship among believers, and an empowering form of spiritual nourishment that strengthens them for the work that lies ahead.

Despite the difference in quantity of food, however, so many of the other elements of a communal meal are in place that the eucharist is bound to create some of the same resonances that are evoked in an everyday mealtime event with members of one's family or friends. The experience of participating in a common project (often involving shared labor), the breaking down of barriers that occurs when people eat together, and the experience of having someone else make abundant provision for one's most basic needs—these elements are present, whether the meal is a multi-course holiday meal at the house of a dear friend, or a eucharistic feast of bread and wine. And, as noted above, both experiences are deeply formative: they are given a particular shape by the presence of regular practices and descriptive narratives; they bring people together in an intimate relationship in the context of satisfying a basic bodily appetite; and they cultivate in their participants a wide range of physical, emotional, and spiritual habits. It should therefore not surprise us that Christians believed, from very early in the history of the faith, that the eucharist was extraordinarily important. It was the most significant opportunity to rehearse the narratives of the faith and to participate in its practices—thereby forming its participants in good habits that would bear fruit throughout their lives.

Eucharistic practices

What, precisely, are the practices into which Christians are habituated by their participation in the eucharist? This question has many possible answers—many more than I can offer here. But for the purposes of this chapter, I want to concentrate on three specific practices that are strongly associated with the eucharist. Part of my rationale for choosing these three is that they echo the habits that are formed around a common table at mealtime. My hope is that those readers who have little direct experience of the Christian eucharist will still recognize the significance of these particular habits, because they *will* have had the experience of other kinds of communal meals. The three habits that I have chosen are: intimate fellowship, bodily giving, and gracious reception. I will then conclude this chapter with a brief discussion of how all these habits are meant to cultivate the virtue of *joy*.

Intimate fellowship

When we eat together, we expose ourselves to one another in ways that are more intimate and more vulnerable than just about any other human act, with the possible exception of sex. When we sit down at a table with other people, many of our physical foibles are fully exposed and on display: any and all of our idiosyncracies—in our speech patterns, gestures, or ways of eating and drinking—cannot be hidden when we are sitting directly beside or across from another person at a meal. When we need something, we have to ask for it, thereby displaying our private desires to all—not to mention our facility (or lack thereof) in the local language. (All those who have eaten a communal meal in which they must speak something other than their native tongue will have experienced this; in such circumstances, our strong desire to have someone pass the salt or the butter often gets subordinated to the embarrassment that we would feel in not knowing how to ask for it.) In addition, when we have been served something we don't like, our choices are to eat it in disgust or to advertise our refusal to do so (since everyone at the table can clearly see what we leave on our plates).

The intimacy of a meal explains why we prefer it to take place with people whom we know well—and why, when we eat with strangers, they do not remain strangers for long. We learn things about others while eating with them; we also realize that they will learn something about us. We can sometimes put on a false personality at a meal, in order to prevent this kind of intimate knowing from taking place; but such work is exhausting and few people can maintain it over the long haul. Meals expose us to one another by bringing us into close proximity during a time when we are carrying out a basic physical necessity. One only need imagine the same kind of exposure during other bodily functions to recognize just how intimate an act a common meal can be.

The eucharist draws strangers together and reminds them that, though they are many, they are one body. They share a common story, engage in a variety of common practices, and come together for a common meal. In doing so, they are forced to recognize that the various barriers that society has constructed in order to separate them from one another—as well as the barriers that they have constructed themselves—have no ultimate significance. The eucharist allows for no retreat into a purely private space; it demands that people eat and drink in one another's presence. It thus demands that Christians become accustomed to the fact that they live in relation to God and to one another.

Recognizing the intimacy of their relationship with one another, Christians are formed in habits that lead them to see other human beings as not so very "other" after all. This is not to dissolve someone else's identity into one's own; it is, rather, to recognize that both oneself and another are members of the same body, and are therefore not so distinct from one another as might be imagined at first glance. No surprise that it was a Christian minister, a priest in the Church of England named John Donne, who wrote the poetic lines, "No man is an island, entire of itself"; he believed that human beings are so connected to one another that we even participate in one another's deaths: "Never send to know for whom the bell tolls; it tolls for thee."

Bodily giving

In order to eat a meal together, people must give of themselves. Someone has to grow or raise the plant or animal life for food, care for it and harvest it, and prepare it in ways that make it edible. People have to run the kitchen and set the table; they have to impose organization on the whole affair so that the meal comes off complete and on time. All of this requires those responsible for the meal to give of themselves: they offer the time, the energy, and the resources necessary to make it all happen. As I have already observed, the significance of this giving is not always clear to us at mealtimes these days, since we usually purchase our food and frequently pay for its preparation as well; but this, too, involves the giving of a gift. Those who pay for the food and its preparation must earn the money with which they do so, and this also requires time and energy and dedication to one's craft. Every time people gather together at a table, someone (and usually quite a few people) have given deeply and bodily of themselves in order for the meal to take place.

The giving of a gift is a complicated matter—much more complicated than it appears at first glance. Even the most selfless givers know that, by giving generously, they will probably be causing the recipients of the gift to feel a certain degree of obligation to the giver; that is, the recipients will want to give something in return. This is one of the things we love about the giving of gifts; it is contagious. But this is also one of its paradoxical flaws, because this imposed sense of obligation ends up making the gift into something more like an *exchange*. This is especially true in contemporary economic culture, where we expect and assume that everything has a price, and that everything that is given creates an expectation that something will be received in return. If we give a birthday present, we may well expect a present of similar significance in return, when the time comes; and even if we don't expect one, we are aware that the recipient is likely to feel a strong sense of obligation to give one. In fact, we sometimes hesitate to give gifts at all—or we limit the significance of the gifts that we give—not so much out of selfishness or a lack of generosity, but because we feel a certain anxiety that others will feel beholden to us.

Common meals can participate in this same paradoxical relationship: we invite others for a meal just for the pleasure of it, but find them asking what they can bring. If we invite someone several times in a row without receiving a reciprocal invitation in return, we assume that something may be wrong with the relationship, or else we receive an embarrassed explanation as to why such an invitation has not been forthcoming. Fortunately, however, this exchange-model understanding of meals has not completely infected the enterprise: within families and among some friends, a particular host can take on the work of offering the gift of a meal together without any expectation of exchange or return. Parents, for example, give the gift of a meal to their children, and spouses give that gift to one another, often without any expectation of return. Some may do so out of duty or under compulsion; but for most families, the gift of a good meal is a genuine pleasure to give. It is one way that we can offer our very selves to one another.

The Christian eucharist seeks to build on this idea of the meal as pure gift, and takes it one step further. It finds its source in Jesus' description of his own last supper as a gift, not so much of his time and energy in preparing the meal, but even more literally as a gift of his own self: his *body*. As the biblical narrative recounts the story, Jesus recognizes that he is about to be handed over to the political and religious officials of the day, and that he will be executed by the particularly gruesome form of capital punishment that was employed by the Roman rulers of Judea at the time. In the face of his imminent death, he describes the bread and wine that his friends are about to eat as his own body and blood. He is, quite literally, giving up his own body so that his followers may become his body in the world.

In the eucharist, therefore, Jesus becomes the model of bodily giving; he gives his time, his resources, and indeed his very life for the sake of others. From his actions, Christians learn to take up a similar posture of giving. In some cases, they may even seek to imitate Jesus in his death; but in any case, they at least seek to imitate him with respect to certain elements of his life: offering themselves up for the sake of others. Some Christians participate in this eucharistic giving in an explicit way in the rite itself: they bake the bread, prepare the table, or clean the linens afterwards; they accompany the event with their talents in music and singing; they help others (particularly their children and godchildren) to understand the significance of the sacrament and to participate in it properly (with "good manners"). But regardless of whether Christians give of themselves bodily in these ways, every participant in the eucharist participates in the gift of self. As I noted in chapter 7, at least one form of the traditional eucharistic rite includes words that make this bodily giving explicit: "We offer and present unto thee, O Lord, our selves, our souls and bodies, to be a reasonable, holy, and living sacrifice." In coming to the table together, Christians learn to give of themselves.

Gracious reception

If giving is difficult in our culture, receiving may be harder still. The giver of a gift experiences the various burdens concerning exchange and reciprocity that I outlined in the previous section; but the receiver of a gift experiences all these difficulties and more. In addition to feeling obligated by a sense of exchange, the receiver is in the socially less acceptable position of being in need, of lacking something that another person must supply. In a world in which "fending for oneself" and "pulling oneself up by one's bootstraps" are taken for granted as actions to be approved and emulated, the acceptance of a gift implies an inability or unwillingness to do these things, and an admission of dependence on others. Children are allowed to assume this posture of dependence, but adults (by and large) are not. Perhaps this is why the sheer pleasure of participating in a meal or attending a party, so evident in the faces of children, can sometimes evaporate among adults: we are all calculating how much this might have cost, and the degree to which we feel obligated to find a way to go about repaying it.

At its best, however, a common meal can provide a space where some of these concerns can, at least temporarily, be set aside—where the focus can be on the grace of receiving another's gift. In my own experience, this can be a difficult lesson to learn: the meal provided to me by a parent or a relative or a friend seems to be something to which I should contribute, actively, in all its stages: purchasing the ingredients, preparing the food, setting the table, washing up afterwards. But I can sometimes get so caught up in my felt need

---

Films and feasts

As many commentators have suggested, the genre of *film* can be very useful in learning about a particular faith, perspective, or worldview. A number of excellent films provide illustrations of various aspects of Christian belief and practice, even when their plots and characters are not explicitly Christian. In my experience, films are particularly useful in helping students think about the Christian sacraments, since these "outward and visible signs" are often already closely connected to some common human experience (such as eating or bathing).

Hence in any film in which meals are shared, and in which these events become opportunities for fellowship, giving, receiving, and joy, certain elements of the Christian eucharist may often come to mind. One of the best examples of this type of film is *Babette's Feast* (1987), in which a French woman's decision to spend her lottery winnings by preparing an extravagant meal for her Danish hosts becomes an opportunity to explore many of the elements of eucharistic practice that are mentioned in this chapter. Other recent films that raise these issues in a significant way include *Chocolat* (2000), *Waitress* (2007), and *Ratatouille* (2007).

A number of other films, while they do not focus on meals and table fellowship as a significant element of the plot, nevertheless include scenes of meals together—from simple fare to extravagant banquets—that can help illustrate the practices of giving, receiving, and fellowship. Here, a very long list of examples could be included; among recent films that seem particularly useful for this purpose are *Witness* (1985), *Under the Tuscan Sun* (2003), *A Good Year* (2006), *Sideways* (2004), and *Harry Potter and the Sorcerer's Stone* (2001).

to "give back" (sometimes even before the gift has been given to me!) that I don't actually allow the giver to be a giver. If the discussion in the previous section is correct—that is, if "bodily giving" is truly a virtue that human beings should cultivate and embody in their lives—then they need to allow space for others to give that gift. This means that they also need to be able to receive, graciously and thankfully, but without moving immediately to the exchange-oriented question of how much the gift cost and how one might go about repaying it.

The Christian eucharist embodies and cultivates this particular practice to a highly significant degree. While Christians are certainly called to imitate Jesus' act of giving, they are also called—more directly and obviously, in the way that the eucharist takes place—to be gracious *receivers* of Jesus' gift to them. Implicit in this idea is the claim that God gives freely, abundantly, and without counting the cost; by receiving the gift that is given, Christians testify to their own dependence on God's provision and their trust that they will continue to be sustained by this divine act of giving.

These latter two practices—of giving and receiving—are obviously dependent on one another: human beings are able to give only because they have first received (they have received the gifts of life, of nourishment and nurture by others, and of the sustenance of their lives by God). At the same time, their continued ability to receive a good gift is strengthened by the experience of giving: they learn how much it means to be able to give a good gift, and give it freely. They may therefore come to understand the importance of gracious reception as something that makes it possible for others to cultivate the virtue of generous giving.

Enduring joy

Allow me to offer a brief thought experiment. Imagine yourself sitting down to a good meal in the company of friends. Imagine either that you have prepared the feast yourself, or that you are simply receiving it as a gift of someone who cares deeply about you. Think about the conversation, the opportunity to catch your breath and catch up on one another's lives, the stories that will be told and retold about the genesis and nurture of these mutual friendships over time. The meal is not particularly elaborate or exotic, but it is good, nourishing food; and your favorite drink is being served as well. The room is warm and full of talk and laughter (and a few tears); the food is plentiful; the company is excellent.

For many people, a scene like this one is the very epitome of *happiness*. Recalling our discussion of that concept in chapter 7, we might say that a meal like this is a place where the two different concepts of happiness inter-sect: it is a moment of intense pleasure, but it is also an appropriate image of the deeper, broader happiness that Aristotle describes: a fulfilled and fulfilling life. (Even those words draw some of their power from their association with the idea of nourishment: a good meal, too, is "fulfilling" in several senses of the word.) No wonder that the Christian eucharist, modeled as it is on a fab-ulous meal, stands at the pinnacle of Christian practices; it is where Chris-tians believe they are most likely to find ways of cultivating good habits that will lead to true happiness and enduring joy.

Regardless of whether a good meal ranks very high on our individual lists of favorite things to do, the kind of scene that I have described above is one from which most of us would find it difficult to turn away. We would need to have a pretty good reason not to join in—and even then, we wouldn't feel particularly good about it. Obviously, not every mealtime gathering has all these warm, glowing elements surrounding it; in fact, for many people, a meal can be a source of tension, chastisement, and an utter *lack* of nourish-ment (physically, emotionally, or both). But at its best, a good meal like this can be one of the highlights of one's life. And just think—many of us already get to do it, or something like it, multiple times every day.

These are the elements of a common meal that the Christian eucharist seeks to capture and exemplify. This is a gathering of friends, with whom one is able to celebrate the best and most important things in life. The table is richly set; the decor is beautifully done; many hours of preparation have gone into readying the feast. People give of themselves and people receive these gifts gra-ciously. The old stories are told, the familiar food is enjoyed, and the experi-ence of fellowship is intense. It would be difficult to imagine a better example of "the good life"—unless, of course, one could imagine it lasting forever.

And perhaps it does. In their efforts to find ways of illustrating their belief in eternal life, Christians have often turned to the idea of a glorious meal—a "heavenly banquet"—as one of the best analogies for that experience of never-ending bliss. The communion, fellowship, and sheer joy that are gen-erated at such an event is about as close to heaven as we can imagine. Thus, by a second analogy, the eucharist is understood to be a foretaste of that end-less heavenly banquet of joy. Hence, the regular practice of the eucharist is one of the ways that Christians can allow themselves to be cultivated in good habits—virtues—that not only orient them toward a fulfilled and fulfilling life, but that ultimately point them toward that glorious vision of perfect and eternal communion with God and with other creatures. Some glimpse of that heavenly vision should be present in every eucharistic celebration: it should evoke the kinds of wonder, fulfillment, and joy that mark the best meal that a person can imagine.

The practices that accompany such a meal—practices of intimacy, of giving, and of receiving—are key elements of the practice of everyday life for Christians. By drawing on the ordinary experience of a meal, and by raising it up to special significance through its inclusion in the worship service, Christians accent its character as a *sacrament*: an outward and visible sign of God's gift of grace to human beings. Like the other major Christian sacrament of baptism, and like the other rites recognized by many denominations as sacraments (such as confirmation, marriage, ordination to the ministry, reconciliation, and anointing of the sick), the eucharist is a form of visible words which emphasizes God's active involvement with the material, created order. As such, it also reminds us that human beings are located at this same intersection: a place that is connected both to God and to the rest of creation, a place of both freedom and limitation, and therefore a place in which the discipline of ethics always demands our attention.

Questions for discussion

1. Do you think of human beings as occupying the kind of space described in this chapter—between God and the rest of the material order? Or do you see them as more like God (or "the gods"), more like the other animals, or something else altogether?

2. What experiences, if any, have you had of Christian sacraments? Have they functioned for you as "outward and visible signs of inward and spiritual grace," as the standard definition would have it? If not, what role have they played?

3. Describe your own experience of communal meals—the best and the worst. In your opinion, what contributes most significantly to a good meal? What factors can make it a bad experience? Do you think that contemporary mealtime practices have changed our general outlook on meals? Why or why not?

4. Discuss your experiences of giving and receiving gifts. Have you felt some of the difficulties described in this chapter (e.g., anxieties about the adequacy of a gift, a sense of obligation to return a gift, slipping into an exchange mentality)? What do you see as the primary obstacles that militate against gift-giving in our culture?

5. Consider the various ways that a common meal brings people into an intimate relationship with one another. What other cultural practices (either in

your own culture, or in others about which you have some knowledge) promote this kind of intimacy? Offer some kind of evaluation of these various practices: in each case, do you consider the practices that you have named to be a positive, negative, or neutral way of promoting closer relationships among human beings?

Sources cited in this chapter and/or recommended for further reading

St. Augustine of Hippo, *De doctrina Christiana (Teaching Christianity)*

Babette's Feast (Babettes gæstebud), dir. Gabriel Axel, 1987

Chocolat, dir. Lasse Hallström, 2000

David S. Cunningham, *Reading Is Believing: The Christian Faith through Literature and Film*

John Donne, *Meditation XVII*

Robert Jenson, *Visible Words: The Interpretation and Practice of Christian Sacraments*

Ratatouille, dir. Brad Bird and Jan Pinkava, 2007

Daniel Sack, *Whitebread Protestants: Food and Religion in American Culture*

Alexander Schmemann, *For the Life of the World: Sacraments and Orthodoxy*

Joel James Shuman, "Eating Together: Friendship and Homosexuality," in Hauerwas and Wells, eds., *The Blackwell Companion to Christian Ethics*

Bryan P. Stone, *Faith and Film: Theological Themes at the Cinema*

Waitress, dir. Adrienne Shelly, 2007

Stephen Webb, *Good Eating*

Samuel Wells, *God's Companions: Reimagining Christian Ethics*

10

Sent forth into the world
Taking character beyond the community

"Class dismissed!" At my elementary school, those words were always eagerly anticipated and offered a sense of freedom and release. Back then, heavy homework demands were rare and, however much one enjoyed one's school classroom, the end of the school day meant that it was time to play. Later on, other responsibilities tended to emerge; then, the dismissal from the classroom often meant that, while one form of work was ending, another form of work was about to begin. By the time we reach college or university, the classroom takes on a different role: although it may be a place where we are asked to concentrate our minds and focus on the subject at hand, we soon learn that most of the work—the reading and the essays and the lab assignments—will be done once we leave the relative comfort of the lecture hall or the seminar room.

Although the word "dismissal" may typically evoke the idea of something coming to an end, its root is actually in the Latin word *missio*, which means "to send forth" (compare the English word "mission"). A dismissal is an ending of sorts, but also a beginning; to dismiss a person or a group of people is not only, or at least not always, to ask them simply to leave their present circumstances; it also involves sending them out into a new set of circumstances. Like the word "commencement," which (in the American context, at least) is used to describe the ceremony at which students receive their degrees from a school or university, it is both an ending and a beginning: a transition from one stage to another. The word "dismissal" thus bears certain similarities to the word "end," as it is used in the subtitle of this book: to speak of Christian ethics as "the end of the law" is both an endpoint—in the sense of a previous dispensation coming to an end—and also a beginning, in that an end is also a goal: it may well demand a new direction and a new purpose.

Dismissal: the "end" of the service

I offer these musings on the significance of the word "dismissal" because it is the name for the concluding rite of the traditional Christian service of worship. The assembled congregation is "dismissed" with words that indicate not only that the worship service has ended, but also that a new "mission" is beginning. A typical form of the dismissal might be, "Go into the world in peace" or "Let us go forth to love and serve the Lord." As in the case where a schoolteacher dismisses the classroom, two things are being said at once: this part is over, and something else—something different but of similar, or perhaps even greater, significance—is about to begin.

We have reached a parallel point in the course of this book. We have examined the narratives and practices that constitute the Christian faith, and we have introduced the excellences of character—the virtues—that constitute the Christian life. Within the tightly compressed space of Christian worship, the significance of these matters is fairly obvious, and they are reinforced by the very specific practices that we described over the course of the last five chapters: professing the faith, confessing and receiving absolution for one's sins, bringing about reconciliation and peace, offering one's self, calling upon God, and being nourished with an abundant gift. But however meaningful these practices and their associated virtues may appear within the context of the worship service, they can sometimes become much more diffuse once Christians leave the relatively safe confines of the Church and encounter the people with whom they live the rest of their lives. This is not to say that such narratives and practices are absent; to the contrary, they would hardly be morally formative influences at all if they were only experienced and performed for one hour each week. Nevertheless, in the broader setting, the contextual clues of the worship service are not present in as concentrated a form. Moreover, in this new environment, Christian narratives and practices will come into direct contact with other narratives and practices that form people in different kinds of habits and according to a different set, or at least a differently defined set, of virtues.

Thus, Christians are likely to discover vast differences in moral formation among those with whom they will, during the course of a typical week, find themselves living, working, and playing. If we think back to the introduction of this book and our discussion of the "thin line" that separates human beings who hold very different moral viewpoints, we will have a fairly good sense of what is at stake when Christians leave the relatively structured space and time of the worship service and go out into the world. There they will work and live and regather alongside people who may have no knowledge of or interest in the specifically Christian forms of moral formation which the worship service has sought to reinforce. Co-workers, neighbors, and fellow participants in all sorts of activities will belong to a great variety of gathering communities, each with its own allegiances and assumptions, its own stories and practices. These features may underwrite a very different process of moral formation than that experienced by Christians. Or, people may find themselves in conversation with people who adhere to the same faith tradition but who have been formed in very different communities; they may therefore find themselves in deep disagreement about specific moral issues. What happens now?

Competing virtues; competing definitions

As we noted in chapters 7 and 8, the virtues are useful descriptive terms, but they have no real meaning until we understand them in the context of the specific narratives and practices of a particular community. The words that we use to name particular virtues may win general agreement, but they remain "hollow" until we fill them out with concrete content; and this can only be done against the backdrop of a set of stories that people live by and practices in which they are habitually engaged.

So, for example, a great many people of diverse backgrounds and circumstances might be able to come to some general agreement about the meaning of the virtue of generosity; if nothing else, they would probably be able to point to a dictionary definition of the term. But such a definition means very little without concrete cases to give it specificity. Do we measure generosity by the sheer quantity of cash or property that someone is willing to give away to others? A quick glance at the news media would suggest that this is, indeed, a significant factor, since gifts that are measured in the millions and billions tend to attract our attention much more readily than those measured in tens and twenties. But some of the narratives of Christianity suggest that the specific amount of one's gift is less important than the *proportion* of one's possessions that one gives (the story of the widow's copper coins, Mark 12:41–44 // Luke 21:1–4), or what one is willing to give up in order to give to others (the story of the wealthy young man, Matt. 19:16–22 // Mark 10:17–22 // Luke 18:18–23), or the *spirit* in which the gift is given (the teaching about gifts, Matt. 5:23–24). Similarly, the practices that we discussed over the last few chapters—confessing one's sins, promoting reconciliation, offering one's self to God, receiving the gift of the eucharist—might shape people to understand the virtue of generosity in very specific ways that may not be shared by those for whom these particular narratives and practices are not part of the ordinary routine.

Because of the many competing sets of narratives and practices that one will encounter in this life, most people find navigating the moral life to be a fairly challenging enterprise. Members of a particular faith community quickly realize that not everyone whom they encounter will have been formed in an identical set of narratives and practices; consequently, they will be likely to have differing assumptions about at least some of the excellences of character that one should cultivate and, therefore, about the proper shape of the moral life.

These differing moral perspectives are part and parcel of the kind of lives we live in the present age: we are highly mobile, are members of a variety of formative communities, and are increasingly aware of the sheer variety of such communities that exist in various parts of the world. In an era in which people rarely traveled far from home and spent most of their lives in a single community (in which religious life, work life, and domestic life were all a part of one another), a fair degree of moral continuity could be assumed. Today, we very rarely find widespread moral agreement across the diverse modes of formation in a mixed society.

This realization sometimes comes as a surprise, and even as a kind of disappointment, to students of ethics. The goal of this discipline (so one might imagine) should be for people to come to broad agreement on significant moral issues. And in fact, one of the goals of the Enlightenment project was precisely to lay a solid foundation for ethics that could win universal, or at least widespread, approval—and to do so without relying on the structures of the (distinctly non-universal) assumptions of a particular church, the nation-state, or some other societal structure. As as we noted in chapter 1, Immanuel Kant sought to develop some kind of philosophical basis for ethics, so that it would not be subject to the whim of a particular community. In a different key, Jeremy Bentham and John Stuart Mill urged people to evaluate the *outcomes* of their decisions in terms of the "greatest good for the greatest number"—in an effort to provide some kind of standard to which all people could subscribe, regardless of their faith commitments and their allegiances to particular communities. These standards were meant to provide a way for all people to judge the relative merits of moral judgment and action—and thereby to come to some agreement on the vexed question of how one should live.

In contrast to the Enlightenment project, the perspective put forth in this book is that ethics depends upon the morally formative structures of particular communities, which help their members develop excellences of character through their habits of telling stories and engaging in common practices. This means, as a necessary corollary, that we must give up the quixotic search for a universal system of morality (and I say this in spite of my appreciation for Don Quixote). We will attain a universal understanding of morality only when we develop a general agreement about what makes for good character, and when we agree on the definitions of these virtues through the acceptance of a common set of narratives and practices. Since this seems an unlikely prospect (at least in the near future), we should probably try to find ways to live within a diverse moral universe.

Why isn't this relativism?

Back in chapter 2, when we first began to explore the moral community as the place where we discover "who we are and whose we are," we observed that this perspective could engender a fair bit of anxiety—since it raises questions about the fixed and permanent quality of moral norms. Some people worry that this perspective makes all moral judgment relative—and so they label it with the term "moral relativism." Here, we need to return to that point and face it head-on.

Because of the fact that every community, people, tribe, and nation will have its own table of the virtues and its own narratives and practices, every group will have its own ethic. Consequently, some critics argue, there will be no good reason for preferring one version over another. All forms of morality (so the critics continue) become relative: the "good" is defined as "what is good for me" or "what is good according to my community," which is tantamount to letting people do anything they want to do.

Although this argument is highly persuasive to many observers, it has a number of significant flaws. These flaws have been alluded to, from time to time, throughout this book; but at this point, we are in a position to examine them more closely. First, this critique is dependent upon at least some residual form of the Enlightenment project; but those who engaged in that project (including Kant and the utilitarians) were never able to find a rational or objective basis for moral norms that could be agreed upon by "all rational men" (and they really did mean *men*). In spite of (what they believed to be) the considerable persuasive appeal of their theories, human beings continued to act in ways that, even though they considered them to be perfectly morally justifiable, other human beings regarded as outrageous offenses. And this occurred even in places like northern Europe, where various peoples, tribes, and nations at least shared a fair bit of common history and culture. Even less successful were those efforts to imagine an objective basis for ethics in a form that would cut across all cultural difference, such that (for example) a Western nation like Great Britain or the United States could venture into a non-Western region like Mesopotamia and expect to find, or to engender, substantive moral agreement.

But the flaws inherent in this charge of "moral relativism" are much deeper; it is not merely that no one has yet developed a successful alternative. The logical gap in the critics' argument is the move from "every community has its own ethic" to "no ethic is any better than another." It may be the case that gathered communities develop their own account of the virtues, based on their narratives and practices. It does not follow, however, that all such communities are "equal" with regard to their morality. We make this assumption because we are schooled in the traditions of liberal democracy, in which we are taught to treat the members of all communities as equal under the law—and this is indeed a good thing to do. But although all communities are equal under the law, they are not equal under ethics. Some ethical frameworks really are better than others.

What worries our hypothetical critic, however—and what worried Kant, Mill, and Bentham, as well as some advocates of a "natural law" position—was that no one would be able to *prove* that one community's ethic was morally superior to another's. And on this point, the critical commentators are absolutely correct. There is no "neutral ground" that we can inhabit, as observers, and that can enable us to make an "objective" judgment about the superiority or inferiority of a particular ethic. This would be similar to a situation in which, with two nations at war against each other, the representatives of one nation are asked to step outside the war into a supposedly neutral space and to make an objective judgment about which side is right. Of course, each nation will see itself as in the morally superior position; this is why they are both fighting the war. Nothing that one side can do will convince its opponents that they are in the wrong. In many cases, even winning the war won't do that; defeated nations and peoples have often continued to believe in the moral superiority of their cause, despite being on the losing side. If the physical destruction and emotional devastation of losing a war cannot convince people that they were wrong, neither will a rational claim about duty, or a supposedly neutral calculus of outcomes, or an appeal to natural law.

What, then, is the alternative? If some communities are morally superior to others, but have no way of proving it, what can they do? Should they just abide in their own moral universe, assured that they are on the right track, but separating themselves from others so that their moral structures are not corrupted by external influences? This is certainly one option, though it has not been all that common through history—primarily because most such communities believe strongly enough in their own ethical framework that they want others to participate in it as well. How do they bring about such a result? Of course, one thing that they can and have done throughout history is to impose moral structures on other communities by force. On occasion, this has even been undertaken through some kind of direct military action—though typically, this kind of "morality imposed by the barrel of a gun" can only be maintained for a relatively short period of time. More frequently, moral structures are imposed by means of the strict enforcement of certain laws, or even simply by exercising a sufficient degree of control over the means of mass communication. Consider, for example, the kind of police state that is described in George Orwell's novel *1984*: here, the population is brought into conformity with a single, universal moral code, not so much by the use of military or police action (although this is employed at key moments), but through a network of communication that strongly encourages all people to agree with, and eventually even persuades them to love, the authorities who control them.

Clearly, however, coercive force is not the only possible approach; we know this, because many communities have managed to convince others of the superiority of their moral claims even though they have no military, no power to legislate or to enforce their laws, and no control over the means of communication. They have instead made their case through *persuasion*: they have used thoughts, words, and deeds to show forth the moral superiority of their understanding of the virtues. In fact, through much of Christian history, this has been the *only* way that Christians have convinced others of the positive value of their ethical claims. As we noted in chapter 6, the earliest Christians were deeply committed to nonviolence; thus any strategy that involved imposing a particular moral perspective by force was not really an option. Moreover, at many times and places in Christian history, views about violence were irrelevant, since Christians had no power to coerce others (by force, law, or censorship). Nor did they imagine, at least before the Enlightenment, that they could appeal to one set of arguments to which all rational people would instantly give their assent (though some thinkers in the Middle Ages came fairly close to this position). Through most of Christian history, theologians and ethicists realized that they simply had to *make their case*: by thinking it through with care, by arguing for it with gusto, and by embodying their convictions in such a way that their entire lives became a living, breathing testimony to their moral claims.

Thus when we observe that the specification of the virtues depends upon the narratives and practices of a particular community, and that the acceptance of these virtues will not be automatic and obvious outside that community, we are not lapsing into moral relativism. That would be true only if we added that it really didn't matter to which community one belonged—that each one is just as good as the next. And in fact, this is a belief that almost no one holds. Many people will begin to argue for such a position—claiming, for example, that one nation is just as morally justified (and as morally culpable) as the next, or that one religion is as good as another, or that one political party is just as good as another. But those who venture down this path soon step away from it, because they will not usually argue, for example, that in Germany

SENT FORTH INTO THE WORLD 215

in 1940, being a Nazi was just as good as being a pacifist, or that in South Africa, being a member of a church that supported apartheid was just as good as being a member of one that advocated racial equality. Very few people actually embrace anything remotely resembling an absolute moral relativism.

So although one community cannot prove its ethic to be superior to another, and although it should not attempt to *force* that ethic onto another group, it can (and should) believe in the rightness of its claims. This is not to say that it should never try to learn anything from other communities; as we have noted, communities need to be open to the criticisms of outsiders so that they do not turn in on themselves and distort even their own best virtues into vices. (In chapter 3, we noted that a community's stories need to provide ways for it to incorporate those who are not yet members; in chapter 9, we observed how a common meal can bring strangers into relationship with one another.) Nevertheless, part of what it means to be a gathered community is to have the courage of one's convictions, and to be able to think about, argue for, and act on one's beliefs in such a way that others—even those outside the community—can recognize that community's virtues.

Completion and purpose

We began this section with a description of the dismissal that closes the typical Christian worship service, noting that it is both an act of completion and a pointer toward something new. The dismissal is the "end" of the service, with the same range of meanings that allowed Paul to describe Christ as "the end of the law." The congregation is sent forth because the worship service is over, but also because a new mission is beginning: they are asked to go out into the world. In doing so, they will fulfill one of the primary purposes of the worship service—namely, to carry the moral formation that they have received, in this time of deep communion with other members of the community, out into an environment in which not all people will be similarly formed. This is done in the hope that those who are sent forth will be, to use a biblical metaphor (Luke 13:21, 1 Cor. 5:6, Gal. 5:9), like *yeast*. Their presence in the world will not remain isolated and without effect on others, but, like a small measure of yeast that leavens an entire batch of dough, they will have an effect throughout the whole.

One of the most frequently misunderstood aspects of the approach to ethics that I am advocating in this book is that it is tantamount to a withdrawal from the world. Because the community's ethical perspective will not automatically be shared by others, its advocates are sometimes labeled "sectarian" and considered to be largely uninterested in what goes on in the rest of the moral universe. But this criticism clearly misses the mark, and an adequate understanding of the dismissal should make this plain. If the worship service ended with the phrase "Now do not go forth, but stay within these walls" or "Now go forth, but avoid anyone who is not part of our community," then these critics would have a point. But in fact, the Christian worship services ends not only with an encouragement, but also with a command, that the congregation go out into the world, where they will encounter others who have experienced differing forms of moral formation. The point is not to withdraw from the world as a separate entity, but to allow the very particular kinds of moral formation that take place within the community to remain with the worshipers as they go forth. As a result, they will have an influence on the wider world—though perhaps not always in ways that are completely obvious, and certainly not in ways that can be measured by some supposedly neutral, universalistic account of the moral life.

As I have already suggested, whatever influence Christians may have on the rest of the world needs to take the form of persuasion, rather than of coercion. Nor can Christians (nor, for that matter, the members of any morally formative community) rely only on arguments that proceed on the basis of logical deduction from some set of general principles. Rather, since not everyone they encounter will agree on those principles, they will have to rely, not on logic and analytic argument alone, but on a wider variety of rhetorical techniques. In fact, such persuasion may be most successful when it takes the form of quiet witness—merely living in a certain way, in the belief that one's way of life will be sufficiently appealing to attract interest. (One ancient writer, Tertullian, remarked on the way that non-Christians were sometimes attracted to the faith simply by observing how believers behaved; they remarked, "Look how these Christians love each other!") And, to take this idea of "quiet witness" one step further, we can imagine that moral formation might be *most* likely to spread beyond the confines of a particular gathering community when those who are formed by that community establish *friendships* with those who are not. The importance of friendship for the moral life has been recognized by many commentators, going at least as far back as Aristotle; thus it deserves our attention here.

The role of friendship

Aristotle regarded friendship as essential for a life of happiness, of *eudaimonia*. Again, his evidence for this was primarily empirical: he saw that the people who seemed to have a happy life—a fulfilled and fulfilling life—were those who had friends. But he also saw friendship as playing an important role in building up a life of virtue. This is because we often come to understand the significance of a particular excellence of character by seeing how it is borne in the life of another person; in other words, we look for exemplars and role-models. Of course, any human being whose life we can observe can be a kind of role-model, but a friend can do something more: friends can have a mutually upbuilding effect *on one another*, each providing both an example and a form of encouragement to the other.

Aristotle differentiated three forms of friendship. First, one can develop friendships for their *usefulness*; a business associate who helps us move up the corporate ladder, or a romantic attachment that I develop primarily because I think that my beloved's popularity will make me more popular as well—these are classic cases of the "useful" friend. Second, one can seek friendship for pleasure: we enjoy our friends' company and feel better when we are in their presence. People who can make others laugh often find themselves with a great many of this kind of friend, for many people take pleasure in those who know how to make a good joke. Both of these types of friendships can be mutual; friends can be useful to one another or take pleasure in one another. Aristotle does not condemn either of these forms of friendship; but at the same time, he believes that they are imperfect forms.

The truest form of friendship—which Aristotle calls "perfect" friendship, or a friendship of virtue—is that in which each friend seeks the good of the other, and is made a better person through the friendship. Such friendships might also be useful or pleasurable, but these aspects are incidental to their true nature; they are identified by the fact that "perfect" friends build each other up in virtue. For this reason, Aristotle believes, such friends must both be good people, and must be similar to one another—or at least, they must eventually *become* similar in their participation in virtue, even if their friendship starts out with certain differences. Ultimately, says Aristotle, "a friend is another self."

A number of Christian theologians have considered Aristotle's account of friendship at length, and have found it to have, with minor modifications, some very important implications for Christian ethics. Some of these implications are simply an application of Aristotle's more general principles to the specifically Christian context. For example, since Christians (like anyone pursuing a life of virtue) need exemplars and role models, friends can provide this; they can also help build one another up toward a good and fulfilled life. But other aspects of Aristotle's account take on new significance when applied to Christian ethics in particular.

The first of these is that Christians are called to be friends, not just of other human beings, but also to be *friends of God*. They believe this to be possible because of God's own decision to take on human flesh and to live alongside other human beings. Jesus of Nazareth is portrayed as becoming friends with a wide variety of people, including a great many whom society had marginalized in one way or another. In his farewell discourse, Jesus makes a point of referring to his followers as his friends:

> This is my commandment, that you love one another as I have loved you. No one has greater love than this, to lay down one's life for one's friends. You are my friends if you do what I command you. I do not call you servants any longer, because the servant does not know what the master is doing; but I have called you friends, because I have made known to you everything that I have heard from my Father (John 15:12–15).

Through their friendship with Jesus, Christians become friends with God. And although this friendship cannot quite meet Aristotle's test of "perfect friendship" (since it is not among equals, and since it is not perfectly mutual—God does not need to be "built up in virtue"), it does cast a whole new light on the significance of Jesus as a moral exemplar. If he is not simply a distant model to be imitated, but a friend with whom we can have a morally formative relationship, his significance for ethics becomes more pronounced.

Second—and this involves some amendment of Aristotle's account—theologians have tended to argue that a Christian account of friendship would have to allow for the possibility of friendship among those who are not particularly similar to one another (at least in the ways that Aristotle would have recognized). This is because the narratives and practices of Christianity often emphasize the importance of embracing others who are different, as well as those who are similar to us. Aristotle's strong and stereotyped notions of (what we would today call) race, sex, and social class made it difficult for him to imagine that perfect friendships could exist across such divisions. But Christianity claims that the faith that is shared by all believers actually outranks these other divisions and indeed renders them irrelevant. As Paul puts it, "There is no longer Jew or Greek, there is no longer slave or free, there is no longer male and female; for all of you are one in Christ Jesus" (Gal. 3:28). Although Christian practice over time has obviously not always adhered to its own best insights in this regard, the faith does seek, at its core, to relativize the categories of race, sex, and class that loomed so large in the ancient world (and today). These categories are understood to have been superseded by the unity of all believers through their faith in Christ. This means that people whom Aristotle would have clearly regarded as quite dissimilar, and therefore not capable of perfect friendship, are—according to the Christian account—not only quite capable of it, but called to it. Their unity in Christ is sufficient to bring them into such a state of friendship, even if other factors would appear, on the surface, to make it more difficult.

A final distinctive feature of friendship within the Christian ethical tradition concerns the topic that we have been discussing in this chapter: namely, what happens when Christians go forth from their gathered communities and encounter others in the world who do not share their same assumptions about narratives, practices, and virtues. When people of two different morally formative communities become friends, they will clearly not share identical definitions of the excellences of character. But through their friendship, they may come to a clearer understanding of one another's perspectives, and may help to build one another up into the life of virtue. Of course, there would always be some question as to the degree to which each person could maintain such a friendship and still remain a member of their own morally formative communities. But if Christians are adequately convinced of the essential rightness of their own moral perspective, they should also be confident about becoming friends with others—knowing that the tendency among friends to build one another up in the moral life will ultimately make a positive difference.

Examining the virtues in practice

Our task for the remainder of this book is to consider how the Christian virtues might shape a person's everyday life, even when Christian narratives and practices must be in conversation with the narratives and practices of other traditions and communities. Therefore, in Part 3, we will focus on various spheres of human action that Christians are likely to encounter. Here, we move out beyond the Christian worship service to examine how the excellences of character that are developed in the very specific context of Christian storytelling and communal practices might be brought to bear on matters that are faced by Christians and non-Christians alike. While one might conceivably propose a very long list of such matters within various aspects of human life, I have chosen to concentrate on five specific spheres of human action that seem to me to give us particularly significant scope for exploration. They also happen to be spheres of action in which questions about good and evil, right judgment, and moral action are very frequently raised: spheres in which we often find ourselves asking the question, "how ought one to live?" These five spheres of action focus on work, the government, medicine, sex, and the environment.

Staying out of the lifeboat

Before we enter into this next part of the book, however, we need to observe one important caution. From very early on, we have criticized the commonly-held idea of "lifeboat ethics," in which the entire enterprise of moral reflection is primarily defined as addressing difficult issues about hard cases. As we turn to particular issues in spheres of life such as medicine, politics, and the environment, we will be sorely tempted to get back into the lifeboat: that is, to focus on difficult dilemmas in which we seem to be presented with only two paths, and where matters of life and death seem to hang in the balance. It would be very easy, in such circumstances, to reduce the entire discussion of ethics thus far to a focus on a few specific cases—particularly since this is precisely how "ethical issues" are raised in popular culture and the media.

If, however, ethics is primarily about excellences of character that are developed through habits that are formed in particular communities—as we have been suggesting throughout this book—then our examination of specific spheres of life will need to be informed primarily by a discussion of virtues, rather than by a set of principles or rules that might be applied in a series of difficult cases. While we may be able to make some generalized judgments about how the virtues would inform particular decisions, we will need to realize that most such discussions will be for illustrative purposes only. The specific circumstances that the moral actor will face cannot be perfectly foreseen, and thus neither can we know exactly how an accounting of the virtues will apply to that case. Like improvisational actors who must develop a certain repertoire of habits and then be willing to make a decision in the moment, so must moral actors rely upon their habits—that is, their formation in specific virtues—in order to address whatever circumstances may eventually arise.

Since time and space will prevent us from elaborating on every possible virtue that could be associated with a particular sphere of influence in the following five chapters, I have chosen three virtues for each. I hope that this will be sufficient to illustrate the kind of moral reasoning that allows us to move from the more abstract language of the virtues to the more concrete questions that we face within these various spheres of life. In adopting this approach, I would like to believe that I am not too far from Jesus' practice when he was asked a specific ethical question: he rarely gave a straightforward answer that indicated precisely what the questioner should do; for this would be simply to reiterate the law that he himself had come in order to fulfill. Instead, he often asked a question in reply, or reflected on the dispositions of those who were asking, or—most frequently of all—told a story. I believe that, by addressing concrete cases in the same slightly elliptical way, we allow space for the ambiguity of the enterprise, and thereby avoid the kinds of abject legalism in which Christian ethics has sometimes found itself entangled.

What to expect

The structure of this last section of the book follows the days of the week. We have thus far focused on the Christian worship service, so let our musings thus far stand for Sunday. We will now turn, day by day, to the days of the week that follows. Each day of the week will point us toward a particular sphere of action and influence; and each sphere of action will serve as an opportunity to explore three of the virtues that have been described over the past several chapters.

Of course, the assignment of certain "spheres of life" to the days of the week is a largely arbitrary convention. This will be obvious in some cases more than others—we deal with medical ethics on "Thursday" only because it doesn't fit anywhere else—but in every case, the association is merely for convenience. Obviously, the point is not that we spend one day each week in a different sphere of influence; quite the contrary. But the structure is useful as a reminder that, as we move through the rhythms of our lives (which, for most of us, includes weekdays and weekends), we move from one sphere of human action to another. We do not face these issues only in isolated moments of crisis; we face them every week (and probably, in some form, every day). I hope that the structure of chapters as "days" can help remind us of this fact.

So: first, on Monday, we will do what most people in the industrialized West do on Monday: they go back to work. Our focus in this first chapter will be on the kinds of questions that arise for us in the midst of our paid employment. This will in turn raise larger questions about the economic order under which we live—a matter that we have mentioned in passing at several points in this book. In this chapter, our reflections on the economy will make use of the cardinal virtue of justice, the trinitarian virtue of particularity, and the fruit of the spirit known as "self-control" (related to the cardinal virtue of temperance) as three dispositions that seem particularly important within the structures of our working lives and in our dealings with the economic sphere more generally.

On Tuesday, we will go "to the ballot box." (Here my status as a US citizen is all too apparent; most of the rest of the world votes on Saturday or Sunday, but in the United States we have a long tradition of holding elections on Tuesdays.) Regardless of what day of the week we might use, however, our focus will be the same: what is the relationship between the excellences of character that Christians seek to cultivate and the governmental structures under which they live? Here we will explore the role of the fruits of the Spirit called faithfulness and peaceableness, as well as the cardinal virtue of courage. What do these Christian virtues mean in the context of the modern nation-state?

In a brief interlude, Wednesday will take us "back to Church." In fact, many

Christian communities do set aside one night a week (in the United States it is often a Wednesday) in which church activities are the primary focus. Although most churches struggle to get a significant number of their members back to church between each week's Sunday services, many Christians do consider this additional point of contact with their communities to be of great significance. We will explore why this is so, and consider how the focus of that mid-week gathering can extend into other spheres of life as well.

By the time we reach chapter 13, we will have arrived at Thursday; and as noted above, for no particular reason (other than the fact that we have an open day), we'll spend it "at the hospital." Here, our sphere of influence is that which we encounter at the margins of life: in birth and in death, in illness and suffering. While most of us do not spend an inordinate amount of our lives in these conditions (or even tending to loved ones who are in these conditions), we do find such encounters to be highly significant. Questions about right and wrong action tend to arise quite dramatically in such circumstances—disproportionately so, compared to the other spheres of action that take up a great deal more time in our lives. Here we will use the virtues of patience, practical wisdom, and faith as our keynotes.

On Friday, we'll go "out on the town," and consider the complexity of our romantic and sexual relationships. While these matters tend to be kept very private in our conversations and discussions, we will need to explore them in some detail to understand the virtues of character that might guide our behavior in this realm. We will use this chapter as an opportunity to expand on the virtues of love and gentleness, as well as the trinitarian virtue of participation, as helpful guides for thinking about how these relationships might be understood as virtuous from a Christian perspective.

Finally, in chapter 15, we will use Saturday to take "a walk in the woods." In recent years, increasing attention has been given to the good and less-than-good actions that we human beings take with respect to the natural environment. What would it mean to articulate a position on these matters with respect to Christian ethics? Here the trinitarian virtue of polyphony, the fruit of the Spirit called kindness, and the theological virtue of hope will be particularly useful in helping us to understand the Christian response to these questions.

Clearly, the assignment of particular virtues to particular chapters is not wholly arbitrary, but neither is it meant to be definitive; for example, while I will examine the virtue of *courage* under the general rubric of politics, it might just as easily be assigned to a discussion of the issues surrounding illness and death—or the issues surrounding our interactions with the natural environment. By assigning a virtue to a specific chapter, I do not mean to suggest that it is only, or even most appropriately, applicable where it is assigned.

In fact, given our earlier discussion of the unity of the virtues, we should theoretically be able to assign all the virtues to all the spheres of human action that are described here, and to all other spheres of action as well—but that would require making this book into a multi-volume work. Therefore, in order to conserve time, space, and my readers' energy, I have limited each chapter to three virtues that seem to me to be particularly salient in each case. All the others could be mapped onto each; and in fact, doing so may often be a helpful exercise in understanding both the unity of the virtues and their applicability to particular spheres of human action. Thus some suggestions in this regard will appear at various points within the chapters.

Each chapter in Part 3 also contains, in a separate textbox, an extended description of someone whose life seems (to me) to have offered us an unusually revelatory encounter with the particular sphere of life being examined in that chapter. In many cases, in fact, that life manifests one or more of the virtues that has been chosen for more detailed examination. I offer these brief vignettes because the ethical tradition, in both its ancient and modern forms (whether Christian or otherwise), has always emphasized the importance of pointing to particular human beings in order to describe precisely what a virtuous life might look like. Christianity, in particular, has a long tradition of naming "the saints" as outstanding moral exemplars. In some Christian traditions, these persons are officially recognized by the denomination's institutional structure; in other traditions, holy lives are lifted up as examples in a less formal way. Throughout these chapters, however, I have generally avoided choosing individuals whose lives have been thus recognized, whether officially or informally. Such persons—whose names may appear after the abbreviation "St." and who may be enshrined in the portraiture of churches or celebrated on a particular day of the year—can certainly offer important examples of the virtues; their absence from these pages is not meant to diminish their significance. Recognizing, however, that many of the readers of this book may not identify themselves as Christians, and wishing to draw as wide a range of experience as possible, I have offered the stories of people who—while relatively well known—are not *primarily* remembered as exemplars of Christian virtue. Some of them, in fact, did not identify themselves as Christians at all (though in many cases, they may have been more deeply formed by Christian narratives and practices than even they themselves realized). To my mind, however, their varying degrees of immersion in the Christian tradition make their witness all the more powerful and appealing. By embodying at least some of the virtues—and by living the kind of life that, at least in some of its aspects, a Christian might hope to live—they remind us that the moral life is not primarily a product of a person's self-declared religious affiliation, an adherence to a particular denomination's "rules," or any other factor that can be mechanically tallied and categorized. From the Christian perspective, any life of virtue is an exemplary life—regardless of which institutions most fervently and successfully claim that person as "one of their own." While not all readers will agree that a life that I describe in a particular vignette is a truly exemplary life, they may at least find themselves in fruitful conversations about lives that *do* embody the virtues; they may even feel inspired to offer some examples of their own. If so, I will have more than accomplished what I sought to do by offering these six portraits.

Throughout the first two-thirds of this book, we have made our way through one version of the Christian worship service. We have considered the way that Christians are formed, both within worship and outside it, by the narratives and practices of the faith. We have come to recognize how these habits form people in particular excellences of character and how these virtues are given concrete content through Christians' understanding of their relationship to God and to one another. At this point, the worship service has reached its "end," in both senses of that word; the time has come for us to go forth into the world.

Questions for discussion

1. In what sense does a "dismissal" (in some context other than worship) seem to imply a beginning as well as an ending? What other kinds of actions that end a particular event or episode of something have this same kind of "initiating" or "sending forth" function?

2. Discuss some of your own experiences in which starkly different moral perspectives have come into conflict with each other. To what extent does the language of "moral formation in a particular community" help to explain these differences? Do you have any experience of such differences being resolved, at least to some degree? If so, what was involved in such resolution? If not, what obstacles prevented it?

3. Do you find this chapter's discussion of the problem of "moral relativism" to be clarifying? To what extent do you consider this to be a genuine problem with the perspective on ethics that is elaborated here? Do you think that ethics should still search for some kind of universal, or at least widespread, agreement on moral matters?

4. Discuss the issue of friendship. Give examples of your own experiences of friendship that illustrate Aristotle's three types. Do you agree with his

judgment that perfect friendship needs to be between equals? Why or why not?

5. Before you read this chapter, was the language of "friendship with God" familiar to you? If so, did any of that familiarity arise out of a specifically Christian insight or tradition, or was it a more general concept? Do you find the concept to be a helpful one? Why or why not?

Sources cited in this chapter and/or recommended for further reading

Aristotle, *Nicomachean Ethics*

Michael Cartwright, "Being Sent: Witness," in Hauerwas and Wells, eds., *The Blackwell Companion to Christian Ethics*

Stanley Hauerwas and Charles Pinches, *Christians among the Virtues: Theological Conversations with Ancient and Modern Ethics*

Stanley Hauerwas and Samuel Wells, "How the Church Managed before There Was Ethics," in Hauerwas and Wells, eds., *The Blackwell Companion to Christian Ethics*

L. Gregory Jones, *Transformed Judgment: Toward a Trinitarian Account of the Moral Life*

Philip D. Kenneson, *Beyond Sectarianism: Re-imagining Church and World*

Alasdair MacIntyre, *After Virtue: A Study in Moral Theory*, 2nd edition

George Orwell, *1984*

Stephen Pope, "Reason and Natural Law," in Meilaender and Werpehowski, eds., *The Oxford Handbook of Theological Ethics*

Paul Wadell, *Becoming Friends: Worship, Justice, and the Practice of Christian Friendship*; *Friendship and the Moral Life*

Part 3

*L*iving the Christian life

11

Monday
Back at the office

It's 6:07 on Monday morning and the alarm is ringing and ringing. The radio came on at 5:30, but it appears to have had no impact whatsoever; in fact, even the alarm—which has now been ringing for seven solid minutes and is beginning to annoy the cat—seems to be having only a negligible effect on the sleep cycles of the house's occupants. Sunday had been a glorious day; no one wanted it to end. Everyone stayed awake much later than might have been prudent, given the next morning's schedule. And now that next morning has arrived, and—by means of the radio and the alarm and the first rays of sunlight streaming in the window—it is virtually shouting: "Get up and get to work!"

For a great many people in Western society, Monday is a day to go back to work. Even though fewer and fewer people are able to claim Sunday as a true "day off," the rhythm of the week still makes Monday morning a time that is dreaded by a large part of the population; even those who profess to "love their jobs" are unlikely to stage a celebration when that alarm starts ringing. And this illustrates a basic fact about work: it's usually something that we have to do, even when we don't want to. We will return to this point later in the chapter; we may even come to see this feature of work as a good thing. But because work includes this element of obligation or compulsion, it raises questions about ethics that are different from those raised in other spheres of life; and so it deserves our attention here, at the very beginning of Part 3 of this book.

Our examination of work will lead us to consider its role within the larger economic system, of which it is only one part. All of us—regardless of whether we work for pay, work in the home without pay, volunteer our services, attend school, or are unemployed—will certainly find ourselves enmeshed in the structures of our economic system. In fact, the depth and degree of that involvement is one of the most pervasive features of the modern world; economic exchange often seems to be a central focus of our lives. Practically everything we do—eating, working, playing, and even sleeping—demands that we enter into the economic realm in order to purchase the goods and services that are associated with each of these activities. At several points in this book, I have turned to examples from our experience of the economic system in order to illustrate a point—partly because it is such a pervasive aspect of human experience and is one of the few things with which practically every reader will be acquainted. Thus it is all the more fitting that we should begin our investigation into the various spheres of human action with an inquiry into work and the economic order. Because this is our first such inquiry, and because it focuses on such a pervasive feature of our lives, this chapter will be among the longest in the book.

Life at work

Most adults spend a considerable portion of their waking lives working. At one time, much of this work would have taken place in (or adjacent to) the home; now, the vast majority of adults work outside the home until they have reached an age in their late 60s or early 70s (and sometimes beyond). Most do so even if they live in households with two or more adults. Questions that arise about ethics in the workplace would have, at one time, affected only a minority of the population; today, however, almost everyone must wrestle with the question of what counts for right judgment and good character within the structures of their paid employment.

What is work?

In spite of our familiarity with work, we may have some trouble defining it in a way that will satisfy us. Most people associate it with paid employment, but there are clearly many tasks in our society—particularly in domestic life—that people regard as *work* even though they are not paid to perform them. Nor does work necessarily involve contractual arrangements; here we can point not only to household tasks, but also to the phenomenon of "self-employment," to illustrate the fact that not all work involves contracts, salary negotiations, and relationships with superiors.

This is why, as I suggested at the outset of this chapter, work might best be understood as comprising those things that we are obligated to do, whether or not we want to do them. Household chores, paid employment, the nurture and care of children, and the homework that students do at school and university—all can find a home under this general description. One may stop doing any of these things, of course; but this will lead to significant consequences. Other things that we do may well seem like "a lot of work"— such as completing the entire Sunday crossword puzzle or transferring all our music from old vinyl albums to the computer. But activities of this sort don't fall under the definition of work that we are developing here, because they involve no obligation and—typically, at least—we face no severe economic consequences, nor even much disapproval from others, when they are not done.

Certainly, in our present cultural context, paid employment does tend to take pride of place among all those activities that we might classify as "work." Most of the other forms of work tend to be undertaken in some relatively close relationship to paid employment: the nurture of children prepares them to support themselves through future employment; schoolwork is designed to prepare us for such employment; household tasks provide an environment in which one can recover from the previous day's work and prepare for the next day's. Moreover, in contemporary Western society in particular, paid employment is a marker of status; those who have not taken it on are typically expected either to be in full-time support of someone who is paid to work (e.g., those who maintain the household), or to have a good reason for being outside the system: student status, military service, or a severe, long-term illness or disability.

Consequently, many of our examples in this chapter will come from the world of paid employment. This will also put us in close proximity to the various tentacles of the economic system, including such matters as employment opportunity, working conditions, wages, consumerism, and debt. These are important aspects of that particular sphere of human action that we are examining here under the general category of "work."

Before we return to those questions, however, we need to examine one particular area of work that is most commonly associated with the field of ethics: namely, those professions (such as medicine, law, business, counseling, and the ministry) that maintain codes of "professional ethics." Since this is the approach to ethics that many people associate most clearly with work, we will need to examine why, in fact, it will not be as useful to us as we might assume.

Professional ethics

A number of professions have recognized the importance of ethical questions, particularly those questions that bear uniquely on people in their particular

232 LIVING THE CHRISTIAN LIFE

line of work. Nurses and physicians must face questions related to medical ethics in ways that are significantly different from the rest of us, who only encounter hospitals and clinics from time to time. Lawyers take courses in legal ethics and people working toward MBA degrees are often required to study business ethics. In recent years, perhaps in the face of workplace-related scandals of various sorts, our culture has witnessed a significant upswing in the emphasis on "ethics" for various professions. Even undergraduates in fields such as laboratory science, communication, or history will sometimes find themselves enrolling in courses that examine the specific ethical issues faced by those who make these fields their careers.

This general increase of interest in the field of ethics is often seen as a positive trend, suggesting that people are becoming genuinely more interested in thinking about right judgment and good action, and even about what makes for a good life with respect to the question of work. Unfortunately, however, most students who have experienced courses in professional ethics tend to report the same depressing fact: their ethics courses are not really about ethics. They are not focused on developing people of good character, nor even—harking back to the commonplace understanding of ethics that we addressed in the first chapter—are they designed to help future professionals to make hard decisions in difficult cases. Rather, these courses teach students *how to follow the rules*—and, more specifically, how to reduce the risk that they will face criminal prosecution for their mistakes. In short, courses in professional ethics teach people how to avoid getting sued.

Even if this turns out to be too cynical a way of putting the matter, many careers and professions do require people to be aware of a wide range of extraordinarily complicated laws, local rules, and codes of conduct. Moreover, these laws and rules have proliferated over the past several decades, as the professions become more specialized and the relationships among the various parties become more complex. In some cases, legislatures and courts have intervened to impose regulations that a profession's practitioners may not consider useful or salutary. Often, as for example in medical science, advances in technology have made widely available many treatments and procedures that were previously not even possible; as a result, new rules must be promulgated to govern the proper use of these new therapies. In law, the increasing complexity of legislation itself makes the field more complex, requiring new rules concerning, say, attorney–client interaction, or access to government documents. In the corporate world, an increasingly globalized market and the addition of thousands of new financial institutions and exchanges worldwide has meant that the potential number of economic transactions has increased exponentially. All this requires regulation and surveillance; therefore, the institutions that train professionals to work in these fields must make them aware of the laws and rules by which the fields are governed, so that they can interpret those rules in ways that will not land them in jail. All this leaves little time for discussing how one might actively pursue the *good*. Unfortunately, even at their best, most professional ethics courses could easily be renamed "How to follow the rules."

In fact, the world of "professional ethics" provides a casebook illustration of the difficulties that ensue when ethics relies too heavily on laws and rules. If ethics is defined as "following the rules" or "obeying the law," then the standard of good behavior will be focused almost exclusively on doing whatever is necessary to avoid breaking the rules. Indeed, this focus will become all the more intense as the rules become more complicated and labyrinthine. As we observed in the introduction and chapter 1 of this book, the rules will not only fail to encourage proactively good behavior; they often unwittingly encourage bad behavior. They also allow us to imagine that, by not breaking any rules, we are doing good. Many students in law, medical, and business schools find themselves profoundly dissatisfied with this approach and with the "ethics courses" that they are required to take. They are looking for some way to explore what it would mean to be a genuinely *good* doctor or lawyer or corporate executive—not just one who follows the rules and thereby stays out of jail. And this is to say nothing of the employees in hundreds of other fields and professions in which there are no "ethics courses." They, too, are wondering what it might mean to be people of right judgment and good character with regard to their particular profession, career, or job.

In chapter 2, we explored questions of communal identity and allegiance—"*who* we are and *whose* we are." We recognized that, regardless of whether people identify themselves as committed to a particular religious faith, they still have beliefs and "ultimate concerns" that will lead them into practices of *worship*—even if not worship of God. But the theological language that we began employing in that chapter, and have continued to refer to throughout this book, is often absent from discussions about the professions and the workplace. As a result, the vocabulary that we have available to discuss ethics in this particular sphere of life is highly attenuated.

This is not to say that the only way to determine whether, for example, a particular doctor is "doing good" is by applying a theological standard to her work. We aren't exactly in a position to ask "what would God do, if God were a doctor?" (Interestingly, though, some writers have made good use of the metaphor: T. S. Eliot evokes the image of Christ as "the wounded surgeon" to powerful effect in his *Four Quartets*.) The real issue here is that, in evacuating our public discourse of *theological* language, we have tended to evacuate it of *all* moral language whatsoever. We have left ourselves without a vocabulary for thinking through questions about moral judgment and the shape of the good life in public spheres (such as the economic order) within which we strive to do our work. We are left instead with a series of rules that are, even at their very best, designed to keep people from doing too much harm.

This again reminds us of why the study of *Christian* ethics is important, even for those who decide not to apply specifically Christian standards to all realms of their lives. Because we are addressing ethics from a very specific theological perspective—namely, that of Christianity—we are reminded that any discussion of morality must work with some conception of the *good*. Different people will hold to different conceptions; but if they do not choose to shape their lives according to a particular set of narratives and practices, they will eventually find that *other* narratives and practices will shape them, all the same—and they may not even realize it. Thus even those who do not ultimately adopt a Christian perspective may nevertheless find that this discussion helps them to examine and evaluate life in terms of what they take to be its highest goods. In other words, they may find that conversations about good and bad character will lead them to develop a richer account of the aims and goals of all that they do. At the very least, the process of exploring this important sphere of life—its purposes, goals, and complications—may help to expand the discussion of "the ethics of work" so that it concerns more than just how to avoid breaking the rules.

Work and the economic order

Thus far, we have made three major observations: first, that work might be best defined as those things that we are obligated to do, even when we don't want to do them; second, that a great many people experience such work primarily in the form of paid employment; but that, finally, the relationship between ethics and work goes well beyond the range of topics typically discussed within the category of "professional ethics." We now need to consider how paid employment is shaped by the economic structure under which we live. This question has been addressed, in passing, in several earlier chapters; here, we need to survey it again in summary form.

First, our economic structure works primarily on strategies of *exchange*: we give something and we receive something. When we give someone money, we expect to get goods or services in return; when we work, we expect to get paid. Our contemporary economic system is hardly unique in this regard; throughout history, people have bartered and exchanged goods and services in order to survive—and eventually, perhaps, even to prosper. But much of this exchange operated at a fairly informal level; people have not always required the assurance of a contract, a receipt, or a promissory note in order to work, buy something, or lend to others. Think of a small town with a volunteer fire department: when the firefighters respond to an alarm at 3:00 am, they do not expect to get paid (they are volunteers, after all); nor do they assume that they will be repaid in kind (their own homes may never catch fire); nor do they have any guarantee that others would respond if the need did arise. One might well point out that a form of exchange is still in effect here; service as a volunteer firefighter is exchanged for the privilege of living in a small town or rural setting, without having to be taxed so that people can be hired to do the same job for pay. But the exchange involved in these two cases differ quite fundamentally: the first is an exchange based on grace (a freely given gift) and trust (a belief that today's victims will become tomorrow's helpers, when their help is needed), rather than on binding contracts, enforced obligations, and a salary sufficient to attract workers.

Today, volunteer firefighters are increasingly rare; like the economic exchanges in most sectors of our society, this work has undergone a process of formalization. Most people live in larger cities and do not know everyone else in town, so the element of trust is often missing. We suspect that if we always volunteered our services freely, without evaluating costs and benefits, we would eventually be drained of all our resources and find ourselves unable to survive. Thus we have cemented our relationships of exchange into formal structures with legally binding contracts and written evidence to make sure that the exchange actually takes place. Since we no longer know the people with whom we are exchanging goods and services, and therefore feel unable to trust them, we must instead place our trust in the governments and the courts that will enforce the rules. As a result, our paid employment—like all our other economic activities—is valued according to whatever we are exchanging for it.

This process of valuation becomes much easier because of the existence of *money*—a universal means of exchange that allows anything to be traded for anything else, just by setting a price on both. Thus an hour of most kinds of work at a typical fast-food restaurant is typically thought to be worth exactly the minimum wage that the government will allow businesses to pay. When a person experiences a painful toothache, the decision to seek healing and relief will be made on the basis of whether one can pay the price charged by the dentist who is able and willing to heal it. The value of a film being shown in a theater is determined by the price of an admission ticket. As these strict economic exchanges come to dominate our lives, it becomes much more difficult to imagine that a particular product, an act of service, or a form of work might actually be worth much more—or much less—than what people are willing to pay for it. Consequently, it becomes difficult for us to know what to do with ethical questions surrounding work, since these questions often do not easily translate into a particular amount of money that can be exchanged. Put simply (and perhaps a bit too simply), one cannot put a price on the virtues.

A second key feature of our economic system is its extreme *efficiency*. It renders the maximum value in an exchange by rewarding those economic actors who operate so as to minimize the waste of time and energy. Consider two scenarios: the first is the old-fashioned lunch counter, where the grill is separated from the dining area by nothing more than a long walkway for the cook—and where everyone can see, hear, and smell everything that anyone else is doing. The second is the fast-food restaurant, in which tasks are broken down into their component parts (one person takes orders and money, another prepares the food, another cooks it, and yet another packages it) and in which much of the work of making the meal takes place out of sight of the person who will eat it. The first scenario is terribly inefficient: at a recent experience of mine at such a setting, the cook had to put on a different pair of disposable gloves for each operation (vegetables with one set of gloves, raw meat with another), and then take the gloves off altogether to handle the register and the cash. The work proceeded extremely slowly, both because one person was doing all the parts of the operation and because food could not be prepared in advance (since the volume of business was small). In the second scenario, the labor is broken up into small tasks, each of which can be done repeatedly in a fraction of the time that it would take one person to do all of them once. This allows food to be prepared more quickly and thus allows a much greater volume of business to be transacted in the same amount of time. Not surprisingly, a particular item of food at the first establishment—even though the quality and quantity of the product are roughly identical—might well cost twice as much as it does at the second. On top of that, the fast-food restaurant will get the food out much more quickly—and often it will not even lack freshness, since its high volume of business often allows food to be served just a few seconds after it is cooked. This explains, of course, why there are so many fast-food restaurants—and so few lunch counters.

What we often miss, in consistently opting for more efficiency, is its effect on those elements of the transaction that are not so easily measured in monetary terms. In the first scenario, the customer and the cook are more likely to get into a conversation; they can see each other, and the waiting time almost demands some kind of interaction. The customer sees the food prepared, and can make judgments about the adequacy of the process. The cook gets to see the customer enjoy the meal, and can even take a certain amount of pride in having done good work. Both the cook and the customer are aware that an exchange has taken place—after all, it was the cook who put the money in the till!—but the transaction becomes much more significant than a mere exchange of food for money, since human interaction is involved.

In the second case, the customer and the worker have no significant interaction. Most of the workers do not even see the customers; only one of them talks to those who are ordering the food, and conversation is limited to placing the order and "have a nice day." The cooks literally cannot see the diners' appreciation for their work, nor does the customer have an opportunity to compliment anyone on the meal having been well prepared. The price that we pay for the market's efficiency is, frequently, that a wedge is driven between the work that we do and the final product of our labor. Whether the work environment is a fast-food counter, a workroom full of cubicles, or a tastefully appointed executive office suite, the results are essentially the same: the more economically efficient the operation, the less frequently we get the opportunity to experience another person's direct appreciation for what we have done, made, or made possible for them. This, again, makes ethical questions very difficult to render. Since ethics is about character, and since we so rarely know anything about the character of those who provide our goods and services, we are not usually in a position to make judgments about what goes on in the workplace; instead, we rely on health inspectors, safety officers, and government attorneys to try to reduce the risk that people of bad character don't use their invisibility to do one another harm.

Finally, the two preceding points—exchange and efficiency—combine to point us toward a third significant feature of our current economic structure: namely, that the final product becomes the exclusive focus of any economic exchange. In less formal or less efficient economic systems, something was always "left over": the pride that the firefighter felt when the whole town knew who saved that family's house from destruction, or the better atmosphere that was created at the lunch counter as a result of the repartee between customer and cook. But formal and efficient systems of exchange work to eliminate this excess, since it often results in higher costs and lower profits. Instead, all of the worker's energy goes into the production of the goods and services; thus, when customers come to judge whether they got good value-for-money, they focus strictly on the product. Questions about working conditions, environmental impact, and the cultivation of good personal relationships among workers or between workers and consumers—all these matters fade into the background because they do not translate easily into a cash equivalent. We look at two roughly identical final products, one of which costs three times as much as the other, and we immediately assume that the excess is making someone extremely wealthy. But in fact, the profit margin on the cheaper goods may be considerably higher than on the more expensive goods—depending on the company's volume of sales, its treatment of employees, and countless other factors that we find difficult to take into consideration (particularly when we have too many needs and too little money). We thus concentrate all our energies on the final product; if it is being sold for a price that we are willing and able to pay, we buy.

This focus on the final product tends to render moot a great many questions with which the field of ethics is primarily concerned. Our judgments about the character of a company, or of one of its workers, are largely rendered irrelevant (unless some cataclysmic event brings to light precisely which corners have been cut). Questions about the virtues with which a particular product is made or a service is rendered are frequently invisible to the consumer, and are rarely signaled in any obvious way by the goods and services themselves. When our automobiles come out of the shops where they have been serviced, we rarely inquire into the character of the workers, the politics of the corporation, or the damage done to the environment in order to complete the repair. Usually we just want to know whether the blasted thing is working again; and if we were to inquire into any other matters, most people would find us rather odd and would probably not understand how such questions had anything to do with the transaction that was just completed. Conversely, few auto-repair workers will ever find out just how much it means to us to have the car working again, nor will they be aware that we may truly appreciate their dedication to their craft. Does the one mechanic who took the extra time to find and replace a small, inexpensive, but nearly worn-out part get any credit for the fact that the car didn't break down in the middle of the next road trip, as it would have done had he not been so conscientious? Such matters are rarely on the table, because our focus is simply on the product: does it work? Does it meet our needs? Do we consider it to be worth the money it cost us? These questions tend to obscure, or even to obliterate, any thoughts we might have about the character of the work that goes into making the product or rendering the service.

In pointing out these features of our economic system, I am not seeking to offer a critique—nor to suggest that there might be a better way to run the economy. I am merely suggesting that we need to *be aware* that these structural elements have a profound influence on the ways that we understand the process of economic exchange, which in turn has a profound influence on how we understand work. Our economic system asks us to operate on the assumption that our work is worth exactly what others are willing to pay for the final product that we (usually together with many co-workers) have produced, as long as we have accomplished this in the most efficient way possible. But what if the significance of our work is something else altogether? We need to explore this possibility, because this is exactly what the Christian tradition has usually held to be the case.

Why work at all?

One way to get at the question of the *significance* of our work is to ask the question of exactly *why* we work. For many of our activities, we can best understand our motives and reasons by examining the role of *desire*; typically, we do things because, at some level, we *want* to do them. But as we have noted, work generally involves tasks that we are obligated to do even when we don't want to do them, so we cannot explain its significance merely by pointing to our desires. For example, if the answer to the question of why we work is simply "to make money," then our economic system has it right: our work is worth exactly the amount of money that someone is willing to pay for it. But very frequently, the mere desire to make money is not, in and of itself, sufficient to motivate us to do what we sometimes wish not to do. Alternatively, we might assume that work is primarily about survival: we work in order to feed, clothe, and house ourselves. This is certainly true; and for much of the world's population, these basic necessities may constitute the very most that the available work opportunities are actually able to provide (and often they may not provide even that much). But most people in the industrialized West work far more than necessary to insure the subsistence of themselves and their dependents. We might therefore amend this description and say that we work in order to purchase more consumer goods; many people find, however, that the extra time spent working to pay for such goods frequently eclipses the time available to enjoy them. In any case, focusing on what our work can "buy" may not ultimately be the most relevant issue. After all, even those who have more money than they need—those who have retired with a good pension, received an unexpected inheritance, or won the lottery—can be quite ambivalent about the life of leisure that is now available to them; instead, they often want to "keep working." All of this suggests that there must be other reasons for work besides a mere instinct for survival and monetary gain.

The Christian theological tradition has offered a number of answers to the question of "why we work." These answers are meant not so much as sociological or psychological descriptions of what motivates people to work, but rather as larger philosophical accounts of why work is actually a good thing. These theological perspectives on human work may help us get beyond the standard economic and cultural answers to the question, providing a broader and deeper portrait of the human condition. This in turn will better prepare us to examine the *virtues* of work in the final section of this chapter. Here, we will explore the theological rationale for work under three headings: habit, hardship, and humanity.

Work as habit

Throughout this book, we have discovered that much human action is the result of habit: we do things because we have been habituated to do them. Sometimes these habits can feel demeaning to us—as though we were mere machines that acted automatically, without the engagement of the brain and the heart. But in fact, much of our habitual action concerns matters about which we wouldn't *want* to spend that much time thinking or caring: I don't really want to pause, every time I leave the room, and have an internal debate with myself as to whether or not it would be a good idea to turn out the light. I'm quite happy to have been habituated to do so (thanks, Mom!); it saves light bulbs, it saves electricity, and while it probably won't save the planet, it's surely better for the environment than leaving the lights on all night. Many of our habits are like this: they concern matters that we don't want to think about too deeply, and they are, in general, good for us.

Work is this kind of habit. At the level of basic survival, we need to be adequately nourished and protected from the elements; so, unless someone else is willing to provide us with these basic human needs, we must work to obtain them. We therefore learn—in early adulthood if not well before—that we would be wise to get in the habit of working enough to make ends meet. Work is, at some level, a result of our basic instinct for survival.

Habits often lead us to take certain things for granted; in this case, we take for granted that we will need to work. We don't have to allow things to get to a difficult pass with regard to our survival (e.g., finding ourselves on the brink of starvation or frostbite) before we go out and seek employment. And this can have a broader effect on our lives; it can help us learn to take for granted that we will sometimes need to do things that we don't particularly want to do. We will need to do these things, not in order to survive, but because achieving some particular good at some point in the future may make it worthwhile to engage in an undesirable activity in the present. This is more than just learning how to delay gratification (though in our present cultural circumstances, that itself is no small achievement); we also need to learn how to recognize that "the good" does not always lie terribly close to the surface. That which appears advantageous to me at the moment—taking the day off work and lounging by the pool instead—may well have deleterious consequences in the future, even if it only amounts to the feeling of frustration that I experience when I find the task-list at the office has only grown longer.

As noted above, these points are not just empirical observations of the human condition; they have roots in a theological claim. Human beings certainly act on the basis of their appetites, so it is hardly surprising that they gravitate toward things that seem to offer positive, pleasurable experiences.

But, theologically speaking, they are also created in the image of God; thus they are able to make judgments and decisions on the basis of a broader perspective. They are not themselves gods, so they cannot see and know everything; but they can take into account the ramifications and eventual consequences of their judgments and actions in ways that go far beyond the breadth and depth of such vision among the other animals. They are able to postulate good ends that may come from getting into the habit of doing things that they do not particularly want to do.

Finally, the habit of work provides human beings with a *structure* for their lives. Again, this is a moot point for much of the world's population, where a full day's labor is necessary just in order to survive. But for much of the industrialized West, a full day's labor produces considerably more resources than is necessary to eke out our basic survival; there is often enough left over for considerable forms of entertainment, non-essential electronic equipment, creature comforts, and the material goods necessary to enjoy hobbies, sports, and a great variety of leisure activities. If we worked only enough to ensure our survival, we would work many, many fewer hours each week; but what would we do with our time? The extra work that we do—along with the many leisure activities in which that additional income allows us to indulge—provide structure and meaning to our lives.

For many religious believers (including Jews, Christians, and Muslims), the habit of work is motivated by one additional factor, which is also related to our need for structure and to the theological claim that we are created in the image of God. To understand this point, we need to return to the narrative of creation in Genesis 1, and consider its description of *God's* work. During the first six days of creation, God undertakes a great deal of work (though it is not exactly like our work, in that God isn't *obligated* to do it). But the next day is different:

> And on the seventh day God finished the work that he had done, and he rested on the seventh day from all the work that he had done. So God blessed the seventh day and hallowed it, because on it God rested from all the work that he had done in creation (Gen. 2:2–3).

From this story arises the Jewish, Christian, and Muslim account of the *Sabbath*: the seventh day as a day on which one does not work, a hallowed day given over wholly to God. While most branches of Christianity shifted their understanding of the Sabbath from Saturday to Sunday and adopted a rather different set of assumptions and practices around it, one key element remained: this was the day that gives all the other days their meaning. All the days of "work" flow from, and flow back into, this day of rest and worship.

Thus, according to the Christian tradition, some of the habits that people develop through their *work* lives can be transferred to their *worship* lives. Work develops in us a certain kind of discipline: a willingness to take on particular tasks and obligations, and to hold fast to them regardless of the desires of the moment. Christians understand worship in a similar way: praying, praising God, and gathering in community may not be the first things that come to mind when one wakes up on a beautiful Sunday morning; but in a larger sense, these are the activities to which Christians are most firmly committed. Often, they may not *want* to do them, just as they may not want to do other elements of their work (chores, job, homework, and so on). But if they are in the habit of recognizing the importance of doing one's work regardless of one's immediate desires, then this same discipline may also come to characterize their worship lives. And since Christianity understands the proper worship of God to be one of the most important purposes of life, worship is seen as one of those disciplines that will turn out to be "good for us" in the long run—no matter how we evaluate it in the moment.

Work as hardship

A second area of Christian reflection on work understands it as something of a punishment—a result of the Fall. After the human beings fall out of right relationship with God in the Garden of Eden (in Genesis 3), God announces that life for them will not be nearly as carefree as it once had been:

> To the woman [God] said, "I will greatly increase your pangs in child-bearing; in pain you shall bring forth children, yet your desire shall be for your husband, and he shall rule over you." And to the man [God] said, ". . . cursed is the ground because of you; in toil you shall eat of it all the days of your life; thorns and thistles it shall bring forth for you; and you shall eat the plants of the field. By the sweat of your face you shall eat bread until you return to the ground, for out of it you were taken; you are dust, and to dust you shall return" (Gen. 3:16–19).

According to Christian theology, therefore, the necessity of work is closely related to the Fall. If, as was the case in the original state of creation, human beings were always in right relationship with God and one another, they would find everything provided for them. But since they fall out of that state, they must expect to do hard labor: for food, for children, and for one another.

Over time, this enforced work came to be seen as a way of avoiding further capitulations to sin. Although there is no definitive Christian teaching about the necessity of work, there does seem to be a general view that those who do not work tend to fall more easily out of right relationship with one another and with God—as is attested by numerous folk-sayings along the lines of "idle hands do the Devil's work." Work reminds human beings of their sinful state, their loss of paradise; that state will only be restored when they return to God completely. Meanwhile, work helps to focus our attention on building up our relationships, rather than tearing them down.

Needless to say, work does not, in and of itself, free people from sin; it just affords them fewer opportunities to dream up new ways of getting into trouble. In fact, our work itself can, and often is, a breeding ground for poor moral judgment and damaged relationships; this is one of the reasons why so many professions have had to create elaborate sets of rules, hoping thereby to restrain the worst offenses. Some theorists have further suggested that the industrial age, in particular, created a new bond between sin and work, since mechanized processes tend to make people feel more distant from their work and therefore less committed to the positive habits that good work can cultivate. (The division of labor, for example, means that each person contributes only a fraction of the work to make a product; similarly, mass production techniques make it more difficult for workers to exercise their creativity and to leave their mark on certain products as particularly excellent.) Karl Marx wrote quite perceptively about the "alienation" that can result from these industrial processes, with workers feeling separated from their work and eventually not caring much about the product; they become just another cog in the machine. A number of Christian theologians have astutely noted the close relationship between this economic account of alienation and the theological account of sin. In contrast, forms of work that give people a sense of purpose and help to cultivate right relationships can bring us back into contact with our true selves. Somewhat surprisingly, then, the "hardship" associated with work may actually turn out to be to our advantage.

Work as a humanizing force

Finally, work is one of the elements of our lives that mark us as distinctively human and distinguish us from the other animals. We are unique in undertaking more work than is strictly necessary for our survival, and in understanding it as something that helps to shape our identity. We can recognize this "humanizing" element of work through three key terms: vocation, socialization, and production.

At least since the time of the Protestant reformation, human work has been associated with *vocation*. This word, which comes from the Latin word *vocare* (to call), suggests that one's work might be understood as something to which one is called by God. The word had formerly been restricted to specifically religious forms of work; priests, monks, and nuns were said to have "vocations," but workers in other fields were not. As one part of Protestantism's attempt to claim a more significant role for the laity, the language of vocation expanded to embrace the idea that God calls all people to their particular forms of work. When secular work is thus aligned with God's claim on particular human lives, that work is endowed with a greater significance and may come to be seen as making human life more noble and fulfilling.

A second element is that of socialization: work often puts us into contact with other human beings, including those with whom we would not otherwise choose to enter into relationships. This might be understood in parallel to the notion that work itself is something that we must do, even when we would rather not; our co-workers, similarly, are people with whom we have to associate, even when we would rather not. One aspect of living in the human community is recognizing that our social relationships are not strictly limited to those that we would choose; sometimes we are drawn into contact with others involuntarily, such that we must learn to negotiate the relationship on the basis of its necessity rather than simply because it is pleasant or useful to us. Our work demands of us a degree of social engagement that may sometimes draw us out of our interior selves and into explicit communal relationships with others.

Third, our work is productive. Some writers have even suggested that work might even be seen as one of the ways that human beings live into their condition of having been created in the image of God—creating as God creates. In contrast, others have argued that the differences between divine and human processes of "creation" are so great that it may be misleading to use the same term to refer to both. Regardless of where a person stands on this terminological dispute, however, one thing is certain: human beings are *productive*. Through their capacities for foresight, insight, and perseverance, they have found ways to structure their work so that it produces. This is not just a matter of the much-sought-after "productivity" of the industrial age, but also of the human energy devoted to horticultural, educational, and artistic pursuits: we produce flowers and fruit in gardens; we produce knowledge and wisdom in colleges and universities; we produce plays in theaters, music in recital halls and living rooms, and paintings and sculpture to decorate private and public spaces. These productive capacities of work are among the features that make it a distinctively human endeavor, through which our lives are given greater meaning and fulfillment.

The broad scope of our work

In our exploration of the Christian tradition's answers to the question of why we work, we have examined three broad categories: work as habit, work as hardship, and the humanizing features of work. While these three answers are hardly exhaustive, they do help us understand that the narrowly economic or financial explanations for why we work are simply not sufficient. We may work in order to eat and to insure a roof over our heads, but—at least in many parts of the world—we undertake a great deal more work than is strictly necessary to fulfill these goals. By exploring some of the other motives that underlie our work, we have better prepared ourselves for the next section: an examination of how certain excellences of character might apply in our work lives—and in our economic encounters more broadly.

The virtues of work

In the first two parts of this book, we examined how the narratives and practices of a community build up certain habits in its members. Among these habits we can identify certain excellences of character—*virtues*—that the community holds to be appropriate and desirable traits. But these character traits remain fairly vague and ambiguous until we fill them with concrete content, so that we begin to understand precisely what it looks like to be, for example, a faithful or grateful or magnanimous person. In this chapter and those that follow, we will undertake some of this "filling in" process with respect to the particular spheres of life that we are examining in each chapter. Here, I will concentrate on three virtues that seem particularly apposite to our work lives: justice, particularity, and self-control.

As I observed in chapter 10, we could theoretically apply any of the virtues to any issue that we might confront. Given our comments about "the unity of the virtues," we would not expect to see any particular virtue completely missing from a consideration of any topic, nor would we expect to see two virtues being set in opposition to one another. Thus it will not surprise us to learn that Martin Luther, for example, focused heavily on *courage* and *patience* as virtues that are cultivated, in significant ways, by our work: courage, because it requires us to take on tasks that we might not desire to do; patience, because a trade may take an entire lifetime to learn well. In choosing to emphasize a different set of virtues than did Luther, I do not mean to suggest that his are wrong, nor even that mine are better; the life of work should, in fact, help people to cultivate *all* the virtues. Thus, throughout this last third of the book, we need only keep in mind that any or all of the virtues could theoretically be applied to each topic. As long as we do that, three or four examples in each chapter should suffice to illustrate how substantive accounts of particular virtues might help us to understand the ethical contours of a particular sphere of life.

Justice

Aristotle defines justice as a habit according to which a person actively chooses and does what is right. This definition strikes most readers as a bit circular, since the notion of "what is right" would seem to be precisely what is in question when we seek to offer accounts of particular virtues (and of morality in general). And this is not far from the truth, since Aristotle regards justice as having a special place among the virtues; at one point, he even says that "justice is all virtue." His reasoning is that the just person chooses and acts rightly not just with respect to him- or herself, and not just with respect to other individuals, but also with respect to the common good. In this sense, justice covers a wider range of matters than does practically any other virtue.

More specifically, however, the account of justice offered in Aristotle and in many of the ancient writers focuses on the idea of rendering to all people *according to their due*. Again, this definition may seem to beg the question, since there will be always be arguments about what someone is "due." But an important point is still being made here, because even in those circumstances where a community comes to agreement about what someone deserves, not everyone has the strength of character needed to render it. Those who are able to do so are the best exemplars of the virtue of justice.

When the word "justice" appears in the English translation of the biblical text, it may refer to one of two different sets of ideas. The first of these is closer to the English word "judgment"; sometimes a call to "seek justice" means something like "ask that a (right) judgment be rendered." This meaning (the Greek root is usually the word *krisis*) focuses on justice as an action that is rendered in a court of law or before a tribunal, rather than justice as a character trait. But *justice* can also focus primarily on human relationships; in the New Testament, the root is often related to *dikaiosunē*—a very important New Testament word, often translated as "righteousness." The meaning of this word is complex, but its primary reference is always to God: righteousness is what God requires of a person, and it is most clearly associated with the idea of being in a right relationship with God and with other human beings.

Throughout Christian history, as writers have sought to unite the ancient virtue of justice with the biblical concept of righteousness, they hit on a number of useful descriptions that may help us get a better grasp of the concept. Augustine, for example, says that "justice is love serving God alone." At first this may appear to take the focus completely away from rendering all people their due; but since Christians believe that God entreats all human beings to love and serve their neighbor, the two ideas are not really mutually exclusive: to allow one's love to "serve God alone" is also to allow it to serve one's neighbors. The Christian bishop and theologian Ambrose of Milan emphasizes this other-directed nature of justice when he writes that "justice renders to each what is his and claims not what is another's; it disregards one's own profit in order to maintain a common equity." Justice, then, is concerned with seeking and bringing about right relationships within the human community, and—according to the Christian account—doing so because it imitates the justice (righteousness) of God.

Justice can be an extremely difficult virtue to cultivate in the economic order under which most of us live. The dominance of market economies means that we have come to believe that the individual pursuit of our own interests—financial, emotional, or spiritual—should take priority in our lives. Faced with a choice between maximizing our own financial gain (say, by selling an item for more than we think it is worth) or diminishing our own profit so that others can prosper, we're certainly more likely to choose the former path. Moreover, some economic theories have suggested that individual profit-maximization really benefits everyone in the long run, as markets work to sort out the disparities and economic growth results. Such theories suggest that we can have our cake and eat it too: while working for our own interests, we bring about justice for others.

In practice, however, things may not work out this way. Even if we accept those economic theories that seek to establish a firm connection between free market economics and general prosperity for all, there is a more immediate sense in which my own efforts to maximize my profits will, at least in the short run, be at someone else's expense. Our economic sensibilities direct us toward ourselves first: if I own something that someone else needs, shouldn't I seek to sell it for the highest possible price? And yet, every unit of currency that comes into my pocket in that transaction comes directly out of the pocket of someone else. Even if some forms of economic exchange lead to higher wages in the long run, those who are disadvantaged by the system of exchange must still make it through the short run.

Hence, no matter what economic theories we employ, we will often find that the virtue of justice is not perfectly served by markets alone. We have no choice but to attend to the particular circumstances in which people find themselves in order to evaluate whether justice is being done. The question will always be—as the ancient writers, both Christian and otherwise, suggest—whether each person receives his or her due. And for those who believe that all human beings are created by God and created in the image of God, it will never be sufficient to imagine that "what a person is due" is necessarily equivalent to "whatever the market will bear" or "whatever that person has worked for" or any other such approach that relies on the economic order alone to mete out perfect justice.

More specifically, a Christian account of justice will always seek to supply each human being with the resources and the opportunities necessary to live into the fullness of the image of God in which she or he was created. This means that basic biological necessities such as food, water, and shelter are "due" to each person, regardless of one's place in the economic order, one's ability and willingness to work, or the fortunes and hardships that a person has faced. Part of what it means to be a community for whom *justice* is a virtue is to seek a social order in which all people have access to such basic necessities—and, in the best case, access to the resources that are needed not only to survive but also to thrive. Jesus said that he came in order that people "may have life, and have it abundantly" (John 10:10). While this notion of abundance does not translate directly into the idea of material wealth alone, it should be clear that a world in which so many human beings lack the basic necessities of life cannot be a world in which Jesus' promise and goal has been fulfilled. Christians, therefore, are called to work for an economic order in which abundant life is possible for all.

George Orwell

Often hailed as one of the finest writers in the English language, the novelist and critic George Orwell (1903–1950) is known to many students as the author of two particularly important twentieth-century novels: *Animal Farm* and *1984*. Although both are cast in narrative form, they are only very thinly veiled critiques of contemporary society: the first, suggesting that those who rise to power in a society can easily become obsessed with, and corrupted by, that power; and the second, suggesting that any society that is allowed to become sufficiently dedicated to controlling the minds of its citizens will certainly succeed in doing so. Orwell was a passionate advocate for the idea that human beings should not be brought under the domination of others—whether those others are well-meaning revolutionaries, faceless bureaucrats, or malevolent and violent dictators. Less well known (particularly outside his native Britain), but just as important, was Orwell's commitment to the idea that human *labor* should be a virtuous endeavor: that it should be marked by, and should help us to cultivate, characteristics such as courage, justice, patience, and self-control. Orwell discovered, much to his chagrin, that these character traits were precisely the opposite of what much work in our society tends to cultivate—particularly at the lower levels of the socio-economic spectrum.

In his late twenties, after having attended Eton, having served with the British Imperial Police in India, and having already published some of his writing, Orwell found himself in Paris doing nothing but giving English lessons. They didn't pay very well; he soon realized that he needed to get a decent job. But just as he began looking for work, his room was robbed and he was left with nothing but the change in his pocket. Instead of escaping back to his life of privilege in England, however, he chose to stay in Paris and to learn what it was like to live on the fringe of poverty. He thereby experienced life as it is known by those who have no significant job skills and who must therefore live in a constant state of transition from one short-term job to the next. He learned that the low pay inherent in such work is only a small part of the problem; one must undertake it while suffering the various other debilitating effects of poverty. These include hunger, fear, boredom, the frequent need to lie and to keep secrets, and a poor person's general susceptibility to disaster as a result of some minor incident. (Dropping a plate full of food or flicking a bug into the milk would be a mere inconvenience to most people; but if that was the only food you had, you then had to go without a meal.) Even though Orwell's experiment was not perfectly analogous to true poverty—he could have "rescued" himself from his condition at any time—he learned a great deal about the relationship between work and character. He published his observations in a very fine memoir entitled *Down and Out in Paris and London* (1933). Some years later he visited the coal-mining areas of northern England during a time of mass unemployment, and offered a devastating account of the poverty that he found there in *The Road to Wigan Pier* (1937).

Orwell's close contact with these marginal spaces in the industrial economy helped him to understand, and to argue for, the place of certain elemental virtues in the world of work. He also suggested—somewhat menacingly, in the eyes of the middle- and upper-class readers who so enjoyed his prose—that many of us contribute to this poverty without even realizing it. If we purchase goods and services that are produced by people who do not earn a living wage, he argued, we are contributing to their poverty. In the light of more recent activism and protests against sweatshops and slave labor, Orwell's insights may seem rather minor; but he wrote at a time when conditions were worse than they are today (at least in the West), and when no one had really taken on the plight of slave-like labor as a worthy cause. His work dramatically altered the general understanding of work and poverty—giving the question a much greater moral intensity in his era, just as writers like Victor Hugo and Charles Dickens had done in theirs.

Particularity

Christians believe that God is three and that God is one. Even though Christianity is, strictly speaking, a monotheistic faith, it nevertheless proclaims an internal differentiation in God that is not perfectly captured by the notion of "oneness" or "unity." According to Christian theology, God is the Source of all that is; at the same time, God gives birth to the Word, who is also God. And God also breathes out the Spirit, who is also God. Human beings experience this threefold quality of God through the mysterious otherness of the Source, the incarnation of the Word in Jesus Christ, and the descent of the Holy Spirit who animates the Christian community.

This unity and multiplicity in God is reflected, in interesting ways, in the human community—which also bears these marks of unity and multiplicity. We are all human beings; we are members of the same species, *Homo sapiens*, and we recognize the essential elements of humanity in one another. On the other hand, the differences among us are also obvious; there is clearly another sense in which humanity is not one, but is multiple. In fact, it has as many facets as there are human beings in the world—and more, since we ourselves are also multi-faceted and since we also change over time. Unfortunately, however, our awareness of this multiplicity sometimes leads us into isolation from one another; we think of ourselves first and foremost as individuals, who may come together from time to time but are always capable of retreating back into our individuality. People in other eras tended to depend much more heavily upon one another and thus had much less confidence in the ability of a single individual to make his or her own way in the world. The modern era has encouraged us to live with the illusion of true individualism—something that was not imagined by our forebears.

The Christian story offers, at its most basic level, a stark contrast to this notion of individualism. In the story related in the first chapter of Genesis, human beings are created as a collective, in a single act of creation: "humankind, male and female." Even the story in Genesis 2, in which a single human creature is "separated" into male and female persons, emphasizes a connectedness and an original unity among human beings that is more basic and more natural than our description of ourselves as potentially isolated individuals.

And yet, even while the Christian story raises questions about some of our more extreme forms of individualism and instead emphasizes the unity that connects us with all other human beings (and with the entire creation), it must also be admitted that human beings differ from one another in significant ways. They cannot easily be transformed into an undifferentiated collective whole; they resist assimilation into straightforward categories. It is therefore incumbent upon us to develop a way of speaking about these differences without obliterating the unity that we share. I have proposed the language of *particularity* as a way of doing this: we are not simply individuals, in that we are not really capable of existing in pure isolation from one another; nevertheless, we *are* particular. We have our own identifying characteristics that allow other people to tell us apart; but this does not mean that we are separated off from the rest of humanity. We are united to others through our common condition as (in Jewish and Christian terms) being created in the image of God. Christians further claim unity with one another through their baptism into the death and resurrection of Jesus Christ and their participation in the ongoing life of the Holy Spirit. To cultivate the trinitarian virtue of *particularity* is to recognize, simultaneously, the degree to which we are bound to other people and the degree to which we differ from them.

What might this mean for our work lives? I suspect that it might help us avoid the kinds of problems that I described in the previous section, on justice: the tendency to set our own profit-maximization in opposition to the interests of others. If we are truly bound to one another (as the language of "particularity" suggests), then we cannot really isolate our own interests from those of others. A better life for me is necessarily related to the kinds of lives that other people live. Indeed—as I have already observed—some economic theories suggest this rather directly, claiming that those who seek to maximize their own personal wealth may thereby contribute to a general condition of economic growth, thereby positively affecting everyone else: "a rising tide lifts all boats." But other writers have suggested that such theories may work only to salve the consciences of those economic actors who are, in the end, really interested only in their own financial success. Those who seek to cultivate the virtue of particularity will not think of the economic condition of others as something that might be improved as a kind of side-effect of maximizing one's own gains. Rather, one's *particularity* is a reminder that one is not an individual actor at all, but merely a node within a much wider network. Rather than bettering oneself and hoping that the whole network will improve as a result, an alternative approach might be to focus on improving the network—recognizing that one's own location within it will be improved in the process.

Self-control

At first glance, this virtue may seem to be in tension with what we have discussed in the previous two sections. If justice requires us to pay attention to the interests of others as well as our own, and if our particularity reminds us that we are not isolated individuals but are inherently connected to other human beings, then it would seem to make little sense to turn in on ourselves, in an individualistic fashion, and focus on the control that we exercise over our own lives.

As some commentators have pointed out, however, Paul the Apostle's word that we translate "self-control" is a bit misleading. It does not mean anything like "self-mastery" or "getting control of one's life"; it is not the virtue that is being cultivated by the thousands of self-help books that one can buy in the bookstores. These and other cultural forces lead us to think of self-control as control of the self, by the self, and for the sake of the self. But Paul, in the context of his comments about the fruits of the Spirit more generally, clearly means something slightly different. His word, *egkrateia*, certainly does include the idea of refusing to be a slave to one's own desires and passions; however, the point of this is not in order to achieve self-mastery or to make oneself the very center of the universe. Rather, Paul's notion of self-control has more to do, surprisingly enough, with the concept of freedom.

Throughout his epistles, Paul regularly observes that human beings are sometimes mistaken about what is good for them; they find themselves desiring things that actually do them harm. (His most concise statement of this claim can be found in Romans 7:19: "For I do not do the good I want, but the evil I do not want is what I do"—try saying that five times fast.) But Paul also insists that human beings have been released from our tendency to pursue that which does us harm—not by our own brilliant work at curbing and subduing our desires, but by God's intervention on our behalf. Paul regularly reminds his readers that God has not held the disordered desires of human beings against them, but has been willing to forgive sin, to redeem the world, and to set human beings free. When people accept that freedom and use it in the service of others, they most profoundly exercise "self-control": they allow the self, which can so often be the center of our attention, to be animated by something greater than itself: by God, who redirects human passions away from mere self-gratification and toward the good of the other. Self-control is thus the recognition that happiness ultimately consists, not simply in pleasing oneself, but in living a life that focuses on others and on one's relationship to those others.

Understood in this way, the virtue of self-control has significant potential to help us think through our work lives and the ethical questions that we face in the midst of those lives. If we focus only on our own interests, on the satisfaction of our desires, we soon discover that they are literally endless. As soon as we achieve the next level of financial, emotional, or spiritual success, our vision grows larger; we seek greater depths, more intense pleasures, and costlier toys. When work becomes nothing more than a way of maximizing profit in order to fulfill our desires, we soon find ourselves on a treadmill that never stops, but only speeds up as we achieve a brisker pace.

All this is common enough wisdom; everyone knows about the reality of rising economic expectations, and we recognize that every new achievement just encourages us to set our sights higher. Nevertheless, these realizations don't seem to have done much to discourage us from continuing to climb the economic ladder; a quick glance at the local bookstore's selection of titles in the "Personal finance" section will make it clear that "making more money" is still the name of the game. In those few instances when someone actually offers a prescription for addressing this illness, it usually involves either over-coming one's desires for more and more "stuff," or else voluntarily lowering one's income, such that our expectations do not continue to rise. But both of these strategies rely on that notion of "self-control" in the old sense of self-mastery: control of the self, by the self, for the sake of the self. An alternative strategy involves the re-ordering of human desire away from one's self (or at least away from one's self in isolation from the rest of humanity), and toward others: control of the self is now neither *by* the self alone, nor *for the sake of* the self alone, but also by and for the sake of those others to whom we are, in spite of appearances to the contrary, always very closely connected.

We can get at this distinction more clearly by reflecting, as have many other commentators, on the relationship between work and artistic production. We often think of the activity of a creative artist as the very opposite of work: such a person does not contribute to the economy in any obvious way, does not manufacture goods or provide services that inspire a large number of people to spend money on those goods and services. But it is precisely these elements that make artistic creation the very best example of work: it is not done merely for the gain of income which can in turn be converted to material objects, pur-chased for the purpose of attempting to fulfill our desires. Instead, the artist's work is for the sake of others, for those who will see the art and enjoy it with-out a focus on its intersection with the economy. This is not to say that mone-tary gain and other forms of culturally-approved success do not motivate artists to create; these elements may often play a role. But most artistic creation pays so poorly and so irregularly that few people would be willing to undertake it for that result alone; and in fact, we often sense that when an artist has become more devoted to financial gain than to the benefit of others, the quality of the art begins to suffer. The work of the artist is, in some sense, its own reward.

This may perhaps suggest that the goal of all work should be to bring it into parallel with the work of artistic creation: done not primarily for the sake of monetary reward, but for the sake of the others who will enjoy the final product, whatever it may be. This can be difficult in some trades and professions, particularly in this era of specialization and industrial division of labor. It will be difficult to think of my work as "art" if I perform the same dull task, over and over again, during every minute of my work life. (This in turn may say something about the relative justice of work that demands this kind of repetitive routine from the workers.) But if I can think of my work as the creation of something beautiful, which others will appreciate as they might appreciate a beautiful sculpture or a brilliant piece of music, then I will have come a long way toward understanding my work as part of who I am— rather than allowing it to alienate me from myself.

How, exactly, is this related to the virtue of self-control? Again, if we think of it as mere self-mastery, the connection will not be terribly clear. But if self-control means a restructuring of our priorities such that our focus on ourselves is "displaced" by a focus on the greater good of others, then the relationship to artistic creation is clearer: artists create, not primarily in order to assert their selfhood as a dominant force in the world, but to shift the center of attention to the work of art itself, so that others might enjoy it and perhaps even become better people in the process. This is "control of the self," but not *for the sake of* the self: it is for the sake of the other.

Conclusion

Throughout this chapter, I have repeatedly observed that, as we know it today, the world of work—and in fact, most of our encounters with the economic order—ask us to focus most of our attention on ourselves. We often imagine that we work primarily in order to earn more money, in order to buy more things, in order to be happier people. The Christian tradition does not deny the significance of work, but it does raise questions about whether happiness is really to be found simply by focusing on what human beings can gain for *themselves*. By redirecting our attention toward other people and helping us to realize the degree to which our lives are entwined with theirs, the virtues of justice, particularity, and self-control can provide our work lives with a new focus and goal. Instead of being little more than an opportunity for profit maximization, our work lives can become a means through which we cultivate habits that bind us more closely to other human beings and put us in right relationship with them. If people could come to see their working lives in this light, they might not find that Monday-morning alarm quite so annoying. Instead, it might serve as a call to participate in a world in which the connections among human beings are more deeply understood, more actively cultivated, and more enthusiastically celebrated.

Questions for discussion

1. Do you agree with the definition offered in this chapter, to the effect that work is "that which we are obligated to do, even when we don't want to"? If not, what alternative definition would you offer? List some experiences in your own life that count as "work" according to this definition (or according to your alternative); then list some things that you have done that were strenuous and demanding ("a lot of work") but that you would not consider to be "work" according to the definition.

2. Do you think that this chapter's description of the key elements of our economic system—exchange, efficiency, and a focus on the final product—provide an adequate description of it? What other elements might be included? Does your own experience of the economic system confirm the importance of these elements? Offer some stories to illustrate your views.

3. Discuss the description of the purposes of work (as habit, hardship, and humanizing force) that are described here as arising from the Christian theological perspective. To what extent do these purposes match your own experience of work? What other purposes would you add?

4. Where have you encountered the language of *justice*? Do those encounters mesh with the description of justice that is given in this chapter? To what extent are various accounts of the virtue of justice dependent upon the stories and practices of the communities that define them? Consider, for example, the ways in which a Christian account of justice might be different from, and similar to, one promulgated by the government of a nation-state.

5. Discuss the concept of self-control. What makes this such a difficult character trait to cultivate in the economic order in which we live? Consider factors across a wide range of spheres of life—not just the economic order, but the political, social, artistic, and cultural realms—that contribute to this difficulty.

6. As a way of exploring our discussion of the "unity of the virtues," pick two virtues that are not discussed in this chapter and describe how they might apply to conversations about work and the economic order.

Sources cited in this chapter and/or recommended for further reading

Aristotle, *Nicomachean Ethics*

David S. Cunningham, "Particularity," chapter 6 of *These Three Are One: The Practice of Trinitarian Theology*

T. S. Eliot, *Four Quartets*

Philip D. Kenneson, *Life on the Vine: Cultivating the Fruit of the Spirit in Christian Community*

Karl Marx, *Selected Writings*, ed. David McLellan

M. Douglas Meeks, *God The Economist: The Doctrine of God and Political Economy*

Gilbert Meilaender, ed., *Working: Its Meaning and Its Limits*

Michael S. Northcott, *Life after Debt: Christianity and Global Justice*

George Orwell, *Down and Out in Paris and London*

R. R. Reno, "Participating: Working toward Worship," in Hauerwas and Wells, eds., *The Blackwell Companion to Christian Ethics*

Dorothy Sayers, "Why Work?" in *Creed or Chaos? And Other Essays in Popular Theology*

Kathryn Tanner, *Economies of Grace*

St. Thomas Aquinas, *Summa Theologiae* IIa–IIae.57–62

Miroslav Volf, *Work in the Spirit: Toward a Theology of Work*

12

Tuesday
At the voting booth

In this chapter we turn to a second sphere of human action about which Christian ethics might have something to say: the relationship between human beings and the structures of government under which they live. In the modern West, the government typically takes the form of the nation-state and its subsidiary governmental units: states, provinces, counties, *départements*, *Länder*, or other regional and local governing bodies. These institutions are in charge of the general social organization of the population, particularly with respect to their interactions with one another and the publicly accessible goods and services that they share. The policies, rules, and regulations of these governments are developed according to certain assumptions about moral judgment and have significant impact on the kinds of questions usually considered under the general heading of ethics.

Within the Christian theological tradition, questions about the relationship of human beings to the government—and, particularly in the modern era, to the nation-state—have tended to provoke uncertainty, anxiety, and vigorous debate. Some Christian groups have argued for a wholesale withdrawal from any more involvement with the government than absolutely necessary—either because of the state's tendency to operate with distinctly non-Christian assumptions in carrying out its work, or because of a concern about the Church's tendency to capitulate to the state's way of seeing things and thereby substituting a very different set of stories and practices for its own. Other Christians have regarded the government and the Church as two distinct realms of authority, each with its own proper ends; thus, rather than withdrawing from any involvement with the state, they seek to live in both realms at once—accepting that the virtues will take a different shape in each, and giving each form of authority the kinds of allegiance that it is due. Still others have argued for a broad Christian engagement in the processes of government, encouraging activism with respect to electoral campaigns, voting, and policy-making; and those who argue for this last position represent a wide range of viewpoints, from reactionary to radical and everything in between.

Given the wide-ranging differences of opinion among Christians concerning their appropriate level of involvement with the state, this chapter will not argue for any one of these approaches as the one that Christian ethics must adopt. Instead, it will attempt to establish a broad account of the relationship between Christians and the state, and will then explore three virtues that can help us understand how the stories and practices of the faith might apply to the kinds of questions that are likely to arise in this particular sphere of human action. Many readers will begin this chapter with strong convictions about which models of Christian engagement in governmental affairs are best; others may decide along the way that some models seem easier to justify than others. But our primary focus will be on how Christians might cultivate the virtues as part of whatever form of engagement they consider most appropriate.

The two cities

Some readers may have noticed that I have thus far avoided the use of the terms "politics" and "political" in this chapter, referring instead to "the government" or "the state." This choice of language was absolutely intentional, and I now need to make clear the reasons for my somewhat cumbersome usage. The word "politics" derives from the Greek word *polis*, which was the word used to refer to the ancient Greek city-state—a self-governing city like Athens or Sparta. But the word *polis* could also be used to refer to a city in a less literal sense: the more general idea of a community, gathered for some particular purpose. We typically think of the population of a city as being gathered for geographical and economic reasons: the delivery of goods and services, as well as the structures of employment, can all be handled more easily when people live in relatively close proximity to one another. But any gathered community can be a "city" in this sense; and when the ancient Greek philosopher Aristotle spoke of the *polis*, he meant any community of human beings who gathered for a common purpose. Hence, his treatise called *Politics* was not just about civil government; rather, it concerned how people might best live together in community, regardless of the specific forms that such life might take.

The city as a metaphor for community

Given the foregoing considerations, we need to recognize that the city (*polis*) and the work of politics are not limited to the governmental entities with which we usually associate these words. In fact, given that we have been considering (ever since chapter 1) the role of the gathered community as the focal point of ethics, we might say that this entire book has been about *politics* just as much as it has been about *ethics*. It has not been about the government of the nation-state, but it *has* been about communities and how they order their lives together: and this is a question of *politics*. The Christian community is as much a *polis* as is a city-state, an empire, or a nation; thus all questions about how Christians should live, as members of the various communities of which they are a part, are *political* questions.

Throughout history, thinkers have often used the language of the city in a somewhat metaphorical way to describe the structure and governance of communities of various sorts. The language gets considerable play in the biblical text, with "Jerusalem" often describing not just a particular city in the geographical entity called Israel, but also describing, in an ideal sense, a properly ordered community: "Jerusalem—built as a city that is bound firmly together" (Ps. 122:3). More than one person has noted the irony of this usage, given that, throughout its history, Jerusalem has been one of the more strife-torn cities on the planet. However, its ideal quality derives not from the specifics of the actual city of Jerusalem, but from its description as an ideal type that included all the qualities that the biblical writers considered essential for good community life: rightly ordered relationships of the people with one another, safety and protection from one's enemies, and—most important of all—a proper acceptance of God as the city's true ruler.

The biblical writers also refer to another city which serves as Jerusalem's opposite: Babylon. Again, the origins of this usage were undoubtedly in the original historical city of Babylon—the capital of the empire that conquered the Jews, the place to which they were sent when they were exiled from their kingdom: "By the rivers of Babylon—there we sat down and there we wept . . . How could we sing the LORD's song in a foreign land?" (Ps. 137:1, 4). But long after the Israelites returned from that experience of exile, the city of Babylon continued to symbolize the kind of community life that was opposed to the beauty and perfection of the idealized Jerusalem. Babylon was described as a city divided and at war with itself, oppressing and subjugating its people, and ruled by those who had no respect for God. It thus served as a metaphor for the disorganized and idolatrous community, even when other actual historical cities arose that could have been used for the same purpose. For example, in the Book of Revelation, even though the author's criticism and outrage is clearly directed against Rome and the Roman Empire (since it was written under Roman rule and probably during a period of severe persecution), Babylon still appears as the city from which all things contrary to God seem to spring.

The strength of the city metaphor would have had something to do with the geographical importance of cities in the Middle East, particularly during the centuries just before and just after the life of Jesus. Cities were fortresses, typically with strong outer walls, that could be used as protection against an enemy. The outside world was often understood as hostile: much of it a dry and dangerous desert, in which the unprotected traveler was at the mercy of pirates and bandits. The appeal of the city was that it might offer a person protection and rest. Of course, because of its great concentration of people and of economic and military structures, it too was a place of danger—including the moral danger inherent in a place where a particular set of stories and practices lead people to form habits that might not be morally salutary. In fact, throughout the history of literature, the city has often served in both these symbolic roles: a place of protection from the dangers of the wilderness, as well as a breeding ground for temptation and degradation.

Christian accounts of the city metaphor

Early Christian writers took up the metaphor of the city, and of the different kinds of cities, as a way of describing the benefits and the dangers of the gathered community in the formation of the moral life. In a good city—well ordered, marked by right relationships, and properly acknowledging the sovereignty of God—good moral formation was possible. In a bad city—one that lacked these features—moral deformation was not only possible but likely. Thus, in similarity with our observation in chapters 2 and 3 that moral formation depends quite heavily on the company we keep, the early Christian thinkers often wrote about the relationship between our moral formation and the city or cities in which we dwell, and to which we give our allegiance.

In particular, the Christian bishop and theologian Augustine of Hippo wrote eloquently and at great length about "the two cities." He called them "the earthly city" and "the city of God." Many people who have only a passing familiarity with Augustine's work often mistakenly assume that he was talking about the difference between earth and heaven—contrasting the day-to-day world in which we live to the heavenly realm to which we are destined in the afterlife. But this is not Augustine's primary meaning. Rather, he is using the language of city metaphorically to help his readers think about their citizenship: to whom do they give their highest allegiance? Should they understand themselves as citizens of the various earthly cities in which they dwell—empires, nation-states, and literal cities, as well as the other kinds of communities to which they are committed? Or should their true allegiance be to the city of God, in which God alone is the only recipient of their devotion?

Augustine found this metaphor to be a fruitful one in sorting out the various forms of wisdom which Christianity had inherited from the Greco-Roman culture into which it was born. He lived well after the conversion of the Roman Empire to Christianity (which had occurred under the emperor Constantine in 313 AD); however, Greek and Roman art, literature, philosophy, and social life still very much dominated his culture. Augustine believed that, if Christians were to make good use of that Greco-Roman wisdom, they would first need to test whether it could be brought into the city of God—that is, whether it was compatible with a citizenship that pledged its full allegiance to God rather than to all the other possible candidates for that allegiance. Some elements of antique culture could be accepted; other elements would need to be rejected; and much of it could be adopted with certain modifications that would bring it under the sway of the Christian perspective.

This last point deserves special emphasis, if for no other reason than to help us avoid another common misinterpretation of Augustine's work. He was *not* using the phrase "the earthly city" to describe ancient Greco-Roman culture, divorced from all connections to Christianity, which would have implied that the city of God was simply another name for the Christian church. This interpretation would too easily lead to the same mistakes that we noted, in chapter 5, concerning H. Richard Niebuhr's book *Christ and Culture*—namely, it would suggest that our goal should be to find just the right "mixture" of the two elements. But this is not what Augustine has in mind: he is suggesting something much more radical.

In order to understand Augustine's point here, we need to employ a pair of diagrams. The first one illustrates the most common modern understanding of the relationship between Christianity and the rest of the world. In this picture, the non-Christian perspective—call it "the secular world" or "the larger culture" or even "the earthly city"—is the larger entity; in fact, it seems to constitute the "whole world." In comparison, the Christian realm—call it "the Church" or "the Christian perspective" or "the city of God"—is an enclave: a small territory within this larger realm, probably struggling to gain a foothold. If we were to create a Venn diagram, it would look like this:

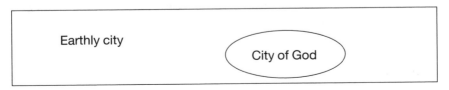

Note that this perspective understands the secular culture as the norm—it is the larger box, the "universe" in Venn-diagram nomenclature, within which the Church is a small subset.

But in fact, this is not what Augustine has in mind at all—precisely the opposite. The "larger" realm, the more comprehensive "city" that takes up the whole of the created universe, is the city of God. The earthly city is created by the choices of fallen humanity, which attempts to block off certain segments of life and to treat them as if they were independent of the sovereignty of God. They are not independent, of course, but those who live in these spaces "wall themselves off" from the guidance and goodness of God, so as to create a hollowed-out space that avoids God as much as possible. A diagram of Augustine's view would look like this:

In Augustine's view, the *earthly* city is the enclave that has pushed back the boundaries of the city of God in order to try to create a "secular" space that is outside God's purview. But of course, if one holds the God-centered view that Augustine held, this kind of position is ultimately impossible to maintain. God's presence and authority is all-encompassing; one cannot escape it. Augustine's vision of the future was that, slowly but surely, the walls of the earthly city would crumble and its citizens would come to realize that their true homeland was the city of God.

All of this may seem completely counterintuitive to those of us who live in a largely secular culture, but it flows quite logically from Augustine's assumptions: that the entire world was created by God, belongs to God, and will ultimately return to God. Thus the "natural" citizenship of human beings is to the city of God. Only when human beings pretend that a part of world is their own, rather than God's, do they find themselves "living in the earthly city."

Here, we need to pause to make one additional important clarification about Augustine's meaning. Too often, he has been misinterpreted as claiming that the city of God is equivalent to "the Christian Church," and therefore that the "earthly city" is a description of everything outside the Church. But Augustine quite specifically argues that this is not the case. Those who call themselves Christians—who proclaim themselves to be members of the Body of Christ, the Church—may be living in the city of God, but they also may be living in the earthly city. Their home will depend on where their allegiances truly lie. Augustine is not interested in what people *declare* themselves to be, nor about what box they mark on the form that says "religious preference"; he is interested in their *true citizenship*. The Church, he believes, is a *corpus permixtum*: a "mixed body," like a field of wheat that includes both grain and weeds. It is impossible to know, when the seeds are germinating and the shoots are beginning to appear, which is which—whether a particular member of the mixed body of the Church is, in his or her heart of hearts, ultimately a citizen of the city of God or of the earthly city. This will depend not just on the person's outward declaration of allegiance, nor even on the person's actions alone (though this, Augustine thought, can certainly give us a clue); it will depend on an alignment of the person's actions with his or her inward disposition. And thus, as Augustine makes very clear (and as Christians have too often ignored, at the cost of great heartache to many): only God truly knows where a person's true allegiances lie.

In one sense, Augustine's argument can be read simply as an extension of the discussion in the opening chapters of this book concerning the importance of the gathering community and the allegiances that it engenders. But I have discussed it at this point because I believe it to be an important key in thinking about the topic of this chapter: the proper shape of the Christian life in its dealings with the state. This is true not only because of Augustine's use of the *city* metaphor and his attention to such politically charged terms as "allegiance" and "citizenship"; it also has to do with his skill in comparing and contrasting two different sets of allegiance, and helping his readers to see them in relationship to each other. He makes it very clear that a Christian's truest and highest allegiance should always be to God; and, as a result, he *relativizes* the importance of other entities to which we are often asked to give our allegiance—including, of course, the state.

Contemporary challenges

The complex relationship between the two cities is an ongoing reality that Christians have faced in almost every era of the Church's existence, and Augustine's work has been highly influential in helping them to understand that reality. But Augustine lived long ago and under a vastly different structure of government from what we experience today. In particular, the last two centuries have brought with them quite fundamental shifts in the prevailing forms of government and in the relationship between the Church and those governments. Consequently, the ethical questions that we are discussing in this chapter have become even more complicated than they were in

Augustine's day. In this section, we need to explore three modern developments that may lead us to look at matters somewhat differently: the rise of democratic political systems, the advent of new technologies, and the appearance of new, non-governmental entities that have partly taken over the former role of governments.

Modern Western democracy

Many people who read Augustine's account of the two cities see it as a useful description of the concerns of his era, but not particularly applicable to our own. Obviously, if Christians living under some form of tyrannical empire were being asked to make sacrifices to the pagan gods or to deny their faith, then of course, they would have to refuse to do these things and, instead, to make it clear that their true allegiance was to God. But many today live in democracies that offer a considerable amount of religious freedom; Christians are allowed to hold firmly to their beliefs and to engage in practices of worship and community life. The democratic form of government (so the argument goes) means that, in practice, one's allegiance to the state and one's allegiance to God need never come into conflict with one another.

Unfortunately, however—as the old song tells us—"it ain't necessarily so." A person's allegiance to the state and to her or his religious faith can certainly be in conflict, particularly when it comes to questions about human judgment and action. Of course, some forms of action that cultivate Christian virtues may be totally unaffected by, or even actively supported by, the government; generosity that has been habituated through Christian stories and practices, for example, may be reinforced and even rewarded by a government's decision to waive all taxes on the money that people give away. But some observers have questioned whether this relationship is quite as cozy as it first appears. The two motives for giving money away—governmental tax policy and generosity motivated by Christian narratives and practices—may appear to be in a mutually reinforcing relationship; but which motive really controls the person's actions? If governmental policy were to change, would we still give as much money away? Questions such as these tend to raise doubts in our minds as to whether an easy synergy between "faith in God" and "faith in government" is always possible.

Another difficulty in this relationship arises from one of its features that most of us think of as a benefit: the "free exercise of religion" that is offered by many western democratic states. Without denying the many positive features of such allowances, we should observe than they can have two troubling consequences. First, the concept of "free exercise of religion" can be used to attempt to prevent people from working for changes in governmental policy that would be favorable to their own religious views. (Whether or not people think this is a good thing usually depends on whether they are on the more successful side of the argument: we tend to appreciate government support for religiously-grounded viewpoints as long as they are *our* religiously-grounded viewpoints!) But a second (and more important) negative consequence is that governments cannot, by their very nature, offer truly free exercise of religion; that exercise has to be limited to those areas that do not interfere too directly with governmental policy. So, for example, a Christian pacifist living in the United States will not be allowed to forgo paying her taxes just because she objects to the government's military policy; similarly, a Muslim schoolgirl in France can be prevented from wearing her *burqa* because the government deems it to have a disruptive effect on the classroom.

Thus, as many commentators have noted, one of the (perhaps somewhat surprising) effects of the rise of modern liberal democracy, which should have allowed religiously motivated action to flourish, has been to closet such action away into the private realm. The "freedom of religion" that most such governments provide is most clearly visible with respect to the citizens' private religious practice: gathering for worship, praying in their homes, and shaping the private elements of their lives according to their faith. In the public sphere, matters are very different: actions that might potentially put people in opposition to the aims of the government, or that would bring differing religious perspectives into conflict with one another, are not nearly so broadly tolerated. As a result, the rise of "modern Western democracy" has not turned out to be as thoroughly positive a development for Christian ethics as some have imagined it to be.

These comments are not meant to suggest, of course, that democracy is a bad idea, or that anyone's life would be improved if modern governments reversed their policies concerning the free exercise of religion. Rather, we simply need to be aware that modern democracies and their proffered "freedoms" are not a cure-all with regard to the relationship between Christianity and the state. The problems that are raised by Augustine's account of the two cities—and the conflicting allegiances that can result from our attempts to maintain citizenship in both of them—are still present, regardless of whether we live under a democracy, a republic, a monarchy, a fascist state, or any other form of government.

New technologies

A second set of contemporary challenges concerns the rise of new technologies. Of course, most of these technologies are available to everyone—not just to governments—and many of them are sufficiently useful and/or entertaining to keep us occupied for hours at a time. This, in turn, tends to distract us from the ways that such technologies are being used to reshape our world.

One of the most prominent forms of new technology is the digital camera, which allows a great deal of human activity to be recorded and observed at all times. Security cameras, traffic cameras, and other forms of "watchfulness" have become so popular that, according to one estimate, the average citizen of Great Britain is now captured on a surveillance camera about 300 times per day. The nightmarish world of George Orwell's haunting novel *1984* may have still seemed quite farfetched even when we arrived at the year designated in its title; but now, a mere twenty-five years later, many of the technologies that his book described have actually been produced and are widely available and in use.

I mention these developments neither to provoke paranoia nor to develop some kind of conspiracy theory about how the government is slowly but surely becoming Big Brother. Rather, my point is that the development of technologies of surveillance can have an extraordinarily powerful influence on our thought about ethics—sometimes without us even realizing it. Such technologies can tend to make us more confident about, and therefore more comfortable with, ethical systems built on rules and laws. This occurs because surveillance helps to ameliorate one of the main problems that we noted throughout this book about such systems: that many people can break the rules and get away with it. In theory, at least, surveillance systems could eventually be extended so broadly that those who break the rules could never expect to avoid punishment; and therefore, we might become even more dependent on such systems of rules than we already are.

And this, I want to suggest, would be a mistake. As we have observed from very early on, Christian ethics has always differed rather profoundly from at least some other systems of morality, precisely because it resists being reduced to a set of rules for good behavior. Like the Greek and Jewish approaches to ethics that preceded it, Christianity has always been highly interested in the *character* with which human people act, and their *motives* for doing what they do—not just with their actions alone. Thus, although we may be tempted by our access to new technology to concentrate primarily on outward human actions and to make ethical judgments on the basis of what people do, we must also remember the importance of character, disposition, and habit in ethical judgment.

The rise of more complex communication technologies also provides human beings with new tools for developing and propagating certain ways of thinking. As a result, viewpoints that would have once been marginalized and unknown can now achieve a wide audience, particularly through the increasingly popular channels of the internet (social networking sites, interactive "alternative worlds," and blogs). On the one hand, this is of course a marvelously positive development; it means that anyone, and not just established institutions and organizations, can play a significant role in the creation of a culture. But it also means that particular systems of ethical thought, including those that have described themselves as Christian, can no longer rely on unspoken alliances with those established institutions and organizations for the widespread propagation of their own ethical perspectives.

The advent of technology, the breadth of access to information, and the rise of *marketing* as a distinct field of study: all these factors have dramatically increased the capacity of human beings to produce and to propagate new narratives—including narratives that can attract the attention of very large groups of people—and to do so at a much quicker pace than has been the case in previous eras. So, for example, a company that wants to sell more of a particular product (let us say, for instance, ethics textbooks!) now has wide access to the channels of communication, an advanced range of technological means and marketing techniques, and (therefore) an opportunity to reach thousands, perhaps millions, of potential consumers. All that is needed is a narrative that can shape people to become more avid consumers of ethics textbooks.

Such straightforward propagation of new narratives was once achievable only by those structures and systems that were able and willing either to demand attention and conformity to the narrative (by force if necessary), or to wait a very long time. Governments were the primary exponents of the first alternative (having, as they did, a means of coercion), whereas religious perspectives usually made use of the latter (having an eternity to make their point). But in recent decades, a range of wholly new structures have emerged, neither strictly governmental nor strictly faith-based, but still able to shape new narratives and practices. These new structures demand our attention for a few paragraphs.

Non-governmental entities in governmental roles

The ready availability of the technological and political means for "re-narrating" reality has given rise to a new kind of enterprise in the modern world. This new structure is dedicated not simply to the traditional patterns of industry (the production of goods and the rendering of services), but to the formation of an entire culture, including a new set of narratives and practices to go along with it. One recent commentator—a political scientist and theologian named Michael Budde—calls them "global culture industries." The goal of these global culture industries is to weave new narratives and to encourage people to participate in an alternative set of practices—and to endow these narratives and practices with such universal appeal that consumers throughout the world will develop needs and desires for the products and services that the same industry produces. These global culture industries seek not so much to produce things that the public already wants, but rather, to make the public want whatever they are already producing.

Thus large media/entertainment/travel conglomerates like Time-Warner and Disney not only produce films; they also saturate markets for everything else with the characters from the films, so that whenever people shop for items that would otherwise be completely unrelated to the film (groceries, underwear, a kid's meal at McDonalds), they are presented with the characters—and sometimes even the plot—of the film. (A cynic once remarked that the entire plot of any animated film made these days needs to fit neatly onto exactly four Burger King souvenir cups.) These same companies also own many of the newspapers in which the films are advertised (and reviewed), and the television stations on which they are promoted. As a result, the story of the film—as well as the larger story that seeing and knowing about the film is urgently important—is learned and acquired almost instantly all around the world.

As a result, the classic narratives and practices of other worldviews and other large-scale systems of thought, such as Christianity, are pushed to the edges. The distinctive stories and practices of Christianity and other long-established worldviews, which once had some power to shape human needs and desires in ways that did not necessarily align with powerful economic and political interests, are frequently eclipsed by the narratives promulgated by the global culture industries—narratives that are usually designed primarily to sell the product. Sometimes, of course, these industries also work very closely with nation-states in order to develop the forms of regulation, taxation, and trade that will be favorable to their own efforts to saturate the market; in such cases, their alternative stories become even more powerful and more persuasive to yet larger numbers of people. As these newly created narratives quickly replace the traditional narratives of Christianity, it becomes very easy for Christians to be drawn into patterns of the moral life that are difficult to differentiate from those of the nation-state.

At one level, of course, this is nothing new; such alignment of the interests of the state with those of particular industries has been a frequent feature of the modern world. What is different in this new situation is, first, that these industries have made marketing and culture-building into a major priority, so that they are able to create an entire world in which "it just seems natural" to want to buy all the new merchandise associated with, for example, the latest hit film. But a second difference—and this is quite unprecedented—is that the global culture industries have so thoroughly saturated so many corners of the global market that they no longer need the cooperation of nation-states in order to create, and to profit from, the culture that they have created. They have developed the power to shape opinion and desire in ways that would be the envy of the rulers of most nation-states.

To summarize: these recent developments—modern democracy, new technologies, and the rise of the global culture industries—have given the earthly city even more ways of building up and fortifying the walls that insulate it from being affected by the city of God. Under such circumstances, Christian ethics cannot simply promulgate a series of rules or laws and expect them to win over the hearts and minds of people who have been shaped by a radically different set of narratives and practices. The only way forward is to consider those excellences of character that ought to shape the citizens of the nation-state, and then to consider whether formation in such virtues is possible under the present cultural and political circumstances. This will be our goal in the remainder of this chapter. Only after such an analysis can we begin to consider to what degree Christians can, or should, be involved in the structures of the nation-state.

Three political virtues

I begin this section by noting once again that, even though I will discuss only a few of the virtues here, I am not thereby dismissing the others. The unity of the virtues reminds us that all of them will affect how Christians engage with the government structures under which they live. Nevertheless, given the limitations of time and space, I have chosen three virtues that seem particularly important to cultivate in this particular sphere of life: faithfulness, peaceableness, and courage. The first virtue, *faithfulness*, is necessary because the nation-state (or its surrogate) constantly threatens to become the first and primary object of our devotion, whereas—at least from a Christian point of view—its authority to demand our loyalty and trust must always remain secondary to that of God. The second virtue in my list, *peaceableness*, is important in this context because of the willingness that nation-states have traditionally shown to use violence when necessary to defend their interests; if Christians are truly committed to peace, they will need to think about how this commitment relates to the use of force by the state. And the third virtue, *courage*, needs to be explored and defined precisely because, at least as it was characterized in the ancient world, it tends to be associated primarily with soldiers in battle and other efforts to defend governing structures with violence. Christians have typically understood courage rather differently, taking account of their commitment to peaceableness and of their alternative understanding of true citizenship.

Faithfulness

Faithfulness is closely related to *faith*, which we discussed briefly in chapter 5 when we considered the Christian use of creeds as statements of faith. As we observed at that point, the creeds serve as declarations that indicate where Christians place their strongest allegiances: in God, as opposed to anything else. When people declare, in the creed, that they "believe in" or "have faith in" God, this is a way of saying that they do *not* place their ultimate allegiance in something else: the state, the market, the numerous other structures that vie for their attention on a regular basis. We will return again to this notion of "faith" in the chapter that follows, as we turn our attention to its role as a theological virtue and its particular applicability to the realm of bioethics.

Meanwhile, we will consider the closely related virtue of faithfulness. These two words—"faith" and "faithfulness"—usually translate the same Greek word in the New Testament: *pistis*. The rationale for the differing translations has a great deal to do with the context in which *pistis* occurs; indeed, it is an extremely multi-faceted word, which sometimes also means *trust*, *persuasion*, or even *proof*. The translation of the word as "faithfulness" is most appropriate in those contexts in which the text's focus is on a relationship of trust that is carried out over the long term; we might also translate it "loyalty" or "constancy." The word suggests a disposition of consistent devotion to another person—a devotion that is not primarily based on the question of whether, or to what degree, that other person is devoted to you.

For Christians, the ultimate example of the virtue of faithfulness is provided by God. God is described as *faithful* to the people: first and foremost to the people of Israel, and then also to God's son Jesus, and finally to the community of believers gathered in the name of Jesus as the Church. God's faithfulness endures, even when those to whom God is faithful offer little or nothing in return. The Old Testament provides a number of illustrations of this faithfulness, describing God as (for example) the spouse of a wayward partner who is disloyal and takes up with others, but whom God does not abandon in spite of these misdeeds (Hosea 1–2). When the people turn away and begin to worship false gods, as in the story of the golden calf, God is angry with them but does not abandon them (Exod. 32:1–14). These repeated stories of God's faithfulness provide the backdrop for the virtue of faithfulness as it applies to human beings—in their relationships both to God and to one another.

Many Christians are quick to assert their *faith* in God, but to exhibit true *faithfulness* to God is another matter. However firmly they may place their trust in God, most believers find that their allegiances are often drawn toward other potential objects of devotion—objects that may eventually compete with God for their attention and their energies, and that may occasionally even seem to displace God altogether. This is especially true in the contemporary context, where relative wealth and a vast array of technological advances have dramatically increased the number of potential objects of our affection and commitment. Many people say that they have *faith* in God, and some will even claim to be unreservedly *faithful* to God, but their actions often suggest otherwise: such single-minded faithfulness can be hard to maintain in the face of opportunities to put one's trust in money, in consumer goods, in military force, in medical technology, and even in the natural environment. When these other elements begin to play a more significant role in a person's life than does God, then that person's life can no longer be characterized by the virtue of *faithfulness to God*.

If so many other possible allegiances capture our attention and our devotion, why should we focus on the virtue of faithfulness in *this* chapter, which is concerned with political structures such as governments? The special relevance of *faithfulness* in this context arises from the particular kinds of allegiances that governments often demand. I may spend a great deal of time playing with my new video game system, and my devotion to it may indeed threaten to eclipse my devotion to God; but if I come to my senses and learn to enjoy my game in moderation, the game itself will not question my loyalty or make any active demands of me whatsoever. On the other hand, if I find myself excessively devoted to the nation-state and try to draw back from that devotion in order to maintain and cultivate my faithfulness to God, the nation-state may well question my loyalty and may even demand that I set my loyalties to God aside in order to give the state the allegiance it considers itself due. Obviously, this does not mean that a Christian cannot have a (secondary) allegiance to other kinds of political and social communities, from nation-states and large institutions to sports teams and good close friends. But Christianity (like Judaism before it) has always been fairly clear about where one's primary allegiance must lie. "You shall love the LORD your God with all your heart, and with all your soul, and with all your might" (Deut 6:5); "Whoever loves father or mother more than me is not worthy of me; and whoever loves son or daughter more than me is not worthy of me" (Matt. 10:37).

A colleague of mine who has written extensively on the relationship between Christianity and the state once commented that, whatever differences we might imagine among various nation-states—big or small, rich or poor, democratic or totalitarian—they all make three demands on their citizens: they demand that people be willing to *die* for them, to *kill* for them, and to *pay* for them. While this comment may be somewhat tongue-in-cheek, it does highlight the *kinds* of demands that nation-states typically place on their citizens: not matters of minor inconvenience, but significant and life-shaping expectations. In at least some instances, the state demands a degree of loyalty from its citizens that far outstrips the demands placed on consumers by manufacturers, on sick people by the health-care system, or on most people by their friends and families. If we decide not to buy a newly released film on DVD, we may regret not getting to see it or even suffer some social disapproval, but we will usually not find our lives or liberty to be in danger. If, however, the state passes a law that requires me to risk my own life, or to put the lives of others under threat, and I am unwilling to do so, then I may well face not only persecution but also prosecution. Because the nation-state exercises police power and can force its citizens to obey its laws, it holds considerably greater sway over the virtue of faithfulness than do most of the other institutions and structures that we experience. In fact, it can actually determine, *for* us, where our loyalties must lie.

Please note that I am not here making the claim that a Christian's primary allegiance to God is *necessarily* incompatible with some kind of secondary allegiance to the state. In fact, particularly in modern Western democracies, many of us go through our lives without the slightest hint that there might be any incompatibilities between these two sets of loyalties. I will return to this point in a moment; meanwhile, it will behoove us to acquaint ourselves with some historical circumstances in which these two sets of loyalties *did* come into conflict. For those of us who have not actually lived through such a situation, we might enter into conversation with someone who has, or read an account written by people who have done so. Consider, for example, the rise of Naziism in Germany, in which Christians who protested against the state's military buildup, or against its treatment of Jews, gypsies, and homosexuals, were very likely to face persecution, imprisonment, or death. This helps to illustrate two elements of our discussion of faithfulness: first, that conflicts between these allegiances can indeed occur; and second, that the considerable power of the nation-state to force people to comply with its demands means that faithfulness to God and to one's religious beliefs can become very difficult to maintain.

Such cases may seem extreme to those of us who live in democratic societies that allow considerable freedom of religion and are relatively tolerant concerning dissent. In the grand scheme of history, however, such free and tolerant societies have been rare; considerably more common have been those regimes in which theologically-grounded opposition to official government

Sophie Scholl

In 1942, a small group of students at the University of Munich created an underground movement which they called "The White Rose." They published pamphlets that criticized the Nazi regime; they did not see themselves as "outside agitators" but as patriotic Germans who loved their country and believed that it was on the road to self-destruction. This was well before full details concerning the concentration camps and other Nazi atrocities had come to light; the students were primarily motivated by the disastrous military strategies that Hitler was pursuing, particularly on the eastern front (for example, the German army had been defeated at Stalingrad, suffering huge losses). The students hoped that their fellow citizens would add their voices and generate a chorus that would erode the government's popular support.

Unfortunately, the students had not fully appreciated the absolutist tactics of the Nazi regime. After distributing their leaflets in one of the university buildings, they were apprehended and forced to confess; their homes were raided and in the process, several of their co-conspirators were also arrested. In a frighteningly short period of time, almost all the members of the group were questioned, convicted in a show trial, and executed.

Eventually, the group was much memorialized, both in Germany and abroad. Two of its members are particularly fervently remembered: siblings Hans and Sophie Scholl. They were the first two students arrested; also, most of those executed were male and, in retrospect, such a swift execution of a relatively innocent young girl was a particularly painful memory for the German people. A popular book focused on her life, her role in the movement, and her execution; it is entitled *Das kurze Leben der Sophie Scholl* (1980; translated as *The Short Life of Sophie Scholl*, 1984). In addition, the incident is the subject of two excellent films: *Die Weiße Rose* (*The White Rose*, 1982), and, more recently, *Sophie Scholl: Die letzen Tage* (*Sophie Scholl: The Final Days*, 2005), which makes use of recently released transcripts of the interrogation and trial.

What comes across clearly—particularly in the most recent film—is the degree to which Sophie, especially, relied on her religious formation in order to stand firm against the government's effort to force her to recant her criticisms of their actions. Not only did she exemplify the virtues mentioned in this chapter—faithfulness, peaceableness, and courage—but she did so, at least in part, from Christian motives. At the young age of 21, she was willing to exercise good moral judgment as to where her allegiances should lie—something that the overwhelming majority of Germans found themselves unable to do, particularly in the face of Nazi repression of all dissent. Reading, watching, and listening to her story, we can only hope that—if one day faced with similar circumstances—we would show ourselves to be people of such character.

policy has been opposed with force. And even an official policy of tolerance and freedom can be manipulated in ways that actually lead most citizens to offer up more allegiance to the government than they realize they are offering. The United States provides a particularly good example of this phenomenon.

In the US context, the separation of church and state and strongly-worded constitutional guarantees about freedom of expression combine to insure that people are rarely imprisoned or executed for their religious beliefs. (There are exceptions; one cannot escape prosecution for sedition by arguing, for example, that one's religion requires one to advocate the violent overthrow of the government.) At the same time, however, a great many US citizens identify themselves both as Christian believers and as loyal citizens of the nation-state. This puts them in a position in which these two sets of allegiances might potentially come into conflict with one another. They therefore usually attempt to deflect this potential conflict by segregating their religious and national commitments into different spheres. Religion is understood to be a private affair, largely related to one's interior state; this allows one's external public persona to be fiercely supportive of the national government, with no apparent conflict between the two. Thus, even though the United States has an official policy of tolerance with regard to religious beliefs, it has maintained a high degree of allegiance among its citizens by encouraging them to relegate all religious belief into a private interior space where it can have little significant impact on one's relationship to the government—or on any aspect of one's external actions.

Obviously, the approach to Christian ethics that we have been exploring throughout this book has little room for such a sharp division between the public and private spheres. If the virtues are to mean anything at all, they cannot be merely interior states that have no bearing on one's public actions and activities. If I am to cultivate the virtue of faithfulness—if I am to remain loyal to God above all else—then this will have to show itself in my outward actions, including my possible rejection of allegiances (including those to the nation-state) when they come into conflict with my primary loyalty: faithfulness to God.

Peaceableness

Another of the fruits of the Spirit is particularly relevant to our discussion of Christian attitudes toward the nation-state: it is that of peaceableness. The Greek word is *eirēnē*, and the Hebrew word that looms large in the background is *shalom*. Many English translations offer the word "peace" rather than "peaceableness," and the former is certainly to be preferred in many contexts. But in modern English, the word "peace" is often used to refer to an interior calmness of mind or a psychological disposition of tranquility; and this is only rarely what the biblical language is seeking to invoke. The focus of the Greek and Hebrew words is on *wholeness* and *well-being*—not only in a person's interior life but in all of his or her dealings: a holistic condition in which all people are in right relationship with one another and with God. In fact, according to the Jewish and Christian perspectives, God is the ultimate source of all peace—a matter on which the biblical witness is fairly consistent. God creates a world in which all creatures are in a peaceable, harmonious relationship to one another (Gen. 1–2); and in the end, they will all gather again into that peaceable harmony (Rev. 21–22).

In short, *shalom* is not just a state of mind; it is a way of life. This is why I prefer to use the term "peaceableness" to name the virtue that is implied by these Old and New Testament words. While "peace" (in the sense of an interior state) may indeed *result* from a life of virtue, "peaceableness" more accurately describes the character trait that Christians are called to embody in their lives.

The express witness of the New Testament is that, in the person of Jesus Christ, God brings peace into the world in a yet more profound way. Through Christ, the world is redeemed from its fall into violence and chaos; right relationships can now be restored. Paul emphasizes this in a passage from his letter to the Ephesians. He accents the importance of *peace* as a product of this restoration, and also sounds a number of other themes that we have stressed throughout this book: the significance of forgiveness and reconciliation; the Christian's true citizenship and allegiance to God, rather than to any earthly kingdom; and the claim that Christ is the end of the law. In this passage, Paul refers to two groups of early Christians: those who were "near," meaning those who already had a close relationship with the God of Jesus Christ (namely the Jews); and those who were "far off," meaning those Gentiles (non-Jews) who had not previously had a close relationship with this God—at least not knowingly so. He describes how both groups are brought into a state of peace:

But now in Christ Jesus you who once were far off have been brought near by the blood of Christ. For he is our peace; in his flesh he has made both groups into one and has broken down the dividing wall, that is, the hostility between us. He has abolished the law with its commandments and ordinances, that he might create in himself one new humanity in place of the two, thus making peace, and might reconcile both groups to God in one body through the cross, thus putting to death that hostility through it. So he came and proclaimed peace to you who were far off and peace to those who were near; for through him both of us have access in one Spirit to the Father. So then you are no longer strangers and aliens, but you are citizens with the saints and also members of the household of God, built upon the foundation of the apostles and prophets, with Christ Jesus himself as the cornerstone (Eph. 2:13–20).

Note carefully the metaphors that Paul uses in this passage: he specifically invokes the language of citizenship to suggest to Christians where their true allegiances should lie. He also uses the phrase "the household of God," which is another way of invoking the social, political, and economic communities of which we are a part: the Greek word here is *oikos*, from which we get our word "economics," which is the science of maintaining a household (whether that of a family or of an entire nation-state). Paul's affirmation of Jesus as the reconciler and restorer of right relationships reminds us that Christians are called to cultivate the virtue of peaceableness and to make peace among those whose relationships have broken down or been distorted into patterns of violence and strife.

(The virtue of peaceableness is obviously quite closely related to the practice of peacemaking that we discussed in chapter 6. While that practice helps Christians to cultivate other virtues as well, it is certainly one of the central means by which they learn to allow their lives to be characterized by peaceableness. Readers may find it useful to return to that discussion at this point and to reread it in light of this chapter's comments on the biblical language for peace and peaceableness.)

This virtue, too, is a particularly challenging one to cultivate, given the context of the modern nation-state. While it would be going too far to describe the state as *inherently* violent, it is certainly the case that states have found it useful to resort to violence to enforce their aims. At various periods of history, the Christian church attempted to mimic the work of the state in this regard, enforcing its own decrees with violence. However, in recent centuries, the Church seems to have given up this rather ill-conceived path. The state has shown very little interest in doing so; and indeed, if my colleague is correct in his threefold description of the state's needs (for people to die, kill, and pay for them), we can expect the state's reliance on violent force to continue and, mostly likely, to increase. (After all, if Thomas Hobbes thought that life outside the protection of the state during the seventeenth century looked like "the war of all against all," what would he think of today's world—more heavily armed, more mobile, more vulnerable to disruption? Our contemporary circumstances give nation-states plenty of excuses to increase their reliance on violent force.)

What does it mean to cultivate the virtue of peaceableness in the midst of such a commitment to violence? As we will note below, it may have implications as to how Christians might want to engage with the government—seeking, for example, to reduce its tendency to rely on military solutions to every problem. But given the depth of that reliance, it would probably be unwise to imagine that enough Christians exerting enough political pressure would convert the state away from its use of violence as an essential element in its approach to governance. A wiser course, as many commentators have suggested, might be for Christians to develop alternative structures to provide the kinds of things that states have sometimes provided—education, health care, social services, and economic structure—and to do so without relying on the violence on which the state depends for the enforcement of its will.

Creating such alternative structures may strike us as a utopian fantasy, but anyone who advocates such an approach can rely on plenty of precedent. Throughout history—including the present day—Christians have created and maintained their own schools, hospitals, social service agencies, and other institutions that are now often taken for granted to be primarily the function of governments. The importance of these alternative structures becomes most obvious under those governments that either do not provide such institutions or do so in ways that Christians consider unjust, inequitable, violent, or otherwise not adequately characterized by the virtues. (Such alternative structures have been particularly prominent in Latin America over the past several decades; Christians living in "base communities" work outside the usual governmental channels to provide one another with the basic necessities of life in ways that are in keeping with their commitments to justice, peaceableness, and hope.) Perhaps unfortunately, most modern Western democracies have provided such services as education, health care, and economic oversight in ways that—while often not particularly virtuous—are just adequate enough that few Christians feel obligated to expend the time, money, and energy that would be necessary to provide these services in ways that truly embody the virtues. Nevertheless, a strong commitment to peaceableness, faithfulness, and courage might well motivate some Christians to give more attention to developing such alternative structures—structures with institutional missions that are motivated, above all, by the One who proclaimed peace to those who were far off and peace to those who were near.

Courage

Courage, also known as fortitude, is usually described as one of the two virtues that help us conform our *will* to our *intellect*. (The other is temperance or self-control.) These two virtues help us commit ourselves to go ahead and *do* those things that we believe, according to our reason, to be the right things to do. Two general categories of obstacles can hinder us from conforming our will to our reason: the first is when we are drawn toward some pleasure that our minds would prefer to reject (which temperance helps us to resist), and the second is when we feel unwilling to face some difficulty which our minds tell us we ought to try to overcome. In this second case, we need courage to surmount whatever obstacles are nudging us to turn away from what the intellect knows we should do.

In the ancient world, courage often stood at the head of the list of cardinal virtues. Its prominence should not surprise us, given the cultural setting in which those virtues arose. In ancient Greece, everything depended on the ability of soldiers to carry out the will of the government—defending the homeland and conquering new territories as needed. Consequently, most of the examples of courage that are offered by the ancient writers derive from the battlefield; military settings provide them with their clearest and most dramatic examples. In fact, almost all of Aristotle's examples of courage come from the field of battle; he even says at one point that courage is chiefly concerned with the danger of death in war.

The heavily military focus of courage in the ancient world presented something of a challenge for Christian authors. They were keen to hold fast to the tradition that named courage among the four cardinal virtues; Gregory the Great, Ambrose, Augustine, and Thomas Aquinas all affirm its significance. But none of these authors believed that Christian virtue was primarily to be demonstrated on the battlefield. Even though they were not "pacifists" as we would define that term today (that is, they believed that Christians could rightly participate in a truly just war), they certainly recognized the degree to which the entire structure of Christian ethics raised serious questions about the heavy focus on combat and violence that marked the ancient Greek and Roman conceptions of the virtuous life.

Compounding this problem was the fact that the word "courage" is so very rare in the Bible (and practically non-existent in the New Testament); its few appearances are mostly in idiomatic phrases of encouragement: "let your heart take courage" (Ps. 27:14 and 31:24); "keep up your courage" (Acts 27:22, 25); "take courage; I have conquered the world!" (John 16:33). With respect to the other ancient virtues, we can usually find approximate parallels in the biblical text, even if the match is not exact (so, as we noted in the last chapter, "justice" often appears as "righteousness" and "temperance" becomes "self-control"). But almost nowhere in the Bible (except in some of the books of the Apocrypha) do we find praise and commendation of the character trait that, for the ancient Greeks, often stood at the forefront of the cardinal virtues. How do the Christian writers face this difficulty?

They do primarily by changing the field of activity in which courage is best exemplified. They hold to the classic definition of the term: it is the virtue that allows our will to overcome the resistance that it sometimes experiences when we face a daunting task that our minds recognize as the right thing to do. But the early and medieval Christian commentators greatly expand the range of circumstances in which such courage is needed. They frequently emphasize, as the ancients did not, that courage is needed to overcome fear of dangers, not just to the body, but also to the soul. They also describe it as essential not just in those fights that take place on the battlefield, but also those that take place in the courtroom, at the hospital, or in a thousand other circumstances of everyday life. Thomas Aquinas, for example, offers two such instances of courage: "when a man does not shrink from attendance on a sick friend for fear of deadly infection, or when he does not shrink from a journey on some matter of duty because of fear of shipwreck or bandits." For the Christian writers, the fact that Aristotle chooses most of his examples from the battlefield does not make this an essential element of the definition of courage; in the Christian reckoning, the very definition of the term means that it clearly must apply—and in fact, apply much more commonly—to other kinds of activities. They therefore call upon examples that are more consonant with the rest of the table of the virtues, in order to demonstrate how Christians must fortify themselves to overcome the temptation to avoid doing what they know to be the right thing to do. The most dramatic of their examples—replacing that of soliders in battle—is that of the *martyrs*: those who, finding themselves faced with demands to deny their faith or to desist from carrying out its obligations, bear witness to the truth of their belief by suffering humiliation, pain, and even death. In this way, the Christian writers are able to acknowledge the ancient descriptions of courage as particularly relevant to life-and-death situations, while still not compromising the Christian commitments to peaceableness, kindness, and love.

In their dealings with the nation-state in its contemporary context, Christians have a wide range of opportunities to embody the virtue of courage —and most of them do not occur on the battlefield. Any time that the government erects an obstacle to undertaking a task that Christians believe to be the right thing to do, they exemplify courage when they choose to pursue that task in spite of the obstacle—whether it be a legal restriction, a complicated bureaucratic procedure, or merely a social stigma. (For many of us, the last of these obstacles—even though it may have no obvious and direct consequences—can be the most difficult to overcome. In the US context, the Supreme Court ruled that no child could be forced, against religious objections, to recite the pledge of allegiance to the country's flag, as is common in many school classrooms; but the fact that those children were protected from criminal prosecution did not eliminate their need for courage. They still had to endure the taunts and abuse of their peers as they enacted their Christian convictions, refusing to participate in what they had been taught to regard as an idolatrous practice.) The virtue of courage is demonstrated by those who face possible jail sentences for their acts of civil disobedience; by those who place themselves under closer government scrutiny by standing in solidarity with an outcast; and by those who find themselves ostracized by their families, friends, co-workers, teammates, or fellow church members (!) when they champion some unpopular cause.

In my view, courage is a particularly important virtue to associate with our dealings with government in the contemporary setting—and this for several reasons. First, as I have already noted, courage is so frequently (and sometimes uniquely) associated with military action that its wider applicability in the Christian context needs to be noted and affirmed. Second—as I will suggest in the concluding section of this chapter—Christians may sometimes need to interact with the state in ways that are significantly different from, and sometimes much more complicated than, the conventional forms of citizenship (supporting candidates for office, voting, and the like). Finding the creativity and the resolve to move beyond these conventional forms of political engagement will often require courage—particularly in the face of the enormous social pressures exerted by a citizenry that can be surprisingly strongly committed (in theory, if not always in practice) to the conventional forms. Finally, because nation-states (and their surrogates, such as the global culture industries) reach so deeply into our lives and wield so much power to enforce their viewpoints, they frequently erect obstacles that discourage people from affirming the ideals and carrying out the deeds that they know to be right. In this realm, more than perhaps in any other sphere of life, we are likely to find ourselves in need of courage in order to steel ourselves against the various ways that powerful interests will attempt to deter us from making right judgments and carrying out good actions.

The state, the virtues, and the redefinition of politics

Given the virtues that Christians seek to embody in their lives, just what degree of Christian involvement in the state is possible? I noted at the outset of this chapter that the answers to this question have been many and various, and that I would not attempt to settle it here. I hope, however, that our discussion of the relationship between Christianity and the state, as well as our exploration of some of the virtues that should mark that relationship, will at least help readers to understand why Christians have so adamantly embraced a variety of positions on this issue. If one believes that the very nature of the modern nation-state—particularly given the various tools that it now has at its disposal—creates a situation in which Christian virtues such as faithfulness, peaceableness, and courage are practically impossible to cultivate, then one will tend to avoid participating in the activities of the state to whatever degree is possible. If, on the other hand, one believes that these (and other) virtues can be maintained and promoted from within the structures of government, then one will tend to seek out ways to use those structures to good advantage. Perhaps one can even hope, in doing so, that the nation-state itself might be made more loving, more peaceable, and more just.

While some would argue for complete withdrawal from the state, and others for wholesale involvement, most Christians probably fall somewhere between these two perspectives. Indeed, they may well shift toward different points on the spectrum, depending upon the particular issue at hand. My own sense is that some degree of political involvement is possible and necessary, but that in many cases, it needs to take a rather unconventional form. The forms of political involvement with which the citizens of modern democracies are most familiar—voting, lobbying one's representatives, or organizing a grassroots campaign to have a piece of legislation enacted or repealed—tend to rely on rules or laws as a means of promulgating an ethics. Moreover, they can only succeed as strategies if they cede a great deal of control to the state. We elect the person that we think will enact the moral platform that we favor, but we often find ourselves on the sidelines as that person is buffeted and swayed by gale-force political winds that may eventually sever the connection between the intention of our votes and the actual result. Or our grassroots campaign is successful and the law that we wanted is passed, but it is interpreted or enforced in such a way as to produce effects that were very different from what we sought in the campaign. Because the workings of the state lie mostly outside their direct control, I believe that many of the changes that Christians would like to achieve will need to be accomplished outside the channels that people have come to rely upon when seeking to bring about change within governments and other powerful institutions. By way of conclusion, I will offer three very brief examples.

One: a group of people had grave concerns about the morality of capital punishment, and particularly about the fact that death sentences seemed to be disproportionately handed down to members of racial minorities. But public opinion remained strongly in favor of keeping the death penalty in place for certain crimes, and the current political leadership of their state had vowed not to budge on the issue. Those who were concerned about the morality of this issue could have waged a campaign to try to change public opinion on the matter, or to vote the current state leadership out of office. Instead, they undertook a significant program of investigative journalism: they proved, beyond the shadow of a doubt, that a number of people who were currently awaiting execution on death row had been wrongly convicted. This led many people to develop grave questions about their own commitment to the death penalty, and eventually led the state's governor—a strong proponent in favor of it—to declare a moratorium on all executions in the state. The ethical issue in question clearly involved the government, but it was addressed through largely non-governmental channels.

Two: a group of Christians were concerned about the number of abortions that were being performed in the large city in which they lived. Some of them considered campaigning for a law to be passed that would tighten the legal restrictions on abortion; others believed that the solution was to elect representatives who would find various ways of reducing the frequency of the procedure. Eventually, however, the group decided on a very different tack. They recognized that most women who were getting abortions were doing so because they felt unable—emotionally, financially, or in some other way—to have a child at this point in their lives. So the group placed regular advertisements in a local newspaper, indicating that any woman who was considering having an abortion could apply to their group for support. The group pledged to pay all the financial costs of carrying the pregnancy to term, and to take responsibility for the placement of the child in a caring home if the mother was unwilling or unable to keep it. Thus, without any involvement with the government, this group of Christians was able to hold firm to its own convictions on this issue and actually to reduce the incidence of abortion—and to do so in ways that not only refused to condemn others for the circumstances in which they found themselves, but actually provided them with some relief and support.

Three: a man found himself strongly opposed to a war in which his government was deeply involved, and particularly opposed to its system for drafting people into military service in order to prosecute that war. Instead of directing his energies toward electing leaders who would end the war, or bringing a lawsuit against the government for its disparate treatment of potential draftees, he instead decided to write a song. Not much of a song, actually: only a chorus, frequently repeated and strung together by a long hilarious narrative telling the story of his arrest for—of all things—littering. But that story led to another story—about his experience with his draft board—and the song became a rallying point for opposition to the war, the draft, and the entire structure of governmental authority at the time; indeed, it remains so to this day. How could a simple chorus of music, the lyrics of which actually had nothing to do with the particular issue at hand, contribute so significantly to a change in government policy? A possible answer to that question is offered at the end of the song, when the singer suggests that people might respond to their draft notices by walking in to the local Selective Service office, singing a few bars of the song's chorus, and walking out. "If three people do it . . . they may think it's an organization . . . And can you imagine, fifty people a day? . . . friends, they may think it's a movement. And that's what it is." It turns out that a work of art—however simple, modest, or apparently irrelevant to a political cause—can become the focal point and inspiration for significant change in the way that a government operates.

All of these examples are true stories of events that have actually taken place. Not all of them were undertaken by Christians, or from specifically Christian motives; but they all demonstrate the possibility of significant interaction with nation-states using means that are not themselves under the direct control of those states. They therefore provide useful examples for people who are wrestling with the question of how one might interact with a government—or, for that matter, with any institutional structure—whose moral assumptions may be vastly different from one's own. Sometimes, at least, that involvement will have to take place on different terms than those promulgated by the institution itself—since such terms may already be profoundly shaped by the alternative moral paradigm within which that institution operates. While these examples certainly do not provide all the answers to the ongoing debate surrounding the appropriate extent of Christian involvement in the affairs of the state, I hope they will provide some food for thought. To me, they offer hope that people who are committed to the cultivation of certain virtues will not need to compromise or undermine those commitments in order to bear witness to their significance for the work of governing the nation-state.

Questions for discussion

1. What comes to mind when you hear the words "political" or "politics"? Have you usually associated politics only with governments, or has it had other meanings and resonances for you?

2. Discuss the account of the two cities that is offered in this chapter. Offer arguments in favor of each of the perspectives represented by the two diagrams showing the relationship between the "earthly city" and the "city of God." Which of these perspectives do you find most convincing, and why?

3. Describe some specific ways that your life is directly affected by the matters discussed in the middle section of this chapter: religious freedom, new technologies, and the global culture industries.

4. Consider some aspects of your own life (outside of any specifically religious context) in which you feel called to be "faithful" to something or someone. What motivates this faithfulness? What are some of the attitudes and practices that allow you to maintain it? What presents the greatest challenge to it?

5. Would "peaceableness" be considered a virtue among your friends and acquaintances? To what degree is violence seen as a necessary element of life today? What factors shape our assumptions about violence and peaceableness?

6. Do you think that our society tends to assume, as did Aristotle's, that most examples of courage take place on the battlefield and in other military contexts? What factors might promote such an assumption? Tell a story about an occasion in your life when you were called upon to show courage. Then think of at least two more examples of courage that arise from circumstances that are *not* related to the courage of soldiers in battle.

7. On the basis of this chapter, engage in a conversation with at least one other person on the question of whether, to what degree, and in what ways Christians should be involved in the affairs of the government. Consider both conventional forms of involvement (running for office, voting, and so on) and alternative forms, such as those implied in the examples at the end of the chapter.

Sources cited in this chapter and/or recommended for further reading

Aristotle, *Politics*

St. Augustine of Hippo, *The City of God*

Robert Benne, "Christian Ethics and Politics," in Meilaender and Werpehowski, eds., *The Oxford Handbook of Theological Ethics*

Michael Budde, *The (Magic) Kingdom of God: Christianity and Global Culture Industries*

William T. Cavanaugh, *Theopolitical Imagination*

William T. Cavanaugh, "Politics: Beyond Secular Parodies," in Milbank, Pickstock, and Ward, eds., *Radical Orthodoxy: A New Theology*

David Clough and Brian Stiltner, *Faith and Force: A Christian Debate about War*

Arlo Guthrie, "Alice's Restaurant"

Stanley Hauerwas, *Against the Nations*

Stanley Hauerwas and William H. Willimon, *Resident Aliens: Life in the Christian Colony*

Eric O. Jacobson, *Sidewalks in the Kingdom: New Urbanism and the Christian Faith*

Nicholas Lash, *Believing Three Ways in One God: A Reading of the Apostles' Creed*

Gerald W. Schlabach, "Breaking Bread: Peace and War," in Hauerwas and Wells, eds., *The Blackwell Companion to Christian Ethics*

Alexander Schmemann, *For the Life of the World: Sacraments and Orthodoxy*

Sophie Scholl: The Final Days (Sophie Scholl: Die letzten Tage), dir. Marc Rothemund, 2005

St. Thomas Aquinas, *Summa Theologiae* IIa-IIae

Hermann Vinke, *The Short Life of Sophie Scholl*

Paul J. Wadell, "Sharing Peace: Discipline and Trust," in Hauerwas and Wells, eds., *The Blackwell Companion to Christian Ethics*

The White Rose (Die Weiße Rose), dir. Michael Verhoeven, 1982

John Howard Yoder, *The Politics of Jesus: Vicit Agnus Noster*; *For the Nations: Essays Evangelical and Public*

*I*nterlude 3

Wednesday

Back to church

Throughout Part 3 of this book, we have been exploring the various spheres of life within which Christian ethics might provide some degree of moral formation and guidance. According to the model we have been developing, Christians experience a certain kind of formation in the narratives and practices of the faith—a process of formation that comes into sharpest focus at the weekly Sunday worship service. Needless to say, such formation will not be very effective if it occurs for only one of the 168 hours in every week; those same narratives and practices, as well as others that provide similar kinds of formation, will need to play a more significant role if they are expected to have a truly formative effect. This is why Christians engage in such practices as Bible study, daily prayer, book discussion groups, and service to others—practices that extend the morally formative effects of Christian worship beyond the specific confines of the Sunday service.

Even with such practices in place, however, those 167 hours between Sunday worship services can present a great many challenges. Thus far, in our journey through the first two "days" of the week, we have encountered a range of circumstances and assumptions that question, challenge, or simply ignore the Christian narratives and practices that address these issues; and over the remaining three chapters, we will discover much more of the same before we arrive again at Sunday. In recognition of the sense of alienation that many Christians feel as they wander through the typical week, the gathering community may need to assemble again, part way through that week, in order to refocus the energies of its members and renew their commitment to a specifically Christian account of the moral life.

These mid-week gatherings can take many forms. Many churches sponsor at least one evening of fellowship each week, in which the entire community—or at number of smaller groups (organized on the basis of demographic categories or mutual interests)—meet for conversation, problem-solving, or perhaps without any particular agenda whatsoever. Other churches organize an ongoing discussion group or educational opportunity, while still others focus on the arts: choirs and bands, acting troupes, sacred dance ensembles, and groups in charge of the visual appeal of the worship space may gather regularly to prepare their work, to enjoy one another's company, and to develop a sense of purpose with respect to their contributions to the community. Even a regular committee meeting—in which members attend to mundane matters that are essential in every institutional structure (such as budgets, personnel, and building maintenance)—can become an opportunity for the community to gather in fellowship and to engage in the process of supporting one another in the Christian life.

The common element in all these forms of mid-week church activity is that of *gathering*. Recalling our observations in chapter 1, we know that part of what binds a community together is the willingness to come into one another's presence on a regular basis. In fact, we can probably gain a fairly good idea of which communities are most important and most formative in our lives by considering the amount of time that we spend in the presence of other members of that community. For many people, the household ranks very high among such communities; co-workers, fellow students, or residents of some kind of shared living arrangement would also be significant in this regard. Given the variety of people with whom we gather on a regular basis, any community whose members hope to offer one another some kind of mutual support in the moral life must expect to see each other more than once a week.

All this talk of mid-week church gatherings may strike some people as a rather dreamy flight into the imagination. With regular Sunday church attendance experiencing a precipitous decline in many parts of the world, and with the rise of individualistic approaches to religion that see no need for any kind of communal gathering of believers, how can anyone expect people to come back to church in the middle of the week? Certainly, in my own experience—both as a church member who has been asked to return to church, and in various leadership roles when I've asked others to do so—I know that any such expectation faces monumental obstacles. Of course, my goal in raising this point is neither to lament these difficulties nor to provide churches with some kind of advice manual for getting people to come back to church. I raise it simply to emphasize the role of such gatherings in the process of moral formation. Since our immediate task is to understand Christian ethics and to examine matters of moral judgment and character formation, we simply need to recognize that regathering the community is a fairly important aspect of this process. Without it—or without something that accomplishes some of the same work of formation—the other cares and concerns of the typical week in the life of a Christian will soon overtake and overrun whatever kinds of moral judgment and character traits are being shaped by specifically Christian narratives and practices.

Martin Luther King, Jr.

The American pastor, preacher, and civil rights leader Martin Luther King, Jr. (1929–1968) was a tireless advocate for improving the lot of African-Americans in the US, most of whom are direct descendants of slaves who were forcibly brought to North America in the slave trade of the 18th and 19th centuries. King sought to raise awareness of the deep and divisive racism that had so profoundly marked the history, the national self-image, and the day-to-day life of the US. He organized people to work through courts and legislatures to enact various forms of legal protection against racial discrimination; but many commentators believe that his greatest achievement was the degree to which he helped shift the attitudes of white Americans concerning the plight of racial minorities in the US.

Less obvious, at least to the casual observer of American life in the 1950s and 1960s, was the degree to which the Christian faith—and in particular, the Church—functioned as the primary vehicle for Martin Luther King's achievements. He appealed regularly to biblical motifs and injunctions in order to make his case; he spoke in the dramatic, high-energy style of black preaching, even when focusing on the technical details of civil rights law; and he employed the extensive networks of deeply committed church members to rally support for his cause. He spoke in churches—indeed, in some communities, churches were the only organizations that would provide him with a venue—and in doing so, he regathered Christians into their communities on a regular basis. Even when he was arrested and jailed, he wrote letters—following the model, and even the style, of the letters of Paul the Apostle, who wrote some of the epistles from inside prison—in order to help ensure that the seeds that he had planted would not fail to produce good fruit.

The life and work of Martin Luther King, Jr. thus provides us with a good example of the importance of bringing Christians "back to church" as an essential element in developing their ethical perspective. Sometimes he literally brought them back, mid-week, to gather at a church to hear an inspirational talk or to learn about what was happening in the country and what they could do to help. At other times, the regathering that he brought about came in the form of a sit-in, a protest march, or even a collective *absence* (such as a boycott of a city's racially-segregated public transportation system). And sometimes the gathering was not physical at all: those who read his "Letter from Birmingham Jail" were, in a virtual sense, "gathered" back into their community through his appeal to specifically Christian stories and practices in his writing.

Put another way, we might say that Martin Luther King found a way of "making Sunday last an entire week." In other words, he inserted the morally formative elements of the Christian community—its worship, its gatherings, its stories and practices—into a wide variety of human activity, including many of the spheres of life that we are discussing in Part 3 of this book (such as paid employment, governmental affairs, and family life). By bringing the essential elements of Christian life and thought into a wide variety of aspects of people's lives, he brought them "back to church" in profound ways—ways that changed the course of human history.

It would be a mistake, however, to imagine that regathering the community only happens when churches design some fascinating program that is sufficiently appealing to lure people away from whatever else they would rather be doing on a Wednesday night (or on any other night, or day). While I would never want to underestimate the importance of face-to-face contact among members of a community, this need not happen in any particular place; groups of Christians gathering on a sports field, around a campfire, or in one another's homes can accomplish the work of ongoing formation just as well as can gathering at a church. And when such face-to-face gatherings are not possible, communities can find other ways of drawing themselves together. Two thousand years ago, Paul the Apostle wrote letters to the far-flung Christian communities that were gathering at various places throughout the Roman Empire, thus establishing a point of contact and a sense of communal purpose even among people who could not be in one another's presence. If that was possible then, how much more are people able today—with the many technological means at our disposal—to gather the community in heart, mind, and spirit.

Even so, a physical gathering of the community is still best—and this for at least three reasons. First, as we will note repeatedly in the next three chapters, our physical bodies play an important role in the Christian faith.

Christianity has always made a strong case that bodies *matter*—that what human beings do with their bodies (where they put them, with what other bodies, under what conditions, and so on) is of great significance. Thus when we explore issue such as medical care, sex, and the natural environment, we will be reminded of the importance of the physical. While letters, the internet, and other forms of "virtual presence" are important alternatives when being in one another's physical company is not possible, they must always be understood as mere substitutes for "the real thing."

Second, when we are in one another's direct physical presence, we can do some things that we simply cannot do otherwise. One of these is an important communal practice that we discussed back in chapter 9: we can eat a meal together. As we observed when discussing the Christian eucharist and its resonances with various aspects of table-fellowship, few practices bind a group of people to one another more effectively than a gathering for a common meal. Not surprisingly, many churches have discovered that a mid-week gathering of Christians will accomplish more of its goals—promoting fellowship, re-establishing commitments, and creating a space where people can mutually build up one another's lives—if food is on the agenda. In fact, some have discovered that food can be the *only* item on the agenda: if people can be persuaded to sit down to a meal together, everything else follows.

Finally, physical presence is the deepest form of contact with other human beings that we know. I have, at several points in this interlude, used the term "face-to-face" to describe the kind of physical presence that brings human beings into direct contact with one another. The usefulness of that phrase is not accidental: it is, in fact, a person's *face* that gives us the most information about their physical identity. We put faces on identification cards and passports; we expect a work of portraiture to show us, if nothing else, a person's face. One important contemporary theologian, David Ford, has written persuasively about the concept of "facing": to place one's face in front of the face of another—to experience another's face, and to have one's own face experienced by the other—is our most profound form of connection to that which is outside ourselves. From a Christian perspective, the only kind of connection and communion that could possibly be more intense is that which comes beyond this present life: the "vision of God." This, too, is a face-to-face encounter, in which human beings are brought into perfect communion, not only with one another, but also with God. Paul puts it this way: "For now we see in a mirror, dimly, but then we will see face to face. Now I know only in part; then I will know fully, even as I have been fully known" (1 Cor. 13:12).

Sources cited in this interlude and/or recommended for further reading

James H. Cone, *Martin & Malcolm & America*

David Ford, *Self and Salvation: Being Transformed*

Philip D. Kenneson, *Life on the Vine: Cultivating the Fruit of the Spirit in Christian Community*

Martin Luther King, Jr., "Letter from Birmingham Jail"

Elizabeth Newman, *Untamed Hospitality: Welcoming God and Other Strangers*

Samuel Wells, *God's Companions: Reimagining Christian Ethics*

Norman Wirzba, *Living the Sabbath: Discovering the Rhythms of Rest and Delight*

13 Thursday
At the hospital

Many of the ethical issues that we have examined thus far are related to elements of human existence with which we are in contact on a day-to-day basis. For example, most adults spend a considerable part of their lives at work, so our discussion of the moral questions that arise around work will be of significance to almost everyone. Similarly, because the structures of government play an ongoing role in our lives, the issues that we examined in the previous chapter will frequently be on the minds of most readers. In this chapter, however, we turn to a set of ethical questions that impinge upon us rarely—and, in the case of some human lives, perhaps not at all. Interestingly, though, the subject-matter of this chapter is often of greatest interest to students of Christian ethics.

Why should a set of topics that will affect so few of us, and so rarely, be of such extraordinary interest? The answer is simple: what these issues lack in frequency and ubiquity, they more than make up for in their intensity and complexity. I refer to those matters that we encounter at the margins of life: at birth and at death, during circumstances of extreme illness, and when faced with medical conditions which, in spite of our technological advances, we still do not fully understand. These matters often involve us in judgments and decisions that impinge quite significantly on our own lives and the lives of other people; moreover, these such weighty judgments will often create, in their wake, emotional and psychological after-effects that will continue to be borne by those who have had to make them—sometimes for the rest of their lives.

The issues that we will consider in this chapter fall under the general heading of "medical ethics" or "bioethics." Many, many entire books have been written on this particular sphere of ethics in general, and on the Christian perspective on bioethics in particular. In the few pages that are allotted to us here, we will not even scratch the surface of this complex and rapidly changing field of inquiry. We will, however, attempt to gesture toward a few structures and concepts that create an environment within which bioethical issues can be addressed. And, even though ethical questions relating to the medical field are often about difficult decisions in particular cases, we will attempt to examine the questions that it raises without resorting to a "quandary ethics" approach. Instead, we will consider how the virtues can serve to guide us, as we venture through the thickets that surround ethical questions related to the margins of life and the mysteries of health and disease. As in the case of the previous chapters, we will focus on three virtues in particular as we seek to chart a course for examining this complex realm of ethical discourse. Before we reach that stage, however, we have some considerable ground to clear.

Some basic assumptions

The Christian faith makes certain assumptions about the nature of life and death that will always bear on the issues that accumulate at the margins of life—by which I mean, those issues relating to sex, conception, birth, maturity, disease, and death. In this section, I want to mention three Christian claims that seem to me most relevant as we address these issues. These three issues are often discussed under the theological headings of "grace," "providence," and "resurrection." We might gloss these three terms by describing our focal issues as follows: the affirmation of life as a gift; the recognition that we have already been given more than we need; and the relativization of death as not having the final word.

Grace

As we noted in chapter 9, the word "grace" comes from the Latin word *gratia*, which means "favor" or "gift." We can recognize its root meaning in many of our related words: if we are pleased with our restaurant service, we leave a gratuity (it's given freely; we don't have to pay it); a *graceful* person seems to have been given the gifts of agility and elegance; we show our thanks for a gift by being *grateful*. In Christian theology, the word refers to one of the chief elements of God's character: namely, that God is a giver of good gifts. The creation of the earth and of humankind, the protection of Noah's family from the flood, the promise to Abraham, the exodus from slavery in Egypt: all these are understood as God's freely given gifts. Even those elements of

God's relationship with humankind that might seem, at first glance, to be a burden to human beings—the giving of the law, the social criticism pronounced by the prophets—turn out to be God's way of caring for the creation and restoring human relationships with one another and with God. Similarly, God's willingness to become flesh and enter into the world, the salvation of the world through death and resurrection of Jesus Christ, and the sending of the Holy Spirit are all understood to be God's freely given gifts. In fact, according to the Christian story, the world is so utterly dependent on God that it is only through God's ongoing gifts that life can be sustained. God's grace is therefore not a one-time event but an ongoing process; some theologians have remarked that it might be better to think of the word "grace" as a verb, rather than a noun. For Christians, the whole created order bears witness to God's ongoing act of "gracing" the world—continuously giving it the gift of life.

With respect to individual human persons, this theological assumption means that Christians seek to understand their own lives, and the lives of their loved ones, as gifts from God: given to us for however long or short a time may be the case, and meant to be accepted as the gifts that they are. This need not be connected to a picture of God as a micro-manager of all human events; God is not necessarily like the ancient Greek notion of the Fates, who cut off individual human lives at a certain time span as if cutting thread from a spool. Nor does it deny the altogether appropriate grief we feel at the sudden death of a young person or, for that matter, the long-expected death of an elderly person. But it does imply a fundamental re-orientation about the nature of life (and death). If all life is a gift from God, then this raises questions about the human tendency to assume that death "takes something (or someone) away." In their better moments, Christians try to think of it as one of the means through which human beings "return the gift" of life back to God. This in turn might imply that they should be somewhat reluctant to improve upon, to alter substantially, or to re-engineer human life in ways that deny its God-given quality.

Again, this point must be carefully nuanced. It is not meant to suggest that one should avoid, for example, using pharmaceuticals to treat illness or injury—or that people should necessarily forgo those medical procedures that might substantially improve the quality or length of their lives. It does mean, however, that improving the quality or length of one's life does not necessarily outrank all other considerations. If human lives are understood to be a gift from God, this raises questions about the assumption that human beings are fully in charge of them—or that they can decide exactly how long they should live, in what state of health, and with what physical and biological capacities.

Providence

Closely related to the theological concept of grace is that of *providence*: the notion that God is ultimately in charge of the way the world goes, and that human beings are not always called upon to revise, repair, or improve upon everything that they take to be wrong with the world. (An exception to this may arise, perhaps, in the case of those things that they themselves do to damage it; more on this in chapter 15.) Again, this claim needs careful inflection; it sometimes leads to a picture of an arbitrary and capricious God, who shortens some lives and lengthens others, without giving the slightest attention to what those particular lives seem to deserve (again, much like the apparently arbitrary decisions of the Fates, cutting each life's length as though it were a piece of string). But rather than seeing the length and quality of one's life as an arbitrary divine decision, one might also choose to view it as a reminder that we human beings do not *cause* God's treatment of us. In other words, we don't make God into a "nice guy" (i.e., one who lets us live a good, long life) simply by being nice people ourselves. According to a much-quoted saying of Jesus, God makes the "sun rise on the evil and on the good, and sends rain on the righteous and the unrighteous" (Matt. 5:45). The apparent lack of any clear relationship between what a particular human being seems to "deserve" and that person's "reward" can easily lead people to imagine a God to be a rather capricious tyrant, arbitrarily meting out rewards and punishments without any attention to who deserves what. But it can also be seen as a way of putting human beings at ease—since it takes matters of their hands. They and their actions are not, in the end, the final deciding factor as to God's disposition; they do not "earn" God's stamp of approval on their lives.

We might arrive at a better understanding of the theological concept of providence if we think about its relationship to the word "provision." The Christian claim is that God is provident in the sense of providing for human beings—giving them everything they need. And what human beings need, more than anything else (according to Christian theology), is to be in right relationship with God and with one another. Consequently, what God gives may not necessarily match up with what human beings think they deserve, or even what they *actually* deserve (whatever that might mean). Nevertheless, according to the Christian perspective on this matter, God's provision for human beings is sufficient and, indeed, abundant: God gives people everything they need, and more. The biblical narrative tells this tale of abundance over and over again; for example, the original creation provides a wealth of food for all the creatures (Gen. 2). Similarly, as Christian ethicist Samuel Wells has recently emphasized, the miracles that Jesus performs are often signs of superabundance: through God's work in the person of Christ, people find themselves with too much wine (John 2), too much food (Mark 5 and Mark 7) and too many fish (Luke 5).

The Christian story, then, is a story of abundance: God's superabundant provision to humankind, in which we are given more than we need. If this seems highly unlikely in the face of the actual conditions of the world, this may be due (at least in the wealthier parts of the globe) to our tendency to imagine ourselves as needing things that we don't actually need, and failing to hold fast to those things that we truly do need. Nor should the language of "divine superabundance" be used as an excuse to turn a blind eye to unjust conditions. As we noted in chapter 11, many people throughout the world are forced to live without the basic necessities of life; this is not because God does not give abundantly, but because human beings are not sufficiently committed to the just distribution of material resources. But in spite of human efforts to the contrary, the consistent witness of the Christian faith is that God's good gifts and God's providence allow human beings to live an abundant life—and to face the end of that life with confidence. This leads us to the third element in our survey of basic Christian assumptions.

Resurrection

Hand-in-hand with the previous two ideas is the Christian claim that the physical death of the body is not actually its final disposition. Instead, Christians claim that human beings are raised up from the dead and that life is not actually limited by the time that elapses between birth and death; in fact, is not limited by time at all. Rather, Christians believe in the *resurrection* of the body, and in *eternal* life.

Once again, we need to exercise caution in coming to an adequate understanding of these central Christian claims. They are *not* meant to imply that one's earthly sojourn from birth to death does not matter, nor that our biological lives are merely the testing ground that determines our disposition in the hereafter. In fact, most Christian theologians have been quite hesitant to speculate on the precise nature of the "eternal life" in which they believe, or in the precise nature of the resurrected body. (Even Paul, addressing this question quite directly in 1 Corinthians, is reticent to provide very much detail.) These theological claims are not designed to provide a road-map for the afterlife, but rather, to make a statement about death: namely, that death is not the definitive and absolute end of human life. This suggests, in turn, that there might be some things worse than death.

This, of course, is a view that is widely held—and not just by Christians. Any time that a human being undergoes some risk of death in order to accomplish something—to save a child from drowning, to defend one's country against an enemy, or even just to experience a momentary thrill or a great adventure—such people are proclaiming, by their deeds, that they believe that some things might be worth dying for. The chief difference offered by the Christian understanding of resurrection is the notion that the decision to take such risks—to go ahead and attempt certain things, even though one might well die in the process—is intimately related to a human being's relationship to God. More specifically, the Christian faith claims that one may, and should, be willing to die for the sake of one's relationship to God. That relationship outranks "avoiding death" in one's list of priorities precisely because that relationship actually *transcends* death: a person is still in relationship with God, even after death. Since life is understood as a gift from God, one ought not to end it, or even to risk ending it, without cause; but on the other hand, if continuing one's life required a person to take steps that would compromise one's relationship with God, then death would clearly be the preferable alternative—since that relationship continues beyond death.

The Christian beliefs in the resurrection of the body and in eternal life have their roots in the claim that Jesus "rose again from the dead." We might well assume, as some commentators have done, that this statement is primarily an empirical or historical claim about the resuscitation of a corpse. Such a claim seems audacious or impossible to some people, and they therefore find it difficult to profess the Christian creed in its traditional form. However, as we suggested in chapter 5, understanding the resurrection in these terms would be to mistake the creed's claim of "believing in" something for a checklist-oriented "believing that" something happened. While people may continue to engage in serious (but often pointless) debate over whether it is or is not possible for a dead person to come back to life, they are missing the essential point of the claim: a belief that God acted, in some definitive and earth-shattering way, to vindicate the life of Jesus and to overcome his death. (After all, Jesus died as a convicted criminal and suffered capital punishment; imagine what it would mean, today, for someone to suggest that an executed criminal was God's chosen messenger. In comparison, a belief in Jesus' resurrection is not nearly so incredible.) Christians believe that Jesus' actions, teachings, and testimony were somehow authenticated, in spite of the humiliating death that he suffered. The form that this authentication takes is that of resurrection; Jesus is raised up from death by God. This in turn provides the warrant for the degree of attention and importance that Christians are willing to give to Jesus as a moral exemplar and a teacher.

In addition, the Christian profession of belief that Jesus rose again from the dead signals the believers' faith in the victory of abundant life over suffering and death. This faith provides a basic orientation for the "life journey" of a Christian: it includes recognition that death is neither final nor the worst thing that can happen to a person. To proclaim that God is able and willing to raise life out of death is to re-order one's own list of priorities, such that extending life and avoiding death at any cost may not be the most important thing that one can do. In fact, according to the Christian tradition, God actually provides a model in this regard: *God* risks death. The very act of becoming a human being ensures that God will face death in some form. As the Christian story describes it, God considers the reconciliation of all people to one another, and the restoration of the relationship between God and humanity, to be more important than the avoidance of death—even more important than the avoidance of God's own death.

The Christian theological claims about grace, providence, and resurrection that I have outlined in this section provide the background against which we can begin to consider the questions that arise in the realm of bioethics. God's freely given gifts, God's willingness to provide more than enough to meet human needs, and the claim that death is not the final word—all these convictions have the potential to reshape, sometimes in rather radical ways, the standard assumptions with which we often face the judgments and decisions that we make at the margins of life. We will see some examples of how those assumptions are likely to be reshaped when we come to examine the virtues that seem particularly salient when facing such judgments. We need to be aware, however, that these theological assumptions will not necessarily lead us to consensus about the most controversial questions in this field. This is because those questions are shaped by some fundamental disagreements among Christians concerning certain key distinctions that human beings make concerning the margins of life and the relationship of health and disease. This will be our focus in the next section.

Some contested distinctions

Questions about medical ethics are often made more difficult by the fact that, in many cases, everything depends on how the observer understands certain fundamental distinctions. For example, if a person believes that pain and suffering are always to be avoided at any cost, then this will make certain procedures and decisions seem obviously appropriate when caring for those who suffer. If, on the other hand, one believes that some forms of pain and suffering may be necessary, or that they must sometimes be endured in deference to some higher good, then those procedures and decisions that seemed "obvious" to one person may seem quite inappropriate to others. The question will depend on how one makes the distinction, if any, between the negative aspects of suffering and those aspects that, while still lamentable, are necessary and proper to human life.

Such distinctions are important, and three of them demand our attention at this juncture. How we make these distinctions will have an enormous impact on the outcome of our deliberations about specific ethical issues in the field of medicine. Even among Christians, however, no clear consensus exists about exactly how to draw these distinctions. Therefore, my goal in exploring them is not so much to argue for one particular way of "drawing the line," but rather to provide a reminder that a person's views on the questions raised here will have a highly significant impact on the analysis of a particular issue in bioethics. The three distinctions that I describe here are those that concern, first, when life begins (and when it ends); second, whether suffering is always to be avoided; and third, whether a particular medical procedure is better described as "repairing" something that has gone amiss, or as "re-engineering" something to make it better than its original design.

The beginning and the end of life

Of all the issues that have vexed the field of bioethics over the years, this one is probably the most significant. The moral issues surrounding abortion, for example, depend upon this question almost completely—and they also provide a nice example of the various paths that Christians have taken over time. For those who argue that life begins at conception, nearly all forms of abortion must be prohibited; the only possible exception would be an abortion to save the life of the mother, and even here, this would be a matter of weighing two lives against one another in roughly equal fashion. Alternatively, for those who believe that human life begins at birth, and that the embryo and fetus are merely "potential" life, most forms of abortion would logically be understood as morally acceptable. Finally, those who think of human life as commencing sometime between these two moments—at the point at which "twinning" has or has not taken place (usually at about 14 days), for example, or at "viability" (the ability of the fetus to survive outside the uterus), or at some distinction based on a certain number of months after conception—then the dividing line between acceptable and unacceptable abortion would fall at that particular point in the pregnancy.

Among these three alternatives, much Christian bioethical discussion has leaned heavily toward the first alternative; this has been particularly the case in Roman Catholic teaching on the subject. This position argues that, once egg and sperm are united, all the conditions are in place for human life; from that point on, the human being's life is best understood as something that *develops*, changing in form but not in essence. This perspective tends to bind the beginning of life very closely to the sexual act that, at least at certain times of the female ovulation cycle, is likely to produce it. It also connects the idea of new human life quite firmly to the biological parents of the embryo.

The second position—that the dividing point is the moment of the passage of the fetus through the birth canal—is one for which few Christian ethicists have argued strongly, if for no other reason than the virtually identical states of a fetus just before birth and an infant just after birth. However, a significant number of Christian thinkers have argued for the third alternative—locating the beginning of life somewhere between conception and birth, but disagreeing with respect to precisely where along this spectrum they would locate it. Such commentators argue that the embryo at the very earliest stages certainly has the *potential* to develop into a human life, but that the same might be said for individual unfertilized egg cells and non-fertilizing sperm cells. At some point, of course, *potential* life becomes *actual* life; that point, however, can be very difficult to identify, which explains why attempts to do so have led to so such division and disagreement.

A slightly different set of questions arises concerning the exact moment of the end of life. Most people would agree that human life does not actually end until the brain stops receiving oxygen, which usually happens only when a person stops breathing. But new technologies have complicated this picture, in two ways. First, we are now able to monitor brain activity in a way that was not previously possible; as a result, we sometimes discover that the brain has ceased to function, even though breathing continues without interruption. Doctors can now identify some individuals as permanently comatose or as being in a "persistent vegetative state"; all the outward signs of biological life continue without interruption, but the brain has essentially been permanently switched off. In such cases, what shall we say of the person—is she "still alive" (because breathing continues), or "essentially dead" (because of the lack of brain activity)?

This matter is further complicated by an additional technological development: namely, our ability to assist people in the process of breathing and receiving nourishment, such that they remain alive—and often with significant continuing brain activity—even though this is only possible because of the mechanical aid that they are receiving. In a previous era, the question would not have arisen; the mechanical assistance would not have been available, and the person would simply have died. To what extent do we deem a person to be "still alive" when that life is provided only by external mechanical stimulation? Does it depend on the extent of the mechanical assistance? (Consider, at one end of the spectrum, a device that allows the patient relative freedom and mobility, such as a heart pacemaker; and, at the other end, a comatose patient aided by a complete system of devices that artificially circulate the blood, aspirate the lungs, and provide intravenous nourishment.) When does life end?

I ask these questions about the beginning and end of life, neither in order to settle them here, nor even to lay out all the relevant issues. I mention them only because of the extraordinarily significant way that they will bear upon questions in medical ethics. Many of the disagreements that so seriously disturb our political and social conversations on these subjects begin with disagreements on this fundamental level. Getting these differences out into the open from the outset will help to clarify the point of disagreement and may well facilitate the progress toward achieving some degree of consensus.

The use and abuse of suffering

A second set of distinctions concerns the example that I offered at the outset of this section: the lengths to which we are willing to go in order to avoid or alleviate pain and suffering. Obviously, pain and suffering are not "good" in any ordinary sense of the word; however, it would be too simple to say that they are simply "bad" or always to be avoided at any cost. Throughout human history, we find examples wherein people are encouraged to endure a certain degree of pain and suffering for some greater good: a painful operation or drug treatment that ensures a longer life; a period of suffering that produces patience and endurance, with positive effects on a person's character for the long haul; or even the pain intentionally inflicted as a punishment, with the expectation that it will lead the perpetrator to choose a better path in the future.

The difficulty with all these forms of pain and suffering, of course, is that they are subject to various forms of abuse. Any positive account of suffering may easily be used, by those who inflict it or ask others to endure it, as a means of subjugating the sufferers and/or elevating one's own position in comparison. Certainly in the case of the last example just offered—meting out punishment in hope of correcting bad behavior—the instances when this has been abused, over the centuries, for the benefit of the punisher would probably well outnumber the instances that it has been truly used for the benefit of the punished. And Christian history is certainly replete with cases in which those in comfortable positions of ecclesiastical power patiently explained to those who lacked that comfort and power that their suffering was appropriate and even to be envied, when in fact this was certainly not the case.

At the same time, Christianity also has a long history of recognizing that taking on suffering—particularly when one does so voluntarily and for the sake of a higher cause—can be a sign of good character. It is also understood as one of the ways that human beings seek to conform themselves to the character of God, whose patient suffering throughout the Old Testament narratives are undertaken for the good of the people whom God loves. Furthermore, by taking on human flesh—as well as (as Prince Hamlet puts it) "the heart-ache and the thousand natural shocks / that flesh is heir to"—God suffers in a dramatic fashion for the redemption of the world. This notion of "redemptive suffering" has played a significant role in Christian theology, in spite of the fact that it can certainly be subject to serious abuse (as already observed). According to the Christian account, suffering represents a certain kind of "giving," and indeed a giving of one's very self—with all the associations evoked by such giving (as explored in our discussion of "offering one's self" in chapter 7, as well as our discussion of grace at the beginning of this chapter).

Flannery O'Connor

As the author of some of the most exquisite short stories in the English language, the American writer Flannery O'Connor (1925–1964) is a permanent fixture in the annals of literary fame. She wrote slowly and with great care, subjecting her work to meticulous revision and throwing away a great deal of material that was probably very good indeed but did not meet her exacting standards. The relatively small corpus of her fiction—two short novels and about thirty short stories—is supplemented by a number of thoughtful essays and a very significant literary correspondence; her letters, in fact, are thought by many commentators to provide every bit as thrilling a read as her fiction. She was a devout Roman Catholic and her theological sensibilities are manifested, for those who know how to look, on every page of her writing; but she was subtle and skilled, and rarely do her religious views hit the reader over the head with a brickbat, as is the case among all too many writers of "Christian fiction." I frequently use her work to teach theology and ethics in the classroom.

She enters our purview here, however, for another reason entirely: namely, that she was very sick for most of her life. She inherited the congenital disease of lupus, and while it was relatively dormant for some of the time, it regularly flared up and caused her severe pain. Through much of her later life, she was an invalid—living at home on her mother's farm and requiring fairly regular care, along with frequent doctors' visits and occasional trips to the hospital. Her chronic illness, and the complications that arose from it, led to her death at a relatively young age. Hers was certainly a life of suffering.

Many commentators have suggested that, as with many great writers, her suffering had something to do with the brilliance of her fiction. She was a person deeply in tune with the pain of the world and of its individual inhabitants; she was therefore able to draw some of the most memorable characters in American fiction, and to endow them with traits and dispositions that were, in turn, a product of their own significant suffering. (O'Connor also understood the difference between real suffering and its imaginary counterpart; her characters also include a number of hypochondriacs, self-pitying and self-identified victims, and "suffering artists"—whose pain was mostly a product of their own egoistical imaginations and who were, in turn, fairly *in*sufferable to those around them.) So at one level, we might remark that, as is the case for many true artists, O'Connor's suffering became a form of self-giving, in which she transfigured her own pain and suffering into an experience of overwhelming joy on the part of her grateful readers.

More than this, though, O'Connor provides us with an example of how one might embody the virtues in the midst of illness. It would have been relatively easy for her to rage against her fate or to complain that God had placed this heavy burden on her shoulders—particularly when she was trying her best to live out her deep devotion to the Church and to glorify God through her fiction. Some people might even imagine that her suffering would eventually cause her to lose her faith in God altogether. Instead, her faith seems to have intensified in the midst of her suffering. From what we can tell by reading her letters and essays—as well as from the personal testimony of those who knew her well—she bore her illness and its accompanying suffering with remarkable patience, courage, and grace. She neither pitied herself for the way that her disease shortened her work hours and curtailed her life, nor transferred any such perspective to her characters. Without a doubt, she was only human and could be frustrated by her condition; "I am sick of being sick," she wrote, in one of her letters, toward the very end. Even so, she taught us—in life and in death—how one might suffer well; and through it all, she somehow found the will to raise up all her talents, as well as whatever energy she could muster on any given day, and devote it all to the greater glory of God.

The fact that Christianity has emphasized both the positive and the negative features of suffering means that well-meaning people are likely to disagree as to precisely where the line is to be drawn between the pain and suffering that is *redemptive* with that which is *abusive*. This has significant implications for medical ethics, since judgments and decisions are sometimes made on the basis of a person having "suffered enough" or being "in too much pain." In spite of disagreements about "how much is enough," however, simply raising these issues can sometimes provide a way forward. For example, our desire (based on compassion) to alleviate a person's pain may help us make better judgments about the relationship between medical intervention and palliative care.

Repairing vs. re-engineering

A third difficult distinction concerns the relationship between a medical procedure that merely repairs something that has gone wrong, and one which effectively redesigns a portion of the body in order to make it function in a way that the designers judge to be "better" than the state in which it was given. Again, the extremes are readily identifiable; at one end are those who would refuse all forms of medical treatment, relying on God to heal the body in God's own time; at the other end we find Dr. Frankenstein of Mary Wollstonecraft Shelley's great novel, assembling a human body and animating it in imitation of God. Few people would argue very strongly in favor of the ethical rectitude of either of these positions, but between the two is a vast field—and this generates a great deal of disagreement about where one might draw the line. Should people agree to donate their vital organs after they die, so that they can save the lives of others? Or does this reduce human beings to mere machines in search of replacement parts? Should we manipulate the genetic structure of a human embryo in order to reduce the likelihood that it will contract certain debilitating diseases? How about doing so in order improve the child's chances of getting into Oxford? Or even in order to change its eye color?

Many Christian ethicists have argued that genetic manipulation for the purpose of developing a "better" human being would be contrary to the claim that human life is a gift from God and therefore not to be re-engineered by human beings themselves. Even prenatal screening may need to be treated with caution, because it may lead parents to consider, or to be pressured to consider, using abortion as a means of selecting the kind of child (gift) that one "wants." The Christian understanding of the relationship between God and human beings raises some significant questions about the idea that some gifts of life should be refused on the basis of their poor quality or potential for adding complexity to the lives of those who would otherwise receive them. On the other hand, genetic research for the purpose of understanding and treating diseases that may develop later in life might lead us to look at the issue somewhat differently. Here, the claim is not that the gift of life is inadequate and must be re-engineered; it is, rather, that accepting a gift does not necessarily exclude the idea of keeping it in good working order.

An example may help us better understand this distinction. Let us imagine that I've been told by a good friend that she is going to buy me a CD player for Christmas. I don't actually want a CD player, however; I want an MP3 player. So, when I see the carefully wrapped package under the Christmas tree, I decide to unwrap it, take the CD player to the store in exchange for the MP3 player, rewrap it, and place it under the tree. That way, on Christmas morning, I will get what I want. Of course, the giver will be disappointed (not to mention a bit shocked!) to see me unwrapping a present that she didn't give me. In this case, I've clearly refused to accept the gift as a gift. I have made it into a means of satisfying my own desires.

Imagine, though, that I was able to resist my desire to engineer a substitute gift and that I accepted the gift of the CD player. I even listened to a few CDs on it, and perhaps came to appreciate some of its features as being rather better than the MP3 player that I thought I wanted. When the CD player's volume control malfunctions, however, I should not feel prevented from having it repaired. I am, admittedly, making a "change" in the gift that was given to me; but it is a change that is in keeping with the original intention of the giver, which was to give me a working CD player.

This analogy is not a perfect one; people are not machines, and the difference between a much-desired MP3 player and a less glamorous CD player is not the same as that between a healthy baby and one born with, say, Downs' Syndrome. Moreover, people will argue about just how "different" a gift has to be before it is no longer in line with the giver's intentions. But the analogy is not meant as a guide to decision-making; it is simply meant to illustrate the difference between replacing an offered gift with a fulfillment of one's own desires and an effort to maintain, in good working order, a gift that one has already accepted.

At the other end of the journey of life, certain questions surrounding death will also be given a different treatment if viewed in the light of these theological assumptions. For example, euthanasia and assisted suicide seem to put the length of one's life into one's own hands, rather than in God's hands; these also lead to questions about the willingness to recognize life, even a life that involves considerable suffering, as a gift from God. The problem with these practices is not their embrace of death; as I noted in a previous section, Christians believe that there may be a number of circumstances in which one should embrace death. The difficulty here is that the embrace of death is not for the sake of something higher, such as one's relationship with God; instead, it is for something lower, namely, one's experience of pain and/or a desire "not to be a burden" to others. These are, in the Christian scheme of things, not adequate reasons to contravene God's particular provision of life—even to a person who is dying. (We might want to distinguish, however, between "killing" and "letting die"; ethical judgments about end-of-life decisions often turn on this distinction. Again, a great many books are devoted in their entirety to precisely this distinction.)

The three sets of distinctions that I have offered here will not be resolved simply because one group or another declares victory and then vacates the scene. The differing perspectives can all call upon various elements in the tradition—from the biblical texts to the teachings of Christian writers to the testimony of theologically-informed medical experts—in order to buttress their views. The differences among well-meaning Christians on these issues may help to explain why, even though Christians rely on a fairly clear set of narratives and practices for their understanding of the moral life, they may still come to radically different conclusions about particular issues relating to the field of medical ethics.

Some healthy virtues

When we (or those to whom we are close) are sick, suffering, or faced with the mysteries of life and death, we often feel particularly vulnerable. We find ourselves faced with enormous forces that we do not fully understand. We therefore need to call upon every resource that is at our disposal in order to bear the pain, the uncertainty, and the grief that often accompanies us in such moments, and to help our loved ones bear these experiences as well. But the process of marshaling these resources is a long-term undertaking; we cannot ignore them for decades and then suddenly have them near to hand when we suddenly find ourselves awash in the issues surrounding suffering, death, and new life. In fact, our vulnerable condition when we are faced with such earth-shattering realities hardly makes this an auspicious time to begin the work of developing the strength of character that we will need in order to wrestle with their complexity. This is why we need to develop, as long-standing habits, certain excellences of character that will strengthen us (and those nearest to us) as we face these complex mysteries. In this final section of the chapter, we will examine three such excellences of character: patience, faith, and practical wisdom.

Patience

You may have heard the joke exchanged in a doctor's waiting room: Ever wonder why the person who needs treatment by a doctor is called a *patient*? It's because you have to have patience if you hope that you'll ever be seen! (I recently learned that doctors and nurses have their own version of the same joke—about *patients* who try the *patience* of the entire medical profession.)

As a matter of fact, the words do draw on the same Latin root, which has the general meaning of enduring, suffering, or bearing something. When we allow ourselves to be treated by a doctor, nurse, or surgeon, we are submitting ourselves to the actions of another—bearing or enduring that action, for our own good. Similarly, the virtue of *patience* is concerned with enduring or bearing something over time. Both uses of the word involve giving up control, yielding it to someone or something else. It means a willingness to relax into a state of allowing something the time that it takes, accepting that complicated matters can't be resolved instantly, and allowing others to set the pace, the conditions, and the goals. (Author's confession: these are all things that I absolutely *hate* to do.)

Like all Christian virtues, patience has its roots in God's character: God is described as "slow to anger" (Exod. 34:6, echoed throughout the Old Testament) and as patient with human beings, "not wanting any to perish, but all to come to repentance" (2 Pet. 3:9). Thus even *God* is willing to submit to the will of another and to yield control—and this in spite of God's own superior knowledge and power. God could, presumably, force our hands and make us do exactly what God desires us to do; but God's commitment to allowing human beings to enjoy a certain amount of free will seems at least as strong as God's commitment to getting them to act rightly. For example, if God had wanted to ensure that the new inhabitants of Eden would not eat from the forbidden tree, God might well have set down some kind of impenetrable force-field (or, as eventually happens, an angel with a flaming sword; see Gen. 3:24), rather than simply telling the man and the woman not to eat from it. Similarly, God could have simply planted a strong sense of assurance inside the mind of Thomas (the apostle who doubted Jesus' resurrection), instead of Jesus appearing beside him in order to fulfill the conditions that he, Thomas, placed on his willingness to believe. Throughout the biblical narrative, God repeatedly validates human freedom—ceding control to others rather than simply exercising power over them. Thus the Christian rationale for patience goes something like this: if God is willing to hand over control to others (in spite of God's superior knowledge and power), how much more should human beings be willing to do so, given that their own knowledge and power is never more than partial at best, and that they are sometimes completely mistaken?

And—we might go on—how much more still should they do so when they are sick, suffering, or simply unsure of the answers to their biomedical questions? In other words: one of the times that we most clearly need to be patient is when we are *patients*. At this point, we really don't have much choice: we have to hand over control to others. Most of us don't have the knowledge and expertise to treat ourselves; moreover, our weakened bodies wouldn't allow us to do so, even if we knew how. But we don't hand over that control very willingly; we want to decide when things will happen, for how long, and under what conditions. In particular, we hate the idea of "becoming a burden" to someone else; we thus impatiently demand an immediate solution to our medical conundrums, even when what is really warranted is some kind of long-term program of waiting (and being cared for). All in all, since we don't have much practice at being patient before we *become* a patient, we often have a hard time of it; after all, as I noted above, it's not easy to develop new habits when you're sick. In order to become more patient patients, we will need to find ways of becoming more patient people in the ordinary course of our lives.

Unfortunately, however, the virtue of patience is in particularly scarce supply in our cultural setting. For one thing, we usually demand a fair amount of control over our own lives and our immediate surroundings; giving up that control to another is something that we do only under duress. We often suspect that our willingness to have patience (or to be a patient) in such circumstances is merely an excuse for other people to take advantage of us. On more than one occasion, I have been tempted to approach the window in a doctor's waiting room and to begin a lengthy complaint: "You know, my time is valuable too. When my students make an appointment to see me, they don't expect to wait 45 minutes beyond the original time, particularly without some kind of explanation or apology." And so on. Of course, when I think about it, I'm pretty sure that the doctors and nurses are not back there playing Monopoly or downloading music; they are taking the time that it takes to see the patients who were there before me, who (no doubt) had to be as patient as I am now asked to be, while they waited for those who preceded them. But stepping into this space requires me to cede control to the doctors and nurses, who (of course) know best how much time it all takes—and that's what I would rather not do.

The analogy of parents and children may be useful to us here. Parents must have an enormous level of patience in order to let a child perform a task that is relatively complicated for her age (say, a four-year-old mixing the pancake batter on Saturday mornings). The parents themselves could do this task much more efficiently, productively, and quickly (and probably with much less mess—though that may depend upon the cooking habits of the adults in question!). Nevertheless, the willingness to cede control to another person is part of the way that we recognize that person's full humanity. Parents know that they need to give children the opportunity to take on certain tasks if they are to grow into the fulness of their lives. Will those who are given such opportunities occasionally bring about catastrophe? Yes, of course. Will they then sometimes take advantage of us? Absolutely—for such results are also part of being human. Again, this is why most of us find patience so challenging a virtue to cultivate as an essential element of our character. But according to the Christian perspective, God's patience reminds us that much is to be gained by doing so.

Another element of our culture deserves mention here: our tendency toward instant gratification. Technology has brought so many things so much closer to our grasp; thus, we really see no good reason to wait. Our music, pictures, and films can be downloaded instantaneously; our communication channels (via cell phone, instant messaging, and e-mail) are open 24/7. We are eager to cram as many units of exciting experience into whatever square footage is available. Since the virtues are *habits*, we would need to be in the habit of being patient in order to cultivate it as an excellence of character; and these days, we rarely wait around long enough to have the opportunity to practice the art of patient waiting.

If we can find ways to cultivate the virtue of patience, however, we will be well rewarded when we or our loved ones get sick—or when we must, in some other way, face the mysteries of life and death, of health and disease. First, we may find ourselves more willing and able to let long-term therapies run their course, instead of insisting on some kind of immediate intervention that turns out to be risky, costly, and altogether unwarranted by anything other than our own lack of patience. Second, we may be able to face the pain and suffering that have been recognized, throughout human history, to be an essential part of the embodied, enfleshed human condition; we may even learn, in the process, that some forms of suffering can actually grace us with some of the redemptive qualities that it is occasionally believed to offer. Finally, we may find ourselves facing less psychological and emotional stress around events at the beginning and end of life—allowing these processes to take the time that they take, learning to bear the challenges that they offer us, and refusing to imagine that we can subject them completely to our own forms of control. I would not want to suggest that any of these activities are easy, or that patience is, in general, a particularly easy virtue to cultivate; in fact, speaking personally, I find it to be one of the most difficult. But just like the various trials that patience can help us to endure, the depth of the hardship that we bear in the process may be closely related to the depth of the happiness that we eventually come to enjoy. As the great Enlightenment philosopher Baruch Spinoza put it, "All things excellent are as difficult as they are rare."

Faith

In the previous chapter we examined the virtue of faithfulness, at which point I remarked that the same Greek word—*pistis*—is sometimes translated as "faith" and sometimes as "faithfulness." For example, if we were to compare the two biblical passages that provide for us the "fruits of the Spirit" (of which "faithfulness" is one) and the "theological virtues" (including *faith*)—Galatians 5 and 1 Corinthians 13—we would find the same Greek word in use. Are these really two different ideas? I believe that they are, but making this case will require us to draw some fairly careful distinctions.

While our discussion of faithfulness in chapter 12 focused on questions of allegiance and loyalty, the theological virtue of faith is somewhat different: the accent here is on confidence and trust. Obviously, the two go hand in hand (as do all the virtues; this is why we speak of their *unity*). But as I noted in the previous chapter, the slight difference in emphasis is important, and may be best illustrated by an example. Imagine two people who consider themselves to be the best of friends (we'll call them Maryann and Wanda, for all you Dixie Chicks fans out there). The virtue of *faithfulness* describes Maryann's devotion to Wanda—her willingness to make whatever sacrifices are necessary to support her and to help her out when she is in trouble. The virtue of *faith* describes Wanda's confidence or trust that Maryann will indeed be there for her. Similarly, in a marriage, I seek to be *faithful* (loyal, constant) to my partner; she seeks to have *faith* (trust, confidence) in my love for her—and vice versa, of course. Faithfulness is one person's devotion to the other; faith is that person's confidence and trust in the other's devotion to oneself. Thus the two virtues mutually reinforce one another; the more my partner demonstrates her faithfulness, the more faith I have in her; and the more faith I demonstrate, the more willing she will be to be faithful.

I chose to discuss the virtue of *faith* in this chapter on issues of bioethics because, at the margins of life, we can most clearly recognize the importance of having confidence and trust in others. When we are conceived and born, we are (obviously) wholly in the care of others; we have almost no ability to influence our environment, and only very limited means to signal distress or to express appreciation. In fact, at these early stages of life, we are not even enough of a "subject" or "agent" to make much sense of the word "faith"; we don't often speak of newborn babies having "faith" in their parents. This lack of usage, however, suggests a theological misunderstanding: we tend to think of faith as a "decision" that we make at a certain point in time, like the person who sees the Christian creed as a checklist of decisions and chooses whether or not to believe each tenet of the statement. But as I have suggested at several points in this book, the character trait that we call "faith"—like the process of affirming a creed—is not so much a mental decision to act, but more of an orientation of life: a condition of trust and confidence, a willingness to put oneself in the hands of another. Viewed in this way, the language of faith is in fact an excellent description of the attitude of an infant to its parents. Moreover, parents respond as one would expect people to respond to one who has demonstrated his or her confidence and trust in them: with care and love, recognizing the infant's degree of dependence and need.

Similarly, when we are sick or dying, we must once again place our confidence and trust in others: in the health-care professionals who provide for us, in our friends and relatives who help us make decisions or, in some cases, make decisions for us; and even in inanimate objects such as medicines, surgical procedures, and mechanical devices. Because of our tendency to think of faith as an act of the will, we imagine that we could, in an instant, decide in favor of it or against it—as though it resulted from a careful, rational process of reflection. But faith is not like that; it is a habit, a character trait that is cultivated over time. Thus, when facing a complex medical situation, one cannot simply "decide" to have it; those who have not developed faith over time usually have some difficulty achieving a high level of trust and confidence in others at such critical junctures. This may also explain why God—who is relatively high on many people's lists of the many possible objects or persons in whom one might have faith—tends to come up in conversation fairly frequently when the subject-matter is suffering, death, or new life. And, as I noted in the previous section, one of the major obstacles that we face in placing our trust in others is our desire not to be a burden to them; we are well schooled in the enthusiastic embrace of rugged individualism. We often try to avoid placing too much confidence or trust in others to take care of us, because we have come to believe that each person ought to take care of him- or herself. This cultural commitment to individualism is sorely tested when we face the circumstances that we are discussing in this chapter.

In what or whom should we place our confidence and trust? For many of us, the medical establishment—in the form of people, technologies, pharmaceuticals, and insurance companies—has become the *de facto* recipient of trust when it comes to questions surrounding the margins of life. These are, after all, the people with the expertise, the information, and the judgment to offer us reliable advice on such matters. The trouble, of course, is that the members of the medical establishment are human beings as well, and they are subject to distraction, temptation, and even corruption. For example, a doctor may tend to prescribe a certain pharmaceutical, not simply because of its usefulness to a patient, but because of pressure that is being applied by the companies that manufacture and market that particular drug. Even if this sort of thing does not happen very often, the fact that it happens at all is a reminder that even the most trustworthy members of the medical establishment are not perfectly trustworthy. Thus, even if we have a fair degree of confidence in the health-care delivery system, we usually recognize that it is not the best choice of an object in which to place the fullest measure of our trust.

This helps to explain why the Christian theological tradition has always been fairly suspicious of the human tendency to place significant trust in someone or something without also placing complete trust in God. Neither people nor systems nor machines are exhaustive of those in whom we should place our trust; this is because they will all, at some level, fail. We are often loathe to acknowledge the possibility of such failure, which is why we are also awash in medical malpractice suits, litigation against drug manufacturers, and complaints about health-care financing systems. Obviously, some of these complaints and lawsuits may express wholly legitimate concerns about some procedure gone awry; but at a more basic level, they express our frustration that the people, processes, and machines in which we have placed our trust have not always come through for us. The Christian response to this claim is, quite frankly, that we should not expect them to do so; the only wholly proper object of a human being's complete and utter trust is God.

What would it mean, for human beings to direct their faith toward God with respect to issues surrounding the margins of life? As I noted in the middle section of this chapter, a small minority of Christians call for a general resistance to all (or almost all) medical practice, insisting on the power of prayer to heal. At the other end of the spectrum, some would tend to set all theological questions to one side, allowing medical practice to become the single, solitary guide to all decision-making concerning treatment. Between these two extremes is a vast space, in which most Christians find themselves: wanting to give attention and respect both to the knowledge that human beings have developed concerning medical practice, and to the beliefs outlined at the beginning of this chapter: that life is a gift from God, that God provides for all creatures, and that death is not the ultimate reality. But most Christians find it difficult, perhaps impossible, to give proper attention to both sets of concerns—theological and medical—at the same time.

In a recent (and very fine) book on medical ethics, *Reclaiming the Body: Christians and the Faithful Use of Modern Medicine*, theologian Joel Shuman and pediatrician Brian Volck have suggested that the best way for Christians to understand modern medicine is through the biblical language of "powers and principalities." This phrase, which comes from a verse in Paul's letter to the Ephesians, suggests that for many Christians, what stands in the way of their true faith in God is not usually just a particular human being, or even a large group of people, but a structure or system of some sort: something which, precisely because it is nameless and faceless, is difficult for us to grasp or to argue against. Paul observes that "we are not contending against flesh and blood, but against the principalities, against the powers, against the world rulers of this present darkness, against the spiritual hosts of wickedness in the heavenly places" (Eph. 6:12, RSV).

Often these "powers and principalities" are assumed to be some kind of mystical force, such as a demon or devil. This is something of a misrepresentation, however; for most people in the contemporary setting, such language is abstract at best and may suggest a failure to be grounded in reality. These days, "demons" are thought to be rather like gnomes in a garden or gremlins in our computer systems—an invented idea that provides an easy explanation for anything that we find inexplicable. But Paul clearly has in mind real, concrete realities—not abstractions or imaginary creatures that fill in the gaps in our knowledge or our ability to offer explanations. The NRSV translation attempts to mitigate this misperception somewhat by translating the words as "rulers" and "authorities." But this language may mislead us in another way, since we tend to assume that "the authorities" are primarily the members of the governmental entities who enforce the laws of the state; and again, Paul has a wider range of reference in mind. More recently, some theologians have suggested that, to modern ears, words like "structures" or "systems" might be a useful description: what concerns Paul is our tendency to allow faith in God to be eclipsed by powerful, concrete systems and structures that get a grip on us, without us even knowing it.

Modern medicine is one such structure or system. It is not necessarily evil, nor is it necessarily good. Rather, it follows the same pattern of existence as do the other powers, principalities, rulers, and authorities: they are potentially good (because they are ultimately shaped by human beings, who are created by God as good); they are fallen (for the same reason: because the human beings who shape them can drift away from God); and they are therefore in need of redemption (being brought back into right relationship with God and with the whole created order). The issue for Christians is therefore not an oppositional confrontation between modern medicine on one side and God on the other; it is between a system of medicine that is in right relationship with God, versus one that is not. The choice is between an idolatrous approach to medicine (in which it replaces God as the proper object of human confidence and trust), and an approach to medicine which allows God to remain the highest recipient of confidence, trust, and worship.

Therefore, faith is a focal virtue for questions of bioethics because here, more than perhaps any other area of life, Christians find themselves tempted to divert their trust away from God and toward whatever technology, procedure, or person seems most likely to offer them relief from suffering, provision of what they desire (youthful features, physical vigor, healthy children), and a better, longer life. Is this because medicine is a wily devil, seducing Christians with its charm? No, it is because such Christians have primed themselves for this treatment by imagining that an absence of pain and suffering, and/or the fulfillment of their desires, and/or a longer or better life, is the ultimate reality: the true object of faith. But of course, these are not the true objects of faith: its true object is God alone.

Here we need to recall the three theological terms with which we began this chapter: grace, providence, and resurrection. According to the Christian theological tradition, any medical decision to extend life, to reduce pain, or to redesign the body must always be made with full attention to these three claims. Grace reminds human beings that their lives are not ours alone, but are ultimately gifts from God. Providence encourages them to place their trust in God's willingness to give them what they need. Resurrection provides them with the assurance that, even in the face of death, their relationships with God and with one another will never be destroyed; they will only be changed in form.

Practical wisdom

Our third virtue was called, by speakers of Latin, *prudentia*; this was their translation of the Greek word *phronēsis*. Our English equivalent, "prudence," does a fairly poor job of getting across the ideas that lie behind these Latin and Greek terms; in fact, as I noted in chapter 7, the word may well mislead us. For us, "prudence" suggests caution, foresight, and discretion; it may also imply careful management of economic resources or even frugality. A prudent investor is one who makes cautious judgments about possible future difficulties; a prudent writer of essays in college does a great deal of advance planning and organizing of material, so as not to be faced with an insuperable task against an impossible deadline. (All my students always do their work in accordance with this approach, of course.) In fact, given the ways that we tend to use the term today, a "prudent" person starts to sound just a little boring! This connotation is only reinforced by the word's association with the word "prude," which—although it has a different root altogether (interestingly, it comes from the same root as *proud*)—gets connected in our minds with the idea of prudence as caution and frugality. Anyone who is consistently prudent just seems like a bit of a prude.

The Latin and Greek roots of the word are actually focused on the idea of wise judgment; another common translation for the Greek version, *phronēsis*, is "practical wisdom." It means being able to make the right judgment, in the right way, in any given situation—neither allowing oneself to be boxed in by an overly narrow interpretation of "the rules," nor simply floating free and doing "what feels right" in the moment, but rather, being *wise* in practical matters. This might often require, as the word "prudence" does suggest, a certain degree of caution and discretion—but not always. There are obviously times when a prudent (wise) investor would need to be quite *in*cautious;

similarly, a prudent essay-writer might recognize that she works very well when up against a deadline. Because these aspects of the term are likely to get lost among the associations of the English word "prudence," I prefer the term "practical wisdom."

As I noted in chapter 7, practical wisdom is something of a master virtue; it names that disposition or habit of mind that allows us to make good appropriations of all the other virtues. In the absence of a concrete set of rules or a specific guide to action, we need a particular faculty of mind: an ability to make the right judgments and to do the right thing, at the right time, for the right reasons. This is the virtue that Aristotle named *phronēsis*: it connects the intellect to the will, so that we can consistently conform our acts of judgment to the reasoning work of our minds. The Christian adaptation of this concept (particularly through the work of Thomas Aquinas) gave it a slightly different emphasis: for Thomas, practical wisdom should also take account of the ultimate end of human beings, which is to live into our true nature, conforming ourselves ever more closely to the image of God in which we were created. Just as they believe God to have a sort of "ultimate" practical wisdom in ordering all things to God's own creative purposes, so should Christians act as imitators of this divine practical wisdom in their own judgment. Thus, according to a Christian account of the virtue of practical wisdom, human beings ought to remain attentive to God's own creative purposes whenever they exercise judgment.

Even though practical wisdom is among the most important of the virtues, it can be a rather slippery concept. In discussions about ethics, it can too easily become a kind of all-purpose answer to every question. ("But how will people know how to face a new medical technology when it arises?" Answer: "They will use practical wisdom.") But it is not meant as a panacea for unresolvable ethical questions, or as a stopgap notion that we use to get along until we can work out a more respectable theory. We can get a better handle on the significance of practical wisdom as a virtue if we remember that the virtues are, first and foremost, *habits*. We need a virtue that allows us to conform the will (judgment) to the intellect (reason), because the only way that we will learn to do so consistently is by *making a habit of it*. By naming practical wisdom as a virtue, we are reminding ourselves that we need to get in the habit of comparing our moral judgments with our mental process of reasoning about moral matters. Since we don't know what kinds of judgments lie ahead, the best that we can do is strengthen the muscles that we will need in order to make them. We are like pianists who, because they cannot know what music they will next be asked to play, get in the habit of sight-reading every day, so that the process of translating the marks on the page to the movement of the hands becomes practically automatic. If we allow ourselves to fall out of such habits—if a musician stops sight-reading, or if we repeatedly make judgments and decisions without consulting our brains—then the two spheres (thought and action) will gradually become detached from one another. Eventually, we may find ourselves making *most* of our moral judgments without attending to our best thoughts on the subject. If, on the other hand, we are in the habit of conforming our judgments to our reasoning, this process will eventually start to seem natural to us; we will begin to take for granted the idea that we should do what our minds tell us to do.

When it comes to questions surrounding the margins of life, we are in serious need of practical wisdom. Given the rapid rate of change in the field of modern medicine, it is simply impossible for any of us to foresee all the judgments that we will need to make about bioethics into the indefinite future. After all, we know that the kinds of assumptions and decisions that today seem appropriate (or even automatic) would not even have been imaginable a few decades ago; and the future seems likely to present more challenges still. We therefore need to develop, as a habit, a faculty that allows us to put our best thought into action.

This again takes us back to our earlier discussion of grace, providence, and resurrection as central concepts in the discussion of issues surrounding the margins of life. If I am correct in identifying these features as central to Christians in this sphere of human activity, then the Christian exercise of practical wisdom will be strongly informed by these ideas. It will mean getting in the habit of allowing these theological ideas to issue in appropriate judgments and actions. Take, for example, the idea that human life is a gift from God and is not something that human beings "deserve" or that they have a "right" to extend indefinitely: practical wisdom is the habit of putting this knowledge into action every time one makes a moral judgment about death. Every visit to the doctor's office, every conversation with a friend facing difficult decisions, and most of the stories that appear in the news—all of these provide opportunities to exercise the muscles that are used to put one's knowledge and beliefs about the nature of life into action. Those who act as though life were a gift, and do so in small ways on a daily basis, will soon be able to make major decisions and judgments in ways that conform with that view. The same is true for the Christian claims about providence—that God provides for human beings, and that they can sometimes be deceived about what they think they need or must have in order to make their lives tolerable—and also about death: that it is not the ultimate fate of human beings, so that avoiding or delaying it, while such actions may be appropriate in some instances, is not something that people should always undertake at any cost.

With these theological principles in mind, Christians are called upon to cultivate the virtue of practical wisdom, so that they will be able to make judgments and decisions about the particular cases that they will face. As most commentators on bioethics have made clear, it is practically impossible to lay down a particular rule or guideline that can and must be adhered to in all cases; even if doing so were possible in some spheres of life (and this book has largely argued that it is not), it would still be impossible in this sphere, where the ground shifts every day. But those who are in the habit of conforming the will to the intellect (because they have done so in small ways, every day) will be better prepared to do when they find themselves in circumstance where "conforming the will to the intellect" will require them to face grief, suffering, or even death. To be able to do so with the courage of one's convictions fully intact is, as Prince Hamlet also says, "a consummation devoutly to be wished."

Questions for discussion

1. Were the theological concepts of grace, providence, and resurrection familiar to you before you read this chapter? If so, offer a brief comparison or contrast between the ways that you thought about these concepts before and after you read this material. If not, describe some aspect of your life or some personal experience (not necessarily connected to religious life) that might illustrate or resonate with each of these concepts.

2. Relate a personal experience that has affected how you think about the distinctions discussed in this chapter concerning beginning and/or the end of human life. Now imagine a different kind of experience—an experience that your or someone else might have had—that would lead to a very different conclusion than the one to which you were led. Consider how, in each case, the experience itself has shaped (or would shape) the person's perspective on the issue.

3. Offer an illustration from something you have read—fiction or non-fiction—that describes someone who endures suffering. (The suffering can be physical, psychological, spiritual, or any combination.) What resources did the person call upon in order to endure it? How did the person's response to these experiences of suffering affect your judgment of her or his character?

4. Find a newspaper story about a new development in medical technology—a device, technique, or medicine that has either recently been put into practice or is currently in development—that is designed to limit the damaging effects of an accident or disease, and/or to reduce the risk of death. Discuss

with one or two other people whether this new technology would best be understood as a "repair" of the human body, as "re-engineering" it, or as some other description. How do you think it might be evaluated in Christian ethics, given the theological assumptions described at the beginning of this chapter?

5. Offer an account, either from personal experience or from something you have read, about someone who either demonstrated extraordinary patience (or who had a difficult time doing so). What factors (specific to your account) made it particularly difficult for the person to be patient? What factors made it easier? Conclude with a description of something about the person's life (assumptions, experiences, habits) that might help us understand why patience was difficult (or easy) to achieve in this case.

6. Give an example from your own life in which you have had to develop something like "practical wisdom"—that is, when you have had to figure out how to align your judgments and actions with what your mind is telling you to do. What challenges did you face in accomplishing this? What helped you achieve it?

7. Choose at least two other virtues, in addition to those discussed explicitly in this chapter, and explain how they might impinge on ethical questions arising from medical procedures, or on decisions relating to the beginning and end of life.

Sources cited in this chapter and/or recommended for further reading

Nigel Biggar, *Aiming to Kill: The Ethics of Suicide and Euthanasia*

David S. Cunningham, *Friday, Saturday, Sunday: Literary Meditations on Suffering, Death, and New Life*

Stanley Hauerwas and Charles Pinches, "Practicing Patience: How Christians Should Be Sick," in *Christians among the Virtues: Theological Conversations with Ancient and Modern Ethics*

M. Therese Lysaught, "Becoming One Body: Health Care and Cloning," in Hauerwas and Wells, eds., *The Blackwell Companion to Christian Ethics*

Gilbert Meilaender, *Body, Soul, and Bioethics*; *Bioethics: A Primer for Christians*

Flannery O'Connor, *The Complete Stories*; *The Habit of Being: Letters*

Paul Ramsey, *Fabricated Man: The Ethics of Genetic Control*

Mary Wollstonecraft Shelley, *Frankenstein, or, The Modern Prometheus*

Joel Shuman and Brian Volck, *Reclaiming the Body: Christians and the Faithful Use of Modern Medicine*

Robert Song, *Human Genetics: Fabricating the Future*

Carol Bailey Stoneking, "Receiving Communion: Euthanasia, Suicide, and Letting Die," in Hauerwas and Wells, eds., *The Blackwell Companion to Christian Ethics*

Darlene Fozard Weaver, "Death," chapter 15 in Meilaender and Werpehowski, eds., *The Oxford Handbook of Theological Ethics*

Samuel Wells, *God's Companions: Reimagining Christian Ethics*

Ralph Wood, *Flannery O'Connor and the Christ-Haunted South*

14

Friday
Out on the town

Alright, show of hands: who wants to talk about sex? The answer, as always, is twofold—everyone and no one. Sex and sexuality are unquestionably a dominant driving force in our lives: built into our physical bodies at a biological level, increasingly on public display in all our cultural structures, and ever-more-easily "experienced," at least in a virtual form, through a wide range of technologies. Yet at the same time, we carry sex and sexuality inside ourselves at the deepest and most inaccessible level: we long to keep it private and sequestered, and we know that opening ourselves up to it makes us as vulnerable as we are ever likely to be. We seem to be of two minds about sex, simultaneously: indeed, our culture seems to demand that we embrace both a prurient celebration of sex and a puritanical disgust about it. No wonder that everyone wants to talk about sex; and, at the same time, no wonder that *no one* wants to talk about it.

But talk about it we must—at least in a book like this, which examines what it means to be people of good character. As was the case with medical ethics, Christian sexual ethics is a very large topic, on which many books have been written; very little of the sheer complexity of the issue will make its way into this brief chapter. Nevertheless, because our sexual desires and the overall shape of our sexuality is so very much a part of who we are, any analysis of human character must necessarily include an analysis of human attitudes and actions with respect to sex and sexuality. Nor can we evade the question by invoking a distinction between the public and private realms. We often hear it said that "sex is a private matter" or "what people do in their bedrooms is no one else's business"; and with respect to laws regulating sexual behavior, good arguments can certainly be made for such claims. But our interest here does not concern legislation, government regulation, or even pronouncements about actions (at least not in the sense of condemning some specific sexual behaviors and condoning others). Our interest is in the relationship between sex and *character*; and character is formed by our private habits as well as our public ones. So we're just going to have to open those bedroom doors and have a look at what's going on inside. It is not a task for the faint of heart.

I have set this discussion on "Friday" in our hypothetical week, and have entitled the chapter "Out on the town"; these decisions require a word of explanation. In Jewish and Christian tradition, the institution of marriage has usually been understood as the structure within which physical expressions of sexual desire are rightly expressed. The extraordinary degree of power, intimacy, and vulnerability that is associated with sex has led many people to conclude that its fullest expression should be reserved to those relationships that entail a lifelong monogamous commitment. In fact, many treatments of Christian sexual ethics begin with a theological discussion of marriage, which then becomes the context within which sex and sexuality can be appropriately discussed. Given the long history and undeniable strength of limiting sex to marriage within the Christian tradition, shouldn't this chapter be labeled "At home with one's spouse" or "In the marriage bed"?

Well, no. First of all, such an account would make sense only if ethics were primarily concerned with law, rules, and constraints. Such approaches to sexual ethics, whether they understand themselves to be strongly restrictive or broadly open-minded, tend to focus on the specific circumstances under which certain physical forms of sexual expression are "allowed," eventuating in a list of rules. But throughout this book, we have been interested in an account of ethics that is focused on *character*: what does a good life look like? What are the excellences of character that are necessary to face any set of circumstances that may arise, to render good judgments, and to acquit oneself in ways that are praiseworthy and rightly emulated? These questions will not be answered by a list of rules—not even rules that precisely limit the times, places, and circumstances under which one can have sex. Having worked so diligently to "stay out of the lifeboat" throughout this book, it would be tragic to climb back in now, just because we have a convenient, long-standing rule that we can grasp hold of, as a kind of life-preserver, as we face these stormy seas.

Second—and this point needs extraordinary emphasis—sex and sexuality are not limited to specific kinds of physical encounters, whether they take place within marriage or otherwise. We are all sexual beings—regardless of whether, and in what circumstances, we choose to enact our sexual desires in physical, bodily ways. Moreover, sexual expression is not limited to those activities in which intimate physical contact is involved; sexuality can be expressed through the ways that we dress, talk, and interact with one another—just as much as it is expressed in bed (and sometimes more so). Because of the infinite variety of sexual expression and the myriad circumstances in which it can take place, it would be a mistake to limit our discussion to questions about "who is allowed to do what, with what parts of their bodies, with whom, and under what conditions." In this chapter, we will try to be attentive to the role of sexuality and sexual desire in *all* aspects of human life—not just during those intense but brief encounters that we commonly refer to as "having sex."

Finally, my decision not to limit this discussion to "sexual intimacy within marriage" should not be taken as an automatic rejection of accounts that embrace that restriction. It may well be that, once we have explored the questions regarding human sexuality and developed an account of the virtues with respect to sex, we may indeed decide that the emotional complexity, the potential exhilaration, and the regular disasters that we face in matters of sex and sexuality are so extreme that only a lifelong monogamous relationship can provide a safe place to encounter them. (I should note in passing, however, that this does not necessarily imply an acceptance of current accounts of what constitutes a marriage; I take it for granted that questions about, for example, same-sex marriage, or the role of the state in certifying marriage, are open to constant scrutiny. As the reader will have come to expect by this point in the book, the ethical test of a relationship is not whether it conforms to culturally-bound notions of what counts as "marriage," but whether it exhibits the virtues.)

Of course, much of what we will be discussing in this chapter applies just as thoroughly to sexual expression within marriage as it does to such expression outside it. (No one should imagine, even for an instant, that restricting physical sexual expression to the marriage bed will ensure that it will be pursued ethically and for the good of all. Within marriages, too, people need to pay attention to making sure their sex is *good*—not just in the sense of pleasurable, but also in the moral sense: responsible, virtuous, and leading not just to momentary elation but to true happiness: a fulfilled and fulfilling life.) Nevertheless, in recent decades—for a wide variety of reasons—sex has become a serious issue of ethical judgment outside the structures of marriage. Whereas the question of "are you married to this person?" would, at one time, have led most people (Christian or otherwise) to a definitive decision about the morality of a potential sexual encounter, it no longer has that effect. Today, people wrestle with the question of what makes for moral sexual expression in many other circumstances—ranging from casual encounters to long-term relationships that, despite not being solemnized as such, may create a considerably more "holy" space for sexual expression than do many marriages. Christian theologians and ethicists have reacted to this socio-cultural development in a variety of ways, ranging from wholesale condemnation to celebratory embrace (and everything in between). One thing is certain, however: for an ever-increasing percentage of human beings, the complex topic of sexual ethics will arise at least as frequently when they are "out on the town" as it does when they are tending hearth and home. Sex and sexuality receive such pervasive attention in our world that it would be irresponsible—theologically, ethically, and pastorally—to attempt to counter it simply by staring people straight in the eye and yelling, "No foolin' around!"

Even Jesus' own specific teachings on this subject are not nearly as definitive as they are sometimes thought to be. While he clearly says some positive things about marriage (Matt. 19:4–6) and leaves very little room for divorce (Matt. 5:32), he also makes it clear that family relationships do not outrank one's relationship with God (Matt. 10:25–37). As for sexual activity outside marriage, Jesus' best known saying runs as follows: '"You have heard that it was said, 'You shall not commit adultery.' But I say to you that everyone who looks at a woman with lust has already committed adultery with her in his heart' (Matt. 5:27–28).

This reminds us of a claim that we have been emphasizing throughout this book: namely, that an interpretation of law that focuses only on outward actions is not a sufficient guide to morality. Rather, one's internal thoughts, judgments, and character are also of enormous significance. In this particular case, Jesus makes it clear that an interior disposition of lust is not excused by the mere fact that one has not yet acted upon it.

For all these reasons, this chapter will not be attempting to pronounce some kind of definitive Christian stance on the moral acceptability (or otherwise) of specific forms of physical sexual expression—whether within the structures of marriage or outside it. Nor will it attempt to offer a Christian account of marriage—an issue that, again because of recent developments, would require a book-length treatment just to address the most basic concerns. Rather, our explorations will begin with an inquiry into the human expression and reception of desire, followed by some considerations about the significance of the physical body as an aspect of Christian ethical deliberation. We will then turn to the virtues, considering how they might apply to our judgments and decisions concerning sexuality and sexual expression.

All desires known

I have always greatly appreciated a particular prayer that occurs near the beginning of the worship service in many churches. In the version of the Book of Common Prayer that is currently used in the United States, that prayer begins as follows: "Almighty God, to you all hearts are open, all desires known, and from you no secrets are hid." I find this a useful turn of phrase for Christian ethics in general, and for sexual ethics in particular; and I think that its usefulness endures, regardless of whether one makes one's home in a church that uses it, or in any church at all—and regardless, in fact, of whether one even believes in God. Its usefulness comes from the idea, central to this opening phrase of the prayer, that our desires are not really private matters hidden deep within our hearts, as we often imagine them to be; they are, rather, open and known—not really secret at all. This is the case for at least two reasons.

First, as the discipline of psychology has often demonstrated, our internal desires become manifested in various concrete ways—even though their outward manifestation does not always seem directly and obviously related to whatever it is that we actually desire. Our desires shape our dreams and affect our behavior; they burst out of our psyche and take shape in our lives, often in distorted and unrecognizable ways. Particularly when we refuse to admit our desires to ourselves, they find ways of appearing in our lives, taking various forms that may appear meaningless or even confusing—to other people and to ourselves. For example, when a person carries around a great deal of anger and frequently lashes out at others, the problem will not always be eliminated simply by "getting it under control." As a good friend of mine always used to say, "people get angry for a reason"—it's just that we often don't know the reason. (In fact, quite frequently, the person who is angry doesn't know the reason either—or is mistaken about the true source of the anger.) It may be, for example, that this apparently angry person carries deeply-seated desires that cannot be realized—perhaps desires that the person has never known were there, or at least has not admitted to him- or herself. A good psychologist can observe the presenting behavior of a patient (in this case, the extreme anger) and, with the proper technique, help that person to discover what actual causes lie behind that behavior. Such causes often have something to do with our unfulfilled desires. This is not to say that those desires should necessarily be fulfilled; nevertheless, burying them or ignoring them will not make them go away. They will find their way to expression in one form or another.

A second reason that our desires are not so deeply buried as we imagine can be gleaned from our investigations, in this book, concerning the formation of character. The desires of our hearts, however private we may consider them to be, will still have an effect on the shape of our character. Moreover, our habits—both in terms of the narratives that we live by and the practices in which we engage—will affect both the shape and the intensity of our desires, regardless of whether we admit those desires to others (or even to ourselves). Burying our desires deeply doesn't make us into different kinds of people, or people of a wholly different character; it just makes it more difficult for us to understand ourselves, and more difficult for us to cultivate the kinds of habits that might lead to true happiness. However deeply buried, potentially embarrassing, and continuously anxiety-producing they may be, our desires are still *our desires*; thus they will still affect our character.

Admittedly, some people develop techniques for compartmentalizing their lives such that a particular set of their desires may be kept far apart from the characteristics that they display in public. But sooner or later, these two worlds are bound to collide; or, at the very least, one of these worlds will spill over into the other's space. Even though a person may put on a mask and play a different character in public, one's true character will eventually become known. Moreover, in a world dominated by increasingly invasive technologies (as signified by surveillance cameras, internet snooping, and the near-permanent nature of cell phone records and credit-card receipts), it has become rather difficult to protect a supposedly "compartmentalized" life against any truly determined investigator. And in any case, the separations that we impose upon the different worlds in which we suppose we live are all ultimately artificial; in the end, they're all part of the same world.

Thus I particularly treasure that prayer's opening phrase, "to you all hearts are open, all desires known, and from you no secrets are hid." Whether or not one wishes to pray this prayer (or any prayer), and whether or not one believes in God at all, this phrase suggests a way of life worthy of emulation: to live as though our hearts were open to others, our desires fully known, our secrets never hidden. This is not to say that we should declare all our desires and our secrets loudly to anyone who will listen; in fact, such public displays of a person's inner life can function as just another way to keep that life hidden by carefully "constructing" exactly what one wants the public to see. Rather, I am arguing that we should resist our tendency to imagine that we can keep our desires tucked away in a private space where they will have no real effect on ourselves or on other people.

Of course, our sexual desires and secrets are only one small subset of all the desires and secrets that we imagine that we keep to ourselves. Why, then, raise this issue here, in a chapter on sexual ethics? First, because our sexual desires are among those that we are most likely to keep hidden away. Given our culture's simultaneous embrace of prurient enthusiasm for sexual expression and of moralizing condemnation of it, bringing issues of sex and sexuality out of their hiding places has become—at the very least—a complicated undertaking. In public settings, we tend to avoid the subject altogether; in private settings, we worry that one wrong word about the shape of our desires might convince our friends to worry about us, our lovers to reject us, and our acquaintances to back slowly out of the room. We sense that our sexual desires will be judged in ways that our other biological drives—for nourishment, warmth, and shelter—will not. And, of course, we're right: they will be judged, sometimes quite harshly, and those judgments will sometimes have serious consequences.

In addition, our sexual desires are often among our most powerful desires. We need a certain amount of food for nourishment, but a desire for just the right kind of food rarely leads us to turn our entire lives upside-down. Admittedly, people may go well out of their way—and occasionally to an extraordinary degree—to satisfy their cravings for, say, the perfect pint of beer or the world's best hot-fudge sundae. But they usually won't have to spend too much time or money in the process, and their efforts will probably not disrupt their own lives or the lives of those around them. Moreover, they will usually find what they were looking for (or at least a reasonable facsimile thereof), and society will rarely disapprove of either the quest or its successful fulfillment. But the active pursuit of our sexual desires is often an extraordinarily time- and money-consuming venture—often meeting with social disapproval and, more often than not, ending in some form of frustration and/or putting us into a permanent state of disequilibrium. No wonder we tend to bury those desires so deeply in our hearts—and no wonder we have so much to gain by living as though our hearts were fully open and our desires truly known.

In advocating this degree of "openness" about our desires, I am *not* attempting to suggest that all of our desires are necessarily *good*, nor that they deserve moral approbation. Our desires are certainly built into us at a biological level, but they are also capable of being shaped—trained and formed in certain directions—just as are the dispositions of our character. We have a biological desire to eat, but that desire is powerfully shaped and formed by parental guidance, peer pressure, and other cultural forces. As a result, precisely *what* we desire to eat—as well as how much, under what conditions, and with what accompanying rituals—will vary greatly from one person to another. Moreover, the process through which desire is shaped is never morally neutral. The ethical traditions have always recognized the possibility of *disordered* desire—as when, for example, a person becomes habituated to eat far too much food (or far too little). Thus we will still have to make judgments about our desires: whether they have been formed in us in a morally appropriate way, whether they are rightly ordered, and to what degree they may have been distorted by the self-interests of other people or by the "powers and principalities" that we discussed in the previous chapter. (In the realm of shaping our sexual desires, those might include culturally dominant constructions of sex and gender, erotically-charged literature and visual imagery, and practically all known forms of advertising. As we noted with respect to medical ethics, such structures and systems are not necessarily good or evil in themselves, but they can have an enormous effect on our basic assumptions about morality.) In the realm of sexual ethics in particular, any question that is raised concerning which desires are "rightly ordered" and which are "disordered" will certainly spark tremendous debate; such matters will not be settled in the small space allotted in this chapter. But we will be unable even to *begin* that discussion unless we are willing to get our desires out on the table—and to admit that they play an extraordinarily significant role in all of our lives.

To summarize our discussion of sexual desire: in no other aspect of our lives are we so likely to hide our desires, and in no other area is it so important to recognize that they are not really hidden at all. We will always find ways to pursue them; they will break through our efforts to bury them; and they will still have a highly significant impact on the formation of our character. Whether we acknowledge it or not, the truth of the prayer is clear: all hearts are open, all desires are known, and ultimately, no secrets can be hidden—at least not for very long.

Why bodies matter

All of this would already be complicated enough if we were wrestling with some kind of abstract, disembodied desire, like a not-terribly-specific desire to be more intelligent or more creative. But our sexual desires, like our other appetites, cannot ignore the reality of our fleshly, physical bodies. To experience sexual desire is to experience an attraction to a physical body—and often, to a very particular body. More than one lover has resonated with the words of the Psalmist, who describes a deeply-felt longing as one in which "my heart and my flesh cry out" (Ps. 84:2).

In fact, we are capable of experiencing a certain kind of sexual desire for bodies alone, as if they were not an integral part of an actual human being. A visual image, a disembodied voice, or a physical human body considered as "merely a body" (without attention to that person's mind, soul, and spirit)— any of these can, under the right circumstances, become the object of our desire. We describe this process as the "objectification" of sexual desire— that is, treating the human person as if he or she were an object, a thing. We ignore the other elements that make that person human (personality, character, intellect, will) and treat her or him as a kind of mechanism, the purpose of which is to fulfill our desires. Such objectification has occurred throughout human history, but our opportunities to engage in it have been significantly amplified over the last century by the advent of certain technologies; photography, recorded sound, moving images, and various advanced forms of "virtual reality" have placed the physical bodies of others—or at least the images of those bodies—within our easy grasp. In such circumstances, it becomes very easy to ignore the other elements that make that person a human being; in fact, in many cases, we may not know a single detail about the person who has become the proximate cause of our desire, other than the shape of his or her physical body: the image that is set before our eyes.

However, in spite of the availability (and the frequent use) of others' bodies as objects, our sexual desires are not limited to physical realities alone. In fact, part of what makes sex so powerful is that it encompasses the whole of our being: physical, mental, emotional, and spiritual. Our desire for physical contact with another body actually signifies a deeper, more persistent desire: a desire for human contact in a more all-embracing sense. We long for relationships of *nearness* to others—allowing us to be present to one another not only physically, but in ways that embrace the whole spectrum of human personhood.

Having said this, however, it can be easy for us to begin to stress the emotional, intellectual, and spiritual aspects of relationships so thoroughly that we set aside the physical aspects, as if these were only tangential to the reality of the relationship. Doing so would be a significant error, because—as already observed—sexual desire usually involves attraction to a physical body, and often, to a very particular body. Thus, while recognizing that we cannot fully understand sex and sexuality by concentrating *only* on the physical body, we must give the body at least some of our attention.

What does Christianity have to say about the body? Here we enter some fairly murky waters, because the churches have not always been particularly clear about their teaching on this subject. In fact, from time to time through Christian history, the physical body has been neglected or ridiculed or pilloried as the primary locus of sin and wickedness. Some Christians feel that they were taught, particularly as young children, to despise their bodies and to avoid the bodies of others at all costs. It was almost as if the Christian faith claimed that our bodies were a tragic nuisance and that we would be better off if we were disembodied souls. Such claims are a monumental distortion of traditional Christian teaching about the body; in fact, the tendency to treat the body as having something of a second-class status—always of less significance than the spirit and happily dispensed with at death—was one of the elements of Greek and Roman thought that both Judaism and Christianity criticized most fervently. What, then, is at the center of Christian beliefs about the body? In answering this question we will be recalling, and in some cases reiterating, some of our earlier discussions concerning particular

Christian beliefs, including the beliefs that God created the world, that Jesus rose from the dead, and that human beings will experience the resurrection of their bodies.

First and foremost, and in keeping with the Jewish roots of their faith, Christians believe that *bodies matter*. Human beings, in their fully embodied and fleshly state, are created by God; this bodily creation is then declared by God to be "very good" (Gen. 1:26–31). The human experience of the world is a *fully embodied* experience; human relationships with other physical realities, from their earliest encounters in the Garden of Eden, are direct bodily relationships. Human beings eat and drink and have sex and give birth; they experience disease and hardship and suffering; and they grow old and die. The extraordinary degree to which Judaism attended to these bodily matters can be seen most clearly in the Levitical laws, most of which have to do with the particular details of this embodied existence: what and how to eat; how to relate to one's physical possessions; what postures to take toward one's fellow human beings. Accordingly, the kings of Israel and the prophets focus their attention on the ways that human beings interact with the physical world. Although the precise rules and claims vary over the course of time, at no point in the biblical narrative is it suggested that the physical bodies of human beings are irrelevant, that we would be better off without them, or that they ought to be despised or neglected. Even Paul the Apostle's occasional critical comments about "the flesh" are offset by his positive account of "the body"; for him, the body is a temple of the Spirit (1 Cor. 6:19), a perfect metaphor for the Christian community (Rom. 12:4–5, 1 Cor. 12–14 and elsewhere), and the vehicle of the resurrection of the dead (1 Cor. 15:35–54).

What *is* suggested throughout the biblical narrative—and corroborated by our everyday experience—is that our physical bodies make us *vulnerable*; this is a second significant Christian claim about bodies. They are vulnerable in and of themselves: sometimes beset by pain and suffering, often weak, always at risk. And the potential weakness and pain of our physical bodies make us vulnerable in other ways as well: psychologically, emotionally, and spiritually. This is most dramatically demonstrated, in the biblical narrative, in the story of God's own sojourn on earth in human form; Jesus is vulnerable to all the insults and injuries of the human condition, including death. Through this story, Christians are reminded that bodies matter—and that they must therefore be cared for and treated with respect. While some bodies are clearly more vulnerable than others, they should not be compared with other bodies merely according to their capacities; that is, a body is not made better or worse, in any moral sense, by the fact that it can or cannot do certain things. While the body can become diseased, and while its healing is clearly understood in positive terms, human personhood is neither augmented by a particular body's extraordinary capacities nor diminished by its incapacities. Because bodies are an integral part of what constitutes a human being, their significance and their goodness transcends their instrumental value as physical entities that are able to do things. In spite of their diverse shapes, sizes, and abilities, all bodies are vulnerable; and this makes them worthy of our attention with respect to questions of morality and character.

A third Christian claim about the body concerns its significance beyond death. The idea of some kind of continued existence after death was certainly not a new idea in the world into which Christianity was born; for example, ancient Greek philosophy believed that the soul was not extinguished at death. But Christians went farther, expressing not just a belief in the immortality of the soul but in the "resurrection of the body." As I noted in the previous chapter, the focus of this claim was not so much on the resuscitation of a corpse, but rather, on the continuing significance of the body after death. The body was understood to be an integral part of the whole human being; therefore, it could not possibly become irrelevant after death. It should continue to be treated with respect and dignity, and the memory of those who have died should always include a memory of their physical reality as well as their intellect and their spirit. Christians accented this belief with their burial practices, which included the burial of bodies in their entirety, rather than their reduction to ashes. This is not to say that they did not understand that a dead body will eventually decay. (After all, the Greek word for a coffin was *sarcophagus*—literally, "flesh-eater"; they knew good and well what happened inside those boxes.) Nevertheless, the practice of burial—carried out at great expense—was a way of emphasizing the enduring significance of the body beyond death, and of affirming the community's belief in its eventual resurrection.

Again, the belief in the resurrection of the body was not so much intended to emphasize a reanimation of a physical body; the emphasis was on the *integrated* reality of human personhood. In ancient thought, the physical flesh and the animating soul were often treated as two distinct realities; their distinction allowed them to be easily separated at death, with the flesh made irrelevant while the soul journeyed on. While one can certainly cite biblical narratives and early ecclesial practices that accepted this distinction, Christianity generally preferred the language of the *body* as a way of emphasizing the integrated reality of human personhood. Thus, when Paul describes the idea of death and resurrection in 1 Corinthians 15, he does not suggest that the flesh simply falls away and the spirit lives on, as would have been standard in many ancient philosophical accounts. Rather, he describes the human being as *dying* in bodily wholeness, as well as being *resurrected* in bodily wholeness. Addressing the hypothetical questions "How are the dead raised?" and "With what kind of body do they come?" (1 Cor. 15:35), Paul suggests that although the resurrected body will be different, it still bears a degree of continuity with what preceded it. He employs an agricultural metaphor to make the point:

> You do not sow the body that is to be, but a bare seed, perhaps of wheat or of some other grain. But God gives it a body as he has chosen, and to each kind of seed its own body. Not all flesh is alike, but there is one flesh for human beings, another for animals, another for birds, and another for fish . . . So it is with the resurrection of the dead. What is sown is perishable, what is raised is imperishable. It is sown in dishonor, it is raised in glory. It is sown in weakness, it is raised in power. It is sown a physical body, it is raised a spiritual body. If there is a physical body, there is also a spiritual body . . . Listen, I will tell you a mystery! We will not all die, but we will all be changed, in a moment, in the twinkling of an eye, at the last trumpet. For the trumpet will sound, and the dead will be raised imperishable, and we will be changed. For this perishable body must put on imperishability, and this mortal body must put on immortality (1 Cor. 15:37–39, 42–44, 51–53).

Even though Paul retains the contrast between the physical and the spiritual, he employs the same word, "body," to describe both. This passage is a reminder of the high degree of continuity that Christians express between flesh and spirit, as well as between the living and the dead.

All in all, then, Christianity offers a very positive account of human bodies and of our embodied condition. It is very unfortunate that so many Christians report having been formed by a theological perspective that denies the significance of the body or regards it primarily as a gateway to sin. Such perspectives can only be maintained through a highly selective reading of the biblical narrative. Why have they had such power over the lives of Christians? My own guess is that such negative accounts of the body have persisted within Christianity primarily because they were considered a useful means of buttressing an overly simplistic, rule-based approach to questions about sex and sexuality (and possibly about health and medicine as well). If people were persuaded to believe that the human body is shameful, ugly, and happily sloughed off at death—rather than being good, beautiful, and of eternal significance—then they might also be more easily persuaded that sexual expression is just an unfortunate biological necessity rather than a potential source of genuine happiness. This is turn could ease their acceptance of a highly restrictive set of rules about sexual ethics. But such an approach is not only untrue to Christianity's affirmation of the body; it also fails to acknowledge the positive significance of desire, as well as the possibility that sexual expression might also serve as one means of cultivating the virtues—a matter that will occupy us for the remainder of this chapter.

How to have good sex

Because Christians hold bodies in high regard, and because they believe that all human desires are known to God, they need to develop an account of how our bodily desires are rightly ordered and appropriately expressed. Unfortunately, the churches have often failed at this task. They have either marginalized sex and sexuality as relevant only to the procreation of children, or they have demonized sexual desire as something to be repressed and rooted out, or else they have followed the surrounding culture by allowing sex to be privatized (thereby removing the subject from theological discourse altogether). None of these approaches is sufficiently attentive to the significance accorded by the Christian faith to the physical body, nor to its recognition that all human hearts are open and all desires known.

This is why I noted, at the very beginning of this chapter, that I would not be offering an account of Christian sexual ethics that was focused primarily on "who can do what with whom." Such approaches have become, in the minds of some people, the sum total of everything that the Christian tradition has to say about sex—most of which can be further summarized in a simple command: "Whatever you're thinking about doing, *don't do it!*" This, I think, is a great travesty—not only because it so thoroughly misrepresents the complexity and the subtle nuance of Christian thought on the subject, but also because it is pastorally unhelpful to the millions of people who live in a world that has become quite thoroughly sexualized and who have no idea how to face it. An approach that concentrates on specific rules about what people can and cannot do with their bodies will always fail to do justice to the depth of theological reflection that can be gleaned from the Christian tradition.

But if we are somehow able to set aside the "rules and regulations" approach to sexual ethics with which we are all too familiar, what then? We need to step carefully, or else we will be too easily persuaded by the culturally dominant voices that privatize sex and sexuality, setting it largely outside the realm of ethical discourse entirely. Our sexual desires are simply too important for us to retreat into the private realm of radical individualism and to act as though they had no effect on the rest of the population. Instead, we need to return to the language of virtue that we have been exploring throughout this book. Here, we will discover a way to think through the complexities of sexual desire and sexual relationships, and to do so in ways that are attentive to the cultivation of good character. Three of the virtues that we named in chapter 7 seem particularly relevant to our discussion of sexual ethics: the theological virtue of *love*; the trinitarian virtue of *participation*; and *gentleness*, one of the fruits of the Spirit.

Love

Perhaps it may seem to go without saying that sex should be clearly related to love; however, this has not always been the case. Historians disagree as to just how recent an invention is our contemporary ideal of "romantic" love, but throughout much of human history, sex has often functioned as a means of pursuing one or both of two goals: a feeling of physical pleasure or a need to procreate. Neither of these goals requires the virtue of *love* to be any part of the equation, from either of the partners. Judaism and Christianity are often credited with bringing love and sex into conversation with one another; Paul the Apostle was drawing on his formation in both traditions when he wrote about how married couples should treat one another. His comments about the need for wives to "be subject to their husbands" are often ridiculed for their apparent capitulation to the male-dominated spirit of his era; but what is less often noticed is the rather radical claim that is embodied in his further demand: "Husbands, love your wives" (Eph. 5:25, 28; Col. 3:19). In suggesting that *love* ought to be a feature of a married relationship, Paul was taking a significant step beyond the standard Greco-Roman view of marriage as something very close to chattel slavery. The idea that men should embody the character trait of *love* toward their wives was a significant step forward— in spite of the fact that Paul and his culture continued to place men in a hierarchical position over women.

Nor should we assume that the theological virtue of *love* is necessarily the same as the emotion that we sometimes experience when we feel romantically attracted to someone. It seems easy enough, when we experience desire for another, to imagine that we have "fallen in love" with the person to whom we are attracted. Of course, the experience can work the other way around as well: we fall in love with someone, experience the giddy emotions that we associate with that state, and then desire to corroborate or perhaps intensify that feeling of love through expressions of sexual desire. But all these accounts describe love as an emotion, a feeling; and, recalling parallels to our discussion of happiness in chapter 7, focusing on "feeling" does not fully capture the moral weight of the concept. Our interest in this book is with love as a *virtue*—an excellence of character. Just as the true happiness that all human beings seek is not merely an experience in which we "feel good" (as in the temporary, hormone-induced moment of pleasure that we experience in sex), so the *love* that we seek to cultivate is not just the temporary infatuation that we feel when we meet someone whose physique, mind, or spirit arouses us in some way.

What exactly is this notion of love as a virtue, then, and what does it mean to bring *love* and *sex* into a more organic relationship with one another? If we remember the roots of the virtue of love in the Greek word *agapē* and the Latin word *caritas*, we will recognize that it will always involve putting the other person in place of priority. Obviously, this is not limited to putting a higher priority on the other person's *sexual pleasure* (though it need not necessarily exclude that!). It means that, in our sexual relationships, we should develop an orientation of care and generosity toward the other. This is a rather counter-cultural notion, since we tend to assume that sex is primarily related to maximizing one's own pleasure; thus placing the desires of the other in a place of higher priority is not something that we are typically taught or encouraged to do. But it seems to be the first and most important feature of "virtuous sex" as the Christian tradition might understand it.

This emphasis on *agapē* as "love for the sake of the other" should not be understood as substituting for, or opposed to, an emphasis on love as *eros*, desire. Too often in the Christian tradition, these two accounts of love were set in stark opposition to one another. In the modern era, this opposition was particularly emphasized under the influence of the Swedish theologian Anders Nygren, whose weighty tome *Agape and Eros* was long considered the definitive work on the subject. According to his account and the tradition that sprang from it, the more strongly one felt physical, bodily desire, the more *unlikely* it was that true agapic love was operating as the essential motivating force. Conversely, human beings were thought to participate in the virtue of love only when they excised all erotic impulses and simply made themselves into a "channel" through which pure, divine, agapic love flowed directly from God to others—uncontaminated by our bodily desires.

This is, admittedly, something of a caricature of Nygren's rather more complex position; nevertheless, his effort to set these two accounts of love in opposition to one another has had a profound and, in my view, largely perverse effect on the Christian account of the relationship between love and sex. Given the Christian faith's positive treatment of rightly ordered desire—as well as its holistic approach to the body as organically interweaving flesh, soul, and spirit—Christianity could hardly counsel a form of love that ignored the role of physical desire. God's willingness to take on human flesh provides a strong warrant against any effort to marginalize its bodily aspects. On the contrary, the incarnation is a clear reminder of the importance of understanding love as an integrated whole—encompassing physical desire, other-directed compassion, and the magnetic attraction of human beings, one to another.

Therefore, good sex—that is, virtuous sex—should be characterized by love for the other that, while certainly motivated by desire, is not exhausted by one's own delight in one's partner. Rather, human beings should love one another in ways that benefit the other person, that seek the other's good, and that ennoble and fulfill the other person's life. That old, time-worn question that is often said to follow a session of passionate lovemaking—"Was it good for you, too?"—might not be too far off the mark; we simply need to expand our understanding of the word "good" beyond its usual connotations (in this context) as referring merely to physical pleasure, and allow the word to assume its full moral breadth and depth. In virtuous sex, one's partner will not only *feel* better, but also *be* better: become a better person, be built up morally, by the encounter. And *that* is an achievement that no sex manual can teach.

This helps us to understand one of the most important roots of the traditional Christian teaching that reserves the fullest forms of sexual expression to monogamous, long-term, deeply committed relationships (traditionally instituted in marriage—though as I have already suggested, some long-held assumptions about marriage may need to be revised in light of the demonstrable virtue of relationships that do not conform to those assumptions). The kind of other-directed love that is being described here is not something that we can extend to an unlimited number of other people simultaneously. Human beings are created in the image of God, and their love can reflect God's love in being directed toward, and offered for the sake of, the other; but we do not possess God's omnipotence and omnipresence, so we cannot extend this kind of love to all human beings, or even to all those whom we meet, or even to all those with whom we develop intimate relationships. If our sexual relationships are to be truly virtuous—if they are to be characterized by a love that not only embodies our passions but is ultimately directed to the good of the other—then we will need to make wise judgments about our own limitations. No matter how strongly motivated we may be, we will be unable to commit ourselves to extending this degree of attention and care to many people simultaneously.

Such an emphasis may seem out of keeping with Christianity's traditional emphasis on abundant life; should we really be so miserly with our affections? On the other hand, the willingness to accept one's own limitations is not itself a denial of the possibility of extending some forms of agapic love to all people. While we do not have the wherewithal to make all such relationships sexual ones, this does not prevent us from loving all human beings in ways that are appropriate to that relationship. And the Christian tradition also emphasizes the importance of placing this love in the context of eternity: given its teachings about the non-finality of death, there really is no limit on the depth and breadth with which human beings can express their love to one another. Jesus says at one point that "in the resurrection," people "neither marry nor are given in marriage, but are like angels in heaven" (Matt 22:30). This has always struck me as a rather joyful claim; it suggests that, freed from our earthly limitations and clothed with the "spiritual body" of which Paul speaks, we will be able to love all people with the same degree of passionate intensity with which, here below, we can love only one.

Mutual participation

The Christian belief that God is both three and one necessarily implies the idea of mutual participation. Each of the persons of the Trinity participates fully in the existence of each of the others, such that they achieve a kind of unity while still maintaining their difference. This puts them in a fully mutual relationship to one another, so that their differences do not become an excuse for setting them up in some kind of hierarchical ordering, one over another. Rather, each of the three trinitarian persons dwells fully in the others, and is, in turn, indwelt by the others. Jesus expresses this mutual indwelling most fully when he says, in John 14:10–11, "I am in the Father and the Father is in me."

This ideal of full mutual participation—a character trait which, according to Christian belief, God has by nature—is not something that human beings find particularly easy to achieve. Especially in our current cultural circumstances, the temptation to treat all human beings as individuals, potentially or actually isolated from one another, is incredibly strong. Like the other virtues, however, the notion that such deep, mutual participation is an essential element of the character of God can help people to understand how their lives, too, might be shaped by a similar kind of mutual indwelling within their interpersonal relationships.

The standard definition of "participate" is "to take part in"; this usually refers to an activity in which we are joined by others. We *participate* in sports, in meetings, in various communal activities. At first glance, then, *participation* would seem to suggest bringing individual human beings together on the basis of their common interests. But this would not make it an excellence of character; it would simply describe a human action or activity. Here, I want to focus on those instances in which human beings take part, not in some*thing*, but in some*one*—an *other*. For example, to "participate in the sufferings of another" is to make another's pain one's own—perhaps by subjecting oneself to similar treatment, or empathizing with someone to the greatest possible degree. Similarly, if I ask you to "take part in" my life, I am asking for a very significant degree of emotional, physical, and spiritual intimacy. This is the element of "participation" that I am trying to evoke in describing it as a virtue: not merely working alongside others in a common activity, but dwelling in, and being indwelt by, one another.

It may help us to set the word "participation" alongside the related words "fellowship" and "communion," in an effort to emphasize this mutual intimacy. Admittedly, these two words have sometimes been understood according to the more "distant" and "disengaged" forms of participation that I have described here—simply coming together on the basis of some common interest, and perhaps exchanging a few words with some casual acquaintances. But communion and fellowship can also be associated with the deep, intimate, mutual indwelling that marks the character of God. When human beings express a true desire to "be in communion with" others, this will certainly require spending time with them and sharing mutual interests; but it also requires a willingness to allow others to shape them in profound and fundamental ways. In such true moments of communion, the lines of identity between "I" and "you" are blurred.

Those who participate fully and mutually in one another's lives are no longer isolated individuals who are fundamentally detachable from the rest of the world. In any event of true mutual participation, we can no longer clearly and permanently distinguish individuals, for this would imply a potentially definitive separation or division. Rather, these supposed "individuals" are best understood as being *particular* persons (in the sense that we used that term in chapter 11): having their own character, yet being so closely related to one another that neither can truly exist without the other. As with our discussion, in previous chapters, of the related trinitarian virtue of *particularity*, the dominant metaphor is one of "nodes in a network": the so-called "individuals" are so reliant upon one another for their true identity that they cannot be isolated from one another without introducing fundamental distortions into the picture.

For Christians, one of the primary experiences of this kind of complete mutual participation is the *eucharist*. No surprise, then, that this rite is sometimes known as "communion"; it provides an outward and visible sign of the deep mutual participation between God and human beings, and of human beings with one another. We have already observed, in chapter 9, the degree to which any common meal can function in this way, as well as observing that the Christian eucharist goes further. It is described as a form of mutual *bodily* participation: believers understand themselves as taking Christ's body into their own—and, at the same time, as being taken up, as members of the body of Christ, into the triune life of God.

This is why the eucharistic rite has traditionally emphasized the very bodily language of flesh and blood. In his last meal with his disciples, Jesus speaks of the bread as his body and says of the cup of wine, "This is my blood of the covenant, which is poured out for many" (Mark 14:24). Even more startlingly, he uses this graphic, physical language as a clear indicator of the profundity of mutual participation: "Those who eat my flesh and drink my blood abide in me, and I in them" (John 6:56). Of course, blood has always served as a reminder of the ways that human beings are connected to one another; we speak of "blood" relatives, we chart genealogical bloodlines, and we know that people once mingled their blood as a sign of their deep bond. We are also reminded of this bodily connection with one another by its potentially negative effects; blood is the carrier of disease from one organism to another. But this too can help us to understand the profound mutual participation that is invoked by the Christian eucharist: it is an event that involves "sharing blood" with other members of the gathered community, with all the anxiety and the elation that such mutual participation should evoke. The lasting power and deep resonances of such language may help us to understand why the eucharist has always been understood as drawing people into a profound state of mutual participation in one another's lives.

I want to suggest that the virtue of mutual participation is of particular importance with respect to our sexual relationships, which should seek to enact it both physically and psychologically. A physical sexual relationship involves taking another person's body into one's own, and/or having one's body received into the body of another. It also involves giving one's self over into the custody of another, and accepting that same gift in return. The sheer depth and significance of such an abandonment of one self to another would seem to call forth several kinds of responsibility and care in return: that the other person be treated with care; that such self-giving never be used as an opportunity for exploitation or control; and that it be truly mutual, with each person fully capable of, and willing to, give to the other. In seeking that their sexual relationships are characterized by this ideal of complete mutual participation, Christians are not only making a general statement about human dignity; they are seeking to reflect the full mutual participation that characterizes the inner life of God. Thus it should not surprise us that a wide variety of Christian writers in the mystical tradition (including Mechtild of Magdeburg, Hadewijch, and St. Teresa of Avila, among many others) have drawn on sexual imagery to convey the mutual intimacy within God's trinitarian life, as well as the profound communion between God and human beings. Understood through the language of the virtues, it can also serve as a disposition that should mark the most intimate encounters of one human being with another.

Gentleness

As I observed in the first part of this chapter, sex makes us extraordinarily vulnerable to one another. In the experience of sex, we lay ourselves open to the other; we are naked—usually, literally so—and without defenses. One of the most profound ways that we can accept and validate the trust that has been placed in us by another person within the context of a sexual relationship is to treat that person with gentleness. Like the closely related virtue of *kindness*, which we will discuss in the chapter that follows, this involves a disposition of tenderhearted care for the other, seeking that person's comfort and avoiding bringing him or her any experience of sorrow, grief, or pain. But the biblical language of gentleness has another element as well—such that this virtue is not exhausted simply by being considerate to one another, or even by maximizing the comfort of others and minimizing their pain.

This additional element can best be understood by examining the various translations of the Greek and Hebrew words for gentleness. These same words (and their cognates) are often rendered as "meekness," "lowliness," or "humility." The common thread running through all these words becomes clearer when we think about their antonyms: they all stand in opposition to any kind of arrogance, haughtiness, or pride. These latter character traits are common when one relies solely on oneself to bring about a desired result; by contrast, the disposition of meekness or humility characterizes those persons who know that they do not have all the answers and that they do not expect to achieve their results single-handedly. A person with these character traits is motivated to exhibit *gentleness* out of a recognition that mistakes may be made, and that those mistakes are less likely to result in harm to others if they are made gently, with tenderness and humility. In contrast, any attempt to proceed with too much force and too much confidence could easily lead to insult and injury.

The specifically Christian element in this virtue is related to our discussion, in the previous chapter, of the theological concept of *providence*. If people are confident that God is ultimately in charge of the way that the world will go, they do not need to base all their actions on their own mastery of the situation; they are able to proceed with more humility and less force. Jesus offers a parable that clearly describes a person whose reliance on his own mastery of the matter at hand leads him to speak roughly and without consideration for others—as contrasted with one who, recognizing that he is utterly dependent on God's mercy, admits his own lowly station and expends no energy castigating others:

> Two men went up to the temple to pray, one a Pharisee and the other a tax collector. The Pharisee, standing by himself, was praying thus, "God, I thank you that I am not like other people: thieves, rogues, adulterers, or even like this tax collector. I fast twice a week; I give a tenth of all my income." But the tax collector, standing far off, would not even look up to heaven, but was beating his breast and saying, "God, be merciful to

me, a sinner!" I tell you, this man went down to his home justified rather than the other; for all who exalt themselves will be humbled, but all who humble themselves will be exalted (Luke 18:10–14).

Note how this parable emphasizes the close connection between humility concerning oneself and gentleness toward others: the humble person is sufficiently convinced of his own problems that he will not expend any energy berating others, whereas the arrogant or haughty person seeks to reinforce his own high view of himself by being distinctly ungentle to those around him.

The virtue of gentleness is particularly relevant to questions of sexual ethics in at least two distinct ways. First, as noted above, the vulnerability that we experience in intimate sexual encounters is so profound that we often find ourselves hurt by some aspect of those encounters. Those who approach sex with an attitude of excessive self-confidence, pride, or haughtiness are very likely to cause pain: perhaps even physical pain, but certainly emotional and spiritual pain. In such cases, the sexual encounter becomes a venue for the building up of one person's ego at the expense of another—rather than embodying the other-directed love and the mutual participation that should characterize all sexual relationships. Thus, when we speak of the importance of entering into sexual relationships with the disposition of gentleness, we are not just emphasizing the physical tenderness that we bring to those encounters; we are also referring (as the biblical language suggests) to a disposition of meekness, in which a person remains aware of his or her own faults and failings. Such a disposition reduces the chances that we will take advantage of the other person's vulnerability as a means of bolstering our own ego. The *gentle* lover will have the humility to remain attentive to the naked vulnerability of his or her partner, recognizing that the encounter always has the potential to bring about not only joy and fulfillment, but also shame, grief, and pain. Finally, the virtue of gentleness encourages a disposition of gratitude toward the other: because this person has given me a profound gift, making herself radically available to me, I will treat that gift with care—considerately, humbly, gently—in recognition of its tremendous beauty and also of its tremendous fragility.

Gentleness should characterize sexual ethics in another way as well—and for many of us, this second aspect will be the more difficult. Whenever we express a strong opinion about some issue in sexual ethics—say, about the advisability of sex outside marriage, or about the use of birth control, or about same-sex relationships—here too, we need to speak and act with gentleness. Not only when we are engaged in physical sexual activity, but even when we are merely *discussing* sex and sexuality, we place ourselves in

Sarah Miles

The fine novel *The End of the Affair* by the brilliant and prolific British novelist Graham Greene (1904–1991) is much praised for its complex and twisting plotline and for his inclusion of a number of memorable characters. But most critics agree that his greatest achievement in this book was his creation of its heroine, a woman by the name of Sarah Miles.

Why should I offer, as an interesting exemplar of Christian sexual ethics, a fictional character? I do so because, partly due to the ways that we try to hide the details of our sex lives, any effort to dissect the sexual structure of an actual human life always creates a faint whiff of exploitation and exposé. In order to understand a person's character, we need access to his or her deepest desires and motives; and as we have noted in this chapter, those desires can be particularly difficult to unearth when it comes to sexual matters. By examining the life of a fictional character, we are granted some access into an interior world of thought and action that helps us better understand the shape of the moral life.

According to most standard accounts of Christian sexual ethics, Sarah is not a particularly exemplary figure. The "affair" of the book's title is, in fact, an adulterous sexual affair that she has with a writer named Maurice Bendrix, while she continues to live in an unconsummated marriage to her husband Henry. So of course, at one level, one might simply declare the relationship to be immoral because it is, by definition, adulterous. In contrast, other people might offer a moral argument in *favor* of the affair, given Henry's tendency to ignore, marginalize, and disregard the needs of his wife; he practically encourages the liaison by asking his friend Bendrix to "take care of Sarah." But I am interested in Sarah's sexual morality not so much because of the affair itself, but because she decides to end it—and because of the reasons she decides to do so.

Again, the reasons are not particularly aligned with traditional Christian claims about the sanctity of marriage and the importance of limiting sexual relationships to that space. Rather, Sarah breaks off the affair because of her commitment to the virtues that we are discussing in this chapter: love, gentleness, and mutual participation. She is so thoroughly in love with Bendrix, so attentive to his vulnerability and his needs, and her life is so deeply integrated with his, that she would not have considered ending the affair under any ordinary circumstances; in fact, in a later era, she would probably have been counseled to have her loveless marriage annulled and to marry her lover. She was certainly completely committed to Bendrix (in spite of his anxieties to the contrary—he imagines that she has broken off the affair in order to take up with someone else).

The real reason that she has ended the affair is for the sake of her beloved. I will not offer too much detail here; doing so would give away one of the wonderful surprises of the plot, and those who have not yet read this marvelous novel should not be denied that discovery. Suffice it to say that, as far as Sarah is concerned, she needed to end the affair in order to save the life of the one she loves. Moreover, in order to remain true to her commitment in that regard, she has to run away from his pursuit of her—to his frustration and to her own great cost.

What is praiseworthy in Sarah's behavior is neither the affair itself nor the decision to end it. It is, rather, the virtues that she embodies with respect to her own sexuality. She loves the other for the sake of the other, wholly and fully, and without counting the cost to herself. She treats her beloved with gentleness, not only in their lovemaking but also in the decision to end the affair: she ends it for his sake and does everything she can to treat him gently even as he clamors for her to resume the relationship. And she provides an excellent example of the mutual participation that I have described in this chapter: a willingness to dwell in the other, and be indwelt by the other, not only physically but in terms of the merging of souls. One of the results of this deep mutual participation is that Maurice Bendrix, an avowed atheist, begins to acknowledge the possibility of the existence of God (though he remains hostile to it, at least as the novel closes); and this is only possible because of the fact that Sarah, a deeply committed if somewhat unconventional Christian, has to some degree "implanted" her belief in her beloved by her willingness to enter into a fully and mutually participative relationship with him.

Because our sexual desires are so very specific to each of us as individuals, it can be extremely difficult to apply the experience of one person to someone else. The same factor probably makes it unwise, at least in many cases, to render detailed and explicit judgments about the morality of another's sexual behavior. In describing the example of Sarah Miles, my intention is only to raise questions about the kinds of indicators that we use to evaluate human action in the sphere of sex and sexuality. A person who utterly fails to abide by the standard "rules" with regard to sexual ethics may still conform his or her life to the virtues; and these are the character traits that are most relevant when we seek to understand human behavior in the deep and mysterious territory of human sexuality.

a condition of extraordinary vulnerability; we also make others more vulnerable, since such discussions expose people's deepest desires to public scrutiny. As we noted at the very outset of this chapter, we would prefer to shield those desires from the gaze of the wider public; indeed, we sometimes hide them even from those who are closest to us. When another human being pronounces on the psychological, moral, or legal appropriateness of those desires, some basic elements of the identity of particular human beings are laid bare and brought under scrutiny. It may well be, as we noted above, that certain desires need to be evaluated as to their morality; the simple fact that I *have* a particular desire does not guarantee that it is a rightly ordered desire. Nevertheless, those who offer moral critiques of real human desires are called upon to do so with the same degree of gentleness that would be exercised in a physical encounter with a lover. We need to offer such critiques with humility, recognizing that we may be wrong, and knowing how much shame, grief, and pain we may be causing those whose deepest desires we are calling into question. Far too much of the ethical discourse around this subject takes place in a strident, arrogant, and harsh tone—the very opposite of the Christian virtue of gentleness. Such voices should be routinely ignored or dismissed until they are willing to allow their arguments to be infused with the same degree of gentleness that characterizes—or that *should* characterize!—their lovemaking.

The significance of gentleness as a virtue may, again, help explain why Christians have traditionally held that physical sexual expression should be reserved for long-term relationships that are publicly recognized as such. A brief, passing, and/or spur-of-the-moment sexual relationship will typically lead us to focus on our own needs first, leaving little room for the kind of consideration of and attentiveness to the other that should characterize all good sexual encounters. Since a short-term relationship does not allow its participants the time and space they need to get to know one another very deeply, they will not have the wherewithal to embody the virtue of gentleness; it's difficult to be fully attentive to others—and even harder to avoid hurting them—if you don't really know what makes them tick. Gentleness requires a couple to have explored the contours of one another's heart, mind, and soul at the same depth, and with the same enthusiasm, that they explore the contours of one another's bodies. Finally, such brief and casual sexual relationships are difficult to approach with the degree of humility and meekness that we have discussed here, since they usually make us feel an urgent need to make a good impression, demonstrating sexual virtuosity as persuasively as possible. Such encounters seem to demand a resolute expression of self-confidence and perseverance on the part of at least one of the participants; whereas a long-term relationship can provide the time and space necessary to enable two lovers to approach sexual encounters in a spirit of humility, meekness, and true gentleness. This is true, I think, regardless of whether that long-term relationship is identified by the term "marriage," and regardless of whether it adheres to all the traditional assumptions about the prerequisites of such a relationship. Its real test is not its name, nor such matters as the biological sex or gender identity of the participants, but the virtues that it embodies and displays.

Judgment and release

The Gospel of John tells a story of a woman who was caught in the act of having sex with someone who was not her husband. A group of people brought her to Jesus and pointed out that the law requires such a person to be stoned to death. At this point, Jesus does something striking: he bends down and writes with his finger on the ground. The text does not say anything about what he wrote, or why; he just writes in the dust. The story continues:

> When they kept on questioning him, he straightened up and said to them, "Let anyone among you who is without sin be the first to throw a stone at her." And once again he bent down and wrote on the ground. When they heard it, they went away, one by one, beginning with the elders; and Jesus was left alone with the woman standing before him. Jesus straightened up and said to her, "Woman, where are they? Has no one condemned you?" She said, "No one, sir." And Jesus said, "Neither do I condemn you. Go your way, and from now on do not sin again" (John 8:7–11).

I have always felt that this passage provides something of a model for dealing with questions in sexual ethics. I say this because the story models two important features which are of extraordinary importance in the Christian ethical tradition: judgment and release. It makes a statement about more and less appropriate forms of sexual behavior; but, in light of everything we know about human beings, their bodies, and their desires, it ultimately counsels forgiveness and refuses to condemn.

Yes, we can identify sexual relationships as being, from a moral standpoint, good or bad, better or worse. Yes, we can enforce certain rules (such as the prohibition against adultery) in ways that seem to us, at least, to improve the probability that good sexual relationships will outnumber bad ones. But human desire is a powerful thing, and human bodies are sensitive, sensuous, and fragile. All human beings are drawn toward sexual expression—good and bad, better and worse, officially sanctioned and socially condemned. If we were to render no judgments about such matters at all, we would be irresponsible; and yet, given the deep and tender places where such judgments will have their effects, we must offer them with care. We need to be attentive to a person's character, and not just whether that person has obeyed the rules. We also need to find ways to address the issues of sex and sexuality that do not resort, first and foremost, to condemnation.

In commenting on the above passage in the Gospel of John, theologian Rowan Williams also emphasizes the dual importance of judgment and release. He considers it significant that, when asked to render a verdict on the situation, Jesus knelt down and wrote in the dust. Williams suggests that when we feel ourselves pulled toward an act of quick condemnation of others, we might want to consider doing some of our own "writing in the dust." Doing so would give us *time*: time to imagine what the life of this other person might really be like; time to consider what virtues, unknown to us, this person might embody; and time to determine whether such condemnation is really in keeping with the virtues that we would like to exhibit in our own lives. As I have already suggested, maintaining a certain degree of humility and reserve seems particularly important in the realm of sexual ethics; however, I think that Williams' advice to "take time" before offering our condemnations applies to the field of ethics quite broadly. When tempted by the desire to castigate and to condemn, we too need to do some "writing in the dust"— and make sure that we do so, as Williams writes, "long enough for some of our own demons to walk away."

Questions for discussion

1. Discuss the phenomenon of desire. It may be best to start outside the specific realm of sexuality and consider, for a moment, the other desires that most strongly motivate us. To what extent are these desires hidden from others? What do you think of the claim that it may be better to act as though all our desires were openly known?

2. Give an example from your own life, or from the life of another whom you know well, in which some kind of "presenting behavior" actually turned out to be a manifestation of an attitude or a desire that was apparently unrelated to its outward signs. If no examples come immediately to mind, consider behaviors such as violent outbursts of anger, extreme talkativeness (or its opposite), or various addictions. What might lie behind such behaviors?

3. Consider examples from your own experience concerning positive and negative evaluations of the body. What elements in our culture treat the body as a problem, and what elements raise it up as positive? To what extent are our perspectives on human bodies influenced by celebrity profiles, advertising, and art? How are our attitudes toward the body affected by unrealistic or idealistic representations of human bodies?

4. How is the word "love" used in common conversation today? Do you find that people use the word frequently or rarely? Which of the various (Greek) words for love do you think lie behind its most common uses? Do you find your peers more or less likely to use the word "love"to describe a romantic relationship? How does love as a virtue differ from love as a feeling?

5. Discuss the relationship between "gentleness" (as we usually use the term) and the idea of humility. Setting aside for a moment the resonances between these two terms in the biblical narrative, do you think that most people today would recognize them as interrelated? Why or why not? Did you find yourself convinced by the argument put forward in this chapter for seeing them as closely connected?

6. On the basis of the virtues discussed in this chapter (and any other virtues that you might want to consider), evaluate the traditional Christian teaching that physical sexual expression ought to be reserved for committed, long-term, monogamous relationships. (Try not to focus on the "rules" that various church bodies might have issued on this topic, or even on the institution of "marriage" as it is practiced today, but simply on the question of whether features such as monogamy, long duration, and public commitment are necessary in order for a sexual relationship to embody the virtues.)

7. Discuss the passage from the Gospel of John that is quoted at the very end of this chapter. Do you think that the twofold movement of "judgment and release" is an appropriate perspective for Christian sexual ethics or for Christian ethics more broadly? Explain why or why not.

Sources cited in this chapter and/or recommended for further reading

Thomas E. Breidenthal, *Christian Households: The Sanctification of Nearness*

Rodney Clapp, *Tortured Wonders: Christian Spirituality for People, Not Angels*

David S. Cunningham, *Friday, Saturday, Sunday: Literary Meditations on Suffering, Death, and New Life* (especially chapter 4 on Iris Murdoch's novel *The Sacred and Profane Love Machine* and chapter 8 on Janet Morley's poetry collection *All Desires Known*)

David S. Cunningham, "Participation," chapter 5 of *These Three Are One: The Practice of Trinitarian Theology*

Michael Duffy, *The Skeptical, Passionate Christian: Tools for Living Faithfully in an Uncertain World*

Graham Greene, *The End of the Affair*

Philip D. Kenneson, *Life on the Vine: Cultivating the Fruit of the Spirit in Christian Community*, chapter 9

David Matzko McCarthy, *Sex and Love in the Home: A Theology of the Household*

Mark A. McIntosh, *Mystical Theology: The Integrity of Spirituality and Theology*

Gilbert Meilaender, *Bioethics: A Primer for Christians*

Janet Morley, *All Desires Known*

Anders Nygren, *Agape and Eros: A Study of the Christian Idea of Love*

Eugene Rogers, *Sexuality and the Christian Body: Their Way into the Triune God*

Joel James Shuman, "Eating Together: Friendship and Homosexuality," in Hauerwas and Wells, eds., *The Blackwell Companion to Christian Ethics*

William Werpehowski, "Anders Nygren's *Agape and Eros*," in Meilaender and Werpehowski, eds., *The Oxford Handbook of Theological Ethics*

Rowan Williams, *The Body's Grace: The 10th Michael Harding Memorial Address*; *Writing in the Dust*

15 Saturday
A walk in the woods

Very few people have failed to be impressed, moved, and inspired by the sheer beauty of the natural world that surrounds us. Whether a person's particular enthusiasms tend toward wide-open landscapes or hidden mountain waterfalls, brightly plumed birds or agile woodland creatures, majestic trees or intricate, fragile insects, there are more than enough opportunities to be astounded by the environment in which we live. From time to time, one may take a more cynical view—in which landscapes are boring, fauna is dangerous, and flora breeds allergies—but such perspectives rarely last an entire lifetime. However expertly we build up our defenses, most of us can still be shocked into a sense of awe and wonder as the train rounds a bend and those snow-capped peaks first come into view.

Even for those of us who are not so inclined to wax eloquent about the wonders of the natural world, the hard fact remains that this planet on which we live is essential to sustain our lives. We are dependent on the natural world to a more extreme degree than we are dependent on anyone or anything else: without its oxygen, we would die within minutes; without its water, in a few days; without its food, in a few weeks. We rarely like to acknowledge our dependence on anything—not even on those elements of life that are under our direct control, and especially not on other people. How much less are we inclined to admit that we are dependent, to such an extreme degree, on so many inanimate objects and elements of the world around us—and yet, that dependence is undeniable.

In fact, that very dependence is part of why we sometimes feel overwhelmed, not just by the earth's beauty and its grandeur, but also by its *otherness*: it can come to feel oppressive and alienating. For one thing, the world is simply enormous; even over the course of a long lifetime, we can experience only a tiny fraction of its grandeur. We may also feel somewhat oppressed by its *givenness*; it was here long before we came to be, and it will remain here (at least in some form) long after we have vanished. We may sigh at the apparently ephemeral lives of some of its species—the animals that live for only a few seasons and the insects that live for only a few days—but the long-term endurance of the physical world makes it seem that even our own relatively lengthy lives will vanish in the blink of an eye.

Moreover, the earth's environment can be as harsh as it is lovely; under certain conditions, its weather patterns and its seismic shifts can put us in grave danger. Some of its plants are toxic to us, and some of its animals are ferocious; we find it difficult to live a long and comfortable life on this earth without building up a significant level of protection against some of its harsher elements. And above all, we find ourselves faced with its secrets: its origins, its destiny, and all those elements of its inner workings that we human beings, despite all our scientific investigations, still do not fully understand.

Glorious beauty, biological necessity, oppressive otherness: even before we begin to tinker with it, the natural world is a complicated place. It should not surprise us, then, that the shape of our character is affected by it, and that our narratives and practices with respect to the natural world can affect our lives just as significantly as do our interactions with people. And given the complexities of our relationship with the earth and all its multifarious inhabitants, the ethical ramifications of that relationship are also likely to be exceedingly complex. Over the course of this chapter, we will consider what Christian ethics might have to say about our relationship with the earth—while keeping in mind the complexity of that relationship, as well as the complexity of the earth itself.

Christian assumptions and Christian arguments

We begin with a survey of some of the theological claims of the Christian tradition that have a significant impact on its account of the natural world and of the place of human beings within it. This survey will lead us into a discussion of some of the disagreements that have arisen among Christians as to the implications of these theological claims. As has been the case for several of the other issues we have examined in the foregoing chapters, the evolving state of our scientific knowledge and the advance of technology has meant that the precise state of our relationship with the environment does not stand still. Nevertheless, the three general categories of theological assumptions that we will examine in this chapter have endured over time—as have the disagreements that have arisen from them. The three claims that we will examine here involve God's creation of the world, God's covenant relationship with its inhabitants, and the metaphor of the corporate body to describe its profoundly interrelated elements.

Creation

First and foremost, Christianity—like Judaism before it—claims that the earth and its inhabitants were created by God. As we have noted at several points in our deliberations, the story that occupies the opening pages of the biblical text tells this tale in a dramatic way: God separates light from darkness, water from land, and sky from earth. Then God creates the lights in the sky, the plants of the earth, the fish in the sea, and the birds of the air. Finally, God creates the animals on the land—and human beings, male and female. Every single element of the universe is described as having its origins in God.

Because of the dramatic way in which the story is told, it is sometimes mistaken for an eyewitness account of the originating physical conditions of the natural world. It is, of course, not an eyewitness account (there were no eyes, let alone witnesses, until the last few days of the week). The text's goal is not to provide a scientific account of the origin of the species. In spite of some claims to the contrary, it is not in any direct conflict with the theory of evolution, or any other theory of the physical processes by which the earth and its inhabitants came to be, because the story of Genesis is not about those physical processes. It is, first and foremost, about God; and secondarily, it concerns human beings in their relationship to God and to the rest of the created order.

Among the original readers of this text and for thousands of years afterwards, no one gave a moment's thought to the idea that Genesis might be some kind of documentary-style account of the origins of the universe. For one thing, that was not how they viewed history; they had a much less definitive distinction in their minds between history and story. It was not until the modern age that people began to imagine historical narratives to be accounts of "what actually happened." In the case of the Genesis story in particular, a close and careful reading of the first two chapters of the text will make it clear just how little the author and original readers were interested in the idea of documentary history. After telling the story of creation in chapter 1, the author turns around and tells it again in chapter 2; moreover, the details of the two accounts are considerably different. Things happen in a different order and the creation of human beings, in particular, is described very differently. This is another reminder that the writer and most of the readers of this story have not read it as a description of the physical processes by which the universe was created. Rather—as I have already emphasized—it is a story about God, about human beings, and about their relationships: to each other and to the rest of the world.

This very important detail is, sadly, often overlooked by those who are seeking to defend God's honor against Charles Darwin, Richard Dawkins, or whomever is presumed to be its latest critic. Those who read the text in this way often get so agitated in their efforts to bend the text into a counter-argument against evolution that they miss its significant *theological* claims—concerning the origin of all things in God and the ultimate dependence of all things on God for their existence and sustenance. This important theological claim—rather than the largely irrelevant question of the length of time that this process took, or the order in which it happened—is the real significance of the accounts of creation that can be found at the very beginning of both the Jewish and the Christian scriptures.

Moreover, the claim that God created the world is not merely a stopgap theory, as though God were being temporarily used as an explanation for something that we do not yet fully understand. Certainly, some people have attempted to use God in this way—a "God of the gaps" whose primary role is to explain the unexplainable and who can eventually retire from the scene once an adequate scientific theory has been found. But such an approach would only be necessary if one were to read Genesis as answering the same kinds of questions that such scientific theories seek to address. If, as I have argued here, Genesis is not so much about the physical processes by which our environment came to be, but is rather a theological account of God's role in that process, then no theory promulgated by the fields of geology, chemistry, or biology is ever going to come along to replace it. No matter how much we learn about our physical universe and its productive and reproductive processes, the Christian belief in the world as created by God will not be changed in any essential way. The claim that God created the world is a different *kind* of claim than is a scientific theory, in that it does not depend upon empirical observation and logical deduction. It depends, rather, on the decision of the faithful to live according to a certain story: a story in which every element of the physical world—from the planets in their courses, to the processes of natural selection, to the next breath taken by a single human being—is wholly dependent upon God.

This claim has some significant implications. First, it suggests that human beings are not "in charge" of the earth and its environment. While we can certainly do it harm or treat it well, its ultimate fate lies outside our hands. Those who argue that human beings should "save the planet" have the right idea, but such language can slip very easily into a kind of idolatry, elevating human beings into the place of God, in whose hands the fate of the earth truly rests. When environmental advocates remain attentive to God's role in the process, their perspective can be an appropriate way of urging human beings to accept responsibility for the effect of their actions on the earth and its inhabitants. Sometimes, however, environmental activism serves primarily as an effort to preserve our own access to the world's beauty: making sure that it remains pleasant to look at and serviceable in sustaining our lives. In such cases, the real motivating factor is not so much concern for the natural environment *per se*, but rather, the desire to attend to the self-interests of human beings. According to the Christian perspective, however, the whole point of caring for the earth is not to ensure our own survival but rather to honor God, who has entrusted its care to human beings.

As an example, consider the recent media attention to the phenomenon of global warming. Human beings are increasingly aware of the significance of this problem, and many people are trying to do something about it. But one can undertake this work with a variety of different goals. First, people can be motivated to address global warming because they fear what may happen to them if they don't: unpredictable weather patterns, rising sea levels, and other forms of environmental change may make it very difficult for human beings to inhabit the planet. This is a purely self-interested approach. Second, people may be concerned not only about human life but about the other inhabitants of the planet as well; in this sense, attempts to address global warming are on a par with other environmental efforts to preserve the habitats of endangered species and to prevent the destruction of rain forests, prairies, and other eco-systems that shelter and sustain life. Here, the motivation is not merely one of self-interest (though that can also play a role; we want to be able to *enjoy* California condors and rain forests); such an approach also expresses a focus on the good of the other, a desire that others survive as well.

But from a perspective that understands the earth to be God's creation and God's gift, a third motive is important as well: people will want to address global warming because this gift has been entrusted to us for its care, and we haven't cared for it very well. Our negligence has brought the environment to its present situation, and therefore we have some responsibility to return it to its original, life-sustaining condition. People do this, not because they consider themselves to be all-powerful saviors of the world, or simply because they fear the consequences of not doing so, but because they seek to honor the gift that they have been given. Such an approach helps to keep Christian claims about God and creation in full view: it serves as a reminder that our responsibility is analogous to that of the recipient of a good gift, rather than that of the creator of life. While we may do things that will make life on this planet very difficult for ourselves, and while we may eventually even manage to wipe ourselves out altogether, God is still in charge: the "fate of the earth" is not ultimately in our hands.

Of course, this claim—that the fate of the earth is not in human hands—leaves us with something of a mixed heritage. On the one hand, it can promote a better relationship between human beings and the rest of creation, by allowing us to recognize its significance beyond its mere usefulness to us and the brief moments in which we pause to take pleasure in it. On the other hand, this same attitude can lead to a certain nonchalance and even wilful abuse of the environment, on the theory that the earth is not, ultimately, our responsibility. In this sense, our relationship to the earth mirrors our relationship to other human beings: in recognizing their otherness, we give ourselves reason to respect them, but at the same time, we also give ourselves leave to ignore them—to use them without attention to their needs, or even to injure them if it suits us. In the next section, as we explore a second theological concept that stands in the background of issues related to the environment, we will discover how Christians have found biblical justification for both of these attitudes.

Covenant

Throughout the biblical narrative, God is represented as entering into relationships with human beings that are usually characterized as *covenants*. A covenant is a mutual pledge between two parties that is typically marked by the promise of each to provide support and care to the other. It is usually contrasted with the similar relationship of a *contract*, which also involves a mutual pledge but usually contains some means of enforcement; anyone who fails to make good on a contractual pledge can be penalized in some way, whereas a covenant is based purely on mutual trust. Moreover, although a covenant usually places two parties into a mutual relationship with one another, the promises of each party are not dependent on those of the other party. In the case of a contract, a broken promise on one side releases the other from the obligation; but a promise made in a covenantal relationship abides regardless of the other party's faithfulness (or lack thereof).

God's relationships with human beings often take the form of covenants. God promises certain gifts and expects certain pledges in return; but if (as often happens) the people fail to be faithful to God, God nevertheless remains faithful to them. So, for example, in one of the most well known covenants of the Old Testament, God promises Abraham and Sarah that, in spite of their childlessness in advanced age, they will become the parents of a great nation—a people who will live in a special and favored relationship to God. These chosen people of God—the Israelites—are not always faithful to God; at various times in their history, they begin to worship idols, or to raise loud complaints against God, or to seek their own glory instead of the glory of their creator. Through it all, God remains faithful to the covenant promise—often reproving the Israelites for their lack of faith or their wayward allegiances, but never abandoning them.

The particular covenant that most interests us here is that into which God enters with human beings concerning their role in the created order. In the initial creation, human beings are given the fruitful garden and all the food that they need; this is God's free gift to them. Their responsibility—their role in this covenantal relationship—is to take good care of what they have been given. The text of Genesis says that, immediately after the creation of human beings, "God blessed them, and God said to them, 'Be fruitful and multiply, and fill the earth and subdue it; and have dominion over the fish of the sea and over the birds of the air and over every living thing that moves upon the earth'" (Gen. 1:28). In this description of the original created order, human beings might be seen as standing at the top of the heap; they are in charge of the entire creation. But as many commentators have noted, the word "dominion" (which appears is this text) is not the same as "domination"; though both words are related to the idea of acting as lord over something (the Latin word *dominus* means "lord"), they express two different stances. *Domination* implies a self-interested claim over the other, enforced by violence if necessary and tending toward the dictatorial and tyrannical. *Dominion* keeps open the possibility that one might exercise one's lordship with the good of the other in mind—in parallel to God's exercise of dominion over the heavens and the earth.

The word that is usually used to describe the human role in the covenant of creation—the proper exercise of lordship in the form of caring for creation for its own sake—is "stewardship." Human beings are the stewards of God's good creation; it has been entrusted to them as a gift, and their role is to be good stewards of its resources. They are permitted the use of the earth, and are even permitted to shape it to their own ends (thus the phrase, "fill the earth and subdue it"); but the lordship that human beings exercise over the rest of creation should be analogous to the lordship that God exercises over them: namely, a lordship that is characterized by the covenantal promise of love and care for the other, rather than by domination as a means of fulfilling one's own self-interest.

But the covenant described in Genesis 1 is a covenant into which God and human beings enter before the Fall. Here, the created order is in its original, peaceful state. Among the other markers of this original peaceable kingdom, all the animals (including the human beings) ate only plants rather than each other (Gen 1:29–30); people were naked and yet unashamed (Gen 2:25); and all the creatures seemed to recognize their complete dependence on God as the provider of all good gifts. At this point in the story, before the Fall, it might still be hoped that human beings—created in the image and likeness of God—would make good use of the dominion that they had been given, and become good stewards of the creation. Soon, however, we find that they make use of their freedom and their power in ways that are directly contrary to the intention of the covenant. They choose to ignore God (Gen. 3:6), to evade responsibility (Gen 3:11–13), and eventually, even to kill one another (Gen 4:8). In fact, the gift of power and dominion to human beings has worked out so badly that God even regrets having created them (Gen. 6:6). Even so, God does not renege on the promise to deliver the earth into human hands; rather than destroying the entire world in the flood, God saves a remnant of creation. Afterwards, God reissues the promise of the covenant, but this time in a somewhat modified form:

> Be fruitful and multiply, and fill the earth. The fear and dread of you shall rest on every animal of the earth, and on every bird of the air, on everything that creeps on the ground, and on all the fish of the sea; into your hand they are delivered. Every moving thing that lives shall be food for you; and just as I gave you the green plants, I give you everything (Gen. 9:1–3).

Note that the word "subdue," which appeared in the earlier passage, is now missing; human beings are no longer expected to shape the earth to their own purposes. Note also that they are no longer asked to exercise *dominion* over the earth; apparently God no longer imagines that they can be expected to rule with the best interests of their subjects in mind. Rather, the animals of the earth will now live in fear of human beings, who will hunt them for food. Human beings have proven themselves unwilling and unable to rule the earth as its benevolent lords; now the best they can expect to be able to do is to terrorize it.

And yet, in spite of the new language that appears in the "Noachic covenant" (the covenant made with Noah after the flood, as quoted above from Genesis 9), the idea that human beings are meant to exercise *stewardship* over the created order does not entirely vanish from the biblical narrative. The agricultural basis of the economy in ancient Israel helped to ensure that people recognized the symbiotic relationship between themselves and the environment. The Levitical law recognized the significance of animals and plants, not just as a means of fulfilling human whims, but as creatures of God in their own right; it therefore expected human beings to make measured use of the entire created order, and imposed penalties on those who would abuse it. In the Psalms and in other poetic writings, as well as in the words of the prophets, this expectation of stewardship is regularly reinforced. In fact, the prophet Isaiah inscribes into the biblical text a vision in which the original harmony of the created order is restored, and human beings are once again the benevolent lords of a peaceable kingdom. Led by one who "with right-eousness . . . shall judge the poor, and decide with equity for the meek of the earth," the entire created order will once again be at peace:

> The wolf shall live with the lamb, the leopard shall lie down with the kid, the calf and the lion and the fatling together, and a little child shall lead them. The cow and the bear shall graze, their young shall lie down together; and the lion shall eat straw like the ox. The nursing child shall play over the hole of the asp, and the weaned child shall put its hand on the adder's den. They will not hurt or destroy on all my holy mountain; for the earth will be full of the knowledge of the LORD as the waters cover the sea (Isaiah 9:5–11).

Even in the midst of the general recognition that, after the Fall, human stewardship of creation would never be the same, the biblical narrative continues to hold up this notion as an ideal and an ultimate goal.

All the same, in spite of the general acceptance of stewardship as a normative concept in the Christian understanding of the created world, a number of tensions still exist. Some Christians continue to argue for a model of human domination of creation, claiming that the rest of the world is ultimately at the disposal of its human inhabitants. At the other end of the spectrum, some have argued strongly against any kind of species hierarchy, suggesting that every living creature, and the creation as a whole, must be treated with the same kind of care that should be accorded to its human inhabitants. This wide diversity of viewpoints has made "environmental ethics" a highly contested field, even among those who operate from a distinctively Christian point of view.

The corporate body

In the previous chapter, we examined Christian teachings about the physical human body—its positive significance and God's affirmation of its importance through the divine activities of creation, incarnation, and resurrection. We now return to the word "body" and note that it also became one of the chief metaphors for describing the new community of believers that was formed, through the power of the Holy Spirit, in the wake of the life, death, and resurrection of Jesus. As we begin to understand the importance of this metaphor, we will also begin to see why it will be useful in our discussion about the relationship of human beings to the rest of the created order.

The word "body"has always been understood as offering particularly rich associations for the Christian theological tradition. First, as already observed, the human body itself is a significant source of theological reflection: created by God as good, taken on by God in the incarnation, raised up by God in the resurrection of Jesus and in the resurrection of the dead. Second, these direct physical references to the body create vivid associations with the physical body of Jesus, particularly at the end of his earthly ministry. During his last meal with his disciples, he refers to the bread and wine as his body and blood (Matt. 26:26–29); the disciples' first experience of his resurrection is the absence of his body from the tomb (Mark 16:1–8 par.), followed by the presence of his (very physical) body among them (Luke 24:26–49; John 20:10–30); and finally, he withdraws from them in bodily form, rising up into the heavens (Luke 24:50–51). Afterward, all these connotations (physical body, eucharistic body, resurrected body) cross over into the word's usage as a description of the community of believers who, empowered by the Holy Spirit, continue Christ's work in the world: the Church, the new "body of Christ."

The smooth, to-and-fro movement of this language among its apparently disparate references—God's body, eucharistic bread, community of believers—is made possible by the complex references of the word "body"itself. First, a *body*, while whole and (in one sense) complete in itself, connects very readily with other bodies; second, a body is typically not an undifferentiated whole, but comprises many parts or "members." Bodies (including our physical bodies) are complex, articulated wholes, within which we can identify many constituent parts; and bodies also connect to other bodies to form yet more complex and articulated wholes. This makes the metaphor of the body extraordinarily useful for those who are trying to emphasize, simultaneously, the ideas of wholeness (completeness in itself) and relatedness (connectedness to others). For Christians, emphasizing both these ideas was important in their understanding of God (as we know from our discussion of the trinitarian virtues); it was also important in their understanding of the unity and diversity of the community of believers.

In his first letter to the Corinthians, Paul offers an extended meditation on the body as a metaphor for both the wholeness and the interrelatedness of the Christian community. Because of its importance in ongoing theological reflection, the passage is worth quoting at some length:

> For just as the body is one and has many members, and all the members of the body, though many, are one body, so it is with Christ. For in the one Spirit we were all baptized into one body—Jews or Greeks, slaves or free—and we were all made to drink of one Spirit. Indeed, the body does not consist of one member but of many. If the foot would say, "Because

I am not a hand, I do not belong to the body," that would not make it any less a part of the body. And if the ear would say, "Because I am not an eye, I do not belong to the body," that would not make it any less a part of the body. If the whole body were an eye, where would the hearing be? If the whole body were hearing, where would the sense of smell be? But as it is, God arranged the members in the body, each one of them, as he chose. If all were a single member, where would the body be? As it is, there are many members, yet one body. The eye cannot say to the hand, "I have no need of you," or again the head to the feet, "I have no need of you." On the contrary, the members of the body that seem to be weaker are indispensable, and those members of the body that we think less honorable we clothe with greater honor, and our less respectable members are treated with greater respect; whereas our more respectable members do not need this. But God has so arranged the body, giving the greater honor to the inferior member, that there may be no dissension within the body, but the members may have the same care for one another. If one member suffers, all suffer together with it; if one member is honored, all rejoice together with it. Now you are the body of Christ and individually members of it (1 Cor. 12:12–27).

For Paul, the body is a perfect metaphor for the various gifts and talents of the members of the community. Its internal differences are not a weakness, but a strength; and all the members, in spite of their differences, contribute significantly to the health of the whole body.

While Paul was focusing on the applicability of this metaphor to the Church, we can easily expand its reference and consider the degree to which the entire created order is also like a body with many members. The obvious differences among the various component parts of the natural world—whether those components are defined broadly (animal, mineral, vegetable) or narrowly (by individual genus and species)—are manifestly different from one another. But this does not make them any less a part of the whole created order, just as the manifest differences among the various parts of the body do not exclude them from membership. The various members of the body fulfill different functions, as do the various parts of the natural environment—some use oxygen and produce carbon dioxide, while for others, the converse is true. The smaller, weaker, and less attractive parts sometimes turn out to be the most important (think of the significance of bees as pollinators, or of the spores of penicillium molds). The members of the body are called to care for one another, because "if one member suffers, all suffer together with it"—a claim that has been repeatedly proven, with respect to the natural environment, over the entire course of its history.

While this is not the place for a detailed description of the applicability of the body metaphor to the natural environment, I hope that I have said enough to suggest the usefulness of Christian reflection on the relationship between the whole and its component parts. By taking this metaphor as seriously with respect to the natural environment as they have taken it with respect to the Church, Christians can offer an important witness to the significance of taking each member of the body seriously and appreciating what it contributes to the whole. This need not require (and in fact, it should not include) making the earth and the natural environment into something divine, as though it were God's own body; while such suggestions occasionally arise within Christian theology, they obscure its long-standing claim that God is ultimately different than, and distinguishable from, the created order. The earth does not need to be "divine" in order to be worthy of respect, any more than do human beings. The simple fact that the various elements of the natural world have been created by God—that God chose to bring them into being—should be sufficient to remind people not to despise them or to injure them. And the fact that these creatures are related to one another in a complex whole—like the various members of a single body—should remind us to respect their interwoven relationships. "If one member suffers, all suffer together with it; if one member is honored, all rejoice together with it."

Now that we have explored the theological significance of Christian claims about creation, covenant, and the corporate body, we need to consider how these notions undergird various excellences of character—which can in turn guide our interactions with the physical environment. Given their claims about God's creation of the world, about God's promises and expectations with respect to the created order, and about the importance of respect for its deeply interwoven strands, what virtues are most important for Christians to cultivate? What kind of people ought they to be, in their dealings with the natural environment?

Some virtues of Earth-care

Throughout Part 3 of this book, we have examined how at least some of the virtues might play a role in structuring the shape of Christian ethics for particular spheres of life: life on the job, at the voting booth, at the hospital, out on the town, and now, during a hypothetical walk in the woods. In each case, I have emphasized that the three examples of virtues that I have offered are clearly not the only ones that could be explored; they are simply those that I considered to be particularly relevant to the topic at hand. Given the unity of the virtues (as described in chapter 8), any one of the excellences of character that we have offered as significant to Christians should apply, at least to some degree, to any of the spheres of life or sets of issues discussed here—or, for that matter, to any other set of issues that we might imagine.

I mention this point again here, not merely because it is my last chance to do so, but because—in the case of environmental ethics—I can point my readers toward a book that very nicely illustrates how this kind of "broadening" of the discussion of the virtues is possible: Steven Bouma-Prediger's *For the Beauty of the Earth*. In addition to being a very fine book on Christian ethics and the environment, it is written by someone with a thorough knowledge of the history of Christian engagements with biblical, theological, and ethical debates. In a chapter entitled "What kind of people ought we be? Earth-care and character," the author sets out a brief account of the virtue ethics tradition, and then goes on to elaborate fourteen specific virtues as they apply to Christian interactions with the environment. His list includes some excellences of character that derive from the traditional lists of the virtues—theological (love and hope), cardinal (justice, courage, and wisdom), and fruits of the Spirit (self-control, patience, and "serenity," which is much like peaceableness). He also offers a few additional virtues that, while they have not been part of our conversation in this book, do have a history in the Christian tradition and have resonances with other biblical themes (respect, honesty, and benevolence).

While it has not been my practice to provide detailed descriptions of the ethical perspectives offered in other books, I have said a bit more about this one because, in addition to being a good book on environmental ethics that I can recommend to those who would like to venture further into this topic, it also illustrates a principle that I am keen to emphasize: the broad applicability of the language of virtue in ethical discussions that focus on particular sets of issues or spheres of life. And because it is a book-length treatment rather than a single chapter, it can also examine a longer list of virtues and thereby underscore the unity of the virtues.

I conclude my own reflections on the relationship of Christian ethics to the environment with a discussion of three of the excellences of character from the table of the virtues that I offered in chapter 7: kindness, polyphony, and hope.

Kindness

To be *kind* is to be considerate of the circumstances of others, sympathetic to their needs and desires, and helpful where help is most needed. The root of this notion in the biblical narrative is, as usual, in the character of God: the Hebrew words that are used in the Old Testament are *hesed* and *tob*, variously translated as kindness, love, loving-kindness, steadfast love, mercy, or devotion. God is described quite frequently as having this characteristic, as we noted in chapter 6 in our discussion of forgiveness: not dealing with others according to what they deserve, nor according to what God could do to them (given God's power), but rather, acknowledging the other's limits and circumstances. The focus, as was the case with the virtue of *love*, is on other-directedness: accepting others for what they are, not seeking to force them into the pattern of what we need or want or would like them to be.

The Greek word that is translated "kindness" in Paul's list of the fruits of the Spirit (*chrēstotēs*) is relatively rare in the New Testament; nevertheless, here too it is understood as a mark of God's character which human beings are called upon to emulate. Jesus tells his followers that by loving their enemies, they demonstrate their close relationship to God, who "is kind to the ungrateful and the wicked" (Luke 6:35). Similarly, Paul counsels the members of the churches to "be kind to one another, tenderhearted, forgiving one another, as God in Christ has forgiven you" (Eph. 4:32). In each case, God's kindness to human beings is taken as a call for human beings to be kind to others. (This last verse was adopted as a motto by the Community of the Cross of Nails, a Christian group formed during and after the Second World War to promote forgiveness and kindness among the citizens of nations that had been at war with one another. The community was founded in the wake of the bombing of the Anglican cathedral at Coventry, England; the original "cross of nails" that became the community's symbol was constructed with nails that were found in the building's wreckage. The ruins are beautifully preserved, immediately adjacent to the beautiful new cathedral; the entire site stands as an outward and visible sign of all three virtues explored in this chapter.)

To whom should our kindness be directed? If we take the kindness of God as a model, we can observe that God, who has infinitely more power and freedom than do we, does not simply use that power and freedom to overwhelm the finite power and finite freedom of human beings, but instead is attentive to the differences between human beings and God. In other words, God doesn't expect people to be God, and doesn't hold them to the same standard; their needs, abilities, and capacities are taken into account. Likewise, then, human beings are called to show kindness to those who lack the power, freedom, or resources that they themselves have: the marginalized, the captive, the poor, the weak. To be kind to such persons is to recognize their need of help and to offer that help as one is able.

This last point helps us understand why this virtue is an especially appropriate one for Christians to cultivate with respect to the rest of creation. According to the story of the creation in Genesis, human beings are at the pinnacle of the created order; they were originally granted dominion over the other elements of creation, in a clear analogy to God's dominion over them. In other words, they are to the rest of creation as God is to them: more knowledgeable, more powerful, and fully capable of overcoming or overwhelming the other. But just as God does not typically use divine power to overwhelm and grind down human beings, so are human beings called to refrain from the use of their own considerable power to exercise tyranny over the rest of the created order. Instead, they are called to recognize that other creatures are different from themselves, and to allow those creatures to take their own proper place within creation—as free as possible from the forces that human beings might potentially bring to bear against them.

Moreover, as I have already observed, the very belief that God created the world should be a sufficient warrant against despising or injuring its creatures. If God willed that these creatures exist, any human action that treats them unkindly is tantamount to a rejection of God's will and of God's gifts. Of course, with respect to the non-human elements of creation, the language of *kindness* may be somewhat difficult to apply; what would it mean, exactly, to be "unkind" to rocks or plants? In these cases, we probably need to distinguish between the *use* of the created order (in keeping with God's covenant and the ideal of stewardship) and the *abuse* of it for selfish human purposes. Environmentally sound uses of the earth's resources would seem to be very much in keeping with God's intentions for the creation; they could be carried out with attention to the virtue of kindness. On the other hand, it is difficult to see how this virtue would be embodied through acts of wanton damage, non-sustainable agriculture, or the active destruction of habitats. Of course, between these two extremes lies a vast field of disagreement and debate; nevertheless, I suspect that if *kindness* is allowed to enter the conversation at all, it would bring a rather different tone to the ongoing discussion of environmental issues.

For example: taking the virtue of kindness seriously, with respect to the environment, might well require Christians to rethink some of the assumptions that they have adopted from the various national and ethnic cultures within which the faith has developed. For example, in contrast to Judaism, which often held very firmly to its own religious claims about what foods should and should not be eaten, Christians eventually tended to merge their own eating habits with those of the people around them. Part of this development was motivated by something that I have stressed throughout this book: a reinterpretation of the Jewish law as something that was fulfilled in Christ, such that dietary laws no longer applied. One can cite many New Testament passages that point in this direction (Mark 7:19; Acts 10:10–15; 1 Cor. 8:1–13). Nevertheless, it may well be that some Christians will want to rethink their assumptions about food, based on the importance of the virtue of kindness with respect to our treatment of the environment. Christians have certainly debated the morality of killing animals for food, given the high esteem in which they have often held virtues such as kindness and gentleness and practices such as nonviolence. Even prescinding from the question of vegetarianism, however, many Christians consider the humane treatment of animals, for whatever purpose, to be a question about which they are ethically concerned. Again, while the great majority of Christian denominations have few or no "rules" on this matter, the application of a virtue such as *kindness* to issues surrounding the rest of the created order must necessarily bring these questions to bear.

Polyphony

A second virtue to consider here is the trinitarian virtue of *polyphony*. As described briefly in chapter 7, this excellence of character arises from the Christian belief that God is one being in three persons, one essence with three "ways of being." This conception of God helps Christians weave together the biblical narratives in which God is understood, simultaneously, as the unbegotten Source who is beyond all human comprehension, as the Word who became flesh and dwelt among human beings, and as the Spirit who animates and enlivens the Christian community in the present day. This simultaneity of threeness and unity is part of God's character, which in turn has implications for the moral life.

One of the metaphors that is often used to describe this simultaneous threeness and unity is that of polyphonic music. Here, multiple sounds can be heard and discerned at once; in fact, entirely different lines of music can cross over one another and intersect in counterpoint and harmony. As listeners, we do not typically find polyphonic music to be contradictory or chaotic; in fact, we often sense that the multiple layers of music have a synergistic interaction that makes the whole greater than the sum of its parts. We can take this music apart and listen to each line separately, but the result is not nearly so satisfying as listening to the symphony of the whole.

In a book that focused on the Christian understanding of God, I suggested that this trinitarian characteristic of polyphony might be understood as one of the virtues: excellences of character that God has by God's own trinitarian nature, and in which we—as human beings created in the image of God—can participate by grace. I suggested that a human being who was willing to live a *polyphonic* life would be characterized by an ease in allowing multiple conceptions and threads of meaning to co-exist side by side. This virtue is marked by a conviction that, in many cases, apparently contrasting perspectives can often conceal a more fundamental state of agreement at some basic level. Thus it is always worth considering the degree to which two or more apparently opposing perspectives can exist alongside one another— rather than doing battle against the rest and assuming that one must always triumph over the others. Again, this notion is modeled on the trinitarian character of God, which is non-hierarchical and in which each person of the Trinity is always about the process of "giving place" to the others.

This metaphor can also guide Christian attitudes toward the environment. The diversity of the biosphere is a positive thing in and of itself; but more significant still is the way that the various elements of the created order work in symbiotic relationships to one another. As I observed earlier in this chapter, even something as simple as the exchange of oxygen and carbon dioxide between plants and animals is a clear indicator of the interdependence of these elements. Just as we cannot remove a single line of polyphonic music without causing significant damage to the whole, neither can we wage war against certain forms of plant or animal life without disrupting their relationships to one another.

The virtue of polyphony is very positively reinforced by the Christian account of the corporate body. In the previous section of this chapter, we explored how the metaphor of the body provided Paul with a useful account of the relationships among human beings within a community. The parts of the body are different from one another, but they also depend upon one another; no part can use its specific characteristics as a means of setting itself above the other parts. As useful as the hand may be, a body that consisted only of hands would not be particularly agile (or attractive!); moreover, it would certainly not be what God intended it to be—namely, a body that comprised many different members. And, as Paul emphasizes, even the apparently weakest members of the body sometimes turn out to be the most important. Any Christian account of environmental ethics must therefore take account of the interdependent relationships among the various elements of the created order; it must allow these diverse elements to sound forth in their polyphonic beauty, rather than allowing one melodic line to overpower, capture, or displace all the others.

This particular virtue calls human beings to seek to overcome those forms of thinking that pit one species against another. In God's harmonious and polyphonic creation, the various forms of life should be able to co-exist without necessarily being in competition with each other. If they appear to be in competition, this probably has more to do with the way that we human beings have ordered the world, rather than some kind of necessary collision within the created order itself. (Readers may here observe an analogy to my repeated invocation of the unity of the virtues: if they appear to be in

Chief Seattle

As the European settlers of North America pushed westward in search of land, lumber, and gold, they encountered native tribes who had lived on the continent for centuries. Because these native Americans had a vastly different conception of land and property rights, and because their weaponry was not as technologically efficient, they were quickly marginalized: lands confiscated, resources plundered, military forces defeated. In a few cases, the United States government made (usually rather woeful) efforts to forge treaties or to "purchase" the land from its occupants. This ugly legacy of the history of the United States is second only to its large-scale importation of slaves from Africa as a blot on its self-image as a morally respectable nation.

During one such "purchase" of native lands, a tribal chief of the Suquamish and Duwuamish peoples named Seattle (?1786–1866) made a celebrated speech. It was given in his native tongue and not transcribed verbatim; it was later reconstructed from a listener's notes and translated.Over the years it has been modified, rewritten, and improvised upon; it has also survived within the oral history of the Suquamish people. Today, it is impossible to determine the degree to which the various versions of the speech cohere with whatever Seattle might actually have said. (One of the most frequently quoted versions of the speech was actually written as part of a film script and took considerable literary license, but still aimed to capture its essence.)

Despite its many forms, and however much it has been modified and reshaped by its transmission over time, the speech has entered into North American folklore as a significant reflection on the relationship between human beings and the rest of the created order. Although Chief Seattle was not himself a Christian, the words that are attributed to him reflect many of the ideas that we have been exploring in this chapter: the luxuriant beauty of the earth; the recognition that human beings are only one part of a much larger reality; and the deep interconnectedness of all things, living and dead, as members of a single body. One version of the speech was published in 1887 and is generally thought to be closest to Seattle's own words, though its editor admitted that it was not an exact account and that it "contained none of the grace and elegance of the original." It runs (in part) as follows:

> Our dead never forget this beautiful world that gave them being. They still love its verdant valleys, its murmuring rivers, its magnificent mountains, sequestered vales and verdant lined lakes and bays, and ever yearn in tender fond affection over the lonely-hearted living, and often return from

the happy hunting ground to visit, guide, console, and comfort them. . . .

But why should I mourn at the untimely fate of my people? Tribe follows tribe, and nation follows nation, like the waves of the sea. It is the order of nature, and regret is useless. Your time of decay may be distant, but it will surely come, for even the White Man whose God walked and talked with him as friend to friend, cannot be exempt from the common destiny. We may be brothers after all. We will see . . .

Every part of this soil is sacred in the estimation of my people. Every hillside, every valley, every plain and grove, has been hallowed by some sad or happy event in days long vanished. Even the rocks, which seem to be dumb and dead as they swelter in the sun along the silent shore, thrill with memories of stirring events connected with the lives of my people, and the very dust upon which you now stand responds more lovingly to their footsteps than yours, because it is rich with the blood of our ancestors, and our bare feet are conscious of the sympathetic touch. . . .

And when the last Red Man shall have perished, and the memory of my tribe shall have become a myth among the White Men, these shores will swarm with the invisible dead of my tribe, and when your children's children think themselves alone in the field, the store, the shop, upon the highway, or in the silence of the pathless woods, they will not be alone. In all the earth there is no place dedicated to solitude. At night when the streets of your cities and villages are silent and you think them deserted, they will throng with the returning hosts that once filled them and still love this beautiful land.

Whatever Chief Seattle may have said, these words accurately reflect some of the significant differences between the native peoples' attitude toward the environment and that of their conquerors. One can only wish that the (supposedly Christianized) Europeans who "settled" North America could have brought with them such a vision of the interrelationships of the living and the dead, of humanity and the rest of creation. Sadly, another part of Seattle's speech offers a rather negative account of "the White Man's god" that has been bestowed on his people—a bitter testimony to the colonizers' utter failure to proclaim the good news of Christianity.

I first encountered a version of Chief Seattle's speech on the wall of a cabin at Barr Camp—a halfway house on a trail leading to the summit of Pike's Peak, on the far eastern edge of the Rocky Mountains in Colorado. The mountain's elevation (14,110 feet) renders it rather mundane by local standards; Colorado alone has thirty peaks that are higher. But its location on the Front Range,

> rising up dramatically from the plains (where the elevation is only 6,000 feet),
> makes it one of the most celebrated mountains in the United States. The trail
> that ascends its western face provides the hiker with a rather spectacular
> encounter with the natural environment. The small camp at the trail's halfway
> point is therefore a superb location for meditating on the interconnectedness
> of all things, and for receiving training—from the mountain itself, from the
> people passing through the camp, and from Chief Seattle—in the virtues of
> kindness, polyphony, and hope.

contradiction with each other, then we have misunderstood the meaning of
one or more of the individual elements, or the overall narratives and practices from which they are derived.) "Peaceful co-existence" might therefore
be an appropriate starting point for Christian considerations of the natural
environment; anything short of this would be insufficiently attentive to God's
polyphonic character, in which qualities that appear to be mutually exclusive
can coexist within one nature.

Hope

The theological virtue of *hope* is the most forward-looking of the virtues,
encouraging Christians to direct their attention to the future with an expectation that, in the words of the medieval mystic Julian of Norwich, "All
shall be well, and all manner of thing shall be well." The source of this positive outlook on the future is not simply a sunny disposition or a tendency
to "always look on the bright side of life" (despite the ending of the Monty
Python film *Life of Brian*!). Rather, hope is intimately related to another theological virtue, that of *faith*. Christians are able to live in *hope* because their
faith (trust, confidence) is ultimately in God. God's grace and providence are
ultimately in charge of the way the world will go; human machinations and
schemes, however powerful they may seem according to the course of history as it is usually told, are only a small blip in the overall arc of the account
of history that matters most. The virtue of hope expresses confidence in the
Christian account of that narrative: confidence in the past (how the world
began, and whence it comes), in the present (how the world proceeds, and
where we currently find ourselves), and in the future (whither the world is
tending, and how it all will end). Each of these modalities—past, present, and
future—is ultimately understood to be a product of God's abundant gift of,
and providential care for, the created order.

Many commentators have noted with interest that the biblical narrative,
in the final canonical form in which it has come down to us, both begins and

ends in a garden. It begins in Eden, where the woman and the man have been placed by God, and which yields up its fruit without effort on their part; it is the very picture of abundance, beauty, and right relationship. The biblical narrative ends in a different kind of garden, now described as located within the walls of a great city—the New Jerusalem—which serves as a symbol of the ultimate convergence of all things within God's providential care. The author of the Book of Revelation describes it in typically dramatic terms:

> Then the angel showed me the river of the water of life, bright as crystal, flowing from the throne of God and of the Lamb through the middle of the street of the city. On either side of the river is the tree of life with its twelve kinds of fruit, producing its fruit each month; and the leaves of the tree are for the healing of the nations. Nothing accursed will be found there any more. But the throne of God and of the Lamb will be in it, and his servants will worship him; they will see his face, and his name will be on their foreheads. And there will be no more night; they need no light of lamp or sun, for the Lord God will be their light, and they will reign forever and ever (Rev. 22:1–5).

These two gardens provide a frame of reference within which the entire biblical narrative is cast. The imagery keeps certain elements of the two gardens consistent; both contain the tree of life, as well as a river that provides the water of life. Like the Garden of Eden that is described as superabundant in its produce, the trees of the New Jerusalem produce their fruit all throughout the year. In both gardens, God finds a dwelling place: walking in Eden in the cool of the day (Gen. 3:8), and seated on the throne at the end of time.

But these two accounts also signal a difference between the two gardens. In the first garden, God's relationship to human beings—while much more direct than what we ordinarily experience—is still mediated through various structures. The inhabitants of the garden encounter God only occasionally; they are distracted by their own appetites and by the cunning of the serpent; and they depend upon the sun, moon, and stars for their light. In the second garden, at the end of time, the relationship between human beings and God is much more direct; it is a face-to-face encounter, with all the implications borne by such language (as we discussed in Interlude 3). The allegiance of the people to God is definitive and clear (after all, they've tattooed God's name on themselves—and not in a particularly discreet location!). They no longer have need of created sources of light, because God provides light and enlightenment in a direct and unmediated way.

In addition, the second garden grows within the walls of a city, rather than in a isolated location of its own. The human beings who live in the

New Jerusalem seem to be part of a vast population—in contrast to the one person, then the two people, who are described in Genesis 2. This difference serves as a reminder that, over the course of history, a human community has been built up to inhabit the new garden; and in this sense, the second garden is superior to the first. Just as, after the creation of the first garden, God recognized that it was not good for the solitary earth creature to be alone (Gen. 2:18), so the possibility of life in community—so often affirmed and praised throughout the biblical narrative—is brought to full fruition in the garden of the New Jerusalem.

In these two accounts, which exhibit elements of both continuity and difference, the biblical narrative suggests a particular kind of movement through time: a movement of a journey forth from a place and a return to the same place, but during which significant positive change has occurred—thereby allowing us to appreciate both the place from which we came and the importance of the journey itself. The great twentieth-century poet T. S. Eliot's oft-quoted words (from the final stanza of "Little Gidding," the last of his *Four Quartets*) seem to apply quite well to this biblically-narrated journey from the first garden to the second:

> We shall not cease from exploration
> And the end of all our exploring
> Will be to arrive where we started
> And know the place for the first time.

The theme is a broad one, and it pervades the entire Christian narrative. Augustine referred to it with the rhyming Latin words *exitus* and *reditus*: all things come forth from God, and they all return back to God as well. They are, of course, not completely unaffected by the journey; they do not return in the same form in which they venture forth. So although the pattern is circular, it is not simply an endless repetition, an eternal recurrence of the same events; in fact, it is more of a spiral, in which we return to the same place but in a wholly different key. Augustine also thought that this motif helped to explain the dissatisfaction we often feel as we are casting about for the "next big thing" in our lives. On this matter, one saying of Augustine's is particularly apposite; I have cited it previously in this book, but it is worth repeating here. Speaking to God, Augustine says: "You have made us for yourself, and our hearts are restless until they rest in you."

The biblical text's journey from one garden to another can be read as a similar kind of venture: a going forth from God and a return back to God. The story begins in the Garden of Eden, with human beings living at peace with the natural world: no labor is required, no hardships are experienced, and no blood is shed (not even that of animals). All that peaceable harmony comes to an end as a result of the Fall, the flood, and the many failures of the earth's human inhabitants; they must venture forth into a world in which the quiet of the garden has been replaced by violence, pain, and bloodshed. In such a world, the relationships among the inhabitants of the earth are strained to the breaking point; as beautiful as the natural order may sometimes be, we are unable to experience it as a wholly positive reality. We often feel confronted by it; its various elements can become warnings, obstacles, or outright threats. We may make our temporary peace with the natural world, learning to live in some kind of manageable but always slightly tense harmony; nevertheless, we do not quite feel at home here. We feel "restless," as Augustine says—longing for a life in that original garden, where everything was at peace.

We have not yet arrived at the final destination—that other garden where peace will once more prevail, and where the leaves of the trees will heal the nations. But the point of the Christian vision of that return is not to proclaim a premature arrival there; it is, rather, to look forward to it in *hope*. As we noted in our discussion of the theological virtues, hope is an excellence of character that involves being directed toward the future, in anticipation of the positive things that are to come. It should not be confused with excessive optimism or with seeing the world through rose-colored glasses; it is not blind to the difficulties embedded in the current state of things. It is, rather, a way of affirming the same point with which we began: that the world is created by God and that God is ultimately in charge of its destiny. Under such conditions, human beings can afford to be hopeful; they can imagine that their journey is leading toward some place in particular, rather than being a random wandering across uncharted territory. Our "journey without maps," to which we referred back in chapter 5, may eventually become an opportunity to arrive at our true destination—from which place we will be able to gain some perspective on the whole of our voyage.

This understanding of the virtue of hope makes it particularly relevant to the relationship between human beings and the environment. Its significance is related to the factors that I mentioned at the very beginning of this chapter: that the natural world is large and complex, and that those who put themselves in the position of trying to keep it all in perfect order, or to "save" it, will quickly be overwhelmed by the enormity (and indeed, the impossibility) of the task. The virtue of hope puts people in a position to offer small contributions toward the overall health of the environment, not as a means of ensuring that "everything will turn out alright," or even under the assumption that they are doing more good than ill, but rather, precisely as a sign of hope. They can offer their small acts of kindness toward the earth and its inhabitants as a way of declaring their belief that, although they are not in control of all its intricate elements, they are confident that it will endure.

Any invocation of the virtue of hope requires a rather exquisite balancing act. Without hope, human beings may fall into its opposite, despair. The many assaults on the natural environment, and in particular the extraordinary selfishness with which people are prone to use and abuse it, makes us wonder how it will survive even into the next decade—let alone through the next century and beyond. On the other hand, an excessive level of confidence and optimism (or a willingness to use the excuse of "leaving it all in God's hands" as a means of taking the easy way out) can discourage people from taking any kind of action on behalf of the natural environment. Cultivating the virtue of hope is a way of expressing one's confidence in providence while not denying the significance of one's own actions. It is, in the terms in which we defined the virtues when we first encountered them, a willingness to accept God's grace in the formation of good habits.

The end of the end

Our comments at the end of the previous section—concerning the virtue of hope as an expression of confidence in God's providential care for the created order—may alert us to a potential problem. Discussions that focus on divine providence and on "the way the world will go" are often connected to beliefs about "the end"—both in an individual sense (what will happen after I die) and in the more general sense (how, exactly, the world will end). Such questions are typically considered under the theological field of *eschatology* (the Greek word *eschaton* means "last" or "end"). This is the study of "the last things": the final destination of the whole created order, and all of the creatures within it. Eschatology is particularly concerned with the questions that we raised in our discussion of *hope*: namely, the "final destination" toward which the world is headed, and the confidence that Christians express that God will be the focal point of the end of history, just as God was the focal point of its beginning.

Unfortunately, Christian accounts of the last things have focused very narrowly on dramatic accounts of the afterlife (with puffy clouds and fiery torments) and on even more dramatic accounts of the end of the world (complete with apocalyptic battles and tales of woe and intrigue). While Christianity has certainly had something to say about the final destiny of human beings and of the whole created order, the imagery that it has used to describe this destiny has too often been interpreted with a kind of wooden literalism that sometimes gets so interested in enumerating the specific tortures of hell, or in pinpointing the time and place where Armageddon will begin, that it quickly misses the whole point. In focusing on the *end* (in the sense of "what happens when we die" or "how the world will end"), it misses the "end" in the sense that we have used the term ever since it appeared in the subtitle of this book: the "end" in the sense of purpose or goal. In short, Christians should be interested less in the question of "what will happen when it's all over" and more in the larger questions of *why*: our focus should be not just on the "end," but on the "end of the end."

The dramatic language that is invoked throughout much of the Book of Revelation has sometimes misled its readers to imagine that they are watching some kind of science-fiction-style prediction of the world's last days. Even the account of the garden in the New Jerusalem is sometimes interpreted as a description of "how nice life will be in heaven, after you die." But both of these readings of the Book of Revelation are far too narrow: they latch on to the dramatic narrative and treat it as the script for a second-rate film, in which the beautiful garden of Revelation 22 is just one more attractive tourist destination. But the significance of the New Jerusalem, and of the Book of Revelation as a whole, is found in its vision of the ultimate course of history: that, in the end, God's reign will be acknowledged and all human beings will be in a right relationship with God, with one another, and with everything that God has made. Keeping this broader picture in mind is the key to understanding Christian eschatology—that is, its accounts of the "ultimate destination" of both individual human beings and of the whole created order.

The biblical writers attempt to maintain this broader perspective by offering a great many different treatments of "what life will be like"—both in terms of our individual destiny and in terms of the final consummation of history. They describe it, variously, as a garden, a city, a banquet, a vision, a face-to-face encounter, an experience of praise and worship, and a mystical union of love. Why so many different images?—because no single vision is adequate to express the ultimate destiny of all creation. If we focus in too tightly on one particular image—the heavenly banquet, say, or the New Jerusalem, or the vision of God on the throne—we run the risk of allowing the image to become the focus of our attention, when the point being made is a rather more significant one. It is, as I noted above, a point about the origin of all things in God and the ultimate return of all things to God. Such a monumental concept could never be embodied in a single image.

Christian ethics must always give adequate attention to these eschatological questions: considerations of the end, not just in the sense of the last thing to happen, but particularly in the sense of the goal and purpose of human life. If its goal were merely to live the longest possible life, or to live with the most pleasure and the least pain, or simply to avoid hurting others, then that would lead to one set of assumptions about ethics. But if the chief end of human life is to return to a perfect relationship with the God who creates, redeems, and sustains us, then the shape of the ethical life will be altered in accordance with our understanding of the character of God. The final destination that we seek will shape the kind of lives we hope to live, the narratives and practices that we seek to embody, and the virtues that we will cultivate. In this way, human beings fulfill our true end—and we do so in right relationship with God, with other human beings, and with the entire created order.

Questions for discussion

1. How does the claim that "God created the earth" affect a person's disposition toward the natural environment? How (if at all) is this claim affected by what one maintains about the physical processes by which the Earth came to be (the Big Bang, evolution, and so on)? Do you agree with the account offered here, to the effect that the accounts of creation offered by Christian theology and by the natural sciences are not ultimately in competition with one another?

2. Describe an occasion in your own life when you entered into a relationship that might be described as a *covenant*. How was that relationship different from other kinds of relationships? Did one party "keep" the covenant to a greater extent than the other? How did things eventually turn out?

3. Offer at least one other metaphor (in addition to this chapter's accounts of the corporate body and of polyphonic music) that stresses the internal relationships and interdependence of the different parts of a whole. How well does your metaphor describe the mutually dependent relationships within the natural environment? What are the limitations of the metaphor?

4. List some of the obstacles present in the contemporary setting that make the virtue of *kindness* a difficult one to embody and to cultivate. To what extent do these obstacles affect the way that we understand our relationship to the world around us, and to questions in environmental ethics?

5. Discuss the virtue of hope. To what extent does it depend upon faith or confidence in someone (or something) being in ultimate charge of things? What causes people to have hope? What factors can make hope difficult to maintain? To what extent does it make sense to have "hope for the past"? (On

this last point, be sure to revisit the textbox on David Ray's poem, "Thanks, Robert Frost," in chapter 6.)

Sources cited in this chapter and/or recommended for further reading

St. Augustine of Hippo, *The Confessions*

Margaret Adam, "More Than We Can Ask or Imagine: Christian Hope beyond Certainty"

Steven Bouma-Prediger, *For the Beauty of the Earth: A Christian Vision for Creation Care*

T. S. Eliot, "Little Gidding," from *Four Quartets*

Eli Gifford, R. Michael Cook, and Warren Jefferson, eds., *How Can One Sell the Air?: Chief Seattle's Vision*

Wes Grandberg-Michaelson, "Earth-Keeping: A Theology of Global Sanctification," in *Sojourners*

John Milbank, "Out of the Greenhouse," in *The Word Made Strange: Theology, Language, Culture*

Julian of Norwich, *Revelations of Divine Love*

Michael S. Northcott, *The Environment and Christian Ethics*

Charles Pinches, "Ecobooks: Journey through the Wilderness," in *Pro Ecclesia: A Journal of Catholic and Evangelical Theology*

Ben Quash, "Offering: Treasuring the Creation," in Hauerwas and Wells, eds., *The Blackwell Companion to Christian Ethics*

Kathryn Tanner, "Eschatology and Ethics," in Meilaender and Werpehowski, eds., *The Oxford Handbook of Theological Ethics*

Stephen H. Webb, *Good Eating*

Sources cited and suggestions for further reading

Adam, A. K. M. *Faithful Interpretation: Reading the Bible in a Postmodern World*. Minneapolis, Minn.: Fortress Press, 2006.

Adam, Margaret. "More Than We Can Ask or Imagine: Christian Hope beyond Certainty." PhD dissertation, Duke University, forthcoming.

Adams, Nicholas. "Confessing the Faith: Reasoning in Tradition." In Hauerwas and Wells, eds., *The Blackwell Companion to Christian Ethics*.

Adams, Nicholas. "Messiaen, Meaning, and the Transmission of Tradition." Paper delivered at the American Academy of Religion, November 2005.

Adams, Richard. *Watership Down*. London: Macmillan, 1972; reprint, New York: Avon Books, 1975.

Adaptation. Dir. Spike Jonze. Beverly Detroit, 2002.

Anscombe, G. E. M. *Intention*. 2nd edition. Ithaca, NY: Cornell University Press, 1963.

Aristotle. *The Art of Rhetoric*. Edited and translated by H. C. Lawson-Tancred. London: Penguin Books, 1991.

Aristotle. *Nicomachean Ethics*. Translated by Martin Ostwald. New York: Macmillan, 1962.

Aristotle. *Politics*. Edited and translated by Steven Everson. Cambridge: Cambridge University Press, 1988.

Auerbach, Erich. *Mimesis: The Representation of Reality in Western Literature*. Translated by Willard R. Trask. Princeton, NJ: Princeton University Press, 1953.

Augustine of Hippo, St. *City of God*. Translated by Henry Bettenson, with an Introduction by John O'Meara. 1972; reprint, London: Penguin Books, 1984.

Augustine of Hippo, St. *The Confessions*. Edited by John E. Rotelle, OSA. Translated by Maria Boulding, OSB. *The Works of Saint Augustine: A Translation for the 21st Century*, vol. I/1. Hyde Park, NY: New City Press, 1997.

Augustine of Hippo, St. *De Musica*. Trans. Robert Catesby Taliaferro. In *Writings of St. Augustine. The Fathers of the Church*, vol. 2. New York: Cima Publishing Co., 1947.

Augustine of Hippo, St. *Teaching Christianity (De Doctrina Christiana)*. Edited by John E. Rotelle, OSA. Translated by Edmund Hill, OP. *The Works of Saint Augustine: A Translation for the 21st Century*, vol. I/11. Hyde Park, NY: New City Press, 1996.

Babel. Dir. Alejandro González Iñárritu. Paramount Pictures, 2006.

Babette's Feast (Babettes gæstebud). Dir. Gabriel Axel. Panorama Film A/S, 1987.

Bach, Johann Sebastian. *Messe in h-moll (Mass in B Minor)*. BWV 232, 1724/1749.

Bach, Johann Sebastian. *Three-Part Inventions*. BWV 772–801, various dates.

Bader-Saye, Scott. *Following Jesus in a Culture of Fear*. The Christian Practice of Everyday Life. Grand Rapids, Mich.: Brazos Press, 2007.

Bader-Saye, Scott. "Listening: Authority and Obedience." In Hauerwas and Wells, eds., *The Blackwell Companion to Christian Ethics*.

Balthasar, Hans Urs von. *Credo: Meditations on the Apostles' Creed*. Translated by David Kipp, with an Introduction by Medard Kehl, SJ. New York: Crossroad, 1990.

Balthasar, Hans Urs von. *Theo-Drama: Theological Dramatic Theory*. Vol. II, *Dramatis Personae: Man in God*. Translated by Graham Harrison. San Francisco: Ignatius Press, 1992.

Begbie, Jeremy. *Theology, Music, and Time*. Cambridge and New York: Cambridge University Press, 2000.

Benne, Robert. "Christian Ethics and Politics." In Meilaender and Werpehowski, eds., *The Oxford Handbook of Theological Ethics*.

Berkman, John. "Being Reconciled: Penitence, Punishment, and Worship." In Hauerwas and Wells, eds., *The Blackwell Companion to Christian Ethics*.

Biggar, Nigel. *Aiming to Kill: The Ethics of Suicide and Euthanasia*. London: Darton, Longman, and Todd; Cleveland: Pilgrim Press, 2004.

Bouma-Prediger, Steven. *For the Beauty of the Earth: A Christian Vision for Creation Care*. Grand Rapids, Mich.: Baker Academic, 2001.

Breidenthal, Thomas. *Christian Households: The Sanctification of Nearness*. Cambridge, Mass.: Cowley Publications, 1997.

Buckley, Michael J., SJ. *At the Origins of Modern Atheism*. New Haven, Conn.: Yale University Press, 1987.

Budde, Michael. *The (Magic) Kingdom of God: Christianity and Global Culture Industries*. Boulder, Colo.: Westview Press, 1997.

Carter, Craig A. *Rethinking Christ and Culture: A Post-Christendom Perspective*. Grand Rapids, Mich: Brazos Press, 2006.

Cartwright, Michael. "Being Sent: Witness." In Hauerwas and Wells, eds., *The Blackwell Companion to Christian Ethics.*

Cavanaugh, William T. "Human Habit and Divine Action in Aquinas' Account of the Virtues." Unpublished paper.

Cavanaugh, William T. "Politics: Beyond Secular Parodies." In Milbank, Pickstock, and Ward, eds., *Radical Orthodoxy: A New Theology.* London and New York: Routledge, 1999, pp. 21–37.

Cavanaugh, William T. *Theopolitical Imagination.* Edinburgh and New York: T. & T. Clark, 2002.

Cavanaugh, William T. *Torture and Eucharist: Politics, Theology, and the Body of Christ.* Challenges in Contemporary Theology. Oxford and Malden, Mass.: Blackwell Publishers, 1998.

Chocolat. Dir. Lasse Hallström. David Brown Productions, 2000.

Cicero, Marcus Tullius. *Tusculan Disputations.* Cambridge, Mass.: Harvard University Press; London: William Heinemann, 1960.

Clapp, Rodney. *Tortured Wonders: Christian Spirituality for People, Not Angels.* Grand Rapids, Mich.: Brazos Press, 2004.

Clough, David, and Brian Stiltner. *Faith and Force: A Christian Debate about War.* Washington, DC: Georgetown University Press, 2007.

Cone, James H. *Martin & Malcolm & America.* Maryknoll, NY: Orbis Books, 1991.

Crash. Dir. Paul Haggis. Bull's Eye Entertainment, 2004.

Cunningham, David S. *Friday, Saturday, Sunday: Literary Meditations on Suffering, Death, and New Life.* Louisville, Ky. and London: Westminster John Knox Press, 2007.

Cunningham, David S. *Reading Is Believing: The Christian Faith through Literature and Film.* Grand Rapids, Mich.: Brazos Press, 2002.

Cunningham, David S. *These Three Are One: The Practice of Trinitarian Theology.* Challenges in Contemporary Theology. Oxford and Cambridge, Mass.: Basil Blackwell, 1998.

The Dave Brubeck Orchestra. "New Wine" from *The Voice of the Holy Spirit* and "Lullaby" from *La Fiesta de la Posada.* Recorded at a festival in 1987/ published in 1992.

Descartes, René. *Meditations on First Philosophy.* Translated by Donald A. Cress. Indianapolis: Hackett, 1979.

Dickens, Charles. *A Christmas Carol in Prose: Being a Ghost Story of Christmas.* 1843; Cleveland: World Publishing, 1946.

The Dixie Chicks. "Thin Line." Special edition of *Taking the Long Way.* Sony, 2006.

Donne, John. *Meditation XVII.* In *The Complete Poetry and Selected Prose of John Donne.* Modern Library Classics. Edited by Charles M. Coffin, with an Introduction by Denis Donoghue. New York: Modern Library, 2001.

Duffy, Michael F. *The Skeptical, Passionate Christan: Tools for Living Faithfully in an Uncertain World*. Louisville, Ky. and London: Westminster John Knox Press, 2006.

Eliot, T.S. "Little Gidding." *Four Quartets*. London: Faber and Faber; New York: Harcourt, Brace, Jovanovich, 1943.

Fletcher, Joseph. *Situation Ethics: The New Morality*. Philadelphia: Westminster Press, 1966.

Ford, David F. *Self and Salvation: Being Transformed*. Cambridge Studies in Christian Doctrine. Cambridge and New York: Cambridge University Press, 1999.

Ford, David F. *Theology: A Very Short Introduction*. Oxford and New York: Oxford University Press, 2000.

Fowl, Stephen E., and L. Gregory Jones. *Reading in Communion: Scripture and Ethics in Christian Life*. Biblical Foundations in Theology. Grand Rapids, Mich.: William B. Eerdmans; London: SPCK, 1991.

Frost, Robert. "The Road Not Taken." In *Mountain Interval*. New York: Holt, 1921.

Frost, Robert. "Stopping by Woods on a Snowy Evening." In *New Hampshire: A Poem With Notes and Grace Notes*. New York: Holt, 1923.

Gadamer, Hans-Georg. *The Relevance of the Beautiful and Other Essays*. Edited by Robert Bernasconi. Translated by Nicholas Walker. Cambridge and New York: Cambridge University Press, 1986.

Gifford, Eli, R. Michael Cook, and Warren Jefferson, eds., *How Can One Sell the Air?: Chief Seattle's Vision*. Summertown, Tenn.: Book Publishing Company, Native Voices, 2005.

Girard, René. *Violence and the Sacred*. Translated by Patrick Gregory. Baltimore, Md.: Johns Hopkins University Press, 1977.

Girard, René, Jean-Michel Oughourlian, and Guy Lefort. *Things Hidden since the Foundation of the World*. Translated by Stephen Bann and Michael Metteer. Stanford, Calif.: Stanford University Press, 1987.

Grandberg-Michaelson, Wes. "Earth-Keeping: A Theology of Global Sanctification." *Sojourners Magazine*, October 1982, pp. 21–24.

Greene, Graham. *The End of the Affair*. London: Heinemann; New York: Viking Press, 1951.

Grossman, Cathy Lynn. "View of God Can Predict Values, Politics." *USA Today*, September 11, 2006, p. 1.

Guthrie, Arlo. *Alice's Restaurant*. Warner Brothers, 1967.

Hauerwas, Stanley. *Against the Nations: War and Survival in a Liberal Society*. Minneapolis, Minn.: Winston Press, 1985.

Hauerwas, Stanley. *Character and the Christian Life: A Study in Theological Ethics*. 1975; reprint, San Antonio: Trinity University Press, 1985.

Hauerwas, Stanley. *A Community of Character: Toward a Constructive Christian Social Ethic*. Notre Dame, Ind.: University of Notre Dame Press, 1981.

Hauerwas, Stanley, and L. Gregory Jones, eds., *Why Narrative? Readings in Narrative Theology*. Grand Rapids, Mich.: William B. Eerdmans, 1989.

Hauerwas, Stanley, and Charles Pinches. *Christians among the Virtues: Theological Conversations with Ancient and Modern Ethics.* Notre Dame, Ind.: University of Notre Dame Press, 1997.

Hauerwas, Stanley, and Samuel Wells, eds., *The Blackwell Companion to Christian Ethics.* Oxford and Malden, Mass.: Blackwell Publishers, 2004.

Hauerwas, Stanley, and William H. Willimon. *Resident Aliens: Life in the Christian Colony.* Nashville, Tenn.: Abingdon Press, 1989.

Haydn, Franz Joseph. *Die Schöpfung.* 1796–1798.

Hays, Richard. *The Moral Vision of the New Testament: A Contemporary Introduction to New Testament Ethics.* San Francisco: Harper/Collins, 1996.

Hobbes, Thomas. *Leviathan, or the Matter, Forme and Power of a Commonwealth Ecclesiastical and Civil,* 1651. Edited by Michael Oakeshott, with an Introduction by Richard S. Peters. New York: Macmillan, Collier Books, 1962.

Jacobson, Eric O. *Sidewalks in the Kingdom: New Urbanism and the Christian Faith.* The Christian Practice of Everyday Life. Grand Rapids, Mich.: Brazos Press, 2003.

Jenson, Robert W. *Visible Words: The Interpretation and Practice of Christian Sacraments.* Philadelphia, Penn.: Fortress Press, 1978.

Johnson, Kelly S. "Praying: Poverty." In Hauerwas and Wells, eds., *The Blackwell Companion to Christian Ethics.*

Jones, L. Gregory. *Embodying Forgiveness: A Theological Analysis.* Grand Rapids, Mich.: William B. Eerdmans, 1995.

Jones, L. Gregory. *Transformed Judgment: Toward a Trinitarian Account of the Moral Life.* Notre Dame, Ind.: University of Notre Dame Press, 1990.

Kant, Immanuel. *Critique of Practical Reason.* Translated by Lewis White Beck. Indianapolis: Bobbs-Merrill, 1956.

Kant, Immanuel. *Foundations of the Metaphysics of Morals.* Translated by Lewis White Beck. 1959; reprint, New York: Macmillan, 1985.

Keillor, Garrison. *Lake Wobegon Days.* New York: Viking Press, 1985.

Keillor, Garrison. *Leaving Home.* New York: Viking Press, 1987.

Kenneson, Philip D. *Beyond Sectarianism: Re-imagining Church and World.* Christian Mission and Modern Culture. Philadelphia, Penn.: Trinity Press International, 1999.

Kenneson, Philip D. "Gathering: Worship, Imagination, and Formation." In Hauerwas and Wells, eds., *The Blackwell Companion to Christian Ethics.*

Kenneson, Philip D. *Life on the Vine: Cultivating the Fruit of the Spirit in Christian Community.* Downers Grove, Ill.: InterVarsity Press, 1999.

King, Martin Luther, Jr. *Letter from Birmingham Jail.* In *A Testament of Hope: The Essential Writings of Martin Luther King, Jr.* Edited by James Melvin Washington. San Francisco: HarperSanFrancisco, 1991.

Lash, Nicholas. *Believing Three Ways in One God: A Reading of the Apostles' Creed.* London: SCM Press; Notre Dame, Ind.: University of Notre Dame Press, 1992.

Lash, Nicholas. "Performing the Scriptures." In *Theology on the Way to Emmaus*. London: SCM Press, 1986, pp. 37–46.

Long, D. Stephen, and Tripp York. "Remembering: Offering Our Gifts." In Hauerwas and Wells, eds., *The Blackwell Companion to Christian Ethics*.

Lysaught, M. Therese. "Becoming One Body: Health Care and Cloning." In Hauerwas and Wells, eds., *The Blackwell Companion to Christian Ethics*.

McCarthy, David Matzko. *Sex and Love in the Home: A Theology of the Household*. London: SCM Press, 2001.

McIntosh, Mark A. *Mystical Theology: The Integrity of Spirituality and Theology*. Challenges in Contemporary Theology. Oxford: Blackwell Publishers, 1998.

MacIntyre, Alasdair. *After Virtue: A Study in Moral Theory*. 2nd edition. Notre Dame, Ind.: University of Notre Dame Press, 1984.

Marshall, Bruce D. *Trinity and Truth*. Cambridge Studies in Christian Doctrine. Cambridge and New York: Cambridge University Press, 2000.

Marx, Karl. *Karl Marx: Selected Writings*. Edited by David McLellan. Oxford: Oxford University Press, 1977.

Meeks, M. Douglas. *God the Economist: The Doctrine of God and Political Economy*. Minneapolis, Minn.: Fortress Press, 1989.

Meilaender, Gilbert C. *Bioethics: A Primer for Christians*. Grand Rapids, Mich.: William B. Eerdmans, 1996.

Meilaender, Gilbert C. *Body, Soul, and Bioethics*. Notre Dame, Ind.: University of Notre Dame Press, 1996.

Meilaender, Gilbert, ed. *Working: Its Meaning and Its Limits*. The Ethics of Everyday Life. Notre Dame, Ind.: University of Notre Dame Press, 2000.

Meilaender, Gilbert, and William Werpehowski, eds., *The Oxford Handbook of Theological Ethics*. Oxford and New York: Oxford University Press, 2005.

Messer, Neil. *SCM Studyguide to Christian Ethics*. London: SCM Press, 2006.

Messiaen, Olivier. *Quatuor pour la fin du temps*. 1940–1941.

Milbank, John. *The Word Made Strange: Theology, Language, Culture*. Oxford: Basil Blackwell, 1997.

Milbank, John, Catherine Pickstock, and Graham Ward, eds., *Radical Orthodoxy: A New Theology*. London and New York: Routledge, 1999.

Mill, John Stuart. *On Liberty and Other Essays*. Edited by John Gray. Oxford and New York: Oxford University Press, 1998.

Mill, John Stuart. *Utilitarianism*. Ed. with an Introduction by George Sher. Indianapolis: Hackett, 1979.

Morley, Janet. *All Desires Known*. Expanded edition. London: SPCK; Harrisburg, Penn.: Morehouse Publishing, 1992.

Morrison, Toni. *Beloved*. 1987; reprint, New York: New American Library, Signet Classics, 1991.

Morrison, Toni. *Song of Solomon*. New York: Alfred A. Knopf, 1977; reprint, New York: Penguin Books, Signet, 1978.

Murdoch, Iris. *The Sovereignty of Good*. 1970; reprint, London: ARK Paperbacks, 1985.

Murphy, Francesca Aran. *God Is Not a Story: Realism Revisited*. Oxford: Oxford University Press, 2007.

Murphy, Nancey, Mark Thiessen Nation, and Brad J. Kallenberg, eds., *Virtues and Practices in the Christian Tradition: Christian Ethics after MacIntyre*. Philadelphia, Penn.: Trinity Press International, 1997.

Newman, Elizabeth. *Untamed Hospitality: Welcoming God and Other Strangers*. The Christian Practice of Everyday Life. Grand Rapids, Mich.: Brazos Press, 2007.

Newman, John Henry. *An Essay on the Development of Christian Doctrine*. With a Foreword by Ian Ker. 6th edition. London, 1878; reprint, Notre Dame, Ind.: University of Notre Dame Press, 1989.

Niebuhr, H. Richard. *Christ and Culture*. New York: Harper and Row, 1951.

Niebuhr, Reinhold. *Moral Man and Immoral Society*. New York: Charles Scribner's Sons, 1932.

Niebuhr, Reinhold. *The Nature and Destiny of Man*. 2 vols. New York: Charles Scribner's Sons, 1941.

Northcott, Michael S. *The Environment and Christian Ethics*. Cambridge and New York: Cambridge University Press, 1996.

Northcott, Michael S. *Life after Debt: Christianity and Global Justice*. London: SPCK, 1999.

Nussbaum, Martha C. *The Fragility of Goodness: Luck and Ethics in Greek Tragedy and Philosophy*. Cambridge: Cambridge University Press, 1986.

Nygren, Anders. *Agape and Eros: A Study of the Christian Idea of Love*. Translated by Philip S. Watson. London: SPCK, 1953.

O'Connor, Flannery. *The Complete Stories*. With an Introduction by Robert Giroux. New York: Farrar, Straus, and Giroux, 1971.

O'Connor, Flannery. *The Habit of Being: Letters*. Edited, with an Introduction, by Sally Fitzgerald. New York: Farrar, Straus, and Giroux, 1979.

O'Donovan, Oliver. *Resurrection and Moral Order: An Outline for Evangelical Ethics*. 2nd edition. Grand Rapids, Mich.: William B. Eerdmans, 1994.

O'Donovan, Oliver and June Lockwood O'Donovan, eds., *From Irenaeus to Grotius: A Sourcebook in Christian Political Thought, 100–1625*. Grand Rapids, Mich.: William B. Eerdmans, 2000.

Orwell, George. *Down and Out in Paris and London*. London and New York: Penguin, 1962.

Orwell, George. *1984*. London: Secker and Warburg; New York: Harcourt, Brace, 1949.

Pinches, Charles. "Ecobooks: Journey through the Wilderness." In *Pro Ecclesia: A Journal of Catholic and Evangelical Theology* 6, no. 4 (Fall), 1997, pp. 488–495.

Pinches, Charles. "Proclaiming: Naming and Describing." In Hauerwas and Wells, eds., *The Blackwell Companion to Christian Ethics*.

Pinches, Charles. *Theology and Action: After Theory in Christian Ethics*. Grand Rapids: William B. Eerdmans, 2002.

Pincoffs, Edmund. "Quandary Ethics" (1971). In Hauerwas and MacIntyre, eds., *Revisions: Changing Perspectives in Moral Philosophy*. Notre Dame, Ind.: University of Notre Dame Press, 1983, pp. 92–112.

Pope, Stephen. "Reason and Natural Law." In Meilaender and Werpehowski, eds., *The Oxford Handbook of Theological Ethics*.

Porter, Jean. *The Recovery of Virtue: The Relevance of Aquinas for Christian Ethics*. Louisville, Ky. and London: Westminster John Knox Press, 1990.

Porter, Jean. "Virtue." In Meilaender and Werpehowski, eds., *The Oxford Handbook of Theological Ethics*.

Prejean, Sr. Helen. *Dead Man Walking: An Eyewitness Account of the Death Penalty in the United States*. New York: Vintage Books, 1994.

Quash, Ben. "Offering: Treasuring the Creation." In Hauerwas and Wells, eds., *The Blackwell Companion to Christian Ethics*.

Ramsey, Paul. *Basic Christian Ethics*. Chicago: University of Chicago Press, 1950.

Ramsey, Paul. *Fabricated Man: The Ethics of Genetic Control*. New Haven, Conn.: Yale University Press, 1970.

Ratatouille. Dir. Brad Bird and Jan Pinkava. Pixar Animation Studios, 2007.

Ray, David. "Thanks, Robert Frost." In *Music of Time: Selected and New Poems*. Omaha, Nebr.: The Backwaters Press, 2006.

Reno, R. R. "Participating: Working toward Worship." In Hauerwas and Wells, eds., *The Blackwell Companion to Christian Ethics*.

Rogers, Eugene F., Jr. *Sexuality and the Christian Body: Their Way into the Triune God*. Challenges in Contemporary Theology. Oxford: Blackwell Publishers, 1999.

Sack, Daniel. *Whitebread Protestants: Food and Religion in American Culture*. New York: St. Martin's Press, 2000.

Saliers, Don, and Emily Saliers. *A Song to Sing, a Life to Live: Reflections on Music as Spiritual Practice*. San Francisco, Calif.: Jossey-Bass, 2005.

Sayers, Dorothy. "Why Work?" in *Creed or Chaos? And Other Essays in Popular Theology*. London: Methuen, 1947.

Schlabach, Gerald W. "Breaking Bread: Peace and War." In Hauerwas and Wells, eds., *The Blackwell Companion to Christian Ethics*.

Schmemann, Alexander. *For the Life of the World: Sacraments and Orthodoxy*. 2nd edition. Crestwood, NY: St. Vladimir's Seminary Press, 1973.

Sedgwick, Timothy. *The Christian Moral Life: Practices of Piety*. Grand Rapids, Mich.: William B. Eerdmans; Cincinnati, Ohio: Forward Movement Publications, 1999.

Sendak, Maurice. *Where the Wild Things Are*. New York: Harper and Row, 1963.

Shelley, Mary Wollstonecraft. *Frankenstein, or The Modern Prometheus*. London, 1818; reprint, Oxford: Oxford University Press, 1998.

Shuman, Joel James. "Eating Together: "Friendship and Homosexuality." In Hauerwas and Wells, eds., *The Blackwell Companion to Christian Ethics*.

Shuman, Joel, and Brian Volck, *Reclaiming the Body: Christians and the Faithful Use of Modern Medicine*. The Christian Practice of Everyday Life. Grand Rapids, Mich.: Brazos Press, 2006.

Song, Robert. *Human Genetics: Fabricating the Future*. Ethics and Theology. London: Darton, Longman, and Todd; Cleveland, Ohio: Pilgrim Press, 2002.

Sophie Scholl: The Final Days (Sophie Scholl: Die letzten Tage). Dir. Marc Rothemund. Broth Film, 2005.

Spohn, William C. "Scripture." In Meilaender and Werpehowski, eds., *The Oxford Handbook of Theological Ethics*.

Stassen, Glen H., Diane M Yeager, and John Howard Yoder. *Authentic Transformation: A New Vision of Christ and Culture*. Nashville, Tenn.: Abingdon Press, 1996.

Steiner, George. *After Babel: Aspects of Language and Translation*. New York: Oxford University Press, 1975.

Stone, Bryan P. *Faith and Film: Theological Themes at the Cinema*. St. Louis, Mo.: Chalice Press, 2000.

Stoneking, Carol Bailey. "Receiving Communion: Euthanasia, Suicide, and Letting Die." In Hauerwas and Wells, eds., *The Blackwell Companion to Christian Ethics*.

Stranger Than Fiction. Dir. Marc Forster. Crick Pictures LLC, 2006.

Tanner, Kathryn. *Economies of Grace*. Minneapolis, Minn.: Fortress Press, 2005.

Tanner, Kathryn. "Eschatology and Ethics." In Meilaender and Werpehowski, eds., *The Oxford Handbook of Theological Ethics*.

Thomas Aquinas, St. *Summa Theologiae*. 60 vols. New York: McGraw-Hill; London: Eyre and Spottiswoode, 1963–1970.

Thomas Aquinas, St. *Treatise on the Virtues*. Notre Dame, Ind.: University of Notre Dame Press, 1984.

Tillich, Paul. *Dynamics of Faith*. New York: Harper and Row, 1957.

Vanhoozer, Kevin. *The Drama of Doctrine: A Canonical-Linguistic Approach to Christian Theology*. Louisville, Ky., and London: Westminster John Knox Press, 2005.

Vinke, Hermann. *The Short Life of Sophie Scholl*. New York: Harper and Row, 1984.

Volf, Miroslav. *Work in the Spirit: Toward a Theology of Work*. Eugene, Ore.: Wipf and Stock Publishers, 2001.

Wadell, Paul J. *Becoming Friends: Worship, Justice, and the Practice of Christian Friendship*. Grand Rapids, Mich.: Brazos Press, 2002.

Wadell, Paul J. *Friendship and the Moral Life*. Notre Dame, Ind.: University of Notre Dame Press, 1991.

Wadell, Paul. *The Primacy of Love: An Introduction to the Ethics of Thomas Aquinas*. New York: Paulist Press, 1992.

Wadell, Paul J. "Sharing Peace: Discipline and Trust." In Hauerwas and Wells, eds., *The Blackwell Companion to Christian Ethics*.

Waitress. Dir. Adrienne Shelly. Night and Day Pictures, 2007

Wannenwetsch, Bernd. "Ecclesiology and Ethics." In Meilaender and Werpehowski, eds., *The Oxford Handbook of Theological Ethics*.

Weaver, Darlene Fozard. "Death." In Meilaender and Werpehowski, eds., *The Oxford Handbook of Theological Ethics*.

Webb, Stephen H. *Good Eating*. The Christian Practice of Everyday Life. Grand Rapids, Mich.: Brazos Press, 2001.

Wells, Samuel. *God's Companions: Reimagining Christian Ethics*. Challenges in Contemporary Theology. Oxford and Malden, Mass.: Blackwell Publishers, 2006.

Wells, Samuel. *Improvisation: The Drama of Christian Ethics*. Grand Rapids, Mich.: Brazos Press, 2004.

Werpehowski, William. "Anders Nygren's *Agape and Eros*." In Meilaender and Werpehowski, eds., *The Oxford Handbook of Theological Ethics*.

The White Rose (Die Weiße Rose). Dir. Michael Verhoeven. Central Cinema Company Film, 1982.

Wicker, Brian. *The Story-Shaped World*. Notre Dame, Ind.: University of Notre Dame Press, 1975.

Williams, Rowan. *The Body's Grace: The 10th Michael Harding Memorial Address*. London: Lesbian and Gay Christian Movement, 1989. Reprinted in Eugene F. Rogers, Jr., ed., *Theology and Sexuality: Classic and Contemporary Readings*, Oxford and Malden, Mass.: Blackwell Publishers, 2002.

Williams, Rowan. *Tokens of Trust: An Introduction to Christian Belief*. Louisville, Ky.: Westminster John Knox Press, 2007.

Williams, Rowan. *Writing in the Dust*. Grand Rapids, Mich.: William B. Eerdmans, 2002.

Wilson, Jonathan R. *Gospel Virtues: Practicing Faith, Hope and Love in Uncertain Times*. Downers Grove, Ill.: InterVarsity Press, 1998.

Wirzba, Norman. *Living the Sabbath: Discovering the Rhythms of Rest and Delight*. The Christian Practice of Everyday Life. Grand Rapids, Mich.: Brazos Press, 2006.

Wood, Ralph C. *Flannery O'Connor and the Christ-Haunted South*. Grand Rapids, Mich.: William B. Eerdmans, 2004.

Wren, Brian. *What Language Shall I Borrow?* New York: Crossroad, 1990.

Yeager, D. M. "H. Richard Niebuhr's *Christ and Culture*." In Meilaender and Werpehowski, eds., *The Oxford Handbook of Theological Ethics*.

Yoder, John Howard. *For the Nations: Essays Evangelical and Public*. Grand Rapids, Mich.: William B. Eerdmans, 1997.

Yoder, John Howard. *The Politics of Jesus: Vicit Agnus Noster*. 2nd edition. Grand Rapids, Mich.: William B. Eerdmans, 1994.

Yoder, John Howard. *What Would You Do? A Serious Answer to a Standard Question*. Scottdale, Penn.: Herald Press, 1992.

Permissions

*I*ndex

abortion 3, 282, 299, 304
absolution 132–133, 138, 166, 209
abundance 33, 92, 191, 248, 295–296, 368
Acts of the Apostles 9, 71, 82, 109, 189, 278, 362
Adam, A. K. M. 102
Adam, Margaret 374
Adams, Nicholas 122, 189
Adams, Richard 64, 75
adultery 12, 178, 323, 341, 344
advertising 63, 152, 282, 327, 346
Aesop 88–89, 91
afterlife 260, 296, 371; *see also* eternal life; resurrection
agapē 161, 334, 347
agnosticism 54, 86
alienation 243, 286
allegiance(s) 49–59, 65, 74, 105, 113, 128–130, 210–211, 258–265, 270–276, 280, 310, 354, 368; conflicting 50, 265
ambiguity 66–67, 74, 86, 89–92, 101, 121, 135, 220, 245
Ambrose of Milan 247, 278
Amos 79
anger 7, 12, 78, 118, 133, 149, 270, 307, 324, 345
anoint(ed) 9, 13, 79, 174
Anscombe, G. E. M. 40
antinomianism 180–181; *see also* law
apocalyptic 67, 84, 371

apostle(s) 81–82, 113, 189, 276, 288–289, 307
Apostles' Creed 58, 113, 122–123, 184
appetite(s) 23, 130, 192, 195, 199, 240, 327, 368
Aquinas, St. Thomas 23, 40, 107, 158, 160, 165, 170–171, 175–176, 184, 256, 278–279, 285, 315
Aristotle 147–157, 165, 169, 176, 178, 205, 216–218, 225, 246, 256, 258, 279, 284, 315
art, artist(s) 25, 65, 67, 97, 100, 107, 159, 244, 253–255, 261, 346
ascension 114, 173
assisted suicide 2, 305; *see also* euthanasia
atheism 52, 54, 58, 342
Augustine of Hippo, St. 102, 158, 175, 184, 189, 193, 207, 246, 260–265, 278, 284, 369, 370, 374
authority 8, 13, 27, 93, 102, 176, 183, 257–258, 262, 269, 283
autonomy 16, 129

Babel 25–26, 40–41
Babylon 78–79, 259–260
Bach, J. S. 187–189
Bader-Saye, Scott 102, 143
Balthasar, Hans Urs von 122
baptism 80, 179, 193–194, 206, 251, 357
Barth, Karl 94

base communities 277
baths, bathing 193–194, 203
battle 21–22, 30, 67, 69, 78, 84, 137, 269, 278–279, 284, 371
beauty 62, 65, 128–130, 143, 187, 254, 259, 331, 340, 348–349, 352, 364–366, 368, 370
Beethoven, Ludwig van 96
Begbie, Jeremy 102, 189
belief *see* creeds; faith
Benne, Robert 284
Bentham, Jeremy 7, 211, 213
Berkman, John 122
Bible: navigating 9–10; *see also* scripture; *under* names of individual books
Biggar, Nigel 318
bioethics 270, 292–319, 347
birth 152, 222, 292–293, 296, 299–300, 329
blessing 77, 146, 172–174, 177, 241, 354
blood 173, 202, 275, 301, 337–338, 357, 370
bodies, bodiliness 23, 28, 46, 71–72, 87, 104, 114, 130, 145–147, 191–193, 199–204, 289, 290, 307, 320–346, 357; *see also* corporate body; embodiment; eucharistic body
body of Christ 40, 180, 262, 337, 357–358
Book of Common Prayer 146, 172
Bouma-Prediger, Steven 143, 360, 374
bravery *see* courage
bread 146, 163–164, 173–174, 186, 196–198, 202, 242, 337, 357
Breidenthal, Thomas 347
Brubeck, Dave 188–189
Buckley, Michael J. SJ 58
Budde, Michael 58, 284
burial 80, 194, 330

canon, canonical texts 69–71, 77, 94, 98, 102, 168, 169, 367
capital punishment 7, 140, 202, 273–274, 281, 297
cardinal virtues 153, 158–159, 278–279
Carter, Craig 122
Cartwright, Michael 225
Cavanaugh, William T. 40, 102, 184, 284
character 13, 21, 26–48, 52–62, 71–75, 109–112, 152–183, 217–224,

230–238, 245–249, 274–279, 301–302, 306–311, 320–327, 336–342, 359–367; formation of 31, 37–38, 55–56, 68, 288, 324; of God 157, 160, 166–171, 174, 182–183, 302, 336–337, 360, 364, 373
child(ren) 32–33, 37, 66–67, 72–73, 120, 131, 174, 177, 201–203, 231, 242, 280, 282, 304, 308, 332, 356
choice(s) 1–7, 17, 22–24, 31, 43–47, 66–69, 104–105, 110–111, 128, 148–149, 154, 159, 199, 262, 355
Christ *see* Jesus Christ
Christ and Culture 106–109, 121–123, 141
church(es) 16, 52, 55, 57, 63, 72–75, 98–99, 114, 117, 131, 133, 140, 145–146, 167–169, 180, 182, 186–187, 189, 209, 211, 215, 221, 222–223, 257, 261–263, 270, 276, 286–290, 323–324, 328, 346, 357–361
Cicero 156, 165
citizen(ship) 52, 63, 67, 221, 248, 260–281, 361; *see also* allegiance(s)
city of God 260–263, 269, 283–284
Clapp, Rodney 347
Clough, David 285
coma 21, 23, 300
combat *see* battle
command(s) 72, 117, 132, 216, 218
commandment(s) 72, 78, 137, 218, 276
companion(ship) 121, 196–198; *see also* friendship
compassion 60, 174, 304, 334
competition 21–22, 33–34, 72–74, 154, 210, 271, 364, 373
Cone, James 291
confession (of sin) 111, 117–119, 131–132, 138, 166, 273, 307
congregation(s) 63, 146, 171–174, 186–187, 209, 215–216
conscience 30, 99
consequences 12, 23–26, 28, 231, 240–241
Constantine 140, 261
contracts 234, 304, 353
contradiction 99, 162–164, 363, 367
conversion 9, 82, 261, 277
convictions 141, 161, 363
Corinthians, First Epistle to 83, 158, 161, 215, 290, 296, 310, 329–331, 357–358, 362

corporate body 356–359, 364, 373
corruption 87, 95, 192, 311
costs and benefits 22–25, 30, 154, 235
courage 30, 36, 153, 156–159, 169, 221–222, 245, 248, 273, 278–281, 284, 303, 360
covenant(s) 173, 337, 353–355, 362, 373
creation 11, 51, 75, 77, 85–88, 93–96, 130–131, 171–176, 182, 188, 191–193, 206, 241–254, 293–295, 312–315, 329, 350–374
creed(s) 112–114, 122, 161, 186–187, 270, 297, 310
crime 6, 28, 232, 280, 297
Cunningham, David S. 75, 122, 165, 184, 189, 207, 256, 318, 347

death 22–25, 77, 83, 129, 141, 151–152, 173, 194, 220, 222, 278–82, 292–298, 302–303, 305–306, 309–317, 328–331; of Christ, 9, 71, 77–82, 114, 173, 178–180, 187–188, 197–198, 202, 251, 356
decisions 2–7, 14–17, 21–26, 29, 33, 36, 38–44, 60, 67–68, 77, 91, 103–104, 110, 113, 135–136, 147–148, 153, 169, 192, 203, 211, 217, 220, 232–235, 241, 258, 264, 272, 282, 292–298, 303–312, 314, 316–318, 321–323, 341–342, 351, 356; difficult 15, 21, 24, 43, 192, 293, 316
democracy 43–44, 50, 52, 213, 264–265, 269, 272
denominations 98, 112, 169, 171, 206, 363; see also church(es)
dependence 16–17, 21, 92, 114, 202, 204, 311, 348, 351–354; on God 92, 354
Descartes, René 108, 122
desire(s) 87, 129, 159, 161, 170–171, 192, 198–199, 239, 242, 245, 252–253, 268–269, 304–307, 311–313, 320–328, 332–335, 341–345, 347, 352, 360
destiny, destination 110, 143, 349, 366, 370–373
determinism 104, 121
devotion 6, 38–39, 55, 78, 129, 140, 244, 253, 261, 269–271, 303, 306, 310, 361

dichotomies 3, 108–109, 135
Dickens, Charles 29, 40, 249
dilemma(s) 21–22, 76, 90, 220
discipline 13, 21, 53, 69, 118, 147, 191, 192, 206, 211, 242, 285, 324
dismissal 208–209, 215–216, 224, 343
disposition(s) 12, 31, 81, 111, 120, 139, 149, 167, 170, 177, 180, 220–221, 263, 266, 270, 275, 295–296, 303, 315, 323, 326, 338–340, 367, 373
diversity 195, 356, 357, 364
division of labor 182, 243, 253
Dixie Chicks 1, 4, 17, 310
domination 88, 248, 354, 356
dominion 88, 354–355, 362
Donne, John 200, 207
dualism 108–109
Duffy, Michael 347
duty 7, 138, 201, 213, 279

"earthly city" 260–263, 269, 283
Eastern Orthodoxy 71
eating 49, 92, 128–129, 159, 166, 194–203, 207, 236, 242, 245, 247, 290, 307, 326, 329, 338, 347, 356, 362, 374; see also meals
economy, economics 16–17, 21–26, 33–34, 40, 47, 53, 74, 79, 92, 98, 107, 113, 116, 118, 154–155, 177, 201, 221, 229–239, 243, 245, 247–255, 258, 260, 268, 276–277, 314; see also abundance; exchange; scarcity
either/or structures 1, 3, 4, 15, 17
elections 221, 258, 281–282
Eliot, T. S. 233, 256, 369, 374
embodiment 96–99, 111, 129, 131, 135, 169–170, 204, 214, 223–224, 275–280, 303, 329, 333, 335, 340–346, 373; see also bodies
embryo 299, 300, 304
emotions 28–29, 78, 97, 100, 139, 151, 154, 189, 197–199, 213, 247, 252, 292, 309, 322, 328–329, 333, 336
employment 17, 37, 40, 149, 164, 221, 230–234, 240, 258, 289
end: of life 299–301, 318; of the law 11, 13, 176, 180, 208, 215, 275; of the world 84, 371–372; of time 128, 188, 368
Enlightenment 154, 168, 176, 211, 212, 214, 309, 368

entertainment 23, 37, 38, 61, 94, 241, 268
environment 10, 16, 21–22, 24, 88, 222, 237–238, 240, 290, 348–374
Ephesians 275–276, 312, 333, 361
epistle(s) 9, 56, 83, 252, 288
eschatology 371, 374
estrangement 83, 135, 136–139
eternal life 114, 152, 205, 296–297
eternity 267, 331, 335, 369
ethos 26; *see also* character
eucharistic body 173, 202, 357
eucharistic prayer 171–174, 182–183, 186, 194
eudaimonia 150–152, 216; *see also* happiness
euthanasia 305, 318–319
evolution 93, 350, 351, 373
excellences of character *see* virtues
exchange 116, 154–155, 201–206, 230, 234–238, 247, 305
Exodus 10, 77, 92, 131, 270, 307

faith 52, 73, 77, 84, 112–117, 161, 211, 218, 264–265, 270–271, 297, 303, 309–314, 367, 373
faithfulness 160–161, 174, 221, 269–272, 274, 277, 281, 284, 309, 310, 353
Fall, the 127–131, 142, 178, 242, 354–356, 370–371
family 39, 42, 47, 60–61, 85, 104, 131, 198, 201, 272, 276, 289, 323
fellowship 194–199, 203, 205, 287, 290, 337
fetus 299–300
finite freedom 104–105, 121–122, 170, 361
flesh 82, 87, 104, 114, 162, 192, 217, 275, 294, 302, 327, 329–331, 334, 337–338, 363
Fletcher, Joseph 7, 18
flood 75, 131, 293, 355, 370
food 117, 130, 191, 194–205, 235–237, 248, 290, 295–296, 326, 354–355, 362–363
Ford, David 123, 290–291
foreknowledge 7, 24
forgiveness 16, 90, 114, 117, 119, 121, 127, 130–138, 142–143, 152, 173, 194, 252, 275, 344, 361
formation, moral 16, 32, 34, 36–49, 52, 57, 63, 66–68, 71–72, 97–98, 155, 187, 198, 209, 211, 216, 218–219, 286–289
fortitude *see* courage
Fowl, Stephen 75
free exercise of religion 264–265, 272
free will 88, 104, 121, 161, 192, 307
freedom 26, 31, 34, 77, 104–105, 121, 131, 170, 206, 252, 264–265, 270, 272, 274, 284, 307, 355, 361
friendship 39, 148, 189, 199–205, 216–219, 224–225, 316; with God 217
fruits of the Spirit 158–160, 221, 252, 275, 310, 333, 360–361
"fulfilled and fulfilling life" 151–152, 162–163, 205, 322

Gadamer, Hans-Georg 123
Garden: of Eden 128, 130–131, 242, 329, 354, 368–372; of the New Jerusalem 368–372
gathering communities 38–39, 42–45, 54–63, 75, 201, 210
gender 118, 177, 326, 344
generosity 30, 33, 90, 152–156, 160–161, 169–170, 201, 210, 264, 334
Genesis 10–11, 25, 77, 87–88, 93–94, 118, 128–131, 136, 175, 188, 191–192, 204, 241–242, 250, 275, 295, 307, 329, 350–355, 361, 368–369
Gentiles 275
gentleness 153, 160, 333, 338–344, 346, 363
global culture industries 267–269, 280, 284
gnosticism 86–87
God: agency of 175; character of 131, 161–162, 167–177, 293, 307, 361, 363; nature of 109, 160, 168; sovereignty of 116, 141; understanding of 15, 51, 56–57, 162, 357, 363; work of 16, 70, 151, 163, 170–182, 241, 296; *see also* Trinity
gods 51–54, 57, 86–87, 113, 115, 191, 206, 241, 264, 270
good, the 13, 29, 54, 131, 155, 161, 167, 172, 212, 233–234, 240, 252, 366
good habits 47, 63, 100, 134, 152, 169–171, 183, 199, 205, 371

good life 12–13, 60, 73, 92, 111, 129, 149, 152, 153, 205, 232, 234, 321
Good Samaritan, parable of 81, 90–91, 96
Gospels 9–10, 69, 79–82, 89
governments 12, 53, 93–94, 139–141, 177, 183, 221, 232, 235, 255, 257–284
grace 83, 167, 177, 179, 182, 193, 203, 206, 235, 293–295, 314–317, 367, 371
Grandberg-Michaelson, Wes 374
gratitude 78, 195, 245, 293, 303, 340
Greene, Graham 341, 347
Gregory the Great 278
grief 78, 294, 306, 317, 339, 340, 343
Grotius, Hugo 176, 184

habits 31–49, 97, 100, 130, 134, 139, 145–148, 152–153, 167–171, 183–184, 196–200, 239–246, 254–255, 306–311, 315–318
happiness 147–156, 163–164, 176, 204–205, 216, 240, 252, 254, 309, 322, 325, 331, 333, 366
Hauerwas, Stanley 18, 41, 58, 75, 102, 122–123, 165, 207, 225, 256, 285, 318–319, 347, 374
Haydn, Franz Joseph 189
Hays, Richard 184
healing 120, 129, 133, 152, 235, 304, 312, 329, 368, 370
health 16, 17, 22, 47, 48, 74, 94, 149, 159, 237, 272, 277, 293–318, 331, 358, 370
heavenly banquet 205, 372
Hebrew (language) 9, 77, 78, 117, 160, 275, 339, 360
Hebrews, Epistle to the 161
hero(ism) 51, 64–65, 67, 90, 341
Hobbes, Thomas 93–94, 102, 128, 143, 276
holiness 171, 183, 192, 223
Holy Spirit 56, 82, 114–115, 159–162, 173–174, 179–183, 189, 250–251, 294, 356–357
homosexuality *see* sexuality
hope 36, 73, 83, 113, 117, 136–137, 161, 222, 277, 360, 367–374
hospitality 61, 291
household 37, 77, 120, 230, 231, 276, 287, 347; of God 276

Hugo, Victor 176, 249
human action 1, 6, 23, 27, 40, 128, 147–148, 170, 240, 266, 336, 342
human will 169, 278, 303, 307, 311, 315, 317
humility 99, 339, 340, 343–346
hunger 88, 117
hymns and hymnody 149–150, 185–188

identity 16, 48–49, 59, 61–65, 71–74, 93, 111, 139, 157, 162, 195, 200, 233, 243, 290, 337, 343–344
idolatry 73, 129, 351, 353
illness 206, 222, 231, 253, 272, 279, 292, 294, 302–303, 306–308, 311, 318
imagination 64, 86, 108, 109, 186
imitation 133, 177, 181, 186, 202, 204, 304; of Christ 177, 181
immortality 114, 330, 331
improvisation 41, 99, 100, 102, 121, 135, 181, 365
incarnation 69, 99, 162, 173, 177, 181, 192, 250, 334, 356, 357
independence 17, 38, 44, 67, 129, 163, 168, 262
individualism 16, 17, 38, 92, 153–154, 162, 250, 252, 287, 311, 332
inspiration, divine 70, 82
instinct 23, 159, 169, 175, 182, 192, 239, 240
intellect 23, 112, 169, 182, 191–192, 278, 315, 317, 327–328, 330
interdependence 163, 364, 373
internet 267, 290, 325
interpretation 10, 16, 27, 66–71, 75, 77, 79, 85–89, 96–101, 105, 109, 121, 154, 158, 181, 188–189, 314, 323, 371–372
intimacy 79, 199–200, 206, 207, 321–322, 335–340
Islam 52, 192, 241, 265
isolation 16–17, 27, 38, 48–49, 163, 192, 250–253, 336–337
Israel(ites) 72, 77–79, 83, 92, 136, 174, 196, 259, 270, 329, 354–355; *see also* Jews; Judaism

Jacobson, David 285
jazz 100, 189
Jenson, Robert 207
Jerusalem 259, 368, 369, 372

Jesus Christ 9, 12–15, 40, 51, 56, 69–72, 77–83, 89–92, 98–101, 106–109, 114, 121–123, 132, 138–147, 150–152, 162, 173–182, 189, 194–195, 215–218, 248–251, 260–262, 270, 275–276, 285, 294–297, 307, 319, 323, 329, 335–339, 344–345, 356–358, 361–362

Jews 69, 77, 79, 83, 140, 160, 175, 177, 218, 241, 259, 272, 275

John the Baptist 80

John of the Cross 189

John, First Letter of 83, 119

John, Gospel of 10, 82, 105, 140, 178, 180, 218, 248, 278, 296, 336, 338, 344–346, 357

Johnson, Kelly S. 123

Jonah 132, 137

Jones, L. Gregory 75, 143, 184, 225

joy 78, 160, 173, 199, 203–205, 340

Judaism 8–14, 51–55, 69, 73, 77–79, 87, 131, 138, 140, 157, 160, 185, 192, 195, 241, 251, 266, 271, 275, 321, 328–329, 333, 350–351, 362

Julian of Norwich 367, 374

justice 79, 115, 153, 158, 166, 178, 221, 225, 245–248, 251, 254–256, 277, 279, 332, 360

justification 87, 179, 353

Kallenberg, Brad 40, 41

Kant, Immanuel 7, 18, 108, 123, 211–213

Keillor, Garrison 61, 75

Kenneson, Philip 41, 58, 123, 165, 225, 256, 291, 347

killing 3, 10, 12, 65, 78, 93, 118, 129, 131, 132, 137, 157, 272, 276, 306, 318, 355, 363

kindness 81, 153, 156, 160, 222, 279, 339, 360–363, 367, 370, 373

King, Martin Luther, Jr. 79, 288–289, 291

kings of Israel 78, 137, 329

Kingsolver, Barbara 33

labor 17, 36, 182, 198, 236, 237, 241–243, 248, 249, 253, 369

Lamb of God 186, 368

Lash, Nicholas 58, 102, 114, 123, 184, 285

law 8–14, 18, 27–28, 46, 72, 81, 83, 118, 132, 135, 175–176, 180–184, 213–215, 220, 233, 272, 275, 276, 288, 294, 321, 323, 344, 355, 362; eternal 176; letter of 12, 81; positive 8, 10, 12; see also end of the law; natural law

legislation 8, 10, 12, 28, 214, 232, 281–282, 321

Leviticus, Levitical 8, 131–132, 329, 355

lifeboat ethics 21–24, 40, 44, 90, 110, 219–220, 321; see also quandaries

liturgy 15–16, 111–112, 121, 127, 146, 168, 171, 175, 182, 186–187; of the Eucharist 16, 121, 127, 171; of the Word 16, 111, 127

Lord 25, 56, 78, 83, 131, 146, 172–173, 186, 202, 209, 271, 354, 356, 368

Lord's Prayer 134

Lord's Supper 194

love 7, 10, 55, 66, 72–73, 140, 160–161, 164, 173–174, 178, 193, 216, 218, 222, 246, 271, 279, 310–311, 333–336, 340–342, 346, 354, 360–361, 365, 366, 372; divine 161, 193, 335, 374; see also agapē

loyalty 73, 161, 269–274, 310; see also allegiance(s)

Luke, Gospel of 79–82, 92, 132, 178, 210, 215, 296, 340, 357, 361

lust 12, 323

Luther, Martin 245

Lysaught, M. Therese 318

McCarthy, David Matzko 347

McIntosh, Mark 347

MacIntyre, Alasdair 41, 58, 225

magnanimity 153, 178, 245

Mark, Gospel of 10, 26, 65, 77–80, 87, 105, 118–120, 128, 157, 164, 182, 205, 210, 215, 243, 263, 281, 296, 335, 337–338, 347, 357, 361–362

marketing 267, 268

marriage 2, 10, 50, 60, 75, 162, 206, 310, 321–323, 333–336, 340–341, 344, 346

Marshall, Bruce 184

martyrs 68, 279

Marx, Karl 243, 256

mass 185–187, 189, 194

material order 87, 192–193, 206
Matthew, Gospel of 10, 12, 79, 80, 82, 105, 132, 138, 140, 210, 271, 295, 323, 357
meals 16, 60, 77, 80, 148, 193–206, 215, 236–237, 249, 268, 290, 337, 357
media 34, 69, 74, 94, 210, 220, 268, 352
medical ethics 55, 149, 162, 221, 232, 233, 271, 290, 292–320, 327
meekness 81, 339, 340, 343, 344, 356
Meeks, M. Douglas 256
Meilaender, Gilbert 18, 102, 123, 165, 184, 225, 256, 284, 318, 319, 347, 374
memory 33, 89, 173–174, 186, 187, 197, 273, 330, 347, 366
mercy 36, 83, 131–135, 173, 178, 186, 260, 339, 361
Messer, Neil 18
Messiaen, Olivier 188–190
Messiah 9, 70, 79, 174, 187; *see also* Jesus Christ
Milbank, John 14, 18, 102, 284, 374
Mill, John Stuart 7, 18, 211, 213
mimesis 133, 137–138, 143
ministry 79, 80, 132, 140, 206, 231, 357
"missing the mark" 118, 120, 215
mission 22, 81, 208, 209, 215, 277
modernity 43, 52, 107, 108, 350
money 22, 30, 35, 53, 73, 145–149, 154, 234–239, 253–254, 264
moral action 1, 23–25, 219
moral relativism 45, 57, 212, 214, 215, 224
Morley, Janet 347
Morrison, Toni 61, 75
murder *see* killing
Murdoch, Iris 58
Murphy, Francesca 102
Murphy, Nancey, 41
music 16, 55, 78, 96–100, 102, 107, 144, 162, 185–190, 202, 231, 244, 254, 283, 308, 309, 315, 363, 364, 373
Muslims *see* Islam
mutuality 71, 77, 92, 127, 162, 204, 217, 287, 336–338, 340–342, 353

narratives 9, 32–45, 55–59, 62–76, 80–111, 114, 118–121, 127–142, 155–162, 166–168, 174, 183–187, 191, 197–199, 202, 209–214, 218–219, 223–224, 234, 241, 245, 248, 264, 267–269, 286, 288, 295, 302, 306–307, 324, 329–331, 346–356, 360, 363, 367–369, 372–373; implicit 33, 63, 85
Nation, Mark 41
nation(-state) 34, 53, 63, 66–67, 73, 94, 211–214, 221, 255–261, 268–283, 365–366
natural law 8, 175, 176, 181, 183, 184, 213, 225
Naziism 98, 188, 215, 272–274
New Testament 9, 56, 79, 83, 84, 141, 184, 246, 270, 275, 278, 361, 362
newcomers 59–62, 65–66
Newman, Elizabeth 291
Newman, John Henry 101–102
Nicene Creed 113, 132, 186
Niebuhr, H. Richard 106–109, 123, 141, 261
Niebuhr, Reinhold 141, 143, 178
nonviolence 127, 130, 135, 139–143, 152, 166, 178, 214, 363
Northcott, Michael 256, 374
nourishment 34, 117, 146, 174, 178, 191, 195, 198, 204, 205, 209, 240, 300, 301, 326
Nussbaum, Martha 165
Nygren, Anders 334, 347

obedience 12, 30, 52, 102, 120, 147, 173, 176, 272, 345
obligation 201–203, 206, 229–231, 234–235, 239, 242, 255, 277, 279, 353
O'Connor, Flannery 302–303, 318–319
O'Donovan, Oliver 181, 184
offering 16, 88, 116, 138, 145–147, 157, 161, 163–165, 173–174, 201–202, 209–210, 302, 357
Old Testament 9, 69, 77, 79, 270, 302, 307, 353, 360
oppression 129, 348–349
Orwell, George 214, 225, 248–249, 256, 265
outsiders 59, 61, 66, 90, 112, 193, 200, 215

pain 129, 242, 279, 298, 301–306, 309, 313, 314, 329, 336, 339, 340, 343, 370, 372; *see also* suffering

parables 73, 89–90, 101, 132
parents 39, 47, 63, 64, 66, 77, 113, 120, 134, 149, 201, 203, 300, 304, 308, 310, 311, 353
participation 17, 35, 46, 162, 199, 217, 222, 251, 333, 336–338, 340–342, 347
particularity 162, 163, 221, 245, 250, 251, 254, 256, 337
Passion narrative 80, 82, 185
Passover 78, 195–197
patience 36, 160, 171, 222, 245, 248, 300–311, 318, 324, 360
Paul the Apostle, St. 9, 12–13, 71, 82–83, 98, 119, 160–161, 175–176, 179, 215, 218, 252, 275–276, 288–290, 296, 312–313, 329–331, 333, 336, 357–358, 361, 364
peace 56, 66, 73, 93, 115, 117, 137, 139, 150, 151, 160, 209, 269, 275–277, 285, 356, 369, 370
peaceable kingdom 354–356
peaceableness 221, 269–270, 273–281, 284, 360
peacemaking 16, 121, 139, 276
performance 71, 85, 96–103, 106, 111, 121, 135, 148, 180, 185, 209, 230, 253, 282, 295, 308
persecution 81, 84, 140, 260, 272
person of Christ 56, 108, 177, 296
personhood 328–330
persuasion 4, 43, 70, 105, 140, 214, 216, 270, 290, 331, 332
Philemon, Epistle to 98
Pinches, Charles 41, 102, 165, 225, 318, 374
Pincoffs, Edmund 41
Plato 153, 157–160
pleasure 10, 34–36, 44, 149–152, 201–205, 217, 240, 249, 278, 322, 333–335, 353, 372
politics 16–17, 26, 40, 48–52, 51, 57–58, 74, 93, 102, 107, 113, 116, 118, 128, 133, 140–144, 165, 177, 184, 202, 214, 220, 222, 238, 257–285, 301
polyphony 162, 189, 222, 360, 363–367, 373
Pope, Stephen 184, 225
Porter, Jean 165
poverty 29, 79, 123, 173, 249, 356, 361
powers and principalities 312–313, 326; see also structures and systems

practical wisdom 153, 158–159, 181–182, 222, 306, 314–316, 318
practices 15–16, 34–65, 68, 71, 74, 79, 84, 88, 90, 98, 100, 107, 109, 111, 113, 115, 119, 121, 127–158, 162, 165–168, 178, 183–192, 198–214, 218–225, 233–234, 241, 245, 247, 255–260, 264–269, 284–290, 305–309, 312, 317, 324, 330, 347, 349, 360, 363, 367, 373
praise 53, 73, 146, 156–157, 171–173, 185–186, 242, 279, 341, 360, 372; see also worship
prayer 71, 78, 81–82, 111, 115–117, 121–123, 132–140, 146, 166, 171–174, 182–189, 194, 242, 265, 286, 312, 323–325, 327, 339
preaching 11, 80–83, 94–97, 101, 137, 179, 189, 288; see also proclamation
pregnancy 3, 282, 299
Prejean, Sr. Helen 133–134, 144
principles 6–8, 13–18, 44–45, 54, 72, 90–93, 135, 147, 154, 216, 217, 220, 316, 360
privacy 27, 38, 52, 73, 153, 169, 199, 200, 222, 244, 265, 274, 320, 321, 324, 325, 332
proclamation 16, 85, 97, 102–103, 121, 131–132, 166, 173, 276–277
procreation 332
Prodigal Son, parable of the 81
profession of faith 111–113, 116, 121
professional ethics 231–234
prophets 9, 78–79, 131, 137, 160, 173–174, 182, 276, 329, 356
Protestant(ism) 70, 71, 98, 146, 243
Proverbs 78
providence 104, 117, 204, 293–298, 305, 314–317, 339, 367–368, 371
prudence 159, 314, 315; see also practical wisdom
Psalms 78, 131, 160, 259, 278, 327, 355
punishment 28–29, 84, 122, 131–133, 202, 266, 281, 295–297, 301

quandaries 21–22, 40–44, 90, 110, 177, 293; see also lifeboat ethics
Quash, Ben 165, 374

race and racism 47, 98, 118–119, 177, 215, 218, 281, 288
Ramsey, Paul 18, 318

rationality 3, 24, 112, 113, 167, 168, 212–214, 311
Ray, David 136–137, 144, 374
receiving, reception 138, 199–204, 206, 209, 210, 300, 319, 323, 367
reconciliation 108, 119, 122, 127, 130, 135, 137–139, 142–143, 152, 174, 178, 206, 209, 210, 275–276, 298
redemption 101, 109, 117, 129, 171, 173, 175, 177–179, 181–183, 252, 275, 302–303, 309, 313, 373
re-engineering 294, 304
regret 129, 134–137, 272, 355, 366
remembrance 16, 32, 49, 61, 64, 89, 145, 171, 173, 174, 183, 198, 266
Reno, R. R. 256
repentance 81–82, 103, 137, 307
responsibility 23, 147, 163, 196, 200, 282, 322, 338, 352, 353, 355
resurrection 9, 71, 77, 79–83, 114–115, 152, 173–174, 178–179, 182, 184, 194, 251, 293–294, 296–298, 307, 314–317, 329–331, 335, 356; of the body, 114, 115, 296–297, 330–331, 357
revelation 80, 167–169, 173
Revelation to John, 9, 84, 128, 188, 259, 275, 368
revenge 131, 133, 137, 153, 178
rhythm 187, 188, 197, 229
right relationship 77, 83, 117–120, 129–134, 136–137, 143, 242–246, 254, 275, 295, 313, 368, 372–373
rights 288, 365
rites 146, 192–194, 197, 202, 206, 209, 337
rituals 63, 77, 138, 146, 192, 194–197
Rogers, Eugene F., Jr. 347
role-models 178, 217
Roman Catholicism 70–71, 146, 188, 299, 302
Roman Empire 82, 84, 140, 260, 261, 289
Romans, Epistle to the 13, 83, 119, 175, 179, 252, 329
rule-breaking 28, 117, 120, 122, 132, 233–234, 266
rules 7–8, 11–14, 18, 21, 27–31, 44–46, 90–91, 104, 110, 117–122, 130–140, 147, 173, 180–181, 220, 223, 232–235, 242–243, 257, 260, 266, 269, 281, 314–317, 321, 329–332, 342–346, 355, 363

Sabbath 241, 291
Sack, Daniel 207
sacraments 192–194, 203, 206–207, 285
sacrifice 6, 24, 65, 146–147, 164, 173, 191, 202, 264, 310
saints 68, 133, 223, 276
Saliers, Don 190
Saliers, Emily 190
salvation 83, 108, 173, 178, 179, 182, 291, 294, 355
same-sex relationships 2, 322, 340; see also sexuality
Sayers, Dorothy 256
scarcity 22, 33–34, 92, 308; see also abundance; economy; exchange
Schlabach, Gerald 285
Schmemann, Alexander 207, 285
Scholl, Sophie 273, 285
science 93, 154, 167, 232, 276, 349–351, 372
scripts 86, 96–99, 365, 372
scripture 68–72, 75, 77, 79, 95–99, 102, 114, 160, 168, 194, 351; see also under individual names of biblical books
Seattle 356–366, 378
sectarianism 123, 215, 225
secularity 53, 102, 107, 244, 261, 262, 284
Sedgwick, Timothy 144
self-control 159–160, 166, 221, 245, 248, 251–255, 278–279, 360
self-deception 12, 14, 119
self-gratification 252
self-reliance 17, 34
Sendak, Maurice 33, 41
sermon see preaching; proclamation
Sermon on the Mount 80; see also Matthew, Gospel of
sex 2, 28, 63, 74, 78, 137, 199, 218–219, 222, 290, 293, 300, 320–347; see also sexuality
sexism 119
sexuality 10, 74, 207, 320–347
Shakespeare, William 96, 186
Shelley, Mary Wollstonecraft 318
Shuman, Joel 207, 312, 319, 347
sickness see illness
sin 83, 108, 111, 114, 117–122, 132, 138, 173, 178–179, 194, 209–210, 242, 243, 252, 328, 331, 344

slavery 7, 66, 67, 98, 136, 174, 195, 218, 249, 252, 288, 293, 333, 357, 365

socio-economic class 25, 28, 47, 218, 248

soldiers 21–22, 30, 269, 278, 284

Sophocles 51

soul 73, 87, 114, 145–147, 149–151, 163, 202, 271, 279, 327–328, 330, 334, 342–343

Spafford, Horatio 150–151

spheres of life (or action) 63, 74, 105–106, 219–223, 229, 233, 245, 269, 280, 286, 289, 317, 359, 360

Spinoza, Baruch 309

spiritual body 331, 336

Spohn, William C. 102

sporting events 37, 42–43, 49, 54

Stassen, Glen H. 123

Steiner, George 41

stewardship 88, 354–356, 362

Stiltner, Brian 285

Stone, Bryan P. 207

Stoneking, Carol Bailey 319

stories *see* narratives

storytelling 32, 61–65, 95, 164, 219, 284, 344

strangers *see* newcomers; outsiders

structures and systems 118, 267, 313, 327

suffering 16–17, 27, 30, 75, 79–80, 114, 115, 138, 141, 222, 249, 253, 272–273, 279, 297–299, 301–303, 305–307, 309, 311, 313, 317, 318, 329, 347, 358–359; *see also* pain

sustaining, sustenance 45, 61, 63, 109, 117, 129, 131, 138, 149–152, 198, 204, 294, 348, 351–352, 373

table-fellowship 195, 290

taking (an action) for granted 30–31, 103, 134, 202, 240, 277, 316, 322

Tanner, Kathryn 256, 374

taxation 4, 8, 264, 268, 339

technology 14, 16, 232, 266–267, 271, 309, 313, 315, 318, 349

television 33–37, 94, 148, 268

temperance 153, 158–160, 221, 278, 279; *see also* self-control

temptation 106, 131, 179, 181, 260, 279, 311, 313, 345

thanksgiving 16, 78, 116, 121, 146

theological virtues 160–161, 310, 370

"thin line" 1, 4–5, 10, 17, 38, 108, 135, 209

Tillich, Paul 58

transcendence 108, 117, 162, 297

Trinitarian virtues 158, 162, 357

Trinity 56, 109, 158, 162, 165–166, 175, 177, 179, 182, 184, 188–189, 221, 222, 225, 251, 256, 333, 336–338, 347, 357, 363–364

truth 119, 153, 172, 279, 327

unity of the virtues 156, 164, 223, 245, 255, 269, 359, 360, 364

universality 7, 44, 83, 135, 194, 211, 214, 224, 235, 268

utilitarianism 7, 18, 212; *see also* Bentham, Jeremy; Mill, John Stuart

value 23, 34, 153–155, 235–237, 330

values 51, 58, 153–155

Vanhoozer, Kevin 102

vices 155, 215, 310

violence 27, 34, 133, 137–143, 214, 248, 269, 274–278, 284, 345, 354, 370

virtues 40–41, 58, 145, 152–171, 175, 177–184, 199, 204, 209–225, 236, 238–239, 245–258, 264, 269–284, 293, 298, 303, 306–310, 313–318, 321–323, 332–346, 357, 359–364, 367, 370–373; content of 153–157, 167; cultivation of 58, 123, 155–159, 165–170, 205, 256, 291, 332, 347, 371; table of 157, 163, 212, 279, 360; *see also* unity of the virtues

"visible words" 193, 206–207

vision of God 290, 372

vocation 133, 243, 244

Volck, Brian 312, 319

Volf, Miroslav 256

voting 66, 221, 257, 258, 280–284, 359

vulnerability 199, 277, 306, 320–321, 329, 330, 338, 340–343

Wadell, Paul 184, 225, 285

Wannenwetsch, Bernd 18

wealth 16, 79, 149, 169, 210, 237, 248, 251, 271, 295

weapons 11, 67, 139–140, 142

Weaver, Darlene Fozard 319

Webb, Stephen H. 207, 374

Wells, Samuel 18, 41, 58, 102, 122–123, 165, 207, 225, 256, 285, 291, 295, 318–319, 347, 374
Werpehowski, William 18, 102, 123, 165, 184, 225, 284, 319, 347, 374
wickedness 11, 30, 95, 129, 132, 312, 328, 361
Wicker, Brian 75
Williams, Rowan 123, 345, 347
Willimon, William H. 285
Wilson, Jonathan 165
wine 146, 163, 173–174, 189, 197–198, 202, 296, 337, 357
Wirzba, Norman 291
wisdom *see* practical wisdom; prudence
withdrawal from the world 105–106, 215–216, 257, 281, 357

witness 82, 216, 223, 279, 283, 294, 350, 359
Wood, Ralph C. 319
Word of God 82, 250, 363
work 22, 229–256
worship 15–18, 41, 54–58, 70–73, 78, 94, 111–113, 119–122, 127–133, 138–146, 163, 171–172, 183–187, 206–210, 215–225, 233, 241–242, 256, 264–265, 270, 286–289, 313, 323, 353, 368, 372
Wren, Brian 190

Yeager, Diane M. 123
Yoder, John Howard 123, 141–142, 144, 178, 285
York, Tripp 165

Related titles from Routledge

Studying Christian Spirituality
David B. Perrin

Readers looking for a comprehensive introduction to the contemporary study of Christian spirituality will be well served by David Perrin's *Studying Christian Spirituality*. This volume offers an ecumenical, interdisciplinary, and thoroughly referenced guide to both method and content in this emerging academic discipline. Perrin knows the issues and the literature as well as anyone in the field, and he clearly writes out of his rich experience of creative teaching and spiritual practice.

Arthur Holder, Dean and Professor of Christian Spirituality,
Graduate Theological Union, USA

David Perrin has written a meticulously constructed introduction to the study of Christian spirituality and its methodologies. What is particularly new, and makes the book required reading, is the way it supplements more familiar biblical, historical, and theological approaches by concentrating on the development of a constructive conversation with the human and social sciences. Perrin is a sure-footed guide, clear, positive, and thorough yet at the same time alert to pitfalls and critical questions.

Philip Sheldrake, Professor, Department of Theology and Religion,
University of Durham

Studying Christian Spirituality is the ideal introduction for students wishing to discover how spirituality can be understood beyond the conventional boundaries that religions have established.

In nine chapters the book includes discussion of a wide variety of issues and questions, including:

  definitions of spirituality
  context
  God
  anthropology
  history
  text

human–spiritual development
spiritual practice
criticism

David B. Perrin explains clearly the traditional relationships between Christian spirituality and theology and history. He also proposes greater connections with the human sciences, such as philosophy, psychology, phenomenology, and sociology, and reshapes the classical approaches to Christian spirituality, its texts, practices, and experience.

Studying Christian Spirituality will enable students to develop a deeper understanding of Christian spirituality's research methods and its relevance to the world today.

ISBN13: 978–0–415–39473–4 (hbk)
ISBN13: 978–0–415–39474–1 (pbk)

Available at all good bookshops
For ordering and further information please visit:
www.routledge.com